ENTREPRENEURSHIP
and
ECONOMIC
DEVELOPMENT

Edited by *Peter Kilby*

ENTREPRENEURSHIP
and
ECONOMIC
DEVELOPMENT

The Free Press NEW YORK

Collier-Macmillan Ltd., London

Library of Congress Catalog Card Number: 79–122279

printing number
1 2 3 4 5 6 7 8 9 10

Preface

THE search for a "missing component" in the growth process of underdeveloped countries is now a long-established tradition. Before World War II lack of natural resources and climatic conditions took pride of place; following the war technical know-how ("Point 4"), capital formation, investment in education, and competitive markets have successively been held to be the critical ingredient for achieving self-sustained growth. Entrepreneurship has emerged—lying at the borders of economics, sociology, and psychology—as a serious contender for being the missing component with the publication of David McClelland's and Everett Hagen's works in the early 1960s. Moreover, theories of entrepreneurship have a direct bearing on the matter of fostering "black capitalism" in the United States. McClelland has already begun to apply achievement motivation training to various potential leadership groups among the Negro community.

Whether or not entrepeneurship is *the* missing component, it is an important component in the process of economic development. The purpose of this volume is to bring together statements of all the major theories of entrepreneurship and a sampling of the best empirical studies which have attempted to apply these theories. In Part II, the empirical section, two studies each for Colombia and Japan propound competing explanations; this has been done both because of the inherent interest of the individual papers and to illustrate the very thorny problems of hypothesis testing. The editor's introductory essay presents a comparative evaluation of the eight theoretical formulations in terms of the kinds of variables employed and methodological approaches. The essay concludes with a modest reformulation of the entrepreneurial problem drawing on the evidence provided in existing empirical studies of business performance in developing countries. Chapters 7 and 14, like the introduction, are original essays.

Many individuals have read and commented upon an earlier draft of my own essay. My debt to these kind and unnamed critics is considerable. However, I must single out four gentlemen—Hans Palmer, Koji Taira, Fritz Redlich, and Frank Young—who variously saved me from serious errors, compelled me to think through all the implications of my own argument, and persuaded me to raise new questions. To all these and my patient wife, I am most grateful.

PETER KILBY

Middletown, Connecticut

Contents

PART II

ENTREPRENEURSHIP
and
ECONOMIC
DEVELOPMENT

1

HUNTING THE HEFFALUMP

Peter Kilby

T HE search for the source of dynamic entrepreneurial performance has much in common with hunting the Heffalump. The Heffalump is a
rather large and very important animal.[1] He has been hunted by many individuals using various ingenious trapping devices, but no one so far has succeeded in capturing him. All who claim to have caught sight of him report
that he is enormous, but they disagree on his particularities. Not having explored his current habitat with sufficient care, some hunters have used as bait
their own favorite dishes and have then tried to persuade people that what
they caught was a Heffalump. However, very few are convinced, and the
search goes on.

In this introductory essay we shall review the major theoretical constructs,
reprinted in the first half of this book, that have been designed for trapping the
entrepreneurial phenomenon. Following a critical evaluation of these theories
and some discussion of the observed entrepreneurial bottlenecks in developing
countries, the writer will present his own description of the Heffalump and
suggest some principles on which future traps might be designed.

[1] See A. A. Milne, *Winnie-The-Pooh* (London: 1926), Ch. 5, and *The House at Pooh
Corner* (London: 1928), Ch. 3.

SECTION ONE

We shall begin our survey of theories of entrepreneurial supply with a very brief glance at the place of entrepreneurship in economic theory. The entrepreneur and his unique risk-bearing function were first identified in the early 18th century by Richard Cantillon, an Irishman living in France, who also coined the term: the "entrepreneur" buys factor services at "certain" prices with a view to selling their product at "uncertain" prices in the future. Thus, the entrepreneur was defined by a unique constitutive function: the bearing of noninsurable risk. A few decades later Jean Baptiste Say described the entrepreneurial function in broader terms, emphasizing the bringing together of the factors of production and the provision of continuing management, as well as risk bearing.

The notion of entrepreneurship, certainly in any significant dynamic sense, did not find a place in the development of English economic thought. Adam Smith, owing to a faulty interpretation of what he observed, set the precedent.[2] Smith's capitalist-employer's primary role was to provide capital for use by his workers and to accumulate. Although the capitalist-employer bore financial risk and was responsible for business coordination, Smith neither analyzed nor emphasized these functions: the term profit was used interchangeably with interest. In his restatement of classical economic theory, the younger Mill, taking his cue from Cantillon and Say, separated the entrepreneurial function (the payment for which is residual profit) from that of providing capital (the payment for which is interest); but the usefulness of this distinction was largely lost when Marshall reaffirmed the Smith–Ricardian tradition of treating profit as a single undifferentiated income flow, relegating entrepreneurship to management, a special variety of skilled labor.

As economic theory has become more formalized, the tendency to discard entrepreneurship as a significant separate factor in the operation of the economy has increased. Thus, in modern growth theory, any contribution of entrepreneurship is typically contained in a catch-all residual factor. This latter residual, variously termed "technical change" or "coefficient of ignorance", includes, among other things, technology, education, institutional organization, and entrepreneurship.

Schumpeter's work, beginning in 1911, is the obvious exception to the above generalizations. His innovation represents not only the first dynamic concept of the entrepreneurial function, but he is the first major writer to put the human

[2] See Fritz Redlich, "Toward Understanding an Unfortunate Legacy," *Kyklos*, XIX (1966), pp. 709–716.

agent at the center of the process of economic development. Perhaps to facilitate the building of a very general theory, Schumpeter posits a single constitutive entrepreneurial function: innovation. Hence, for most of his life the business leader is engaged in non-entrepreneurial "managerial" activities. This contrasts with the less narrowly defined, more empirical conceptualization of entrepreneurship employed by the other writers whose work appears in this volume. They broadly identify the entrepreneur with the modern industrial businessman. And it is in this generic sense that the term will be used throughout this essay.

In the literature on the historical experience of economic growth in Europe and America, the prominence given to the entrepreneur has varied greatly. Joseph Schumpeter, A. H. Cole, and T. C. Cochran have attributed to him the critical role in economic expansion. In contrast, H. J. Habakkuk, Phyllis Deane, and Douglass North, whether explicitly or simply by virtue of omission, consider entrepreneurial supply to have played a passive part in the drama whose major themes were invention, changing factor prices, and new market opportunities.[3] However, the majority of economic historians have eschewed the solitary rigour of either of these extremes in preference to a more realistic (if overdetermined) multicausal model embracing economic, sociological, and historical determinants. The paradigm for this group of studies is T.S. Ashton's *The Industrial Revolution 1760–1830*.

It is worth noting the not altogether surprising fact that the importance given to the entrepreneur as a causal variable in the growth process is strongly conditioned by the particular scholar's field. As we shall see, the economist who operates in the mainstream of his discipline assumes that the supply of entrepreneurial services is highly elastic and that failures in entrepreneurship are attributable to maladjustments in the external environment. Thus, the determinants of entrepreneurial performance lie on the demand side, in the structure of economic incentives found in the market environment—the home ground of the economist. Similarly, while acknowledging that extreme economic inducements or impediments will significantly affect entrepreneurial activity, the psychologist holds that over the normal range of variability of pecuniary incentives, the prime movers for risk bearing and innovation are certain non-

---

[3] Douglass North, who earlier was himself an entrepreneurial historian, makes explicit the reasons for his omission of the entrepreneur in United States development: ". . . productivity changes stemming from technological innovations, are, in part at least, a nearly autonomous response to successful expansion of industries in an acquisitive society under competitive market conditions. . . . The role of entrepreneur and innovator is an important one, but I would downgrade its significance for the study of growth in economies which: (1) followed in the process of industrial development and (2) were acquisitive oriented under competitive market conditions." *The Economic Growth of the United States 1790-1860* (New York: 1961), p. 8.

materialistic, inner, psychic concerns—the analysis of which falls in the domain of the psychologist. The sociologist sees economic incentives as but one part of a larger system of sanctions based on the society's value and status hierarchy, which in its entirety will determine the extent of entrepreneurial activity. In short, practitioners in each of the social sciences tend to define the problem so that the principal determinants of entrepreneurial performance fall within their discipline.

Before turning to the individual theories of entrepreneurial supply, it is important to recognize explicitly that there is a prior question as to the nature of the entrepreneurial function. The kinds of tasks to be performed obviously have a strong influence on the type of individual to be recruited. The array of all possible entrepreneurial roles encompasses the perception of economic opportunity, technical and organizational innovations, gaining command over scarce resources, taking responsibility for the internal management and for the external advancement of the firm in all its aspects. In any particular time and place, the skilled performance of certain of these tasks by the entrepreneur is critical while other tasks demand little attention or can be safely delegated to subordinates. Thus, different settings may call for markedly dissimilar entrepreneurial personalities.

This temporal variability in the skills and motivations of the successful entrepreneur has been recognized in the context of the evolution of developed economies. To cite a single example, Redlich and Chandler have pointed out that the personality type and behavior characteristics of the American industrialist in 1850 bears little resemblance to his counterpart in 1950.[4] A comparable morphology has not been developed at the inter-nation level. Theories of entrepreneurial supply are primarily concerned with the early take-off period. By postulating a unique set of personal qualities which define the entrepreneurial type, they tacitly imply that the situational factors during the modernization period are roughly similar wherever and whenever it occurs.

Yet, on the face of it, the nature of the entrepreneur's function in contemporary underdeveloped countries seems to differ considerably in a number of respects from that in nineteenth-century Europe and America. These differences stem from a single source—the existence of a very large stock of proven technical innovations in the advanced economies which has not yet been applied in the developing economies. Thus, original technological innovation, which was frequently the heart of nineteenth-century industrial entrepreneurship, is

---

[4] A. D. Chandler and Fritz Redlich, "Recent Developments in American Business Administration and Their Conceptualization," *Business History Review*, No. 35 (1961); see also Redlich's review of McClelland's *The Achieving Society* in *Explorations in Entrepreneurial History* (Fall: 1963), pp. 15, 19, 25.

not an activity for which there is now much call. Far simpler adaptations are the principal requirement so far as new production processes are concerned. Moreover, the availability of foreign technical assistance in its various forms has the potential to facilitate the transfer process.

Set against the less exacting entrepreneurial task in this province, the windfall of innovations also means that there is an extreme technological disparity. This disparity between existing semitraditional modes of production and the modern techniques that the entrepreneur seeks to introduce necessitates an upgrading of factor inputs of a magnitude many times greater and in a far shorter interval than that which faced entrepreneurs of the pre-1900 period. Consider the average capital requirement per worker.[5] In late eighteenth-century England, this investment requirement was the equivalent of about four months' wages; in early nineteenth-century France it was six to eight times the average monthly wage. By contrast, in India and Turkey in the mid-1950s, the capital requirement of competitive modern technology represented from 220 to 350 times the monthly wage. There is a similar disparity in the gap between existing labor skills and those needed for the new technology. Working from the relatively advanced practices existing in blacksmithing and watch and instrument making, it was a manageable distance to creating the engineering skills required for Watt's steam engine; from rural blacksmithing to the L–D oxygen steel-making process is a very much greater distance. Finally, and perhaps most significantly, in the currently developing countries the requisite changes in the organization of work are much greater than in the earlier era.

Adding to these relatively greater difficulties on the production side, the fledgling entrepreneur in an open economy faces price and quality competition in his product market of a degree unknown to his predecessors. Not only does the comparative superiority of seasoned manufacturers—commanded by teams of functionally specialized entrepreneurs—in the advanced countries surpass that of England over her early imitators, but the drastic reduction in the cost of ocean transport has reduced natural protection to approximately one-fifth its early nineteenth-century level. While trade barriers can offset this vulnerability, the advanced producers frequently circumvent these barriers by investing in a local subsidiary plant.

What do these differences imply about the nature of the entrepreneur's function in the contemporary underdeveloped world? In this writer's view, the

---

[5] This point and the following discussion of natural protection is drawn from Chs. 11 and 13 of Paul Bairoch's very insightful *Révolution Industrielle et Sous-Développement*, 2nd edition (Paris: 1964). I am indebted to Bruce Johnston for bringing this book to my attention.

backlog of unapplied production techniques and the existence of large, well mapped out import markets means that perceiving truly *new* economic opportunities and the carrying out of fundamental, pioneering innovations of the type envisaged by Schumpeter are largely irrelevant. On the other hand, the operational problems of matching advanced technology with qualitatively ill-fitting local factors of production are considerably greater than in the nineteenth century. To obtain adequate financing, to adapt techniques and organization, to maximize factor productivities and minimize unit cost, to improvise substitutes for nonavailable skills and materials—these tasks on the production side will more often than not represent the critical entrepreneurial function in the modernizing economy of the twentieth century.

SECTION TWO

Having made all the necessary preparations, we are now ready to begin our search for the Heffalump. Theories of entrepreneurial supply are constructed from either psychological or sociological elements. We are considering seven such theories in this book: four psychological theories (Schumpeter, McClelland, Hagen, Kunkel) and three sociological theories (Weber, Cochran, Young). In this section, we set out what each of these authors postulates as the defining qualities of the entrepreneur and the noneconomic variables which govern his appearance. The theories are further examined for the role played by social groups and the mechanisms by which individuals are recruited into business occupations.

The theories of Max Weber and Joseph Schumpeter have much in common. Both are comparatively simple constructs in terms of the number of variables and the articulation of causal sequences and interactions. And as Ronan Macdonald's essay makes clear, Schumpeter's central vision of the process of economic development was much influenced by Weber's 1904 paper. In both theories, the energized entrepreneur appears in the traditional economy and sets in motion a revolutionary process of creative destruction. The key to competitive success for Weber's entrepreneur is his innovation in a thoroughgoing rationalization of every aspect of his enterprise. In Schumpeter's schema, the key is also innovation but of a much bolder sort, including changing the basic technological and demand parameters of the economy.

In the Weberian system, the driving entrepreneurial energies are generated by the adoption of exogenously supplied religious beliefs. For the faithful these beliefs, both in their direct implications for practical conduct and in the entrained anxiety to generate signs of a favorable predestination, produce intensive exertion in occupational pursuits, the systematic ordering of means to ends, and the accumulation of productive assets.[6] These are for Weber the critical characteristics of the successful entrepreneur; however, they will also be present in the supervisors and workmen who support and are lead by the entrepreneur and in the larger community whose approval reinforces his behavior. In terms of its applicability to underdeveloped countries, the community-wide influence of this ethic, which operates irrespective of personality type, gives Weber's explanation an advantage over Schumpeter's and McClelland's.

Contrary to Weber's and to all other theories of entrepreneurial supply, the appearance of Schumpeter's entrepreneurs is not a function of some social, cultural, or religious variable. Schumpeter's economic leaders are individuals, motivated by an atavistic will to power, who occur randomly in any ethnically homogeneous population. Their special characteristics are an intuitional capacity to see things in a way which afterwards proves correct, energy of will and mind to overcome fixed habits of thought, and the capacity to withstand social opposition.[7] These attributes would seem closely related to the nineteenth-century experience in which original innovations were important, and social institutions were comparatively permissive.

Whether because of the intuitive appeal of their basic postulates or the descriptive realism of their larger explanation of European socioeconomic development, the theories of Weber and Schumpeter still command at least as much respect as their more elaborate successors. Later theories which explicitly include non-Western countries have sacrificed some of the earlier realism for attempted generality.

David McClelland's theory, as set forth in *The Achieving Society*, can be seen as a development of Weber's Protestant ethic in which an intermediating psychological motive (the need for achievement) is introduced. Weber's causal

---

[6] The translation of Weber's religious imperatives of an occupational calling, rationality, and asceticism into their economic behavioral counterparts suggests that a formally more accurate description of Weber's paradigm might be "the development ethic and the spirit of religion." Indeed, it is common among sociologists to speak of the "functional equivalent of the Protestant Ethic." David McClelland's review of the world's apparently entrepreneurial religious sects and the nature of their religious beliefs (*The Achieving Society*, New York 1961, pp. 364–372) leads him to conclude that asceticism and a commitment to a calling are seldom present, but that all these religions do share an emphasis upon unmediated confrontation between the individual and God in which the individual is accountable for each and every action of his life.

[7] J. A. Schumpeter, *The Theory of Economic Development* (Cambridge, Mass.: 1934), pp. 85–87, 89. In light of the writer's experience in West Africa that entrepreneurs tend to get involved in second and third ventures before they master important operational problems in their first project, we might add as a fourth attribute "a certain narrowness which seizes the immediate chance and *nothing else*."

sequence producing entrepreneurial behavior is extended by McClelland in the following manner:

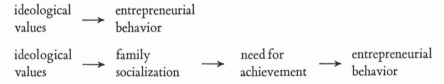

ideological values $\longrightarrow$ entrepreneurial behavior

ideological values $\longrightarrow$ family socialization $\longrightarrow$ need for achievement $\longrightarrow$ entrepreneurial behavior

McClelland, much like Everett Hagen, ascribes the inculcation of the achievement motive to child-rearing practices which stress standards of excellence, maternal warmth, self-reliance training, and low father dominance. The special entrepreneurial qualities cited by McClelland derive from those characteristics demonstrated by participants with a high need for achievement during test-taking experiments (pp. 44–46, 211–32).[8] These characteristics include little interest in performing routine tasks or in situations of high risk in contrast to keen interest in situations involving moderate risk where skill counts, a desire for responsibility, and a desire for a concrete measure of task performance. All these attributes seem to be relevant to successful business endeavor in the developing countries, save for the lack of interest in carrying out tasks of management control which are critical even though of routine nature. Indeed, although factory manager is later treated by McClelland as one of the principal entrepreneurial occupations, the ambitious need achiever who is always seeking new challenges is contrasted with the "conscientious, efficient, forward-looking, *managerial* type" (p. 277).

The emphasis in *The Achieving Society* is on the empirical: developing need for achievement as a quantifiable variable, measuring the level of this motive in societies past and present (scoring folk literature, children's readers, and fantasy essays for achievement imagery), and correlating the latter with various indices of economic growth. Thus, only one of ten chapters in the book, chapter 9, is concerned with articulated theory building. Here McClelland states that the achievement motive is formed during middle childhood and is produced by "reasonably high standards of excellence imposed at a time when the son can attain them, a willingness to let him attain them without interference, and real emotional pleasure in his achievements short of overprotection and indulgence" (p. 356). The prime determinant of these aspects of the child-parent relationship, the author argues, is the parents' religious world view (p. 341); two less important, indirect influences are the father's occupation and

---

[8] These and later page references given in parentheses are all from *The Achieving Society*.

living arrangements (the presence of slavery, polygamy, serial monogamy). Finally, McClelland finds a very high statistical association, unconnected with child-rearing patterns, between need for achievement and climate.[9]

An interesting variant on McClelland's 1961 theory concerning the factors determining the child-parent relationship is provided by Robert LeVine.[10] LeVine argues that the socialization of children will be regulated by the type of status mobility system that prevails in that society. Where higher status is attained through outstanding performance in one's occupational role, parents will try to foster in their children initiative, industriousness, and foresight through self-reliance and achievement training. He postulates that this is what occurs in Ibo society in Nigeria. In contrast, in hierarchical societies, such as the

---

[9] To a degree unmatched by any other investigator, McClelland considers alternative theories to his own in explanation of the empirical findings. These alternatives are developed fully and sympathetically. In this particular matter McClelland lives up admirably to his claim to a rigorous scientific methodology. Of course, in many cases it is not possible to disprove the alternative. The most recurrent of these, not easily dismissed, is that achieving behavior is aroused by the immediate external environment (e.g., social structural factors) rather than being a consequence of the prior existence of a psychic need.

One such instance of environmental arousal is climatically conditioned energy levels. (The writer's three years in West Africa have perhaps prejudiced the selection of this instance!) Ellsworth Huntington defined regions of high climatic energy by a mean temperature of approximately 40° F in winter and 64° F in summer, relative humidity of about 60 per cent at noon and frequent but not extreme changes in weather. Although it is not possible to confirm that changes in long-run weather conditions coincided exactly with the rise and fall of advanced civilizations as Huntington has tried to show, the preponderance of these civilizations have occurred in his predicted regions. McClelland finds an even closer fit between need achievement scores of fifty-two preliterate tribes and Huntington's climatic variables. "Thus the general picture is quite clear. Low n Achievement is associated particularly with tropical climates which are hot, humid and show little temperature variation. High n Achievement is associated with moderate, dry climates which also tend to have poor soil, so that growing conditions for agriculture are not optimal." (p. 386).

McClelland suggests that the effect of climate might not be on energy levels so much as on promoting polygamy which in turn operates on child rearing. However, whatever the nature of its influence, it would seem incumbent upon the investigator, rather than simply dropping the subject at this point, to consider climate as a prime contender or co-determinant with religious values.

McClelland is exceptional in giving a full and accurate statement of the climatic thesis. Climate, like natural resource endowment, is unalterable and hence is usually dismissed in a paragraph or two with a short list of exceptions, e.g., Switzerland and Incan civilization. These exceptions are typically fewer in number than those which can be cited in contradiction of the hypothesis being advanced. In statistical terminology, theories based on unalterable causal factors are evaluated against fully deterministic criteria, whereas other theories are judged on stochastic or probabilistic standards.

[10] Robert LeVine, *Dreams and Deeds: Achievement Motivation in Nigeria* (Chicago: 1966), Ch. 2.

Hausa, upward mobility is attained through loyalty, obedience, and sycophancy; here the parents subject their children to obedience training, instructions in the use of flattery, and the suppression of tendencies that might antagonize superiors. Because alternative explanations of need achievement fantasy scores predicted the same ordering, it was not possible to get an unambiguous test of this theory. In any case, LeVine's variant shifts the "first cause" from religious values to social structure.

In his most recent book, written with D. G. Winter and others, McClelland alters his earlier position on the importance of child rearing as the intrinsic determinant of the achievement motive. Changes in motivation are now seen to be primarily a result of the ideological arousal of latent need for achievement among adults, typically associated with a new sense of superiority;[11] this raises the possibility of training programs to stimulate achievement-oriented behavior. This reevaluation by McClelland *et al.* appears to have been induced by several considerations: the desirability of a theory with more favorable implications for policy intervention, the apparent changes in adult motivation achieved by evangelical missionaries, and criticisms of McClelland's earlier book with regard to the inseparability of arousal and motive strength.[12] McClelland's new formulation brings him very close to the purely sociological theories; indeed, his explication of motive acquisition provides a needed, semiautomatic linkage between the sociologists' group-level variables and individual behavior.

Everett Hagen's *On the Theory of Social Change: How Economic Growth Begins* has much in common with *The Achieving Society*. Not only is Hagen's theory a mediating psychological explanation, but his "creative personality" is an individual characterized by a high need for achievement, order, and autonomy. However, Hagen's work is set off from that of McClelland and all the other entrepreneurial theorists by the fact that its central vision was formed against the background not of the European and American experience but rather in the context of contemporary backward economies of Asia and Latin America. Paradoxically for an economist, Hagen's view of economic development does not stress the spread of markets, capital accumulation, the perception of profitable opportunities, willingness to save, and the like—indeed, factors such as these are rarely mentioned in his 500-page book. Rather, economic development is seen almost exclusively as a process of technological change which is brought about by the technological creativity of individuals in the society. Thus, Hagen sees the entrepreneur as a creative problem solver interested in things in the practical and technological realm and driven by a duty to achieve.

[11] McClelland *et al.*, *Motivating Economic Development* (New York: 1969), p. 35.
[12] Ibid., pp. 2, 34, 42.

Hagen and McClelland share certain conceptual difficulties. Hagen's central construct is the authoritarian–creative personality dichotomy. Do these ideal types in their descriptive accuracy approximate modal personalities in all traditional and all modernized societies respectively? Second, is there a necessary association between an authoritarian personality and non-innovative behavior? In his review of Hagen's book, Alexander Gerschenkron observed that the description of child rearing in Burma would serve equally well for the entre-preneurially advanced countries of Germany, Sweden, and Austria.[13] Since McClelland's theory makes fewer assumptions about values, cognitions, and motives other than the need for achievement, it is less open to the criticism of relying upon unverified psychoanalytical constructs concerning man's internal state. Although there is no consensus among psychologists as to what constitutes a motive, John Kunkel's criticism of the need for achievement as "nothing more than an abstraction of concrete behavior" would not appear to be correct when the motive is measured by dreams and fantasy stories, evidence of a very different kind from concrete behavior.

Reversing McClelland's balance between empirical testing and theoretical articulation, Hagen's attempts at verification are limited to five case studies,[14] whereas the major emphasis is upon developing a comparatively complex and detailed explanation of how child-rearing practices change over time in response to an initial external disturbance. Hagen postulates that the sequence of changes separating the typical authoritarian personality of a stable traditional society from the emergence, many decades later, of creative entrepreneurial activity is as follows:[15]

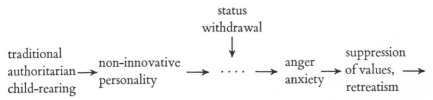

[13] *Economica* (February, 1965), p. 179. Gerschenkron's view of the entrepreneurship issue is a sophisticated version of the economist's model considered later. He holds that the normal variation in child-rearing practices and in IQ will produce enough potential entre-preneurs in every society; the critical question is the opportunities available for entre-preneurial endeavor.

[14] A sixth case study of two Indonesian communities, written by Clifford Geertz and contributed as Ch. 16, is based on a sociological theory of change which has no reference to psychological preconditions. See especially E. E. Hagen, *On the Theory of Social Change: How Economic Growth Begins* (Homewood, Illinois: 1962), p. 406. As in the preceding case, further page reference in parentheses pertain to this book.

[15] He admits the highly speculative nature of this theorizing. Ibid., p. 201.

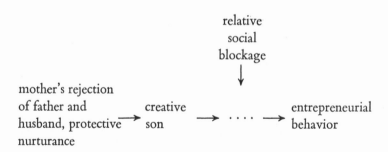

Withdrawal of status respect, also described as group subordination, is one of two exogenous variables in Hagen's system (the other is relative social blockage) and is the trigger mechanism for changes in personality formation. Status withdrawal "is the perception on the part of the members of some social group that their purposes and values in life are not respected by groups in the society whom they respect and whose esteem they value" (p. 185).

Hagen postulates that four types of events can produce status withdrawal: (1) displacement by force, *e.g.*, the Norman invasion of England or the derogation of merchants, samurai, and wealthy peasants in seventeenth-century Tokugawa Japan; (2) denigration of valued symbols, *e.g.*, suppression of religious sects in seventeenth-century Russia and England; (3) inconsistency of status symbols with a changing distribution of economic power; and (4) nonacceptance of expected status on migration to a new society, *e.g.*, the Antioqueños in seventeenth-century Colombia (pp. 187–190). Once status withdrawal has occurred, the sequences of change in personality formation are set in motion with the creative personality emerging after a minimum retreatist interval of five generations.[16]

Interestingly, status withdrawal, like Frank Young's reactive subsystems, is a purely intergroup phenomenon and is independent of religious beliefs or cultural values which figure so prominently as "first causes" in the psychological theory of McClelland or the sociological theories of Weber and Cochran. About values and religious beliefs, Hagen has this to say:

New values are not adopted by a process of rational choice either by children or adults. Rather, the process is a largely unconscious one of responding to needs and finding the mental model which will justify holding the values that promise to satisfy the needs. The environmental pressures which initiate the process of adaption of new values are not those of the larger society but the complex of pressures which impinge immediately upon the individual in childhood (p. 234).

[16] The maximum interval noted by Hagen is 800 years in the case of England. He puts the interval in Japan and Colombia at about 250 years (pp. 218–219).

Religious systems are in general a projection of the need structure of the members of society, although there is no reason to deny them a reciprocal influence of their own. The case studies illustrate the point that presence of one or another religious dogma is in no sense a necessary accompaniment to economic growth, to say nothing of being a cause. The presence of Protestant dissent in England is matched by the presence of pious Catholicism in Antioquia and of little fervor associated with any religious dogma in Japan. When elite groups in traditional society no longer provide a satisfactory object to which to attach one's need dependence, there emerges a reinterpretation of religion by which one visualizes a more direct personal dependence on a deity. Such a reinterpretation may sanction changes in social values conducive to economic growth (pp. 257–258).

A second sociological theory of entrepreneurial supply, in the Weberian–Parsonian tradition, is of the type that Thomas Cochran has applied extensively to Latin America–United States comparisons.[17] The key elements in his system are cultural values, role expectations, and social sanctions. Entrepreneurs are not seen as being deviant or supernormal individuals, but rather as representing society's modal personality. This modal personality is shaped by prevailing child-rearing practices and schooling common to the culture. The individual's performance as a businessman will be influenced by three factors: his own attitudes toward his occupation, the role expectations held by sanctioning groups, and the operational requirements of the job. Society's values are the most important determinants of the first two factors. Changes over time in such exogenous variables as population, technology, and institutional drift will impinge on the role structure by creating new operational needs—whether the entrepreneurial response will be creative as in the United States or largely abortive as in much of Latin America will be determined primarily by cultural values.

A third sociological theory, related to Durkheim and Levi-Strauss, is that of Frank Young. Although Young shares Cochran's position as to the unimportance of personality factors, he does not share Cochran's focus on values and society-wide phenomena. Young is solely concerned with intergroup relations. As contrasted to the Parsonian equilibrium comparative statics approach, Young's theory is a theory of change based on society's incorporation of reactive subgroups. A group will become reactive, in Young's schema, when two conditions coincide: a group is experiencing low status recognition and denial of access to important social networks, and it possesses a greater range of institutional resources than other groups in society at the same system-level. Although similar to Hagen's subordinated groups, Young's schema avoids Hagen's problematic assumptions about sequential changes in personality.

[17] See also S. M. Lipset, "Value, Education and Entrepreneurship," in S. M. Lipset and A. Solari, eds., *Elites in Latin America* (New York: 1967).

The last theory of entrepreneurial supply considered in this volume is the behavioralistic model elaborated by John Kunkel. In contrast to Young's treatment of psychic needs and values as passive phenomena reflecting group-level activity, Kunkel, following Skinner and Homans, moves in the opposite direction reducing values and personality types to the behavioral patterns from which they are inferred. Behavioral patterns in this model are determined by reinforcing and aversive stimuli present in the societal context, such rewards and punishments not being limited to the child-rearing period. Hence, entre-preneurial behavior is a function of the surrounding social structure, both past and present, and can be readily influenced by manipulable economic and social incentives. So Kunkel's theory, based upon experimental psychology, identifies sociological variables as the determinants of entrepreneurial supply while at the same time implying a much more optimistic, economist-like view as to the efficacy of short- and medium-term policy intervention.

In order to assess these theories for their completeness, it is worth clarifying somewhat further the role played by the social group in each of these constructs. It is also useful to do this as a means of showing the relationship of these theories to Bert Hoselitz's well-known observations on the importance of culturally marginal groups in promoting economic development (*e.g.*, the Jews and Greeks in medieval Europe, the Lebanese in West Africa, the Chinese in Southeast Asia, the Indians in East Africa). Hoselitz, borrowing from the earlier work of Stonequist and Park, hypothesizes that marginal men, because of their am-biguous position from a cultural or social standpoint, are peculiarly suited to make creative adjustments in situations of change and, in the course of this ad-justment process, to develop genuine innovations in social behavior.[18]

In three of the seven theories presented in Part I, the influence of groups, be they marginal or elite, is seen as causally unimportant. Kunkel's thorough-going behavioralism denies the independent existence of group phenomena and their interaction with the larger social structure. Schumpeter (in his later work) and Cochran acknowledge the reality of status groups but conceive of them as responding passively, and with no significant reciprocal influence, to shifts in the economic and political functions that these groups perform.

In the remaining four theories, groups are given the critical role in trigger-ing economic change, although all the theorists save Young would probably exclude Hoselitz's alien minorities as being incapable of causing major trans-mutations in the host country's social structure. Hagen holds that scattered individuals from the elite groups are induced to imitate the technological

[18] B. F. Hoselitz, "A Sociological Approach to Economic Development," in D. Novack and R. Lekachman, eds., *Development and Society* (New York: 1964), p. 157.

leaders from the subordinated group whose new wealth threatens the status of the accepted elites and that, by this process, innovation gradually spreads throughout the society. "If on the other hand the innovators are an alien minority group, lacking deep and acknowledged roots in the society, distaste for their behavior is apt to be such that, if through innovation they threaten to gain too much power, the defensive reaction will not be to imitate them but to expel or suppress them."[19] Weber sees changes in cultural values and beliefs, the key to economic growth, as the outcome of competition between various status groups each with their own world view.[20] McClelland is frequently concerned with the differential need for achievement between religious groups. The logic of his theory seems to require an explanation of what regulates the influence any particular group will have in shaping the growth—determining *national* values and attitudes—but none is given.[21] Only in Young's model, in which a social system is defined solely in terms of communications networks, would Hoselitz's alien minorities qualify as candidates for the reactive subsystem.

An important question for any theory of entrepreneurial supply is to identify the channels by which entrepreneurial personalities or groups are directed into business pursuits. According to Weber, whose focus was Protestant Europe, the Calvinist notion of the advisability of proving one's faith in measurable worldly activity no doubt enhanced the choice of business as an occupation, but he felt that the principal effect of ascetic Protestantism was to transform those leisurely, satisficing traditional capitalists who happened to adopt the new beliefs into unrelenting, ever-expanding modern capitalists. The question of "what channels" is especially pertinent in Schumpeter's theory because of the relative infrequency of his heroic entrepreneurial types. Yet, as Schumpeter himself acknowledges, two of the three motivational drives of the innovator—

---

[19] Hagen, *On the Theory of Social Change*, p. 248. Recent history of the Indians and Lebanese in Africa and the Chinese in Malaya and Indonesia would appear to support Hagen; the pent-up hostility is released during periods of stress.

Although ethnic minorities have done little to promote creative social change, they have made important contributions to the development of indigenous entrepreneurial capabilities. Because these marginal groups typically command less capital, a less sophisticated technology, and fewer import licenses than other (corporate) private foreign investors, they have been compelled to employ more labor-intensive, domestic resource-using production techniques. As a result, the activities of these resident minorities have had far greater educative externalities for indigenous entrepreneurs in terms of the diffusion of appropriate technologies and organizational skills.

[20] From Weber's sociology of religion which is articulated in his later work. See Reinhard Bendix, *Max Weber an Intellectual Portrait* (New York: 1960), pp. 258–262.

[21] The absence of a discussion of this subject and of how sources of need for achievement change over time represent the major lacunae in McClelland's work insofar as it purports to be a general theory.

the will to conquer and the joy of creating—may "be taken care of by other arrangements not involving private gain from economic innovation" (p. 94).

Of all the writers represented in Part I, Hagen provides the most complete specification as to how and under what conditions creative personalities from the subordinated group will be directed into modern business activities. First, the individual, unless he himself comes from the simple folk, must have overcome that antipathy to manual labor and work with tools which is the principal sign of "super-menial" class status (p. 96). Second, advancement in the economic sphere must not be blocked, as it was for first and second generation immigrant groups to the United States who were accepted only "as hewers of wood and drawers of water" (p. 242). And finally, the conditions of relative social blockage must be such as to make an entrepreneurial activity the most attractive of all possible alternative channels to social recognition.

> If traditionally honored roles are not open to an individual or if prowess in them does not win him recognition because his other characteristics bar him from being honored, and if armed rebellion is impossible because of the preponderance of strength of the new dominant group or because of the growth of effective social sanctions against the use of force, and if migration is not a feasible solution, then the pressure of unsatisfiable values and frustrations may be expected over a number of generations to inculcate new values. In short, the requisite for economic growth in a traditional society is not merely that upward social mobility by new means is possible but also that upward social mobility by traditional channels is not possible [p. 242].

McClelland, like Hagen, expounds an explicit mechanism by which individuals with high need for achievement are directed into entrepreneurial occupations (pp. 239–253). It is worth reconstructing his argument in some detail because the exposition gives a good taste of much of the analysis in *The Achieving Society*—analysis characterized, on the one hand, by its ingenuity and empirical orientation the ot and, onher, by problems arising from loosely defined variables, biased sample data, and weakly linked multistage arguments.

McClelland begins with the simplest proposition that boys with high need for achievement will tend to be attracted to business occupations because they perceive the occupations as calling for characteristics which they possess. A sample of boys was scored by McClelland for need achievement and then asked to indicate whether they liked, disliked, or were indifferent to twelve occupations, four of which (including "factory manager") were in business. The sample consisted of 254 Wesleyan freshmen from the United States, 150 Japanese, 392 German, 378 Brazilian, and 152 Indian high school students

fourteen to eighteen years old.[22] There was a positive correlation coefficient of
.16 between need for achievement and business occupations for the Wesleyan
students; for the students from the other countries, the correlations were very
small, not statistically significant, and in two cases were zero and negative. In
short, viewed at the aggregate level, there is no evidence that achievement-
motivated individuals are especially attracted to entrepreneurial occupations.

Trying a second tack, McClelland hypothesizes that the prestige of business
occupations determines whether people with high need for achievement are
attracted to them. Having no direct measure for prestige, the "average liking"
for the twelve occupations was used as an indirect measure for the same five-
country sample of students. (It is not clear that liking is a valid proxy since the
respondents were told to disregard considerations of ability required, salary,
and social standing in making their choices.) In all countries, the liking for
business occupations was below average and the cross-country correlation
between liking business occupations and need for achievement was negative,
although not statistically significant. In other words, "boys with high need for
achievement (if anything) prefer business occupations more when those
occupations are in general less well liked."

The need for a more analytical approach having been indicated, McClelland
next hypothesizes that occupational preference is a function of the level of
need for achievement times the difficulty of achieving success in the occupation.
"Since more difficult occupations are ordinarily more prestigeful," McClelland
uses prestige rankings as a proximate index of difficulty. The only test of the
hypothesis was a test conducted by Litwin with twenty-nine Japanese
thirteen-year-olds. Unfortunately Litwin "was hampered by not having clear-cut
status or prestige ratings available, but by putting together information contained
in a number of sources and by analyzing the nature of the job he was able to arrive
at four distinguishable occupational levels." Litwin then found that high need
achievers' liking for occupations was significantly more skewed toward the high
prestige occupations than was that of low need achievers.*

The penultimate step in McClelland's analysis is a test he conducted with

[22] Notice that this liking for an occupation is quite different from occupational preference. Instructions to respondents contained the following: "You are not asked if you
would take up the occupation permanently, but merely whether or not you would enjoy
that kind of work, regardless of any necessary skills, abilities or training which you may
or may not possess. Disregard considerations of salary, social standing, future advancement, etc." (p. 241).

* Reservations are in order concerning the validity of Litwin's analysis. Explorer and
poet, along with scientific research worker, constitute the highest occupational level. On
the other hand, clergyman, civil servant, and stockbroker appear in the two lowest occupational levels. It is not at all obvious, taking innate talents as given, that an achievement-

twenty Harvard juniors in which need for achievement showed a $-.39$ correlation coefficient, significant at the 10 per cent level, with business occupations and a .46 correlation for law, medicine, and research scientist. Noting that this result is inconsistent with the test on Wesleyan freshmen in which need for achievement did correlate positively with business preferences, McClelland rather improbably postulates, "The chief difference between the two groups of students is their class status, the Harvard students being more upper class in fact *or in aspiration.*"[23] This, McClelland argues, is consistent with the previous hypothesis about perceived difficulty of success: "Boys of middle class background should have a lower estimate of their probability of success at high-level occupations [the professions] than boys of upper-class background" and thus those "with high need achievement should prefer middle-level occupations [business] representing 'moderate risk' for them." "In upper class boys need achievement should be negatively correlated because business occupations are 'easy' for them or, if anything, represent a step downward in the prestige hierarchy."

The mechanism by which individuals with high need for achievement are directed into entrepreneurial careers can now be stated in full. Occupational choice is a multiplicative function of the individual's need for achievement, the difficulty of the occupation, and the probability of success as affected by one's social class status. The difficulty of an occupation can be measured by its prestige. Business occupations hold a middle prestige level, ranking after the professions. Business pursuits represent the desired moderate risk situations for achievement-motivated individuals coming from the lower and lower-middle classes.[24] Somewhat surprisingly, in *Motivating Economic Achievement*, McClelland

---

motivated individual would find exploring and versifying appreciably more difficult than being a civil servant, clergyman, or stockbroker.

[23] McClelland, *The Achieving Society*, pp. 249, 252. Italics added. There are serious questions here about the validity of both the comparison and the imputation of differential class status. With regard to the comparability of the two sets of preferences, the Wesleyan students were freshmen, the Harvard students juniors; the two groups were presented with a different schedule of job choices; the first group was specifically instructed to disregard social prestige whereas the second was not. It becomes clear on page 252 that McClelland identifies class status by the very thing he is trying to predict when he classifies Cornell, a diverse land-grant university, as an upper class school because only 6 per cent of its students want to go into business!

[24] To complete our critique, in addition to the problems inherent in McClelland's prestige orderings, the equation of prestige with degree of difficulty and social class imputation, all the samples are biased, correlation coefficients small, and levels of significance low from a statistical point of view. These criticisms are called for by McClelland's immodest claims in Ch. 1 of *The Achieving Society* that he is the first investigator of economic development to apply an empirically-based, rigorous scientific methodology.

refers only to the Wesleyan sample and states as a previously established fact that individuals high in need for achievement are predisposed toward business careers (pp. 12, 23).

The remaining theories of Cochran, Young, and Kunkel do not deal with the recruitment problem specifically. In Cochran's case, it is quite clear that for him, as for Weber, the main effect of a change in values is to transform the performance of business men already in place. In Kunkel's system, as in the economist's model, changes in the structure of social incentives would attract more individuals into entrepreneurial pursuits. Young's theory is perhaps the least satisfactory in this regard—it provides no predictive mechanism as to the direction in which the reactive group's energy is likely to be channeled; something like Hagen's relative social blockage would seem to fit best.

SECTION THREE

We have examined the seven theories of entrepreneurial supply for their conceptions of our Heffalump and for their formulation of the key relationships governing the appearance of dynamic entrepreneurs. The final and critical test of any theory is whether it works—does it predict behavior? In light of the complexity of the problem and the nature of the data, it is perhaps not surprising that none of the theories can be judged to achieve an acceptable level of empirical verification. On the other hand, none of the theories can be rejected as demonstrably false.

Of all the explanations put forth, McClelland makes the most ambitious claims for systematic hypothesis testing. Yet, closer inspection reveals that the indices that are correlated are *not* economic growth and need for achievement. In his most important test covering twenty-two countries in the twentieth century, his independent variable is achievement imagery in primary school textbooks. This measure shows a negative correlation with national samples of individual's fantasy story scores (pp. 77–79)—the only valid test of need for achievement. Indeed, these school readers show that under-developed countries in 1950 exhibited higher achievement scores than developed countries.[25]

[25] McClelland rationalizes this finding as follows: "It is as if many of the backward countries realize their backwardness and are now motivated to close the gap between themselves and the more industrially developed countries. Such an interpretation will surprise no one. What it suggests once again, however, is the need for achievement score [which it is not] is a sensitive barometer of concern felt in a country for economic development" (p. 102). This Gerschenkronian interpretation is, of course, in direct contradiction to McClelland's theory as to the factors causing changes in child-rearing practices.

McClelland's use of achievement imagery in primary school textbooks as his primary explanatory variable raises a serious question as to the validity of all his empirical tests. As just mentioned, scores from these school books do not correlate with the sample data of fantasy story scores. In other parts of his work McClelland repeatedly points out that what people say in interviews or write for public consumption does not reflect their spontaneous inner needs but rather the normative social expectations pertaining to the particular situation (1961, pp. 38–41, 243–244, 331–334; 1969, p. 10). Hence children's readers measure a sociological variable relevant to the theories of Cochran and Young. On page 79 of *The Achieving Society* McClelland briefly acknowledges the problem but fails to grasp its implications for the validity of his theory.

Comparison of reader *n*-Achievement levels with levels obtained from individuals has raised some interesting questions as to just what the readers are measuring. It has even thrown some doubt on whether they are measuring anything of importance; but in the end, the proof of the pudding is in the eating: Do they enable us to predict which countries will develop more rapidly economically?

The problems with McClelland's empirical analysis do not end here. The predicted variable is not growth in national output (which is not related to the explanatory variable as demonstrated in Sayre Schatz's paper reprinted in Part II) but rather a twice-modified measure of electricity production. Similarly for societies in the past, McClelland's ingeniously manufactured proxi-variables (changes in design on Grecian urns and Incan pottery measuring shifts in the need for achievement, with area of empire and volume of public building measuring economic development) and his interpretation of results do not stand up to the most sympathetic scrutiny.[26] Paralleling Hagen's problem, in McClelland's study of achieving societies in the past the interval between the appearance of high need for achievement and the onset of economic growth varies from 1 to 250 years.

The empirical results of the motivation training project reported by McClelland and Winter in 1969 are no more convincing. The training technique for stimulating greater achievement orientation has much intuitive appeal: compelling the business man through self-analysis (1) to define his hierarchy of goals, (2) to acknowledge the sacrifices in familial and social relationships that determined achieving behavior requires, and (3) to think through the specific changes in behavior needed in his daily life to attain greater entrepreneurial effectiveness.[27] This regime bears a close resemblance to the rationalized be-

[26] See Benjamin Higgins *Economic Development*, 2nd edition (New York: 1968), pp. 245–246. Higgins' Ch. 12 contains many incisive criticisms of both Hagen and McClelland.

[27] McClelland et al., *Motivating Economic Achievement*, Ch. 2.

havior induced by migration to an unfamiliar environment or Weber's Pro-testant ethic. However, the Indian experiment appears too casual to provide a reliable test. The training consisted of eleven $2\frac{1}{2}$ hour sessions, given at night after work, over a six-week period. The performance measures of the partici-pants in the course and a control sample were oral estimates of annual employ-ment, investment, sales, and the like, over the preceding five years—all based on the respondent's memory! Given the nature of the "data" and given the con-tinuous and apparently successful attempts to generate a "Hawthorne effect" (which also tends ᵗ ᵒ obscure any personality change), there is a strong presump-tive bias favoring positive results for the training. As expected, for the course participants there are substantial differential increases in the entrepreneur's time input, attempts to establish new businesses, labor hired, and capital invested. Unexpectedly, there is no significant differential increase in gross output. Thus, if the test were to be treated as valid, it would indicate that motivational training engenders a willingness to increase inputs while at the same time it reduces entrepreneurial efficiency and, thereby, the returns to entrepreneurial effort.

In the case of Hagen's theory, beyond the issue of indeterminate lags, status withdrawal is defined so broadly that one suspects that it must occur in all societies rather frequently, say once or twice every decade. And as with McClelland's selection of data for measuring need for achievement, one occasionally suspects that Hagen identifies a particular event as constituting status withdrawal because it is followed by the emergence of economic crea-tivity. His documentation of sixteenth-century status withdrawal for the Antioqueños is particularly unconvincing; the only evidence is nineteenth-century public opinion which held that the Antioqueños were socially inferior—evidence just as plausibly explained by the fact that they were frequently of lowly esteemed Basque origin. Basque separatism, with its origins in early Iberian history, is not characterized by a sense of inferiority or a need to prove Basque worthiness to other condescending groups.[28] No evidence exists on Hagen's postulated sequential changes in personality formation and in his three success cases—England, Japan, Colombia—there are equally compelling sociological hypotheses to explain the same phenomena.

Aside from a few limited examples neither Young nor Kunkel has yet attempted to verify his hypothesis empirically. Cochran's model, like most of its type, is not operational because the explanatory variable, cultural values, is

---

[28] One qualification to Leonard Kasdan's persuasive reinterpretation of Antioqueñian dynamism is that Basque descendants, although they are overrepresented in Hagen's entrepreneurial census compared to their 16 per cent share in the Antioqueñian population, still account for only 23 per cent of the entrepreneurs.

inferred from the variable to be predicted, namely, the way people behave.[29] (When confined to scoring achievement imagery in dreams and fantasy stories, McClelland's indices for need for achievement are derived independently from the aggregative measures they predict and thus avoid hidden tautology.) Moreover, Cochran (perhaps because he is a good historian) has no satisfactory explanation as to how values change. Although *The Protestant Ethic and the Spirit of Capitalism* has stimulated many studies, none of them can be considered as providing a satisfactory test of Weber's theory as originally propounded.

Economists and others may feel that Schumpeter has not received his rightful share of attention. The reason is simply that the great bulk of Schumpeter's analysis is concerned not with the supply of entrepreneurship but rather with the reactions of the economic system. Thus, the circular flow, innovation clusters, creative destruction, forced savings through inflationary credit creation, and so on, have been the aspects of Schumpeter's theory to be investigated.[30] No one, to the writer's knowledge, has ever attempted to test Schumpeter's theory of entrepreneurial supply—indeed, it could be accomplished only by a team of biographers trained in psychoanalysis.

This discussion of Schumpeter ties in closely with a further difficulty in verifying any psychological or sociological entrepreneurial theory. Almost invariably the investigator faces a pervasive identification problem of the supply and demand type. When a change in entrepreneurial performance is observed, how can it be ascertained whether this has happened because of a shift in the supply of entrepreneurial effort or because of an improvement in the economic environment? This issue is well illustrated by the Colombian case. In addition to the competing entrepreneurial supply explanations of Hagen and Kasdan, it is possible that changes in the external environment were the key factor in explaining the flowering of Antioqueñian entrepreneurial activity. William Long has argued that the emergence of coffee growing in Antioquia from the early

[29] A minor inconsistency in "The Entrepreneur in Economic Change" occurs in Cochran's comparison of Henry Ford with Torcuato Di Tella. In his diffused ambitions to be a business leader, family head, intellectual, and patron of the arts, Di Tella is seen as presenting a typical pattern. He was able to do this and have successful businesses because he "delegated most of the purely technological work to trusted subordinates." But Cochran has already described the central management characteristic in Latin America as excessive individualism leading to little delegation of authority, mutual distrust between the entrepreneur and his managers, and inability to cooperate. Given Di Tella's deviance from the norm here, how much weight should we give to the typicality of his behavior in the first area?

[30] Despite the wide popularity of Schumpeterian notions among economists, comparatively few of them have survived rigorous empirical testing. For an excellent review of the literature on this subject see Edgar Salin, "The Schumpeterian Theory and Continental

1880s is virtually the entire cause of the development pattern described by Hagen.[31] Having the best soils in the country for this crop, Antioquia was soon producing nearly half of Colombia's leading export. Export earnings provided both the investment resources and a regional demand for industrial consumer goods. The transportation network constructed by the government (1874–1929) primarily to evacuate coffee greatly extended the market for factories in Antioquia but did not do so for the rival Bogota area. How can we identify the influence of these external conditions as distinct from changes in the quantity and quality of entrepreneurial effort?

This identification problem can be formalized in a conventional supply and demand diagram.[32] On the horizontal axis we would like to measure, ideally, the quantity of entrepreneurial services in standard units; as an imperfect proxy we will use output, positing somewhat unrealistically a fixed entrepreneurial input coefficient. On the vertical axis is the entrepreneur's "wage"—residual profit per standard unit of entrepreneurial service; our substitute measure for this variable is the rate of return on investment, P/K.[33] The supply schedule is a function of sociopsychological variables and, to some extent, the past amount of entrepreneurial "training." The derived demand for entrepreneurial services at any point in time is a function of the price of all cooperating factors of production, the stock of known or transferable technology, the level of managerial organization, and consumer income.

A possible objection to a downwards sloping demand schedule is that entrepreneurs create their own demand. Although this holds for original innovation, with very few exceptions entrepreneurial activity in developing countries is directed to expanding production or import substitution in response to existing price signals. However, it is true that the downward sloping demand curve will be different for each entrepreneur, varying with his command over technical knowledge and his managerial efficiency in combining factor inputs.

As shown in panel A of Figure 1-1 we are never able to observe either the supply or demand schedules: all we see at a point in time is a certain level of production associated with a certain profit rate. Suppose we want to measure

Thought" and the comments by Alexander Gerschenkron and Serge-Christophe Kolm in *The Transfer of Technology to Developing Countries*, eds. D. L. Spencer and A. Woroniak (New York: 1967).

[31] Unpublished seminar paper, summarized by Benjamin Higgins, op. cit., pp. 253–257.

[32] For a differently specified and more sophisticated mathematical treatment of the supply and demand issue than that which follows, see J. R. Harris, "Industrial Entrepreneurship in Nigeria," doctoral dissertation (Northwestern University: 1967), Ch. 2.

[33] The use of the profit rate surrogate entails the assumption of uniform risk in all projects and a linear relation between the amount of capital and entrepreneurial services.

the extent to which the supply of entrepreneurship has shifted over a given time period. We would observe two points such as t_1h_2 or t_1t_4 or h_2t_4, and so on as shown in panel A. Without a considerable quantity of additional information we have no way of knowing whether the growth in output is attributable to (1) primarily a shift in the supply schedule of entrepreneurial effort—panel B, (2) entirely a demand shift—panel C, or (3) some intermediate combination of the two. Only in the case of the set h_2t_4 can we be sure that there has been, *de minimum*, a shift in supply.

Panel D depicts a closed, Hirschmanesque economy[34] where an outside disturbance (in this case pushing demand out to h_2) induces an increase in output, O_aO_b, which in turn generates new investment opportunities through backward and forward linkages and creates expansion-inducing external economies for existing producers. The result of these positive externalities is an endogenously powered outward movement in the demand for entrepreneurial services via successively diminishing steps to the point h_3. The extent of this induced demand shift will depend upon the size of (1) the original disturbance, (2) the output-positive externalities ratio, (3) countervailing external diseconomies, and (4) the elasticity of entrepreneurial supply. At the same time that this latter factor is influencing the shift in demand, it is also determining the extent of the output response, O_bO_c. Thus, the effective strength of Hirschman's linkages depends critically upon the elasticity of entrepreneurial supply.

From this formulation of the identification problem, it is a very short step to an eighth and final model of entrepreneurial performance. We shall term this the economist's model; it stands as a counter-hypothesis to all the theories of entrepreneurial supply. It is most frequently encountered in an implicit form in empirical studies such as those of G. F. Papanek, J. R. Harris, and Kozo Yamamura reprinted in Part II of this volume.[35]

In this construct, one constant factor is given exogenously and is assumed to be present in all societies: the psychological drive for pecuniary gain, or in its more formal guise, the desire to maximize real income. The effect of this psychological constant conjoined with a particular definition of the entrepreneurial role provides the highly elastic supply schedule of entrepreneurial services noted above. All the other elements in the model lie on the demand

[34] A. O. Hirschman, *The Strategy of Economic Development* (New Haven: 1958).

[35] Three explicit statements of at least part of the economist's model propounded here are H. G. Aubrey, "Industrial Investment Decisions: A Comparative Analysis," *Journal of Economic History* (December, 1955); Nathan Rosenberg, "Capital Formation in Under-developed Countries," *American Economic Review* (September, 1960); and W. J. Baumol, "Entrepreneurship in Economic Theory," *American Economic Review*, Supplement (May, 1968).

FIGURE 1-1 **Entrepreneurial Services: Demand and Supply**

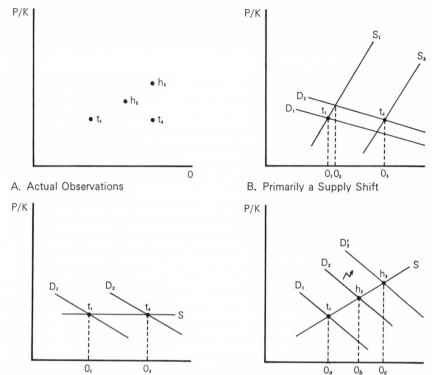

A. Actual Observations

B. Primarily a Supply Shift

C. Demand Shift

D. Endogenous Demand Shift

side and can be described as economic environment variables. These comprehend the level of demand for industrial products, availability of required labor and raw material inputs, degree of inflation, level of company taxation, ease of importing essential inputs, regulatory environment, political stability, and security of property. Given well-functioning product and factor markets and an otherwise favorable setting, the entrepreneur's role is reduced to decision making under uncertainty.

Within the context of this model, lack of vigorous entrepreneurial response in manufacturing is explained by various kinds of market imperfections and inefficient policy making. High rates of inflation induce rational profit maximizers to invest in real estate, consumer goods inventories, precious metals, and the like where sure capital gains far exceed moderate and less reliable industrial profits. Abrupt changes in political administration, devaluation, restrictions on imported ingredients, and sudden wage increases by political fiat result in windfall losses to industrial producers, but such losses are not shared by those who have invested in urban housing or stocks of imported goods.[36] Add to these malfunctions the normally greater risks of industrial enterprise, its more extensive management requirements, and its greater dependence upon potentially scarce inputs, then limited entrepreneurial activity in manufacturing is not to be wondered at.

In most instances, the economist's claim cannot be disproved, although neither can he establish an undisputed primacy for market incentives.[37] The economist's remedies for poor entrepreneurial performance are well known: pursue appropriate monetary and balance-of-payments policies, remove all market impediments, stimulate demand for local production by import tariffs or government purchasing programs, and supplement markets by providing complementary inputs on a subsidized basis (e.g., technical education, loan capital, technical assistance). These and other measures are carefully spelled out in the selection in Part II by Eugene Staley and Richard Morse.

A major problem with the economist's model is its excessively narrow definition of the entrepreneurial function. This definition is based upon implicit assumptions about the nature of a well-functioning underdeveloped economy. These assumptions are that factors of production possess a relatively high degree of mobility; that inputs and output are homogeneous; that producers, consumers, and resource owners have knowledge of all the possibilities open to them; and that there are no significant indivisibilities. These assumptions conveniently produce a situation where risk and uncertainty are minimal, where change is continuous and incremental, and where the influence of social institutions is neutral. When the assumptions are relaxed, and ignorance, hetrogeneity (segmented markets), impeded factor mobility, lumpiness, pervasive administrative controls, and input nonavailabilities are brought into the model, then the extraordinary qualities required of the entrepreneur—and the possibility of their limited supply—become apparent.[38]

[36] John Harris has pointed out to the writer that a partial offset to these negative incentives will occur when commodity prices rise faster than factor prices; that is, wage lags and an over-valued foreign exchange rate will tend to favor industrial profits.

[37] Thus, Papanek does not examine the sociological history of Pakistan's innovating groups and so cannot preclude supply factors as possible prime determinants. Although Yamamura raises questions about the reliability of Hirschmeier's entrepreneurial characterizations, he avoids the evidence that profits rates in Meiji Japan were exceedingly low (e.g., the return on Yasuda's assets was 4.4 per cent); nor does Yamamura attempt to explain the behavior of the two most influential figures in Meiji entrepreneurial history—Shibusawa Eiichi and Fukuzawa Yukichi.

[38] Two economists who do emphasize the importance of these kinds of departure from the competitive model are Albert Hirschman and Harvey Leibenstein. While both authors discuss incentives and other arrangements to minimize these difficulties, neither of them

SECTION FOUR

Although we have traversed considerable terrain and have learned much about the hazards of attempting to trap our Heffalump, he has not been caught and, indeed, we may still lack a reliable description of what he looks like. Where then, do we go from here? Our starting point is the following observation: all the theory builders, despite many sensitive insights and distinctions with regard to specific problems, end up by positing that the creative (or achievement-oriented, or rational, or innovative) entrepreneur with his special facility is either *present* or *absent*, and that business performance is uniformly lackluster and tradition-bound or it is innovative and expansive in all aspects. The writer's own experience in West Africa and a perusal of the empirical literature on this subject for other underdeveloped countries suggest that this binary conception of the entrepreneurship problem is neither fruitful nor in accord with what we observe.

Let us start by sketching the potential scope of the entrepreneurial task in an underdeveloped economy. Widening the typical three- or four-function description of the industrialist's job to a more appropriate degree of articulation, thirteen roles or specific kinds of activities that the entrepreneur himself might have to preform for the successful operation of his enterprise are given below. It will be convenient for later discussion to categorize these roles into four sub-groupings: exchange relationships (1–4), political administration (5–7), management control (8–9), and technology (10–13).

1. Perception of market opportunities (novel or imitative).

2. Gaining command over scarce resources.

3. Purchasing inputs.

4. Marketing of the product and responding to competition.

5. Dealing with the public bureaucracy (concessions, licenses, taxes).

---

attempts to develop a theory of entrepreneurial supply. See A. O. Hirschman, op. cit. and *Journeys Through Progress* (New York: 1963); and H. Leibenstein "Entrepreneurship and Development" *American Economic Review*, Supplement (May, 1968).

6. Management of human relations within the firm.

7. Management of customer and supplier relations.

8. Financial management.

9. Production management (control by written records, supervision, co-ordinating input flows with orders, maintenance).

10. Acquiring and overseeing assembly of the factory.

11. Industrial engineering (minimizing inputs with a given production process).

12. Upgrading processes and product quality.

13. Introduction of new production techniques and products.

Under the strict assumptions of the economist's model the entrepreneur himself (or the entrepreneurial team in the case of a large corporation) will only perform activities 1 and 2; the skills for the remaining eleven functions will be purchased in the market place. In practice, the economist may attribute as many as the first four functions to the entrepreneurial unit. The extent to which the entrepreneur can *actually* parcel out activities to competent lieutenants depends upon the following four factors:—

i. The scale of production—the larger the enterprise the more scope there is for utilizing specialized executive personnel, in so far as factors 2 to 4 permit.

ii. The degree of development of the high-level manpower market.

iii. Social factors governing the amount of responsibility with which hired personnel will perform.

iv. The entrepreneur's comparative efficiency in utilizing high-cost managerial employees.

While one can observe greater delegation of entrepreneurial tasks in the more advanced and socially disciplined economies, by and large the effect of the latter three factors has been to hold to a maximum the number of activities per-formed by the entrepreneur, in whole or in part, up to a threshold firm size somewhere between 100 and 200 employees. Because of the greater importance of firms falling below this threshold, in conjunction with underdeveloped factor input markets, the demands placed upon the entrepreneurial unit are considerably more extensive in low-income as compared to high-income economies.

This conceptualization of entrepreneurship as the performance of services that are required but not available in the market (or not available in sufficient divisibility) can usefully be contrasted with other formulations. The entrepreneurial function is defined in terms of activities rather than in terms of attributes such as innovation or risk-taking which may or may not characterize a particular activity. No invariable set of activities, such as investment decisions or designing market strategy, is identified as constitutive of the entrepreneurial function. The entrepreneurial unit provides the variable, residual non-marketed services and receives the residual profit income as payment. But let us return now to our principal objective of empirically assessing differential role performance.

Evidence from contemporary underdeveloped economies for evaluating entrepreneurial performance in the thirteen roles we have enumerated is found in a number of descriptive studies of on-going industrial entrepreneurship and in studies of productive efficiency in factory enterprise. The former are cross-sectional surveys covering one or a number of industries in individual countries. investigators report energetic and skillful performance in roles 1 to 7: these business men are highly responsive to economic opportunities, they are willing to risk their own capital in long-term ventures, they are adept at marketing, and (with the exceptions noted) they maintain harmonious relations with their staff, suppliers, and the public bureaucracy.[39] Moreover, making allowance for capital entry requirements, these entrepreneurs are recruited from a broad range of occupational and social strata; there is no evidence of blocked mobility which would lead to inadequate numbers of entrepreneurs.

Seeming to bear out the speculations made in section I about the critical entrepreneurial tasks in late developing countries, the domain where performance is reported to be least satisfactory is that of technology and production

---

[39] J. J. Berna, *Industrial Entrepreneurship in Madras State* (New York: 1960), Chs. 4–6; J. J. Carroll, *The Filipino Manufacturing Entrepreneur* (Ithaca: 1965), Ch. 6; T. C. Cochran, *The Puerto Rican Businessman* (Philadelphia: 1959), Ch. 4; J. R. Harris, *Industrial Entrepreneurship in Nigeria*, unpublished doctoral dissertation (Northwestern University: 1967), Ch. 8; Peter Kilby, *African Enterprise: The Nigerian Bread Industry* (Stanford: 1965), Chs. 7–8; E. W. Nafziger, *Nigerian Entrepreneurship: A Study of Indigenous Businessmen in the Footwear Industry*, unpublished doctoral dissertation (University of Illinois: 1967), Chs. 3–5; G. F. Papanek, *Pakistan's Development, Social Goals and Private Incentives* (Cambridge, Mass.: 1967), Chs. 2–3; Y. A. Sayigh, *Entrepreneurs of Lebanon* (Cambridge, Mass.: 1962), Chs. 1–4. Limited information on role performance can be gleaned from A. P. Alexander, "Industrial Entrepreneurship in Turkey: Origins and Growth," *Economic Development and Cultural Change* (July, 1960), pp. 349–365.

management. Cochran, Harris, Kilby, and Nafziger identify this area as the major bottleneck to indigenous industrial development. Papanek also views in-factory managerial efficiency as the principal problem in Pakistan but considers it to be of manageable proportions even in the near-term. In his fifty-two machinery-making firms, Berna ranks inadequacies in industrial engineering and technological betterment with rigid attitudes toward labor relations as the principal impediments to further industrial expansion. Sayigh and Carroll, because of the type of data they collected, do not mention any "internal" deficiencies in entrepreneurial performance.

All but two of these investigators interpret these shortcomings as transient and as being a function of the scarcity of market supplied skill inputs, lack of competitive pressures (especially in Pakistan, Turkey, and the Philippines), and inexperience. In short, these authors take the position that there is little or no problem of entrepreneurial supply, rather that the difficulties lie primarily in external market conditions. Only Thomas Cochran and the present writer see managerial and technological shortcomings as enduring impediments rooted in sociological variables on the supply side. One can isolate two factors that might have biased the majority of investigators toward their predominantly demand interpretation. First, by and large they all approached their subject with an economist-like conception of what constitutes the entrepreneurial function, *i.e.*, a primary emphasis on roles 1 to 4. Second, because their studies are cross-sectional rather than longitudinal and their descriptive data on entrepreneurial performance are limited to a single point in time, actual observation of persisting managerial and technological problems is precluded.[40] In contrast, the effect of differing market circumstances on intra-sample entrepreneurial performance is clearly seen. Moreover, even when measurements of entrepreneurial performance are obtained on a time-series basis, the influence of slow-changing supply variables will be obscured unless the period is long enough to average out shifts in economic conditions.

The writer's own perception of the *persistence* of very substantial managerial and technological shortcomings originated with a study of development lending and other relatively comprehensive business assistance measures in Nigeria which began in the late 1940s.[41] Although there has been some improvement over a twenty-year period with accumulated experience and rising levels of entrepreneurial education, the problem remains a crippling bottleneck to

[40] Harris' cross-sectional analysis does control for ethnic background, but because the critical cultural factors have a common set in all Nigerian tribes their significance is not detected.

[41] See Peter Kilby, *Industrialization in an Open Economy: Nigeria 1945–1966* (Cambridge: 1969), Ch. 10.

industrialization based on indigenous entrepreneurial resources.[42] In expatriate industry, the prime constraint on labor productivity is the proficiency of Nigerian supervisors.[43] Similarly, poorly carried out managerial functions appear to be the main causes of inefficiency in state enterprise and government departments.[44] What is the nature of this organizational slack in Nigeria and how important is it? In the baking industry the writer documented the loss of three-quarters of potential profits to raw materials wastage, damaging of bread during baking, and extensive employee pilferage.[45] Lawrence Okigbo found that over half of Nigeria's sawmills were operating at less than 50 per cent efficiency during the hours in which they were in use; and Harris and Rowe report that, combining efficiency with hours utilized, "most Nigerian sawmills are producing only 10 to 20 per cent of the lumber that the installed machines are capable of producing."[46] Comparable magnitudes of underutilization were found in the rubber creping industry.

The factors which lie behind such poor performance are, on the production side, failure to regularly maintain equipment, inadequate coordination of raw material purchases with product orders, a disinclination to utilize written records for purposes of control, and the absence of conscientious supervision in the work place. Profits are further reduced through pilferage and embezzlement of funds by the senior clerical staff.[47] We will conclude this description by quoting John Harris reporting on a survey he and Mary Rowe conducted in 1965 which covered 269 of Nigeria's leading indigenous industrial firms:

Generally, the level of efficiency within the firms was very low. Substantial increases in output could be achieved without additional investment. Closer supervision, better organization, improved layout, and quality control are desperately needed on the production side. Low levels of capacity utilization are largely a result of management deficiencies.

The general standard of financial management is also very low. Although 249 of the firms had some kind of accounting systems, they were not systematically used as

[42] Thus, Harris finds that degree of entrepreneurial success (an index combining profitability and rate of growth of firm) is only weakly and not significantly associated with the individual's education, Goodman-Krushkal's Gamma = 0.154. Kilby and Nafziger found the relationship even weaker.

[43] Kilby, *Industrialization in an Open Economy*, pp. 224–225.   [44] Ibid., pp. 77–79.

[45] Kilby, *African Enterprise: The Nigerian Bread Industry*, pp. 57–67.

[46] Both citations from J. R. Harris and M. P. Rowe, "Entrepreneurial Patterns in the Nigerian Sawmilling Industry," *Nigerian Journal of Economic and Social Studies* (March, 1966), p. 78.

[47] See particularly Kilby, *African Enterprise*, Ch. 5; W. T. Newlyn and D. C. Rowan, *Money and Banking in British Colonial Africa* (Oxford: 1954), pp. 97 ff; and E. K. Hawkins, *Road Transport in Nigeria* (London: 1958), Ch. 4.

management tools. The larger firms had annual statements prepared by outside auditors for the purposes of establishing tax liability (thus avoiding arbitrary assessment), but for the most part these documents were lying on the shelf gathering dust. Surprisingly, records of asset values were more available than records of output and sales. . . .

This widespread lack of financial control was reflected in the fact that barely more than half of the entrepreneurs had an adequate understanding of depreciation, and only one-half of them could make a reasonable estimate of the minimum production per day needed to break even. Only 31 of them had any organized system of cost accounting, and separation of business and personal accounts was rare.

Most of the firms were one-man operations. When the business expands beyond the point that the owner can control everything himself, serious problems are encountered. The ability to delegate responsibility and authority, while still keeping control, is generally lacking. Admittedly, it is difficult to find capable subordinates and managers in Nigeria, but little has been done by these entrepreneurs to train and develop such personnel. Several cases were encountered of successful small firms foundering badly after major expansion. Experience of the entrepreneurs with hired expatriate managers has been largely unhappy.[48]

In his 1962 article reprinted in this volume, Papanek states that Pakistani entrepreneurs were little concerned with raising productive efficiency since greater returns to their effort could be had from promoting new ventures and evading government regulations. In his 1967 book,[49] he reports that from the late 1950s circumstances changed (both the level of protection and the amount of government regulation declined drastically) so that it was then maximizing behavior to expend effort on increasing technical efficiency. Papanek advances a few pieces of evidence to show that there have been significant increases in productivity. If this were so, it would indicate that, as Papanek claims, there is no entrepreneurial supply problem in Pakistan. However, it is the validity of just this point that reviewers have questioned:

Dr. Papanek's assertion about improvement of efficiency in industries since the late 1950's is not based on reliable empirical evidence. It may be granted, however, that efficiency began to improve at a slow rate, but more important is the level of efficiency in industrial production. Several studies indicate that wastage and misallocation of scarce resources was and continues to be very large, real income could be considerably increased through greater efficiency, and the transfer of resources from some industries to others. For instance, Soligo and Stern [1965] have shown that for a large number of industries including cotton textiles, jute textiles, sugar and tobacco, the net subsidy received through

[48] J. R. Harris, "Factors Affecting the Supply of Industrial Entrepreneurship in Nigeria," mimeograph (December, 1966). A paper read at the Yale Growth Center seminar.
[49] See footnote 39.

tariff protection exceeds the total value added. Islam and Malik [1967] have shown that there is a very high degree of underutilisation of capacity which is another indicator of inefficient use of scarce capital. These studies should not be considered conclusive, but they strongly suggest a high level of inefficiency. Nor, after more than a decade's operation, can this inefficiency be passed off by the infant industries argument.[50]

There is much scattered evidence on organizational slack and remediable technical inefficiency for individual industries in developing countries, although the findings are seldom completely free of other influences. In the Brazilian textile industry, measured input productivity is just half that United Nations experts judge is obtainable under Latin American conditions; in a sample of twenty-five spinning mills, with scale effects held constant, average operational efficiency was 54 per cent of best-practice performance—two-thirds of the short-fall was attributed to management factors.[51] W. Paul Strassmann cites numerous examples from Puerto Rico and Mexico in his recent book; he also identifies the extreme scarcity of supervisors who can do their jobs well as "perhaps the greatest bottleneck for economic development."[52] One can also cite testimony on the quantitative importance of organizational shortcomings given by A. O. Hirschman and F. H. Harbison.[53]

Probably the best single set of data on the matter is that provided by ILO Productivity Demonstration Missions which reveals directly the quality of entrepreneurial performance on our role 11, industrial engineering.[54] By the introduction of simple alterations in plant layout, materials handling, waste control, work method, and the like, the ILO Missions achieved capital and labor savings averaging about 35 per cent. These results are shown in Table 1-1. They imply a very high level of managerial inefficiency. Even more revealing, despite the large contribution to profits, most of the demonstration firms— Israel excepted—slipped back into their original inefficient ways within a year's time.

[50] S. R. Bose, *Pakistan Development Review* (Summer, 1968), p. 269. S. R. Lewis makes the same point in the December, 1968 *American Economic Review*, pp. 1395–1396.

[51] United Nations, *The Textile Industry in Latin America, II Brazil* (New York: 1963), p. 76 and Chs. 5 and 6. The other third was attributed to age of machinery.

[52] W. Paul Strassmann, *Technological Change and Economic Development* (Ithaca: 1968), p. 93.

[53] A. O. Hirschman, *The Strategy of Economic Development* (New Haven: 1958), Ch. 8; and F. H. Harbison, "Entrepreneurial Organization as a Factor in Economic Development," *Quarterly Journal of Economics* (August, 1956).

[54] For a full discussion of the ILO data, see Peter Kilby, "Organization and Productivity in Backward Economies," *Quarterly Journal of Economics* (May, 1962).

TABLE 1-1
ILO Productivity Mission Results

Factory or Operation	Method[a]	Increase in Labor Productivity %	Impact on the Firm (Unit Cost Reduction) Labor Savings %	Impact on the Firm (Unit Cost Reduction) Capital Savings[b] %
India				
Seven textile mills	n.a.	5-to-250	5–71	5–71
Engineering firms				
All operations	F, B	102	50	50
One operation	F	385	79	79
All operations	F, B	117	54	54
All operations	F, B	34	25	25
All operations	F, B	44	31	31
One operation	F, B	21	17	17
One operation	F	44	31	31
One operation	F	120	55	55
One operation	F	116	54	54
One operation	F	500	83	83
Vehicle maintenance	A, F	161	62	62
Burma				
Molding railroad brake shoes	A, F, B	100	50	50
Smithy	A	40	29	29
Chair assembly	A, B	100	50	50
Almirah assembly	A, B	65	39	39
Biscuit wrapping	F	45	31	–
Cutting hosiery	F	40	29	–
Packing towels	A, F	20	17	–
Match manufacture	A, F	24	19	–
Indonesia				
Knitting	A, B	15	13	–
Radio assembly	A, F	40	29	29
Printing	A, F	30	23	–
Cement block	A, B	50	33	33
Enamel ware	F	30	23	–
Singapore				
Vegetable oils	A, E, D, F	63	38	–
Malaya				
Furniture	A, D	10	9	9
Engineering workshop	A, D	10	9	9
Pottery	A, B	20	17	17
Thailand				
Locomotive maintenance	A, F	44	31	31
Saucepan polishing	E, D	50	33	–
Saucepan assembly	B, F	42	30	–
Cigarettes	A, B	5	5	–

TABLE 1-1 *(continued)*

Factory or Operation	Method[a]	Increase in Labor Productivity %	Impact on the Firm (Unit Cost Reduction) Labor Savings %	Capital Savings[b] %
Pakistan				
Textile plants	C, H, G			
Weaving		50	33	33
Weaving		10	9	9
Spinning and weaving		30	23	23
Bleaching		58	37	37
Over-all operations		400	80	80
Spinning waste		36	26	26
Weaving		5	5	5
Weaving		141	59	59
Israel				
Locomotive repair	F, B, G	30	23	23
Diamond cutting and polishing	C, B, G	45	31	–
Refrigerator assembly	F, B, G	75	43	43
Wire insulation	n.a.	44	31	31
Wire insulation	n.a.	50	33	–
Cleaning clothes	n.a.	30	23	23
Ironing trousers	n.a.	50	33	33
Packing textiles	n.a.	40	29	–
Processing textiles	n.a.	140	58	–
Flush tank assembly	n.a.	100	50	–
Orange picking	F	91	47	–

[a] A = plant layout reorganized   E = waste control
   B = machine utilization and flow   F = work method
   C = simple technical alterations   G = payment by results
   D = materials handling   H = worker training and supervision
   Limited to plant and equipment, excluding increased depreciation costs.

SECTION FIVE

Summarizing the foregoing review of available empirical evidence from under-developed countries, it was found that with a few exceptions entrepreneurial performance in those roles involving exchange relationships and "political administration" is vigorous and effective. On the other hand, entrepreneurs typically do not apply themselves with equal intensity or skill to their tasks in the realms of management control and technology. Deficiencies in these latter areas represent in many instances the operational bottleneck to indigenous industrial development.

This essay will have achieved its major goal if section IV has succeeded in establishing a reasonable case for the existence of differential entrepreneurial role performance. Hopefully, this will entice future investigators in developing countries to widen their research design vis-à-vis the basic entrepreneurial roles to be studied. In this concluding section, we will very briefly speculate on the much more complex and elusive question of the sources of observed managerial and technological deficiencies.

One can identify at least four levels at which the problem may be rooted. At the first level, it is hypothesized that these deficiencies are superficial and can be remedied over a relatively short period by providing conventional education and training inputs. This is the position John Harris takes in his Nigerian study. Interpreting this position in terms of the economist's model, the supply schedule of efficient entrepreneurial services can be shifted or flattened by an appropriate investment in training facilities. At a second level, it is argued that, despite the modest results obtained from conventional training, a properly designed technical education program which stresses simultaneously theory, practical participation, and individual experimentation starting in the seventh school year—is potentially capable of producing the necessary skills and attitudes. Proponents of this position note that indigenous cultures frequently lack both the concept and the vocabulary of many technological relationships;[55] post-secondary training built upon earlier noninternalized education by rote results in narrow skills and the complete absence of technical problem-solving (creative) abilities. At a third level, general environmental technological deprivation in semitraditional societies, particularly in the rural environment where most children's perceptions of the physical world are formed, is postulated as the principal root cause. Finally, at the fourth level, technological and managerial weaknesses in the entrepreneur's performance are seen to be a function not only of the technological environment but also of the social structure which supports and is pervasively intermeshed with traditional technology.

The explanation offered here is based on the conviction that the described differential role performance is rooted at the fourth level. The efficacy of remedies aimed at the primary, secondary, and tertiary level manifestations are not denied; the sufficiency of such remedies *is* denied. The argument will be developed for traditional societies, an ideal type which applies with diminishing force to contemporary Africa, Asia, and Latin America. Modifications will be introduced later.

Our thesis concerning entrepreneurial task performance is as follows: where similar activities have existed in traditional or semitraditional society, as

[55] To cite one striking example, R. G. Armstrong has pointed out that for various eco-logical reasons the simplest mechanical principles embodied in the wheel, the inclined plane, and the lever have never found their way into West African societies. "Some Technical Gaps in Nigerian School Curricula," *Proceedings of the West African Institute of Social and Economic Research* (Ibadan: 1953).

in the case of exchange relationships and "political administration," those social mechanisms which transmit the required skills and attitudes from one generation to the next provide the necessary conditioning for effective performance in parallel if somewhat more complex roles in the modern entrepreneurial setting. Where there are no transmutable antecedent roles, particularly if the absence of a positive tradition is reinforced by inhibitory social structural influences (as with supervision), then we may expect low levels of intensity and proficiency in carrying out these particular functions. This applies to the entrepreneur's lieutenants and labor force as well as to himself. Some specific tasks will now be considered.

A basic managerial function in any productive enterprise is to synchronize the work of various individuals or groups, each of whom is performing a particular subset of operations, and to control for quality, standardization, materials wastage, and rate of throughput. In other words, coordination and control are a necessary corollary of division of labor. Where a single individual produces a commodity in its entirety and at a pace and quality of his own setting, no such managerial ability is called for. "Only rarely is any division of labour for the production of a given commodity encountered among non-literate folk."[56] "Neither is it [production] organized in a manner requiring clear specifications of direct producer, supervisor and policy-maker which underlie the bureaucratic structure of a modern intensive and extensive division of labour.[57] The absence of intra-commodity specialization is not surprising insofar as one of the principal attributes of a simple technology is the lack of divisibility of the production process. Although cooperative work organization is widespread, in most cases each individual is performing the same kind of work and is not subject to any direct controls. In sum, in traditional society there are no antecedents for the coordination and control functions which are central to the management of an industrial enterprise.

It is instructive to contrast the situation of eighteenth-century Europe (Tokugawa Japan was not markedly dissimilar[58]) to that of contemporary semi-traditional societies. Charles Wilson in his discussion of English entrepreneurship during the industrial revolution observes "that abrupt change is not in fact characteristic of the economic process, certainly not in the 18th and 19th century. Late 18th century Britain was an old commercial society, highly skilled and sophisticated in certain economic techniques. The new industrial changes were linked organically and personally with an older economic world at every

---

[56] Melville J. Herskovits, *Economic Anthropology* (New York: 1952), p. 126.
[57] Manning Nash, *Primitive and Peasant Economic Systems* (San Francisco: 1966), p. 21.
[58] See particularly the writings of R. P. Dore and T. C. Smith.

stage."[59] Wilson spells out the continuity in terms of sources of capital, marketing channels, and technology. In his exhaustive study of the origins of industrial management, Sidney Pollard documents the presence of strong antecedent traditions—codified estate management, putting-out, and subcontracting. "It should be stressed how much of the older system was left in the interstices of the new factory organization, making adjustment easier and postponing, to that extent, the development of modern management techniques."[60] And yet, even with these traditions to build upon, it was not until the beginning of the nineteenth century that a reasonable level of control was obtained over careless operation of equipment, irregular product quality, theft by operatives, and embezzlement by paid managers.

Paralleling the absence of any significant commutable managerial roles in premodern technology, certain aspects of traditional social structure also impede adaptation to the behavioral requirements of specialized production processes. The most significant feature of traditional labor viewed from this perspective is its plurality of purpose: the provision of purely economic services is intertwined with the performance of other basic social functions. Thus, for the individual participating in group work, in addition to the economic returns of food and a claim on reciprocal labor, he is also at the very minimum expressing his kinship loyalty to the wider group, affirming bonds of friendship for the individual, and seeking personal prestige.[61] This relatively heavily laden social situation is governed by canons of etiquette which preclude the use of direct sanctions to correct undesired work performance. After completion of the work and in ways that avoid direct confrontation, indirect sanctions may be invoked (smaller portion of food at the feast, no invitation to the next communal project, veiled satirical verses). Thus, for the factory worker and supervisor who have been socialized in the traditional or semitraditional setting, there is likely to be a reluctance to accept supervision and a disinclination to exercise it.[62]

There is another factor, related to the status system, that operates against effective managerial supervision. Reported in Latin America and Asia, as well as in Africa, there is a strong antipathy among superiors to concern themselves on a continuing and constructive basis with the task performance of subordinates.

[59] "The Entrepreneur in the Industrial Revolution in Britain" (1955), reprinted in B. E. Supple, ed., *The Experience of Economic Growth* (New York: 1963), p. 173.

[60] Sidney Pollard, *The Genesis of Modern Management: A Study of the Industrial Revolution in Great Britain* (London: 1965), p. 18.

[61] Herskovits, p. 123.

[62] Evidence on this point for Pakistan and Ethiopia can be found in J. A. Lee, "Developing Managers in Developing Countries," *Harvard Business Review* (November–December, 1968), pp. 58, 61–63 and for Nigeria in the writer's *Industrialization in an Open Economy*, pp. 224–225.

Although Hagen interprets the phenomenon in terms of authority protection and LeVine in terms of status-enhancing conspicuous leisure, both agree that genuine concern with the task performance of a subordinate is viewed as socially degrading.[63] The consequence of this status factor for the operation of a business enterprise (or any similar organization such as governmental departments, cooperatives, and the like), is to undermine the imperatives of supervisory activity both for the entrepreneur and for all his supervisory staff. Against the obvious longer term gains in technical efficiency and commercial aggrand · isement, any supervisory actor must balance the immediate cost in lost status respect.

The continuing effect of traditional social structure on the propensity to innovate, once the environmental conditions no longer hold, is far less clear than the impact in the managerial sphere.[64] Traditional society exhibited very little technological innovation because of its small scale and customary patterns of distribution. The small scale of traditional society meant (1) it had limited access to new technical knowledge and limited internal information-processing capacity, and (2) it could not absorb innovations involving interdependencies extending beyond the communal boundaries of trust. Customary patterns of distribution of output for consumption blocked innovation wherever the latter involved an absolute loss in the share of product going to any claimant or where the extent of sharing was such as to remove any reasonable incentive for undertaking the expense and uncertainty entailed by the innovation. To what extent these factors of scale and communal obligation survive in the semimodern period and operate to dampen innovation remains problematical.

Not all the preceding sociological propositions fit every underdeveloped country. Social structure barriers to effective entrepreneurship can be conceptualized as being of two kinds. On the one hand, where existing society is characterized by low levels of role differentiation there will be problems of *role discontinuity* when a complex technology is introduced which requires extensive division of labor (differentiation) and managerial coordination (integration). The multipurpose goals involved in rendering labor in peasant society, with its implications for supervision, is an example of an undifferentiated role. On the other hand, where the society is characterized by high structural differentiation— the modern sector of Latin American countries and of some Asian countries— there may be problems of *role incongruency* in relation to the requirements of industrial technology. A considerable amount of such incongruency appears to obtain in Latin America. By contrast, in the hierarchical, Confucian societies of

[63] Hagen, *On the Theory of Social Change*, p. 80; and LeVine, *Dreams and Deeds*, Ch. 1.

[64] The propositions in this paragraph owe much to discussions with Victor Uchendu.

Japan, Korea, and Taiwan (countries also characterized by a rice-paddy agricultural technology), surging entrepreneurial performance indicates that incongruencies are minimal.

And so our search for the Heffalump draws to a close. We have attempted to convince the reader that we have caught sight of the entrepreneurial phenomenon. Although the evidence leads us to reject the economist's agnosticism concerning the variability of entrepreneurial supply, so too do we reject those theories which postulate a binary presence or absence of entrepreneurial capabilities. Rather, we have argued that the various activities required of the industrial entrepreneur are individually reinforced or impeded by prior techno-economic traditions and social structure factors. We have further argued that in late modernizing economies, the critical entrepreneurial inputs are related to achieving and maintaining efficient production, in contra-distinction to innovation or marketing activities. The same sociological variables of role continuity and role congruency also condition the behavior of certain non-entrepreneurial personnel (*e.g.*, technicians, foremen) whose effective cooperation the business leader must win; however, in order to maintain an operational focus on the problem, it is most fruitful to view these matters in terms of what they imply for successful entrepreneurial action.[65] If these conclusions can claim a reasonable measure of validity, then hopefully we have made a modest contribution toward designing a better trap and pointing to that part of the wood where future hunters will eventually succeed in capturing the Heffalump.

[65] There are a number of interesting similarities between the conclusions presented here and what Hugh Aitken identifies as the areas of agreement that emerged from the studies of the entrepreneurial historians who worked at Harvard in the 1950s. See H. G. J. Aitken, "The Future of Entrepreneurial Research," *Explorations in Entrepreneurial History* (Fall, 1963), pp. 5–7. A major reason why the Harvard effort has had such a limited impact on entrepreneurial theory was the failure to relate social role analysis in a rigorous and concrete way to the behavioral requirements of the business leader in performing his entrepreneurial functions.

PART

I

2

THE FUNDAMENTAL PHENOMENON OF ECONOMIC DEVELOPMENT

J. A. Schumpeter

SECTION ONE

OUR problem is as follows. The theory we gave earlier describes economic life from the standpoint of a "circular flow," running on in channels essentially the same year after year—similar to the circulation of the blood in an animal organism. Now this circular flow and its channels do alter in time, and here we abandon the analogy with the circulation of the blood. For although the latter also changes in the course of the growth and decline of the organism, yet it only does so continuously, that is by steps which one can choose smaller than any assignable quantity, however small, and always within the same framework. Economic life experiences such changes too, but it also experiences others which do not appear continuously and which change the framework, the traditional course itself. They cannot be understood by means of any analysis of the circular flow, although they are purely economic and although their explanation is obviously among the tasks of pure theory. Now such changes and the phenomena which appear in their train are the object of our investigation. But we do not ask: what changes of this sort have actually made the modern

Reprinted by permission of the publisher from The Theory of Economic Development *(Harvard University Press, Cambridge, Mass. 1934), pp. 62–94.*

economic system what it is? nor: what are the conditions of such changes? We only ask, and indeed in the same sense as theory always asks: how do such changes take place, and to what economic phenomena do they give rise?

The same thing may be put somewhat differently. The theory of the first chapter describes economic life from the standpoint of the economic system's tendency towards an equilibrium position, which tendency gives us the means of determining prices and quantities of goods, and may be described as an adaptation to data existing at any time. In contrast to the conditions of the circular flow this does not mean in itself that year after year "the same" things happen; for it only means that we conceive the several processes in the economic system as partial phenomena of the tendency towards an equilibrium position, but not necessarily towards the same one. The position of the ideal state of equilibrium in the economic system, never attained, continually "striven after" (of course not consciously), changes, because the data change. And theory is not weaponless in the face of these changes in data. It is constructed so as to be able to deal with the consequences of such changes; it has special instruments for the purpose (for example the instrument called quasi-rent). If the change occurs in the non-social data (natural conditions) or in non-economic social data (here belong the effects of war, changes in commercial, social, or economic policy), or in consumers' tastes, then to this extent no fundamental overhaul of the theoretical tools seems to be required. These tools only fail—and here this argument joins the preceding—where economic life itself changes its own data by fits and starts. The building of a railway may serve as an example. Continuous changes, which may in time, by continual adaptation through innumerable small steps, make a great department store out of a small retail business, come under the "static" analysis. But "static" analysis is not only unable to predict the consequences of discontinuous changes in the traditional way of doing things; it can neither explain the occurrence of such productive revolutions nor the phenomena which accompany them. It can only investigate the new equilibrium position after the changes have occurred. It is just this occurrence of the "revolutionary" change that is our problem, the problem of economic development in a very narrow and formal sense. The reason why we so state the problem and turn aside from traditional theory lies not so much in the fact that economic changes, especially, if not solely, in the capitalist epoch, have actually occurred thus and not by continuous adaptation, but more in their fruitfulness.[1]

[1] The problems of capital, credit, entrepreneurial profit, interest on capital, and crises (or business cycles) are the ones in which this fruitfulness will be demonstrated here. Yet it is not thereby exhausted. For the expert theorist I point, for example, to the difficulties which surround the problem of increasing return, the question of multiple points of intersection

By "development", therefore, we shall understand only such changes in economic life as are not forced upon it from without but arise by its own initiative, from within. Should it turn out that there are no such changes arising in the economic sphere itself, and that the phenomenon that we call economic development is in practice simply founded upon the fact that the data change and that the economy continuously adapts itself to them, then we should say that there is *no* economic development. By this we should mean that economic development is not a phenomenon to be explained economically, but that the economy, in itself without development, is dragged along by the changes in the surrounding world, that the causes and hence the explanation of the development must be sought outside the group of facts which are described by economic theory.

Nor will the mere growth of the economy, as shown by the growth of population and wealth, be designated here as a process of development. For it calls forth no qualitatively new phenomena, but only processes of adaptation of the same kind as the changes in the natural data. Since we wish to direct our attention to other phenomena, we shall regard such increases as changes in data.[2]

Every concrete process of development finally rests upon preceding development. But in order to see the essence of the thing clearly, we shall abstract from this and allow the development to arise out of a position without development. Every process of development creates the prerequisites for the following. Thereby the form of the latter is altered, and things will turn out differently from what they would have been if every concrete phase of development had been compelled first to create its own conditions. However, if we wish to get at the root of the matter, we may not include in the data of our explanation elements of what is to be explained. But if we do not do this, we shall create an apparent discrepancy between fact and theory, which may constitute an important difficulty for the reader.

If I have been more successful than in the first edition in concentrating the exposition upon essentials and in guarding against misunderstandings, then further special explanations of the words "static" and "dynamic," with their innumerable meanings, are not necessary. Development in our sense is a distinct phenomenon, entirely foreign to what may be observed in the circular flow or

---

between supply and demand curves, and the element of time, which even Marshall's analysis has not overcome.

   [2] We do this because these changes are small per annum and therefore do not stand in the way of the applicability of the "static" method. Nevertheless, their appearance is frequently a condition of development in our sense. But even though they often make the latter possible, yet they do not create it out of themselves.

in the tendency towards equilibrium. It is spontaneous and discontinuous change in the channels of the flow, disturbance of equilibrium, which forever alters and displaces the equilibrium state previously existing. Our theory of development is nothing but a treatment of this phenomenon and the processes incident to it.[3]

SECTION TWO

These spontaneous and discontinuous changes in the channel of the circular flow and these disturbances of the centre of equilibrium appear in the sphere of industrial and commercial life, not in the sphere of the wants of the consumers of final products. Where spontaneous and discontinuous changes in consumers' tastes appear, it is a question of a sudden change in data with which the business-man must cope, hence possibly a question of a *motive* or an opportunity for other than gradual adaptations of his conduct, but not of such other conduct itself. Therefore this case does not offer any other problems than a change in natural data or require any new method of treatment; wherefore we shall neglect any spontaneity of consumers' needs that may actually exist, and assume tastes as "given." This is made easy for us by the fact that the spontaneity of wants is in general small. To be sure, we must always start from the satisfaction of wants, since they are the end of all production, and the given economic situation at any time must be understood from this aspect. Yet innovations in the economic system do not as a rule take place in such a way that first new wants arise spontaneously in consumers and then the productive apparatus swings round through their pressure. We do not deny the presence of this nexus. It is, however, the producer who as a rule initiates economic change, and consumers are educated by him if necessary; they are, as it were, taught to want new things, or things which differ in some respect or other from those which they have been

[3] In the first edition of this book, I called it "dynamics." But it is preferable to avoid this expression here, since it so easily leads us astray because of the associations which attach themselves to its various meanings. Better, then, to say simply what we mean: economic life changes; it changes partly because of changes in the data, to which it tends to adapt itself. But this is not the only kind of economic change; there is another which is not accounted for by influence on the data from without, but which arises from within the system, and this kind of change is the cause of so many important economic phenomena that it seems worth while to build a theory for it, and, in order to do so, to isolate it from all the other factors of change. The author begs to add another more exact definition, which he is in the habit of using: what we are about to consider is that kind of change arising from within the system *which so displaces its equilibrium point that the new one cannot be reached from the old one by infinitesimal steps.* Add successively as many mail coaches as you please, you will never get a railway thereby.

in the habit of using. Therefore, while it is permissible and even necessary to consider consumers' wants as an independent and indeed the fundamental force in a theory of the circular flow, we must take a different attitude as soon as we analyse *change*.

To produce means to combine materials and forces within our reach. To produce other things, or the same things by a different method, means to combine these materials and forces differently. In so far as the "new combination" may in time grow out of the old by continuous adjustment in small steps, there is certainly change, possibly growth, but neither a new phenomenon nor development in our sense. In so far as this is not the case, and the new combinations appear discontinuously, then the phenomenon characterizing development emerges. For reasons of expository convenience, henceforth, we shall only mean the latter case when we speak of new combinations of productive means. Development in our sense is then defined by the carrying out of new combinations.

This concept covers the following five cases: (1) The introduction of a new good—that is, one with which consumers are not yet familiar—or of a new quality of a good. (2) The introduction of a new method of production, that is, one not yet tested by experience in the branch of manufacture concerned, which need by no means be founded upon a discovery scientifically new, and can also exist in a new way of handling a commodity commercially. (3) The opening of a new market, that is, a market into which the particular branch of manufacture of the country in question has not previously entered, whether or not this market has existed before. (4) The conquest of a new source of supply of raw materials or half-manufactured goods, again irrespective of whether this source already exists or whether it has first to be created. (5) The carrying out of the new organisation of any industry, like the creation of a monopoly position (for example, through trustification) or the breaking up of a monopoly position.

Now two things are essential for the phenomena incident to the carrying out of such new combinations, and for the understanding of the problems involved. In the first place it is not essential to the matter—though it may happen —that the new combinations should be carried out by the same people who control the productive or commercial process which is to be displaced by the new. On the contrary, new combinations are, as a rule, embodied, as it were, in new firms which generally do not arise out of the old ones but start producing beside them; to keep to the example already chosen, in general it is not the owner of stage-coaches who builds railways. This fact not only puts the discontinuity which characterizes the process we want to describe in a special light, and creates so to speak still another kind of discontinuity in addition to the one mentioned above, but it also explains important features of the course of events. Especially in a competitive economy, in which new combinations mean the competitive elimination of the old, it explains on the one hand the process by which individuals and families rise and fall economically and socially and which is peculiar to this form of organization, as well as a whole series of other phenomena of the business cycle, of the mechanism of the formation of private fortunes, and so on. In a non-exchange economy, for example a socialist one, the new combinations would also frequently appear side by side with the old. But the economic consequences of this fact would be absent to some extent, and the social consequences would be wholly absent. And if the competitive economy is broken up by the growth of great combines, as is increasingly the case to-day in all countries, then this must become more and more true of real life, and the carrying out of new combinations must become in ever greater measure the internal concern of one and the same economic body. The difference so made is great enough to serve as the water-shed between two epochs in the social history of capitalism.

We must notice secondly, only partly in connection with this element, that whenever we are concerned with fundamental principles, we must never assume that the carrying out of new combinations takes place by employing means of production which happen to be unused. In practical life, this is very often the case. There are always unemployed workmen, unsold raw materials, unused productive capacity, and so forth. This certainly is a contributory circumstance, a favorable condition and even an incentive to the emergence of new combinations; but great unemployment is only the consequence of non-economic events—as for example the World War—or precisely of the development which we are investigating. In neither of the two cases can its existence play a fundamental role in the explanation, and it cannot occur in a well balanced circular flow from which we start. Nor would the normal yearly increment meet the case, as it would be small in the first place, and also because it would normally be absorbed by a corresponding expansion of production within the circular flow, which, if we admit such increments, we must think of as adjusted to this rate of growth.[4] As a rule the new combinations must draw the necessary means of production from some old combinations—and for reasons already mentioned we shall assume that they *always* do so, in order to put in bold relief what we hold to be the essential contour line. The carrying out of new combinations means, therefore, simply the different employment of the economic system's

---

[4] On the whole it is much more correct to say that population grows slowly up to the possibilities of any economic environment than that it has any tendency to outgrow it and to become thereby an independent cause of change.

existing supplies of productive means—which might provide a second definition of development in our sense. That rudiment of a pure economic theory of development which is implied in the traditional doctrine of the formation of capital always refers merely to saving and to the investment of the small yearly increase attributable to it. In this it asserts nothing false, but it entirely overlooks much more essential things. The slow and continuous increase in time of the national supply of productive means and of savings is obviously an important factor in explaining the course of economic history through the centuries, but it is completely overshadowed by the fact that development consists primarily in employing existing resources in a different way, in doing new things with them, irrespective of whether those resources increase or not. In the treatment of shorter epochs, moreover, this is even true in a more tangible sense. Different methods of employment, and not saving and increases in the available quantity of labor, have changed the face of the economic world in the last fifty years. The increase of population especially, but also of the sources from which savings can be made, was first made possible in large measure through the different employment of the then existing means.

The next step in our argument is also self-evident: command over means of production is necessary to the carrying out of new combinations. Procuring the means of production is one distinct problem for the established firms which work within the circular flow. For they *have* them already procured or else can procure them currently with the proceeds of previous production as was explained in the first chapter. There is no fundamental gap here between receipts and disbursements, which, on the contrary, necessarily correspond to one another just as both correspond to the means of production offered and to the products demanded. Once set in motion, this mechanism works automatically. Furthermore, the problem does not exist in a non-exchange economy even if new combinations are carried out in it; for the directing organ, for example a socialist economic ministry, is in a position to direct the productive resources of the society to new uses exactly as it can direct them to their previous employments. The new employment may, under certain circumstances, impose temporary sacrifices, privations, or increased efforts upon the members of the community; it may presuppose the solution of difficult problems, for example the question from which of the old combinations the necessary productive means should be withdrawn; but there is no question of procuring means of production not already at the disposal of the economic ministry. Finally, the problem also does not exist in a competitive economy in the case of the carrying out of new combinations, if those who carry them out have the necessary productive means or can get them in exchange for others which they have or for any other property which they may possess. This is not the privilege of the possession of property *per se*, but only the privilege of the possession of disposable property, that is such as is employable either immediately for carrying out the new combination or in exchange for the necessary goods and services.[5] In the contrary case—and this is the rule as it is the fundamentally interesting case—the possessor of wealth, even if it is the greatest combine, must resort to credit if he wishes to carry out a new combination, which cannot like an established business be financed by returns from previous production. To provide this credit is clearly the function of that category of individuals which we call "capitalists." It is obvious that this is the characteristic method of the capitalist type of society—and important enough to serve as its *differentia specifica*—for forcing the economic system into new channels, for putting its means at the service of new ends, in contrast to the method of a non-exchange economy of the kind which simply consists in exercising the directing organ's power to command.

It does not appear to me possible to dispute in any way the foregoing statement. Emphasis upon the significance of credit is to be found in every textbook. That the structure of modern industry could not have been erected without it, that it makes the individual to a certain extent independent of inherited possessions, that talent in economic life "rides to success on its debts," even the most conservative orthodoxy of the theorists cannot well deny. Nor is the connection established here between credit and the carrying out of innovations, a connection which will be worked out later, anything to take offence at. For it is as clear *a priori* as it is established historically that credit is primarily necessary to new combinations and that it is from these that it forces its way into the circular flow, on the one hand because it was originally necessary to the founding of what are now the old firms, on the other hand because its mechanism, once in existence, also seizes old combinations for obvious reasons.[6] First, *a priori*: we saw previously here that borrowing is not a necessary element of production in the normal circular flow within accustomed channels, is not an element without which we could not understand the essential phenomena of the latter. On the other hand, in carrying out new combinations, "financing" as a special act is fundamentally necessary, in practice as in theory. Second, historically: those who lend and borrow for industrial purposes do not

[5] A privilege which the individual can also achieve through saving. In an economy of the handicraft type this element would have to be emphasised more. Manufacturers' "reserve funds" assume an existing development.

[6] The most important of which is the appearance of productive interest, as we shall see elsewhere here. As soon as interest emerges somewhere in the system, it expands over the whole of it.

appear early in history. The pre-capitalistic lender provided money for other than business purposes. And we all remember the type of industrialist who felt he was losing caste by borrowing and who therefore shunned banks and bills of exchange. The capitalistic credit system has grown out of and thrived on the financing of new combinations in all countries, even though in a different way in each (the origin of German joint stock banking is especially characteristic). Finally there can be no stumblingblock in our speaking of receiving credit in "money or money substitutes." We certainly do not assert that one can produce with coins, notes, or bank balances, and do not deny that services of labor, raw materials, and tools are the things wanted. We are only speaking of a method of procuring them.

Nevertheless there is a point here in which, as has already been hinted, our theory diverges from the traditional view. The accepted theory sees a problem in the existence of the productive means, which are needed for new, or indeed any, productive processes, and this accumulation therefore becomes a distinct function or service. We do not recognize this problem at all; it appears to us to be created by faulty analysis. It does not exist in the circular flow, because the running of the latter presupposes given quantities of means of production. But neither does it exist for the carrying out of new combinations,[7] because the productive means required in the latter are drawn from the circular flow whether they already exist there in the shape wanted or have first to be produced by other means of production existing there. Instead of this problem another exists for us: the problem of detaching productive means (already employed somewhere) from the circular flow and allotting them to new combinations. This is done by credit, by means of which one who wishes to carry out new combinations outbids the producers in the circular flow in the market for the required means of production. And although the meaning and object of this process lies in a movement of goods from their old towards new employments, it cannot be described entirely in terms of goods without overlooking something essential, which happens in the sphere of money and credit and upon which depends the explanation of important phenomena in the capitalist form of economic organisation, in contrast to other types.

Finally one more step in this direction: whence come the sums needed to purchase the means of production necessary for the new combinations if the

[7] Of course the productive means do not fall from heaven. In so far as they are not given by nature or non-economically, they were and are created at some time by the individual waves of development in our sense, and henceforth incorporated in the circular flow. But every individual wave of development and every individual new combination itself proceeds again from the supply of productive means of the existing circular flow—a case of the hen and the egg.

individual concerned does not happen to have them? The conventional answer is simple: out of the annual growth of social savings plus that part of resource which may annually become free. Now the first quantity was indeed important enough before the war—it may perhaps be estimated as one-fifth of total private incomes in Europe and North America—so that together with the latter sum, which it is difficult to obtain statistically, it does not immediately give the lie quantitatively to this answer. At the same time a figure representing the range of all the business operations involved in carrying out new combinations is also not available at present. But we may not even start from total "savings." For its magnitude is explicable only by the results of previous development. By far the greater part of it does not come from thrift in the strict sense, that is from abstaining from the consumption of part of one's regular income, but it consists of funds which are themselves the result of successful innovation and in which we shall later recognize entrepreneurial profit. In the circular flow there would be on the one hand no such rich source, out of which to save, and on the other hand essentially less incentive to save. The only big incomes known to it would be monopoly revenues and the rents of large landowners; while provision for misfortunes and old age, perhaps also irrational motives, would be the only incentives. The most important incentive, the chance of participating in the gains of development, would be absent. Hence, in such an economic system there could be no great reservoirs of free purchasing power, to which one who wished to form new combinations could turn—and his own savings would only suffice in exceptional cases. All money would circulate, would be fixed in definite established channels.

Even though the conventional answer to our question is not obviously absurd, yet there is another method of obtaining money for this purpose, which claims our attention, because it, unlike the one referred to, does not presuppose the existence of accumulated results of previous development, and hence may be considered as the only one which is available in strict logic. This method of obtaining money is the creation of purchasing power by banks. The form it takes is immaterial. The issue of bank-notes not fully covered by specie withdrawn from circulation is an obvious instance, but methods of deposit banking render the same service, where they increase the sum total of possible expenditure. Or we may think of bank acceptances in so far as they serve as money to make payments in wholesale trade. It is always a question, not of transforming purchasing power which already exists in someone's possession, but of the creation of new purchasing power out of nothing—out of nothing even if the credit contract by which the new purchasing power is created is supported by securities which are not themselves circulating media—which is added to the existing circulation. And this is the source from which new combinations *are* often financed, and from which they would have to be financed *always*, if results of previous development did not actually exist at any moment.

These credit means of payment, that is means of payment which are created for the purpose and by the act of giving credit, serve just as ready money in trade, partly directly, partly because they can be converted immediately into ready money for small payments or payments to the non-banking classes—in particular to wage-earners. With their help, those who carry out new combinations can gain access to the existing stocks of productive means, or, as the case may be, enable those from whom they buy productive services to gain immediate access to the market for consumption goods. There is never, in this nexus, granting of credit in the sense that someone must wait for the equivalent of his service in goods, and content himself with a claim, thereby fulfilling a special function; not even in the sense that someone has to accumulate means of maintenance for laborers or landowners, or produced means of production, all of which would only be paid for out of the final results of production. Economically, it is true, there is an essential difference between these means of payment, if they are created for new ends, and money or other means of payment of the circular flow. The latter may be conceived on the one hand as a kind of certificate for completed production and the increase in the social product effected through it, and on the other hand as a kind of order upon, or claim to, part of this social product. The former have not the first of these two characteristics. They too are orders, for which one can immediately procure consumption goods, but not certificates for previous production. Access to the national dividend is usually to be had only on condition of some productive service previously rendered or of some product previously sold. This condition is, in this case, not yet fulfilled. It will be fulfilled only after the successful completion of the new combinations. Hence this credit will in the meantime affect the price level.

The banker, therefore, is not so much primarily a middleman in the commodity "purchasing power" as a *producer* of this commodity. However, since all reserve funds and savings to-day usually flow to him, and the total demand for free purchasing power, whether existing or to be created, concentrates on him, he has either replaced private capitalists or become their agent; he has himself become the capitalist par excellence. He stands between those who wish to form new combinations and the possessors of productive means. He is essentially a phenomenon of development, though only when no central authority directs the social process. He makes possible the carrying out of new combinations, authorizes people, in the name of society as it were, to form them. He is the ephor of the exchange economy.

SECTION THREE

We now come to the third of the elements with which our analysis works, namely the "new combination of means of production," and credit. Although all three elements form a whole, the third may be described as the fundamental phenomenon of economic development. The carrying out of new combinations we call "enterprise"; the individuals whose function it is to carry them out we call "entrepreneurs." These concepts are at once broader and narrower than the usual. Broader, because in the first place we call entrepreneurs not only those "independent" businessmen in an exchange economy who are usually so designated, but all who actually fulfil the function by which we define the concept, even if they are, as is becoming the rule, "dependent" employees of a company, like managers, members of boards of directors, and so forth, or even if their actual power to perform the entrepreneurial function has any other foundations, such as the control of a majority of shares. As it is the carrying out of new combinations that constitutes the entrepreneur, it is not necessary that he should be permanently connected with an individual firm; many "financiers," "promotors," and so forth are not, and still they may be entrepreneurs in our sense. On the other hand, our concept is narrower than the traditional one in that it does not include all heads of firms or managers or industrialists who merely may operate an established business, but only those who actually perform that function. Nevertheless I maintain that the above definition does no more than formulate with greater precision what the traditional doctrine really means to convey. In the first place our definition agrees with the usual one on the fundamental point of distinguishing between "entrepreneurs" and "capitalists" —irrespective of whether the latter are regarded as owners of money, claims to money, or material goods. This distinction is common property to-day and has been so for a considerable time. It also settles the question whether the ordinary shareholder as such is an entrepreneur, and disposes of the conception of the entrepreneur as risk bearer.[8] Furthermore, the ordinary characterization of the

[8] Risk obviously always falls on the owner of the means of production or of the money-capital which was paid for them, hence never on the entrepreneur *as such*. A shareholder *may* be an entrepreneur. He may even owe to his holding a controlling interest the power to act as an entrepreneur. Shareholders *per se*, however, are never entrepreneurs, but merely capitalists, who in consideration of their submitting to certain risks participate in profits. That this is no reason to look upon them as anything but capitalists is shown by the facts, first, that the average shareholder has normally no power to influence the management of his company, and secondly, that participation in profits is frequent in cases in which everyone recognizes the presence of a loan contract. Compare, for example, the Graeco-Roman *foenus nauticum*. Surely this interpretation is more true to life than the other one, which,

entrepreneur type by such expressions as "initiative," "authority," or "foresight" points entirely in our direction. For there is little scope for such qualities within the routine of the circular flow, and if this had been sharply separated from the occurrence of changes in this routine itself, the emphasis in the definition of the function of entrepreneurs would have been shifted automatically to the latter. Finally there are definitions which we could simply accept. There is in particular the well known one that goes back to J. B. Say: the entrepreneur's function is to combine the productive factors, to bring them together. Since this is a performance of a special kind only when the factors are combined for the first time—while it is merely routine work if done in the course of running a business—this definition coincides with ours. When Mataja (in Unternehmergewinn) defines the entrepreneur as one who receives profit, we have only to add the conclusion of an earlier chapter, that there is no profit in the circular flow, in order to trace this formulation too back to ours.[9] And this view is not foreign to traditional theory, as is shown by the construction of the *entrepreneur faisant ni bénéfice ni perte*, which has been worked out rigorously by Walras, but is the property of many other authors. The tendency is for the entrepreneur to make neither profit nor loss in the circular flow—that is he has no function of a special kind there, he simply does not exist; but in his stead, there are heads of firms or business managers of a different type which we had better not designate by the same term.

It is a prejudice to believe that the knowledge of the historical origin of an institution or of a type immediately shows us its sociological or economic nature. Such knowledge often leads us to understand it, but it does not directly yield a theory of it. Still more false is the belief that "primitive" forms of a type are also *ipso facto* the "simpler" or the "more original" in the sense that they show their nature more purely and with fewer complications than later ones. Very frequently the opposite is the case, amongst other reasons because increasing specialisation may allow functions and qualities to stand out sharply, which are more difficult to recognize in more primitive conditions when mixed with others. So it is in our case. In the general position of the chief of a primitive horde it is difficult to separate the entrepreneurial element from the others. For the same reason most economists up to the time of the younger Mill failed to

---

following the lead of a faulty legal construction—which can only be explained historically—attributes functions to the average shareholder which he hardly ever thinks of discharging.

[9] The definition of the entrepreneur in terms of entrepreneurial profit instead of in terms of the function the performance of which creates the entrepreneurial profit is obviously not brilliant. But we have still another objection to it: we shall see that entrepreneurial profit does not fall to the entrepreneur by "necessity" in the same sense as the marginal product of labor does to the worker.

keep capitalist and entrepreneur distinct because the manufacturer of a hundred years ago was both; and certainly the course of events since then has facilitated the making of this distinction, as the system of land tenure in England has facilitated the distinction between farmer and landowner, while on the Continent this distinction is still occasionally neglected, especially in the case of the peasant who tills his own soil.[10] But in our case there are still more of such difficulties. The entrepreneur of earlier times was not only as a rule the capitalist too, he was also often—as he still is to-day in the case of small concerns—his own technical expert, in so far as a professional specialist was not called in for special cases. Likewise he was (and is) often his own buying and selling agent, the head of his office, his own personnel manager, and sometimes, even though as a rule he of course employed solicitors, his own legal adviser in current affairs. And it was performing some or all of these functions that regularly filled his days. The carrying out of new combinations can no more be a *vocation* than the making and execution of strategical decisions, although it is this function and not his routine work that characterizes the military leader. Therefore the entrepreneur's essential function must always appear mixed up with other kinds of activity, which as a rule must be much more conspicuous than the essential one. Hence the Marshallian definition of the entrepreneur, which simply treats the entrepreneurial function as "management" in the widest meaning, will naturally appeal to most of us. We do not accept it, simply because it does not bring out what we consider to be the salient point and the only one which specifically distinguishes entrepreneurial from other activities.

Nevertheless there are types—the course of events has evolved them by degrees—which exhibit the entrepreneurial function with particular purity. The "promoter," to be sure, belongs to them only with qualifications. For, neglecting the associations relative to social and moral status which are attached to this type, the promoter is frequently only an agent intervening on commission, who does the work of financial technique in floating the new enterprise. In this case he is not its creator nor the driving power in the process. However, he *may* be the latter also, and then he is something like an "entrepreneur by profession." But the modern type of "captain of industry"[11] corresponds more closely to what is

[10] Only this neglect explains the attitude of many socialistic theorists towards peasant property. For smallness of the individual possession makes a difference only for the petit-bourgeois, not for the socialist. The criterion of the employment of labor other than that of the owner and his family is economically relevant only from the standpoint of a kind of exploitation theory which is hardly tenable any longer.

[11] Cf. for example the good description in Wiedenfeld, *Das Persönliche im modernen Unternehmertum*. Although it appeared in Schmoller's *Jahrbuch* in 1910 this work was not known to me when the first edition of this book was published.

meant here, especially if one recognizes his identity on the one hand with, say, the commercial entrepreneur of twelfth-century Venice—or, among later types, with John Law—and on the other hand with the village potentate who combines with his agriculture and his cattle trade, say, a rural brewery, an hotel, and a store. But whatever the type, everyone is an entrepreneur only when he actually "carries out new combinations," and loses that character as soon as he has built up his business, when he settles down to running it as other people run their businesses. This is the rule, of course, and hence it is just as rare for anyone always to remain an entrepreneur throughout the decades of his active life as it is for a businessman never to have a moment in which he is an entrepreneur, to however modest a degree.

Because being an entrepreneur is not a profession and as a rule not a lasting condition, entrepreneurs do not form a social class in the technical sense, as, for example, landowners or capitalists or workmen do. Of course the entrepreneurial function will *lead* to certain class positions for the successful entrepreneur and his family. It can also put its stamp on an epoch of social history, can form a style of life, or systems of moral and aesthetic values; but in itself it signifies a class position no more than it presupposes one. And the class position which may be attained is not as such an entrepreneurial position, but is characterized as landowning or capitalist, according to how the proceeds of the enterprise are used. Inheritance of the pecuniary result and of personal qualities may then both keep up this position for more than one generation and make further enterprise easier for descendants, but the function of the entrepreneur itself cannot be inherited, as is shown well enough by the history of manufacturing families.[12]

But now the decisive question arises: why then is the carrying out of new combinations a special process and the object of a special kind of "function"? Every individual carries on his economic affairs as well as he can. To be sure, his own intentions are never realized with ideal perfection, but ultimately his behavior is moulded by the influence on him of the results of his conduct, so as to fit circumstances which do not as a rule change suddenly. If a business can never be absolutely perfect in any sense, yet it in time approaches a relative perfection having regard to the surrounding world, the social conditions, the knowledge of the time, and the horizon of each individual or each group. New possibilities are continuously being offered by the surrounding world, in particular new discoveries are continuously being added to the existing store of knowledge. Why should not the individual make just as much use of the new possibilities as of the old, and, according to the market position as he understands

---

[12] On the nature of the entrepreneurial function also compare my statement in the article "Unternehmer" in the *Handwörterbuch der Staatswissenschaften*.

it, keep pigs instead of cows, or even choose a new crop rotation, if this can be seen to be more advantageous? And what kind of special new phenomena or problems, not to be found in the established circular flow, can arise there?

While in the accustomed circular flow every individual can act promptly and rationally because he is sure of his ground and is supported by the conduct, as adjusted to this circular flow, of all other individuals, who in turn expect the accustomed activity from him, he cannot simply do this when he is confronted by a new task. While in the accustomed channels his own ability and experience suffice for the normal individual, when confronted with innovations he needs guidance. While he swims with the stream in the circular flow which is familiar to him, he swims against the stream if he wishes to change its channel. What was formerly a help becomes a hindrance. What was a familiar datum becomes an unknown. Where the boundaries of routine stop, many people can go no further, and the rest can only do so in a highly variable manner. The assumption that conduct is prompt and rational is in all cases a fiction. But it proves to be sufficiently near to reality, if things have time to hammer logic into men. Where this has happened, and within the limits in which it has happened, one may rest content with this fiction and build theories upon it. It is then not true that habit or custom or non-economic ways of thinking cause a hopeless difference between the individuals of different classes, times, or cultures, and that, for example, the "economics of the stock exchange" would be inapplicable say to the peasants of to-day or to the craftsmen of the Middle Ages. On the contrary the same theoretical picture[13] in its broadest contour lines fits the individuals of quite different cultures, whatever their degree of intelligence and of economic rationality, and we can depend upon it that the peasant sells his calf just as cunningly and egotistically as the stock exchange member his portfolio of shares. But this holds good only where precedents without number have formed conduct through decades and, in fundamentals, through hundreds and thousands of years, and have eliminated unadapted behavior. Outside of these limits our fiction loses its closeness to reality.[14] To cling to it there also, as the traditional theory does, is to hide an essential thing and to ignore a fact which, in contrast

[13] The same *theoretical* picture, obviously not the same sociological, cultural, and so forth.

[14] How much this is the case is best seen to-day in the economic life of those nations, and within our civilization in the economics of those individuals, whom the development of the last century has not yet completely drawn into its stream, for example, in the economy of the Central European peasant. This peasant "calculates"; there is no deficiency of the "economic way of thinking" (Wirtschaftsgesinnung) in him. Yet he cannot take a step out of the beaten path; his economy has not changed at all for centuries, except perhaps through the exercise of external force and influence. Why? Because the choice of new methods is not

with other deviations of our assumptions from reality, is theoretically important and the source of the explanation of phenomena which would not exist without it.

Therefore, in describing the circular flow one must treat combinations of means of production (the production-functions) as data, like natural possibilities, and admit only small[15] variations at the margins, such as every individual can accomplish by adapting himself to changes in his economic environment, without materially deviating from familiar lines. Therefore, too, the carrying out of new combinations is a special function, and the privilege of a type of people who are much less numerous than all those who have the "objective" possibility of doing it. Therefore, finally, entrepreneurs are a special type,[16] and

---

simply an element in the concept of rational economic action, nor a matter of course, but a distinct process which stands in need of special explanation.

[15] Small disturbances which may indeed, as mentioned earlier, in time add up to great amounts. The decisive point is that the businessman, if he makes them, never alters his routine. The usual case is one of small, the exception one of great (*uno actu* great), disturbances. Only in this sense is emphasis put upon "smallness" here. The objection that there can be difference in principle between small and large disturbances is not effective. For it is false in itself, in so far as it is based upon the disregard of the principle of the infinitesimal method, the essence of which lies in the fact that one can assert of "small quantities" under certain circumstances what one cannot assert of "large quantities." But the reader who takes umbrage at the large-small contrast may, if he wishes, substitute for it the contrast adapting-spontaneous. Personally I am not willing to do this because the latter method of expression is much easier to misunderstand than the former and really would demand still longer explanations.

[16] In the first place it is a question of a type of *conduct* and of a type of *person* in so far as this conduct is accessible in very unequal measure and to relatively few people, so that it constitutes their outstanding characteristic. Because the exposition of the first edition was reproached with exaggerating and mistaking the peculiarity of this conduct, and with overlooking the fact that it is more or less open to every businessman, and because the exposition in a later paper ("Wellenbewegung des Wirtschaftslebens," *Archiv für Sozialwissenschaft*) was charged with introducing an intermediate type ("half-static" businessmen), the following may be submitted. The conduct in question is peculiar in two ways. First, because it is directed towards something different and signifies doing something different from other conduct. One may indeed in this connection include it with the latter in a higher unity, but this does not alter the fact that a theoretically relevant difference exists between the two, and that only one of them is adequately described by traditional theory. Secondly, the type of conduct in question not only differs from the other in its object, "innovation" being peculiar to it, but also in that it presupposes aptitudes differing *in kind* and not only in degree from those of mere rational economic behavior.

Now these aptitudes are presumably distributed in an ethically homogeneous population just like others, that is the curve of their distribution has a maximum ordinate, deviations on either side of which become rarer the greater they are. Similarly we can assume that every healthy man can sing if he will. Perhaps half the individuals in an ethically homogeneous group have the capacity for it to an average degree, a quarter in progressively diminishing measure, and, let us say, a quarter in a measure above the average; and within

their behavior a special problem, the motive power of a great number of significant phenomena. Hence, our position may be characterized by three corresponding pairs of opposites. First, by the opposition of two real processes: the circular flow or the tendency towards equilibrium on the one hand, a change in channels of economic routine or a spontaneous change in the economic data arising from within the system on the other. Secondly, by the opposition of two theoretical *apparatuses*: statics and dynamics.[17] Thirdly, by the opposition of two

---

this quarter, through a series of continually increasing singing ability and continually diminishing number of people who possess it, we come finally to the Carusos. Only in this quarter are we struck in general by the singing ability, and only in the supreme instances can it become the characterizing mark of the person. Although practically all men can sing, singing ability does not cease to be a distinguishable characteristic and attribute of a minority, indeed not exactly of a type, because this characteristic—unlike ours—affects the total personality relatively little.

Let us apply this: Again, a quarter of the population may be so poor in those qualities, let us say here provisionally, of economic initiative that the deficiency makes itself felt by poverty of their moral personality, and they play a wretched part in the smallest affairs of private and professional life in which this element is called for. We recognize this type and know that many of the best clerks, distinguished by devotion to duty, expert knowledge, and exactitude, belong to it. Then comes the "half," the "normal." These prove themselves to be better in the things which even within the established channels cannot simply be "dispatched" (erledigen) but must also be "decided" (entscheiden) and "carried out" (durchsetzen). Practically all business people belong here, otherwise they would never have attained their positions; most represent a selection—individually or hereditarily tested. A textile manufacturer travels no "new" road when he goes to a wool auction. But the situations there are never the same, and the success of the business depends so much upon skill and initiative in buying wool that the fact that the textile industry has so far exhibited no trustification comparable with that in heavy manufacturing is undoubtedly partly explicable by the reluctance of the cleverer manufacturers to renounce the advantage of their own skill in buying wool. From there, rising in the scale we come finally into the highest quarter, to people who are a type characterized by super-normal qualities of intellect and will. Within this type there are not only many varieties (merchants, manufacturers, financiers, etc.) but also a continuous variety of degrees of intensity in "initiative." In our argument types of every intensity occur. Many a one can steer a safe course, where no one has yet been; others follow where first another went before; still others only in the crowd, but in this among the first. So also the great political leader of every kind and time is a type, yet not a thing unique, but only the apex of a pyramid from which there is a continuous variation down to the average and from it to the sub-normal values. And yet not only is "leading" a special function, but the leader also something special, distinguishable—wherefore there is no sense in our case in asking: "Where does that type begin then?" and then to exclaim: "This is no type at all!"

[17] It has been objected against the first edition that it sometimes defines "statics" as a theoretical construction, sometimes as the picture of an actual state of economic life. I believe that the present exposition gives no ground for this opinion. "Static" theory does not assume a stationary economy; it also treats of the effects of changes in data. In itself, therefore, there is no necessary connection between static theory and stationary reality. Only in so far as one can exhibit the fundamental form of the economic course of events with the maximum

types of conduct, which, following reality, we can picture as two types of individuals: mere managers and entrepreneurs. And therefore the "best method" of producing in the theoretical sense is to be conceived as "the most advantageous among the methods which have been empirically tested and become familiar." But it is not the "best" of the methods "possible" at the time. If one does not make this distinction, the concept becomes meaningless and precisely those problems remain unsolved which our interpretation is meant to provide for.

Let us now formulate precisely the characteristic feature of the conduct and type under discussion. The smallest daily action embodies a huge mental effort. Every schoolboy would have to be a mental giant, if he himself had to create all he knows and uses by his own individual activity. And every man would have to be a giant of wisdom and will, if he had in every case to create anew all the rules by which he guides his everyday conduct. This is true not only of those decisions and actions of individual and social life the principles of which are the product of tens of thousands of years, but also of those products of shorter periods and of a more special nature which constitute the particular instrument for performing vocational tasks. But precisely the things the performance of which according to this should involve a supreme effort, in general demand no special individual effort at all; those which should be especially difficult are in reality especially easy; what should demand superhuman capacity is accessible to

---

simplicity in an unchanging economy does this assumption recommend itself to theory. The stationary economy is for uncounted thousands of years, and also in historical times in many places for centuries, an incontrovertible fact, apart from the fact, moreover, which Sombart emphasized, that there is a tendency towards a stationary state in every period of depression. Hence it is readily understood how this historical fact and that theoretical construction have allied themselves in a way which led to some confusion. The words "statics" and "dynamics" the author would not now use in the meaning they carry above, where they are simply short expressions for "theory of the circular flow" and "theory of development." One more thing: theory employs two methods of interpretation, which may perhaps make difficulties. If it is to be shown how all the elements of the economic system are determined in equilibrium by one another, this equilibrium system is considered as not yet existing and is built up before our eyes *ab ovo*. This does not mean that its coming into being is genetically explained thereby. Only its existence and functioning are made logically clear by mental dissection. And the experiences and habits of individuals are assumed as existing. How just these productive combinations have come about is not thereby explained. Further, if two contiguous equilibrium positions are to be investigated, then sometimes (not always), as in Pigou's *Economics of Welfare*, the "best" productive combination in the first is compared with the "best" in the second. And this again need not, but may, mean that the two combinations in the sense meant here differ not only by small variations in quantity but in their whole technical and commercial structure. Here too the coming into being of the second combination and the problems connected with it are not investigated, but only the functioning and the outcome of the already existing combination. Even though justified as far as it goes, this method of treatment passes over our problem. If the assertion were implied that this is also settled by it, it would be false.

the least gifted, given mental health. In particular within the ordinary routine there is no need for leadership. Of course it is still necessary to set people their tasks, to keep up discipline, and so forth; but this is easy and a function any normal person can learn to fulfil. Within the lines familiar to all, even the function of directing other people, though still necessary, is mere "work" like any other, comparable to the service of tending a machine. All people get to know, and are able to do, their daily tasks in the customary way and ordinarily perform them by themselves; the "director" has his routine as they have theirs; and his directive function serves merely to correct individual aberrations.

This is so because all knowledge and habit once acquired becomes as firmly rooted in ourselves as a railway embankment in the earth. It does not require to be continually renewed and consciously reproduced, but sinks into the strata of subconsciousness. It is normally transmitted almost without friction by inheritance, teaching, upbringing, pressure of environment. Everything we think, feel, or do often enough becomes automatic and our conscious life is unburdened of it. The enormous economy of force, in the race and the individual, here involved is not great enough, however, to make daily life a light burden and to prevent its demands from exhausting the average energy all the same. But it is great enough to make it possible to meet the ordinary claims. This holds good likewise for economic daily life. And from this it follows also for economic life that every step outside the boundary of routine has difficulties and involves a new element. It is this element that constitutes the phenomenon of leadership.

The nature of these difficulties may be focussed in the following three points. First, outside these accustomed channels the individual is without those data for his decisions and those rules of conduct which are usually very accurately known to him within them. Of course he must still foresee and estimate on the basis of his experience. But many things must remain uncertain, still others are only ascertainable within wide limits, some can perhaps only be "guessed." In particular this is true of those data which the individual strives to alter and of those which he wants to create. Now he must really to some extent do what tradition does for him in everyday life, *viz.* consciously plan his conduct in every particular. There will be much more conscious rationality in this than in customary action, which as such does not need to be reflected upon at all; but this plan must necessarily be open not only to errors greater in degree, but also to other kinds of errors than those occurring in customary action. What has been done already has the sharp-edged reality of all the things which we have seen and experienced; the new is only the figment of our imagination. Carrying out a new plan and acting according to a customary one are things as different as making a road and walking along it.

How different a thing this is becomes clearer if one bears in mind the impossibility of surveying exhaustively all the effects and counter-effects of the projected enterprise. Even as many of them as could in theory be ascertained if one had unlimited time and means must practically remain in the dark. As military action must be taken in a given strategic position even if all the data potentially procurable are not available, so also in economic life action must be taken without working out all the details of what is to be done. Here the success of everything depends upon intuition, the capacity of seeing things in a way which afterwards proves to be true, even though it cannot be established at the moment, and of grasping the essential fact, discarding the unessential, even though one can give no account of the principles by which this is done. Thorough preparatory work, and special knowledge, breadth of intellectual understanding, talent for logical analysis, may under certain circumstances be sources of failure. The more accurately, however, we learn to know the natural and social world, the more perfect our control of facts becomes; and the greater the extent, with time and progressive rationalization, within which things can be simply calculated, and indeed quickly and reliably calculated, the more the significance of this function decreases. Therefore the importance of the entrepreneur type must diminish just as the importance of the military commander has already diminished. Nevertheless a part of the very essence of each type is bound up with this function.

As this first point lies in the task, so the second lies in the psyche of the businessman himself. It is not only objectively more difficult to do something new than what is familiar and tested by experience, but the individual feels reluctance to it and would do so even if the objective difficulties did not exist. This is so in all fields. The history of science is one great confirmation of the fact that we find it exceedingly difficult to adopt a new scientific point of view or method. Thought turns again and again into the accustomed track even if it has become unsuitable and the more suitable innovation in itself presents no particular difficulties. The very nature of fixed habits of thinking, their energy-saving function, is founded upon the fact that they have become subconscious, that they yield their results automatically and are proof against criticism and even against contradiction by individual facts. But precisely because of this they become drag-chains when they have outlived their usefulness. So it is also in the economic world. In the breast of one who wishes to do something new, the forces of habit rise up and bear witness against the embryonic project. A new and another kind of effort of will is therefore necessary in order to wrest, amidst the work and care of the daily round, scope and time for conceiving and working out the new combination and to bring oneself to look upon it as a real possibility and not merely as a day-dream. This mental freedom presupposes a great surplus force over the everyday demand and is something peculiar and by nature rare.

The third point consists in the reaction of the social environment against one who wishes to do something new. This reaction may manifest itself first of all in the existence of legal or political impediments. But neglecting this, any deviating conduct by a member of a social group is condemned, though in greatly varying degrees according as the social group is used to such conduct or not. Even a deviation from social custom in such things as dress or manner arouses opposition, and of course all the more so in the graver cases. This opposition is stronger in primitive stages of culture than in others, but it is never absent. Even mere astonishment at the deviation, even merely noticing it, exercises a pressure on the individual. The manifestation of condemnation may at once bring noticeable consequences in its train. It may even come to social ostracism and finally to physical prevention or to direct attack. Neither the fact that progressive differentiation weakens this opposition—especially as the most important cause of the weakening is the very development which we wish to explain—nor the further fact that the social opposition operates under certain circumstances and upon many individuals as a stimulus, changes anything in principle in the significance of it. Surmounting this opposition is always a special kind of task which does not exist in the customary course of life, a task which also requires a special kind of conduct. In matters economic this resistance manifests itself first of all in the groups threatened by the innovation, then in the difficulty in finding the necessary cooperation, finally in the difficulty in winning over consumers. Even though these elements are still effective to-day, despite the fact that a period of turbulent development has accustomed us to the appearance and the carrying out of innovations, they can be best studied in the beginning of capitalism. But they are so obvious there that it would be time lost for our purposes to dwell upon them.

There is leadership *only* for these reasons—leadership, that is, as a special kind of function and in contrast to a mere difference in rank, which would exist in every social body, in the smallest as in the largest, and in combination with which it generally appears. The facts alluded to create a boundary beyond which the majority of people do not function promptly by themselves and require help from a minority. If social life had in all respects the relative immutability of, for example, the astronomical world, or if mutable this mutability were yet incapable of being influenced by human action, or finally if capable of being so influenced this type of action were yet equally open to everyone, then there would be no special function of leadership as distinguished from routine work.

The specific problem of leadership arises and the leader type appears only where new possibilities present themselves. That is why it is so strongly marked among the Normans at the time of their conquests and so feebly among the Slavs in the centuries of their unchanging and relatively protected life in the marshes of the Pripet. Our three points characterize the nature of the *function* as well as the *conduct* or behavior which constitutes the leader type. It is no part of his function to "find" or to "create" new possibilities. They are always present, abundantly accumulated by all sorts of people. Often they are also generally known and being discussed by scientific or literary writers. In other cases, there is nothing to discover about them, because they are quite obvious. To take an example from political life, it was not at all difficult to see how the social and political conditions of France at the time of Louis XVI could have been improved so as to avoid a breakdown of the *ancien régime*. Plenty of people as a matter of fact did see it. But nobody was in a position to *do* it. Now, it is this "doing the thing," without which possibilities are dead, of which the leader's function consists. This holds good of all kinds of leadership, ephemeral as well as more enduring ones. The former may serve as an instance. What is to be done in a casual emergency is as a rule quite simple. Most or all people may see it, yet they want someone to speak out, to lead, and to organize. Even leadership which influences merely by example, as artistic or scientific leadership, does not consist simply in finding or creating the new thing but in so impressing the social group with it as to draw it on in its wake. It is, therefore, more by will than by intellect that the leaders fulfil their function, more by "authority," "personal weight," and so forth than by original ideas.

Economic leadership in particular must hence be distinguished from "invention." As long as they are not carried into practice, inventions are economically irrelevant. And to carry any improvement into effect is a task entirely different from the inventing of it, and a task, moreover, requiring entirely different kinds of aptitudes. Although entrepreneurs of course *may* be inventors just as they may be capitalists, they are inventors not by nature of their function but by coincidence and vice versa. Besides, the innovations which it is the function of entrepreneurs to carry out need not necessarily be any inventions at all. It is, therefore, not advisable, and it may be downright misleading, to stress the element of invention as much as many writers do.

The entrepreneurial kind of leadership, as distinguished from other kinds of economic leadership such as we should expect to find in a primitive tribe or a communist society, is of course colored by the conditions peculiar to it. It has none of that glamour which characterizes other kinds of leadership. It consists in fulfilling a very special task which only in rare cases appeals to the imagination of the public. For its success, keenness, and vigor are not more essential than a certain narrowness which seizes the immediate chance and *nothing else*. "Personal weight" is, to be sure, not without importance. Yet the personality of the capitalistic entrepreneur need not, and generally does not, answer to the idea most of us have of what a "leader" looks like, so much so that there is some difficulty in realizing that he comes within the sociological category of leader at all. He "leads" the means of production into new channels. But this he does, not by convincing people of the desirability of carrying out his plan or by creating confidence in his leading in the manner of a political leader—the only man he has to convince or to impress is the banker who is to finance him—but by buying them or their services, and then using them as he sees fit. He also leads in the sense that he draws other producers in his branch after him. But as they are his competitors, who first reduce and then annihilate his profit, this is, as it were, leadership against one's own will. Finally, he renders a service, the full appreciation of which takes a specialist's knowledge of the case. It is not so easily understood by the public at large as a politician's successful speech or a general's victory in the field, not to insist on the fact that he seems to act—and often harshly—in his individual interest alone. We shall understand, therefore, that we do not observe, in this case, the emergence of all those affective values which are the glory of all other kinds of social leadership. Add to this the precariousness of the economic position both of the individual entrepreneur and of entrepreneurs as a group, and the fact that when his economic success raises him socially he has no cultural tradition or attitude to fall back upon, but moves about in society as an upstart, whose ways are readily laughed at, and we shall understand why this type has never been popular, and why even scientific critique often makes short work of it.[18]

We shall finally try to round off our picture of the entrepreneur in the same manner in which we always, in science as well as in practical life, try to understand human behavior, viz. by analysing the characteristic motives of his conduct. Any attempt to do this must of course meet with all those objections against the economist's intrusion into "psychology" which have been made familiar by a long series of writers. We cannot here enter into the fundamental question of the relation between psychology and economics. It is enough to state that those who on principle object to *any* psychological considerations in an

[18] It may, therefore, not be superfluous to point out that our analysis of the role of the entrepreneur does not involve any "glorification" of the type, as some readers of the first edition of this book seemed to think. We do hold that entrepreneurs *have* an economic function as distinguished from, say, robbers. But we neither style every entrepreneur a genius or a benefactor to humanity, nor do we wish to express any opinion about the comparative merits of the social organization in which he plays his role, or about the question whether what he does could not be effected more cheaply or efficiently in other ways.

economic argument may leave out what we are about to say without thereby losing contact with the argument of the following chapters. For none of the results to which our analysis is intended to lead stands or falls with our "psychology of the entrepreneur," or could be vitiated by any errors in it. Nowhere is there, as the reader will easily satisfy himself, any necessity for us to overstep the frontiers of observable behavior. Those who do not object to *all* psychology but only to the *kind* of psychology which we know from the traditional textbook, will see that we do not adopt any part of the time-honored picture of the motivation of the "economic man."

In the theory of the circular flow, the importance of examining motives is very much reduced by the fact that the equations of the system of equilibrium may be so interpreted as not to imply any psychic magnitudes at all, as shown by the analysis of Pareto and of Barone. This is the reason why even very defective psychology interferes much less with results than one would expect. There may be rational *conduct* even in the absence of rational *motive*. But as soon as we really wish to penetrate into motivation, the problem proves by no means simple. Within given social circumstances and habits, most of what people do every day will appear to them primarily from the point of view of duty carrying a social or a superhuman sanction. There is very little of conscious rationality, still less of hedonism and of *individual* egoism about it, and so much of it as may safely be said to exist is of comparatively recent growth. Nevertheless, as long as we confine ourselves to the great outlines of constantly repeated economic action, we may link it up with wants and the desire to satisfy them, on condition that we are careful to recognize that economic motive so defined varies in intensity very much in time; that it is society that shapes the particular desires we observe; that wants must be taken with reference to the group which the individual thinks of when deciding his course of action—the family or any other group, smaller or larger than the family; that action does not promptly follow upon desire but only more or less imperfectly corresponds to it; that the field of individual choice is always, though in very different ways and to very different degrees, fenced in by social habits or conventions and the like: it still remains broadly true that, within the circular flow, everyone adapts himself to his environment so as to satisfy certain *given* wants—of himself or others—as best he can. In *all* cases, the *meaning* of economic action is the satisfaction of wants in the sense that there would be no economic action if there were no wants. In the case of the circular flow, we may also think of satisfaction of wants as the normal *motive*.

The latter is not true for our type. In one sense, he may indeed be called the most rational and the most egotistical of all. For, as we have seen, conscious rationality enters much more into the carrying out of new plans, which themselves have to be worked out before they can be acted upon, than into the mere running of an established business, which is largely a matter of routine. And the typical entrepreneur is more self-centred than other types, because he relies less than they do on tradition and connection and because his characteristic task—theoretically as well as historically—consists precisely in breaking up old, and creating new, tradition. Although this applies primarily to his economic action, it also extends to the moral, cultural, and social consequences of it. It is, of course, no mere coincidence that the period of the rise of the entrepreneur type also gave birth to Utilitarianism.

But his conduct and his motive are "rational" in no other sense. And in *no* sense is his characteristic motivation of the hedonist kind. If we define hedonist motive of action as the wish to satisfy one's wants, we may indeed make "wants" include any impulse whatsoever, just as we may define egoism so as to include all altruistic values too, on the strength of the fact that they also mean something in the way of self-gratification. But this would reduce our definition to tautology. If we wish to give it meaning, we must restrict it to such wants as are capable of being satisfied by the consumption of goods, and to that kind of satisfaction which is expected from it. Then it is no longer true that our type is acting on a wish to satisfy his wants.

For unless we assume that individuals of our type are driven along by an insatiable craving for hedonist satisfaction, the operations of Gossen's law would in the case of business leaders soon put a stop to further effort. Experience teaches, however, that typical entrepreneurs retire from the arena only when and because their strength is spent and they feel no longer equal to their task. This does not seem to verify the picture of the economic man, balancing probable results against disutility of effort and reaching in due course a point of equilibrium beyond which he is not willing to go. Effort, in our case, does not seem to weigh at all in the sense of being felt as a reason to stop. And activity of the entrepreneurial type is obviously an obstacle to hedonist enjoyment of those kinds of commodity which are usually acquired by incomes beyond a certain size, because their "consumption" presupposes leisure. Hedonistically, therefore, the conduct which we usually observe in individuals of our type would be irrational.

This would not, of course, prove the absence of hedonistic motive. Yet it points to another psychology of non-hedonist character, especially if we take into account the indifference to hedonistic enjoyment which is often conspicuous in outstanding specimens of the type and which is not difficult to understand.

First of all, there is the dream and the will to found a private kingdom, usually, though not necessarily, also a dynasty. The modern world really does not know any such positions, but what may be attained by industrial or commercial success is still the nearest approach to medieval lordship possible to modern man. Its fascination is specially strong for people who have no other chance of achieving social distinction. The sensation of power and independence loses nothing by the fact that both are largely illusions. Closer analysis would lead to discovering an endless variety within this group of motives, from spiritual ambition down to mere snobbery. But this need not detain us. Let it suffice to point out that motives of this kind, although they stand nearest to consumers' satisfaction, do not coincide with it.

Then there is the will to conquer: the impulse to fight, to prove oneself superior to others, to succeed for the sake, not of the fruits of success, but of success itself. From this aspect, economic action becomes akin to sport—there are financial races, or rather boxing-matches. The financial result is a secondary consideration, or, at all events, mainly valued as an index of success and as a symptom of victory, the displaying of which very often is more important as a motive of large expenditure than the wish for the consumers' goods themselves. Again we should find countless nuances, some of which, like social ambition, shade into the first group of motives. And again we are faced with a motivation characteristically different from that of "satisfaction of wants" in the sense defined above, or from, to put the same thing into other words, "hedonistic adaptation."

Finally, there is the joy of creating, of getting things done, or simply of exercising one's energy and ingenuity. This is akin to a ubiquitous motive, but nowhere else does it stand out as an independent factor of behavior with anything like the clearness with which it obtrudes itself in our case. Our type seeks out difficulties, changes in order to change, delights in ventures. This group of motives is the most distinctly anti-hedonist of the three.

Only with the first groups of motives is private property as the result of entrepreneurial activity an essential factor in making it operative. With the other two it is not. Pecuniary gain is indeed a very accurate expression of success, especially of *relative* success, and from the standpoint of the man who strives for it, it has the additional advantage of being an objective fact and largely independent of the opinion of others. These and other peculiarities incident to the mechanism of "acquisitive" society make it very difficult to replace it as a motor of industrial development, even if we would discard the importance it has for creating a fund ready for investment. Nevertheless it is true that the second and third groups of entrepreneurial motives may in principle be taken care of by other social arrangements not involving private gain from economic innovation. What other stimuli could be provided, and how they could be made to work as well as the "capitalistic" ones do, are questions which are beyond our theme. They are taken too lightly by social reformers, and are altogether ignored by fiscal radicalism. But they are not insoluble, and may be answered by detailed observation of the psychology of entrepreneurial activity, at least for given times and places.

3

SCHUMPETER AND MAX WEBER: CENTRAL VISIONS AND SOCIAL THEORIES

Ronan Macdonald

SECTION ONE: INTRODUCTION

IT is the purpose of this paper to compare Schumpeter and Max Weber, with respect to their "central visions" and their social theories. Schumpeter always emphasized the importance of identifying "prescientific vision," and in his own case the task is relatively easy. It is clearly related to his "entrepreneur—mere manager," "circular flow—developing system" contrasts. In Weber's case, identification is scarcely more difficult. Not only is his treatment of the Protestant ethic and the spirit of capitalism his most famous contribution —it is also the primary focus of most commentators, and the point of vantage from which his other wide-ranging explorations are usually surveyed.

Both writers, in spite of their very different interests, had social theories and economic sociologies which, though incomplete, are similar in scope and theoretical conclusions. Much of this similarity can be attributed to the common influence of Marx, acknowledged by both writers, but much also remains unexplained thereby. Schumpeter in particular invoked Marx to considerable advantage in explaining his own social analysis, but his approach and conclusions

Reprinted by permission of the author and the publisher from Quarterly Journal of Economics, *(August, 1965), pp. 373–396.*

are often so un-Marxian that a similar comparison with Weber, who also treated the same set of social phenomena, is justified.

Weber published his *Die Protestantische Ethik und der Geist des Kapitalismus* in the form of two articles in the *Archiv für Sozialwissenschaft und Sozialpolitik* (1904 and 1905).[1] To quote Tawney:

On their first appearance they aroused an interest which extended beyond the ranks of historical specialists, and which caused the numbers of the *Archiv* in which they were published to be sold with a rapidity not very usual in the case of learned publications.[2]

At that time, Schumpeter was twenty-two, a brilliant graduate student at Vienna. The echoes of the *Methodenstreit* were rumbling, and relations between the Austrian and German camps were still somewhat strained. Moreover, Weber's thesis, primarily an attack on Marx's materialistic interpretation of history, was also a challenge to the autonomy of economics as a science. In the opinion of Reinhard Bendix, Weber had demonstrated that ". . . economic conduct was inseparable from the ideas with which men pursued their economic interests, and these ideas had to be understood on their own terms."[3] In itself this was nothing new. Members of the German historical school had been asserting it for years, on empirical and methodological grounds, and rejecting classical economic theory on the strength of it. What was new was Weber's assertion of it on *theoretical grounds*.

Precisely how this development might have appeared to Schumpeter is not known. It is clear, however, that he formulated his own theoretical structure about this time or very shortly thereafter. Professor Smithies estimates that at the end of Schumpeter's five years at the University (1901–06), the "essentials of his vision of the social and economic process had already been formed,"[4] and certainly in his first book in 1908 he states that his "exposition rests on the

---

[1] The first article, Part I (here called Section I), appeared in the autumn of 1904 (XX, 1–54), the second in the spring of 1905 (XXI, 1–110). It was reprinted with considerable revision and some new material in 1920, as the first study in Weber's series *Gesammelte Aufsätze zur Religionssoziologie*. Parsons' translation is from the latter printing, but the sections on Weber's central vision remain unchanged, and may be found on pages 27–29 of Part I of the original article. The corresponding pages in Parsons' translation are pages 66–69. For convenience, the citations on Weber's central vision will be to Parsons' translation rather than to the original article. Max Weber, *The Protestant Ethic and the Spirit of Capitalism*, trans. by Talcott Parsons with a foreword by R. H. Tawney (New York: Charles Scribner's Sons, 1930). It is cited in this paper as *Prot. Ethic.*   [2] *Prot. Ethic*, p. 1 (b).

[3] Reinhard Bendix, *Max Weber: An Intellectual Portrait* (Garden City, N.Y.: Doubleday, 1960), p. 52.

[4] Arthur Smithies, "Memorial: Joseph Alois Schumpeter, 1883–1950," in *Schumpeter, Social Scientist*, ed. Seymour Harris (Cambridge: Harvard University Press, 1951), p. 11.

fundamental distinction between 'statics' and 'dynamics'."[5] What is being presented here, then, is a comparison of two theoretical structures, formed at about the same time, one the product of a representative of the German historical school, the other by a young man trained in the Austrian tradition of economic theory.

SECTION TWO: CENTRAL VISIONS

Weber was specifically attacking Marx's view that the capitalist, armed with new techniques and driven by rational acquisitiveness, had swept away the old traditional methods and attitudes, and had imposed on society his own ethos or *geist* as well as the specific capitalist mode of production.[6] This, for Weber, was not a realistic picture of the process of capitalist development. A more typical sequence, occurring even within Weber's lifetime, was one in which the new man broke into a completely adapted traditional environment in which the mode of production was specifically capitalist. Moreover, the new man was not armed with a new invention, capable of revolutionizing the industry, but with a new spirit.

Until about the middle of the past century the life of a putter-out was, at least in many of the branches of the continental textile industry, what we should today consider very comfortable. We may imagine its routine somewhat as follows. The peasants came with their cloth . . . to the town in which the putter-out lived . . . and . . . received the customary price for it. The putter-out's customers, for markets any distance away, were middlemen, who also came to him . . . seeking traditional qualities, and bought from his warehouse, or . . . placed orders which were in turn passed on to the peasants. Personal canvassing of customers took place, if at all, only at long intervals. The number of business hours was very moderate, perhaps five to six a day, sometimes considerably less . . . Earnings were moderate; enough to lead a respectable life and in good times to put away a little. On the whole, relations among competitors were relatively good, with a large degree of agreement on the fundamentals of business. A long daily visit to the tavern, with often plenty to drink, and a congenial circle of friends, made life comfortable and leisurely.[7]

Weber then goes on to emphasize that the form of organization was capitalistic,

[5] Quoted in Fritz Machlup. "Schumpeter's Economic Methodology," in *Schumpeter, Social Scientist*, p. 99.

[6] Cf. note 1, [p. 72]. The passages chosen as representative of Weber's central vision of the economic process are found on pages 27–29 of Part I of his original article.

[7] *Prot. Ethic*, p. 66.

with capital turning over in the business, entrepreneurial business activity and rational bookkeeping. But it was also traditionalistic in every respect.

> . . . the traditional manner of life, the traditional rate of profit, the traditional amount of work, the traditional manner of regulating the relationships with labor, and the essentially traditional circle of customers and the manner of attracting new ones.[8]

In this passage we find, expressed in a common-sense way, all the essentials of Schumpeter's circular flow. There is the same emphasis on the routine, on prices and wages which are completely adjusted, and on entrepreneurial functions rendered almost automatic. Schumpeter's own description, stripped of its technical considerations, may be set down in truncated form for comparison.

> For our present argument we may thus visualize an economic process which merely reproduces itself at constant rates; a given population, not changing in either numbers or age distribution . . . . The tastes (wants) of households are given and do not change. The ways of production and usances of commerce are optimal from the standpoint of the firms' interest and with respect to existing horizons and possibilities, hence do not change either, unless some datum changes or some chance event intrudes upon this world.
>
> No other than ordinary routine work has to be done in this stationary society, either by workmen or managers. Beyond this there is, in fact, no managerial function—nothing that calls for the special type of activity which we associate with the entrepreneur . . . Such a process would turn out, year after year, the same kinds, qualities, and quantities of consumers' and producers' goods; every firm would employ the same kind and quantities of productive goods and services; finally, all these goods would be bought and sold at the same prices year after year.[9]

It is fairly clear that Weber's type of "traditional capitalism" and Schumpeter's circular flow are essentially the same thing. Weber's "We may imagine its routine . . ." and Schumpeter's "we may thus visualize . . ." indicate that both were presenting an "ideal type" refined from their general vision of the economic process.

After presenting the traditional picture, Weber then goes on to introduce the "new" businessman into the picture of tranquil routine.

> Now at some time this leisureliness was suddenly destroyed, and often entirely without any essential change in the form of organization, such as the transition to a

---

[8] *Prot. Ethic,* p. 67.

[9] J. A. Schumpeter, *Business Cycles: A Theoretical, Historical, and Statistical Analysis of the Capitalistic Process* (New York: McGraw-Hill, 1939), pp. 40–41. Cited herein as *Business Cycles.*

unified factory, to mechanical weaving, *etc.* What happened was, on the contrary, often no more than this: Some young man from one of the putting-out families went out into the country, carefully chose weavers for his employ, greatly increased the rigour of his supervision of their work, and thus turned them from peasants into labourers. On the other hand, he would begin to change his marketing methods . . . . At the same time he began to introduce the principle of low prices and large turnover. There was repeated what everywhere and always is the result of such a process of rationalization: those who would not follow suit had to go out of business. The idyllic state collapsed under the pressure of a bitter competitive struggle, respectable fortunes were made, and not lent out at interest, but always reinvested in the business . . . . And, what is most important in this connection, it was not generally in such cases a stream of money invested in the industry which brought about this revolution—in several cases known to me the whole revolutionary process was set in motion with a few thousands of capital borrowed from relations —but the new spirit, the spirit of modern capitalism, had set to work . . . . Its entry on the scene was not generally peaceful. A flood of mistrust, sometimes of hatred, above all of moral indignation, regularly opposed itself to the first innovator. Often—I know of several cases of the sort—regular legends of mysterious shady spots in his previous life have been produced.[10]

Here we have, in its essentials, the view of the capitalist process which Schumpeter made the center of his economic analyses—the circular flow disturbed and transformed by the innovator and his imitators. One of Schumpeter's many descriptions of the innovation process is included here for comparison.

The matter then appears as follows. If anyone in an economic system in which the textile industry produces only with hand labor sees the possibility of founding a business which uses power-looms, feels equal to the task of overcoming all the innumerable difficulties, and has made the final decision, then he, first of all, needs purchasing power. He borrows it from a bank and creates his business.[11]

Then, given certain technical economic conditions, the business begins to make profits, even when market prices fall as a result of increased output.

But now comes the second act of the drama. The spell is broken and new businesses are continually arising under the impulse of the alluring profit. A complete reorganization of the industry occurs, with its increases in production, its competitive struggle, its supersession of obsolete businesses, its possible dismissal of workers, and so forth.[12]

[10] *Prot. Ethic*, p. 68.
[11] J. A. Schumpeter, *Theory of Economic Development*, trans. by Redvers Opie from the third German edition (1926) (Cambridge: Harvard University Press, 1934), p. 129. Cited herein as *Economic Development*.   [12] Ibid., p. 131.

There is no denying that this view of the capitalist process is identical with Schumpeter's. The aggressive entrepreneur breaking into the placid circular flow, equipped with nothing but will, energy, and the idea for the innovation; his success against the resistance of the old firms; their forced liquidation or adaptation; this is the theme on which Schumpeter played a thousand variations in the course of his career. But what is of importance here is not the superficial similarities, but rather the underlying differences—what each man made of this vision. Weber, of course, saw in the innovator the "ideal type" of the Protestant worldly ascetic. Schumpeter on the other hand, chose to regard him as the supernormal entrepreneur. This was a distinct analytical advance, because, in explaining the rise of capitalism, it is more plausible to postulate the appearance of men of supernormal ability as causes of change, than to postulate the appearance of Calvin or some similar charismatic leader. More important is the fact that, since supernormal entrepreneurs are always present, an increase in the frequency of occurrence of innovations and waves of adaptation could be assumed.

Still another implication follows from Schumpeter's postulate of leadership. Weber's model of change, like Marx's, was essentially one of comparative statics—what Parsons has called a "mosaic theory."[13] Into an era of "intact" feudalism Weber introduces the Protestant leaders. Their followers pursue their careers with the intensity, rationalism, and frugality of the true worldly ascetic until all is swept before them and the period of high capitalism begins. For Schumpeter the picture is different. His business leaders can appear at any time— as early as the twelfth century or earlier—can conquer their territory and force the tradition-bound firms to adopt the new methods. Each innovation confronts an economy fully adapted to traditional methods, forces it to adapt again, and a new period of "traditionalism" ensues, but with a higher level of efficiency and output. Traditionalism appears here as an *ex post* concept—the traditional methods being merely the up-to-date, efficient methods of yesterday, before the innovator came. This gives Schumpeter a *dynamic* model, in which capitalism proceeds gradually, yet by discontinuous steps, and each wave of improvement is succeeded by a period of relative quiet, a new position of equilibrium. At this point Schumpeter has the germ of both his business cycle theory and his theory of the rise of capitalism, although he was to spend the rest of his life providing the theoretical articulation for them.

However, Weber had anticipated this appeal to the supernormal leader. Certainly these early capitalists could arise and even have a limited success.

[13] Talcott Parsons, *The Structure of Social Action* (Glencoe, Illinois: The Free Press, 1949), p. 607.

"Capitalist acquisition as an adventure has been at home in all types of economic society which have known trade with the use of money."[14]

But such institutions were inherently barren. They could never grow and spread and inspire loyalty. The mass of mankind has never rallied behind the skull-and-crossbones banner. The spirit generated here, ". . . the inner attitude of the adventurer, which laughs at all ethical limitations . . .",[15] could never have prevailed against the medieval Catholic *zeitgeist*. As Weber is at pains to show, the practice of acquisitiveness, the *auri sacra fames*, was held in particular abomination. What was required was a countervailing *geist,* the *geist* provided in fact by the Protestant ethic.

Here Schumpeter's second fundamental postulate comes into play—the postulate of "overlapping *geists.*" "There is no single *zeitgeist.*"[16] "Social structures, types and attitudes are coins that do not readily melt."[17] This implied, on the one hand, that the innovator did not in fact have to face a solid phalanx of ethical opposition, although he certainly encountered resistance. On the other, it meant that the innovator might himself be inspired by combinations of values, ideals and attitudes inherited from previous eras.

At the same time, it implied the restoration, in modified form, of Marx's economic interpretation of history. If the "ideal superstructure" or *geist* of a social system could be analyzed as the reflection, not merely of the current structure of production, but also of previous structures of production, an invaluable economy of postulational structure would be obtained, as well as a fruitful new area of investigation. Moreover, it provided another element of dynamism in Schumpeter's picture of the social process, a picture of gradual, cumulative growth and change which was a considerable improvement over the implausible (though dramatic) sequence of thesis-antithesis-and-synthesis which marked both Weber's and Marx's models. Finally, the postulate was to have important implications for Schumpeter's theory of entrepreneurial motivation, and for his broader social system.

The argument above has indicated how Schumpeter, starting from Weber's central vision of the capitalist process as found on pages 27–29 of his 1904 article, could proceed by two postulational steps to something very like his developed theory. Next to be considered are some important theoretical similarities in the two writers' views of the innovator.

First, both theories are clearly based on the principle of antinomic balance,

[14] *Prot. Ethic*, p. 58.   [15] Ibid.

[16] J. A. Schumpeter, *Imperialism and Social Classes*, trans. Heinz Norden, intro. by Bert Hoselitz (New York: Meridan Books, 1955), p. 111. Cited herein as *Imperialism.*

[17] J. A. Schumpeter, *Capitalism, Socialism and Democracy* (3rd ed.; New York: Harper and Brothers, 1950), p. 12.

a construct which has been used by a variety of thinkers since earliest times.[18] This method involves the contraposition of opposites—for Weber, the type of modern capitalist enterprise, sparked by the Protestant economic ethic, is set against the traditional enterprise, governed by the Catholic ethic. Schumpeter sees his position as "characterized by three corresponding pairs of opposites"— the circular flow and the developing economy, "statics and dynamics," and the entrepreneur versus the mere manager.[19]

Second, both theories are "elitist" in concept. For Schumpeter this is clearly so. Weber's innovator, a Calvinist, is indeed a member of the elite in one of its original senses, and Gerth and Mills even went so far as to suggest for Weber a "great man" theory in the tradition of Carlyle and Lecky.[20]

Third, of more significance, is the fact that the innovator is at once a man of unusual will and energy, and a man with no capital. Schumpeter says "What have the individuals under consideration contributed to this? Only the will and the action."[21] The "unusually strong character" and the "clarity of vision and ability to act"[22] of Weber's innovator is matched by Schumpeter's emphasis on "the capacity for making decisions" and the "vision to evaluate forcefully."[23] Here Marx's view of the capitalist is completely reversed. Instead of "The man who has the capital creates the business" we have "The man who creates the business gets the capital." Both authors clearly reject the Marxist and the classical view of investment as virtually an automatic process.[24]

Fourth, and even more significant, is the rejection of hedonism as the underlying motive of entrepreneurial action and capital accumulation. Throughout the nineteenth century all economists, Marxists and others, had viewed the entrepreneur as motivated by simple greed—"a homogenous globule of desire of happiness"[25] in Veblen's words. Weber, of course, saw the case "where a man

[18] Cf. the discussion by Professor Stolper, who suggests that applications of this can be traced back to early Christian and Greek philosophers. W. Stolper, "Reflections on Schumpeter's Writings," in *Schumpeter, Social Scientist*, p. 108.

[19] *Economic Development*, p. 82. The fundamental similarity between the two models, and some methodological implications of the difference between them, are noted by Edward Carlin in "Schumpeter's Constructed Type—the Entrepreneur," in *Kyklos*, IX (Fasc. 1, 1956), 27–40.   [20] Bendix, op. cit., p. 329n.

[21] *Economic Development*, p. 132. Cf. also *Essays of J. A. Schumpeter*, ed. R. V. Clemence (Cambridge, Mass.: Addison-Wesley Press Inc., 1951), p. 65. Cited herein as *Essays*. "Successful innovation . . . is a feat, not of intellect, but of will."

[22] *Prot. Ethic*, p. 69.   [23] *Imperialism*, p. 121.

[24] This is true, in Weber's case, only for the original innovator. Once capitalism and its attitudes have established themselves, the process of capital formation does become almost automatic, as Marx depicted it.

[25] Thorstein Veblen, "Why is Economics Not an Evolutionary Science?", *Quarterly Journal of Economics*, XII (July, 1898), 389.

exists for the sake of his business instead of the reverse"[26] as a result, first of religious impulse, and later as simply the effect of an irrational sense of duty. Schumpeter's position is also clear: ". . . his conduct and his motive are 'rational' in no other sense. And in no sense is his characteristic motive of the hedonist kind . . . typical entrepreners retire from the arena only when and because their strength is spent and they feel no longer equal to the task. . . ."[27]

Fifth, related to the above, is the question of what the motive is, if not hedonism. Weber explains it as an atavism—the grin without the cat, ". . . the idea of duty in one's calling prowls about in our lives like the ghost of dead religious beliefs."[28] Schumpeter offers his well-known "the dream and the will to found a private kingdom," "the will to conquer," "the joy of creating," and observes that ". . . it points to another psychology of non-hedonist character."[29] He does not tell us what that psychology is, and, in that context, it is irrelevant to his argument. Nevertheless, it is essential to the understanding of his system to recognize that all of these motives, as well as the others he mentions, are atavisms. In a master stroke of postulational economy, Schumpeter was able to bring in his "psychology of the entrepreneur" as a special case of his principle of "overlapping *geists*." This is only indirectly revealed when he uses this principle to analyze the problem of imperialism. The blood-thirsty Assyrian, the perspiring tennis champion, Veblen's conspicuous consumer, and the executive planning the newest merger, may all have something in common. They are all acting, in part, ". . . to gratify activity urges springing from capacities and inclinations that had once been crucial to survival, though they had now outlived their usefulness."[30] Weber himself had noted that after the religious motivation is exhausted, other motives emerge; ". . . the resort to entailed estates and the nobility . . . is a product of later decadence."[31] "In the field of its highest development, in the United States, the pursuit of wealth . . . tends to become associated with purely mundane passions which often give it the characteristic of sport."[32] In effect, the motives Weber mentions as support for his "waning of charisma" fit perfectly into Schumpeter's "psychology of non-hedonist character," so that he might well argue that these were the "true" motives throughout the whole period, only concealed by the religious garb.

As a final point in the comparison of the two theories, it is worth noting that Weber refers to his entrepreneur as an "innovator"[33] and that the innovation described fits Schumpeter's definition perfectly, even emphasizing the

---

[26] *Prot. Ethic*, p. 70. [27] *Economic Development*, p. 92.
[28] *Prot. Ethic*, p. 182. [29] *Economic Development*, p. 93.
[30] *Imperialism*, p. 33. [31] *Prot. Ethic*, p. 71.   [32] Ibid., p. 182.
[33] "Dem ersten neuerer" in his original article. Cf. note 10 [p. 75] and note 1 [p. 72].

absence of any particular element of invention. Weber had not intended this. He in fact deprecates the novelty of the action in order to emphasize the necessity of "an unusually strong character" and "highly developed ethical qualities." The young man of his story did ". . . no more than . . ." turn peasants into laborers, adapt the quality of his product, and introduce the principle of low prices and large turnover.[34] It is clear that the action described is a good example of Schumpeter's fifth cause of innovation—the carrying out of the new organization of an industry.[35]

In summary, the lesson Weber drew from his vision of capitalist change emphasized the difference in the *motives* of the participants. Marx's postulate of rational self-interest was clearly inadequate to account for the dedication, will and energy required and actually observed. Some extra-economic spur was necessary to accomplish the transition from feudalism to capitalism, and the Protestant ethic filled this theoretical gap perfectly. The acceptance of Weber's view would thus imply the inadequacy of any purely economic theory of economic development.

From essentially the same central vision, Schumpeter drew an entirely different inference, by emphasizing the difference in the *economic acts* being carried out. The traditional capitalists were behaving in routine fashion, but the innovator was changing the routine itself—an act of economic leadership. A succession of such acts of leadership could account for the transition from feudalism to capitalism, without assuming any other motive than the ordinary desire for profit. Consequently, the mechanism of the circular flow, the motives and methods involved in changing it, and the resulting adaptations can all be explained without invoking extra-economic elements, and a purely economic theory of economic change is possible.

However, at a higher level, economic theory must be embedded in an economic sociology or social theory, which provides criteria for weighing the relative significance of economic and noneconomic elements. At this level Schumpeter's postulate of social leadership, his modified economic interpretation of history, and his "psychology of non-hedonist character" come into play, and his social theory bears comparison with Weber's.

SECTION THREE: SOCIAL THEORIES

From his treatment of the Protestant ethic, Weber moved to explore the economic ethic of other civilizations, China, India and ancient Palestine. In the

[34] *Prot. Ethic*, p. 68.   [35] *Economic Development*, p. 66.

process he studied the sociology of their religions, and later used the analytical tools he had developed to attack the problems of law, democracy, music. On these problems he spent the fifteen years remaining to him after his famous article, and many of his studies were unfinished at his death.

Throughout his later work he continued to use his relatively static method of "ideal types," and among the most important of these were his three types of authority: the Charismatic, the Traditional and the Rational (legal). These had already appeared implicitly in his analysis of the Protestant ethic, the traditional methods being swept away by the dynamic of charisma, which was in turn eroded away by the rational methods enjoined by Protestant asceticism. They continued to dominate his general approach to other problems. In his work he seems to have used the concept of rationalism as analogous to the principle of entropy, *i.e.*, ideas and methods were to be analyzed in terms of this guide line.[36] Combined with this he used many of the categories explored and made explicit by Marx.

Schumpeter's theory was framed primarily for economic analysis, but, as he noted, had been found valuable ". . . even beyond the boundaries of economics, in what might be called the theory of cultural evolution."[37] He had little interest in developing theory for its own sake, and in consequence its broader implications are observable only in the context of specific social problems such as those treated in his *Capitalism, Socialism and Democracy*, or in his essays on imperialism and social classes.

Professor Usher recognized, perhaps more clearly than any other scholar, the significance of Schumpeter's contribution to social science research. It was, above all, an integration of theory and history.

> Even in its most abstract formulation, *The Theory of Economic Development* opened new vistas in the interpretation of economic history. When expanded in *Business Cycles,* all these features of the theory became explicit. Nothing less is at stake than a massive revision of the interpretation of economic history of Europe since the age of discovery.[38]

To complete the framework of Schumpeter's social theory, and make it comparable with Weber's, one postulate must be added to those already

[36] Bendix, op. cit., p. 299 note 22; p. 327. For a brief and clear outline of Weber's "image of society" cf. his Chap. VIII. Although the present argument regarding Weber was formulated before the appearance of Professor Bendix's book, it has benefited from his presentation, and is not intended to be inconsistent with his interpretation of Weber.

[37] *Economic Development*, p. xi. For an example of this, cf. his reference to the circular flow in *Imperialism*, p. 112.

[38] A. P. Usher, "Historical Implications of the Theory of Economic Development," in *Schumpeter, Social Scientist*, p. 127.

mentioned—his contraposition of rationalism and magic. These concepts are mentioned only once—in the analysis of the erosion of precapitalist traditions[39]—but they are implicit in the remainder of his writings. His use of the concept of rationalism is identical with Weber's, and his concept of "magic," including as it does all methods and attitudes resting on nonempirical grounds, seems to cover essentially the same set of phenomena as Weber's *charisma*.[40]

The present comparison starts from Usher's view of Schumpeter's place in social science. What "new vistas" were opened up by his theory, and how were they related to his central vision? In what respects can Schumpeter's theoretical structure be considered superior to Weber's?

The Problem of Historic Change

Professor Usher has given eloquent testimony to the most important of Schumpeter's contributions:

> Historical analysis cannot rise above the level of wholly subjective narrative until there is some defensible and workable concept of process.[41]

Schumpeter's concept of process, obtained by placing his entrepreneurial leader in the context of the circular flow, provided him with a tool vastly superior to the "comparative statics" analysis of Marx and Weber. In Usher's words:

> The romantic idealists and the various historical sociologies identified change with the transition from one stage to another. The discontinuities of history were, thus, restricted to long-term movements dated in terms of centuries. In *The Theory of Economic Development*, change became a completely pervasive feature of social life.[42]

By increasing the expected frequency, and reducing the individual impact of change to the point of associating it with business fluctuations, Schumpeter was able to present a picture of relatively continuous, cumulative economic expansion. This made it possible for him to accept Marshall's cherished "Principle of Continuity"[43] as consistent with his own view of development, and by means

---

[39] *Capitalism, Socialism and Democracy*, pp. 121 ff.

[40] Ibid. Cf. in particular the "collective and affective attitudes" which Schumpeter's term embraces, and Weber's "communal" and "associative" relationships in Bendix, op. cit., p. 292, n. 7.

[41] Usher, op. cit., in *Schumpeter, Social Scientist*, p. 125.

[42] Ibid., p. 127.

[43] A. Marshall, *Principles of Economics* (8th ed.; London: Macmillan, 1938), pp. vi ff.

of it show that Weber's problem of the origin of the capitalist spirit was spurious.[44]

On the other hand, Schumpeter did not accept the Marshallian theory of economic change. For Marshall, the system adapted incrementally to shifts in preference and production functions, the result being a continuous improvement in moral qualities, tastes and economic techniques. This provided no theoretical room for business cycles,[45] and Marshall was forced to include separate postulates of human error and monetary misbehavior to account for them. Moreover, Marshall's approach implied a theory of unilinear evolution, while Schumpeter's did not.[46]

In effect, Schumpeter's theory of change occupies a position somewhere between the extremes represented by Marshall and Weber. Weber's is a picture of rapid transition punctuating long periods of continuity, while Marshall's is one of relative continuity throughout. Thus both Marshall's and Weber's pictures of entrepreneurial activity in developed capitalism are quite similar, and different from Schumpeter's.

The Problem of Individual Volition

Marx had made a considerable contribution to social science analysis by showing how difficult it was for individuals to think and act outside their own classbound routines. However, in claiming that historic change was completely determined, he overstated his case, and Weber took advantage of the overstatement. If this were so, how was it possible for the "new capitalist" to so transcend the attitudes of his own traditional capitalist class? By postulating a non-hedonistic, religious motive for the new capitalist, Weber was able to restore the element of human volition, but at a considerable methodological price. For economics, at least, he opened a Pandora's box of human motives, any one of which might have significance for economic action.

[44] Cf. *Business Cycles*, pp. 226 ff., and *Essays*, p. 185 f., for Schumpeter's argument here. For his view that this constituted a misuse of the method of ideal types, cf. Schumpeter, *History of Economic Analysis* (New York: Oxford University Press, 1954), p. 80n.

[45] "There is the 'theory' that the economic process is essentially non-oscillatory and that the explanation of cyclical . . . fluctuations must therefore be sought in particular circumstances . . . which disturb that even flow. Marshall stands out in the large crowd that represents this 'hypothesis'." Schumpeter, *Ten Great Economists from Marx to Keynes* (New York: Oxford University Press, 1951), p. 252.

[46] Cf. Marshall, op. cit., p. 86 f., for his treatment of "wants and activities." For his views on evolution, ibid., pp. ix and xiii. For his treatment of business cycles, cf. A. and M. Marshall. *The Economics of Industry* (London: Macmillan, 1879), pp. 114 ff. and pp. 152 ff. For the methodological implications of Marshall's approach, cf. Parsons, op. cit., pp. 155 ff.

Schumpeter attacked the problem on two levels. First, in any economic system there existed entrepreneurs who, driven by the usual profit motive, would be willing to use new *methods*. These new methods, if successful, would enforce economic adaptation, and the whole sequence could be treated as an economic problem. In Schumpeter's words, "Economic activity may have *any* motive, even a spiritual one, but its *meaning* is always the satisfaction of wants."[47]

However, second, there remains the overwhelming empirical evidence that successful entrepreneurs are not motivated merely by hedonistic impulses; in particular, there is the dedication to business which Weber describes so vividly and attributes to the remains of religious belief. Here Schumpeter's postulate of overlapping *geists* plays its part again. Men are inclined to adopt, or to continue to use, methods and motives which formerly had survival or prestige value, even though the application might not seem appropriate under existing circumstances. Thus successful entrepreneurs continue to accumulate more wealth than they can ever enjoy; thus, too, they imitate the nobility by building castles and establishing dynasties, even though these no longer have the survival or prestige value they once possessed.

Schumpeter, by this postulate, was able to give recognition to human volition, without invoking, as Weber did, the ". . . unconditional acts of great men, to whom underlying truths are directly revealed."[48] In addition to the general methodological advance implied in this injunction to look first at the economic environment, past and present, in ascribing motives, it provided a single explanation of entrepreneurial motivation where Weber had assigned two or more. In Weber's view, the contemporary entrepreneur was being driven partly by the ghost of his dead religious beliefs, and partly by "more mundane passions,"[49] such as the urge to ape the nobility or to engage in business as in sport. Schumpeter was able to use the precise psychological characteristic invoked by Weber—the persistence of behavior patterns long after their rationale had vanished—to account for all these motives, Weber's "sense of duty" included.

Rationalism, Traditionalism and Charisma

Schumpeter's model also throws new light on Weber's famous triad and reveals some of its deficiencies. First, since Schumpeter's is a process model, in contrast to Weber's "mosaic" structure, he is able to use a two-element postulate

[47] *Economic Development*, p. 10.
[48] Usher, op. cit. in *Schumpeter, Social Scientist*, p. 126.
[49] *Prot. Ethic*, p. 182.

—his concepts of rationalism and magic—to cover the same theoretical ground. In his model of development by small increments, traditional methods and attitudes are merely yesterday's rational ones, now superseded by the innovation. Second, his model provides a theoretical expectation of the rise of charisma, at least in its secular aspect, "glamor." The aristocracy who for centuries exacted awe and obedience on pain of sudden death, continued to receive it even after its real power had vanished. Moreover, traditional attitudes and values may be transmuted by new relations of production, and play a new role, as in the case of the aristocrat "who hurls himself into an election campaign as his ancestors rode into battle."[50]

Third, although Schumpeter, like Weber, sees modern history as a "slow though incessant widening of the sector of social life"[51] within which rational methods are used, the process is by no means irreversible or unilinear. Rationalist criticism, which erodes away institutions and values having no clear empirical relevance, may in fact be mistaken, and, when the mistake becomes obvious, the way is clear for social leadership to reinstate them. In contrast, Weber's theory emphasizes the "waning of charisma,"[52] but has no room for its revival except by the rise of some new prophet.[53]

Class and Status

As Bendix points out,[54] Weber's "image of society" recognizes the existence of several social strata, each stratum having its own *geist*. There is a sharp distinction between actions and attitudes arising from social status, and those arising from the economic class to which the subject belongs. In effect, Weber accepts Marx's doctrine regarding class conflict, insisting only that other kinds of conflict, just as fundamental, but proceeding from status positions and ideals, can exist.[55] Here again, Schumpeter's more continuous view of social development exhibits its superiority. The rank of a social class, and its class privileges

[50] Ibid., p. 167. Cf. also ibid., p. 34.

[51] *Capitalism, Socialism and Democracy*, p. 122.

[52] Ibid., He notes the errors of the rationalist criticism of the enlightenment period. Their possible reinstatement, however, is a conclusion of the theory, and is not mentioned by Schumpeter himself.

[53] This is, as Bendix shows, partly a consequence of ". . . an artifact of exposition," and Weber approaches Schumpeter's position in several respects. He implies the existence of "innovating activity" in the development of legal institutions, and emphasizes the contribution to political leadership sometimes made by aristocratic traditions. Nevertheless it is true that Weber had no general theory of the rise of leadership. Bendix, op. cit., pp. 327 f., 432 ff.

[54] Ibid., p. 267.

[55] Cf. ibid., pp. 105 ff. for an explanation of Weber's notion of "class" and "status."

and perquisites, relate to the socially necessary function[56] its members perform as entrepreneur, commissar or leader in battle. When the structure of production changes, the older attitudes and functions are either eroded away or transmuted as above. In Schumpeter's system of continuous change, status follows function, but with a lag, and conflict can develop here, as well as among purely economic interest groups. Thus no unalterable class conflict need be postulated, and distinction between status and class becomes one of convenience in relation to the problem under study.

A further implication of Schumpeter's theory of social classes is that of symbiosis. Although the class performing the "most socially necessary function" will normally use its power in order to arrogate to itself other prerogatives and functions, these other functions may require aptitudes and values antithetical to those of the leading class. In such cases there may develop two or more leading classes, each depending on the others to perform functions it cannot perform for itself.[57]

Economic Determinism

Professor Usher points up the true value of Schumpeter's contribution to the understanding of history. Because of his work, history and theory mesh, and "the processes of history are neither transcendental and unknowable, nor mechanical and foreordained."[58] Weber's work does display an awkward conflict between these two tendencies. He is able to break through the mechanical and foreordained determinism of Marx only by postulating a relatively "transcendental" charismatic influence. Schumpeter avoids determinism by accepting goals and attitudes from prior relations of production, coupled with a full recognition of the creative impulse in human history. Development proceeds through innovation—"not an adaptive but a creative response to a changing environment. It was not uniquely determined by it and might have failed to come about."[59] In contrast, Weber left the impression that the system again lapsed into determinism after the charismatic force had spent itself.

The Puritan wanted to work in a calling; we are forced to do so. For when asceticism was carried out of monastic cells into everyday life, and began to dominate worldly

[56] *Imperialism*, pp. 137 ff.
[57] For Schumpeter, symbiosis was both an essential element in the capitalist system, and an actual, though perhaps not a necessary, feature of all historical epochs. Cf. *Capitalism, Socialism and Democracy*, p. 139.
[58] Usher, op. cit., in *Schumpeter, Social Scientist*, p. 125.
[59] *Business Cycles*, p. 229.

morality, it did its part in building the tremendous cosmos of the modern economic order .... Victorious capitalism, since it rests on mechanical foundations, needs its support no longer.[60]

Although Weber did not explore systematically the question of the future of capitalism, he held out at least two possibilities, one the development of a socialist bureaucracy, the other the rise of new charismatic leaders.[61] Schumpeter's model is somewhat richer in implications, of which three may be distinguished. The first proceeds from his concept of the erosive effects of rationalism (corresponding to Weber's "waning of charisma"), and involves, among other things, the destruction of the nonhedonist impulses of the capitalist class, and of the feudal aristocracy which had protected it. The second type of change follows from his notion of the function of social leadership. The capitalist class provides the dynamic of capitalism through constant innovation, and the class may decline in status either because its function is made automatic and routine, or because additional increases in productivity are no longer of first importance.

A third possible type of change derives from his postulate of overlapping *geists*. Methods, values and aptitudes called for by one structure of production will often persist into the next. Even though they play no useful part there, they may not be eroded away. Instead they may turn against the system, either destroying it or causing it to develop in a different direction. One example cited by Schumpeter attributes the apparently objectless rise of Assyrian imperialism to the persistence of hunting aptitudes and traditions beyond their period of usefulness.[62] Another provides the basis for his sociology of the intellectual,[63] in which the capitalist system develops more intellectuals than it can usefully absorb, and these help to destroy the system by their criticism and persuasion. Although Schumpeter himself concluded that socialism was the most probable outcome of capitalist change, it is nevertheless true that his model suggests other possibilities as well.

Religion and Social Science

It is perhaps paradoxical to assert that Schumpeter, an economist and an exponent of the economic interpretation of history, could have made a

[60] *Prot. Ethic*, p. 175.

[61] Cf. his references to the possibility of new prophets or a lapse into traditionalism. *Prot. Ethic*, p. 182. Cf. also Bendix, op. cit., pp. 451 ff., for a discussion of his later work on bureaucracy.   [62] *Imperialism*, pp. 32 f.

[63] *Capitalism, Socialism and Democracy*, pp. 146 ff.

contribution to the field of study for which Weber was so famous. In fact, his contribution may be more correctly described as a reaction against, and a supplement to Weber's analysis. As an economist, he was concerned with tracing the interaction of economic motives and economic action, and it was his duty to continue until motives and effects could be unmistakably identified as non-economic in nature.

For Schumpeter, the economic interpretation of history is always invoked as a methodological convenience, and never as a philosophical conviction.[64] If, by itself, it provides a sufficient explanation of a social phenomenon, any further postulate would be redundant. If it does not, the postulate is supplemented. In the few cases where the religious element came into question in his analysis (i.e., in "religious imperialism" and in Protestantism as the causal element in the rise of capitalism), he denies its significance as an explanatory element.

His position is stated fairly clearly in his work on imperialism. First:

Conscious motives—no matter whether, in the concrete case, they were always religious in character—are seldom *true* motives . . . and they are never the *sole* motives.[65]

Nothing is more difficult in the social sciences than the judging of an actor's true motives for action, particularly because of the human tendency to rationalize.

Second, the attribution of religious motives to action may reverse the causation.

The 'true' prophet recognizes the necessities of the existing situation—a situation that exists quite independently of him—and when these necessities subsequently change, he manages to adopt a new policy.[66]

Third, the appeal to religious beliefs or to the charismatic leader should be avoided except as a last resort, because (a) it may well be redundant, and (b) as in attributing a man's argument to his ideological bias, it brings analysis (at that level) to a close. In the case of Islamic imperialism,

It is pointless to insist that the Word of the Prophet is an ultimate fact beyond which social science cannot go . . . . When that fact becomes easily understandable from the very social, psychic, and physical background that is itself quite adequate to explain fully

---

[64] His comments on the economic interpretation are found, among other places, in: *Economic Development*, p. 58; *Capitalism, Socialism and Democracy*, pp. 11 f.; *Imperialism*, pp. 6, 111, 172, 178.

[65] *Imperialism*, p. 32.   [66] Ibid., p. 40.

what the Word of the Prophet is otherwise left to explain alone. Quite apart from trying to explain the unknown through the still less known, we would be resorting to a crutch that is quite unnecessary.[67]

In brief, Schumpeter held the view that all problems of motive in the social sciences be submitted to two tests: (a) Is the observed action consistent with the rational self interest of the actor? If not, (b) is the action consistent with Schumpeter's "psychology of nonhedonist character"? That is, can the action be explained as an atavism, stemming from preceding relations of production? If the action were consistent with neither of those assumptions, then other motives, including religious, might be explored. He certainly did not deny that religious motives do have important effects on action. For example, the missionary activity in the medieval church must be analyzed primarily, although not necessarily exclusively, as a product of religious beliefs. This is the case of "the religious idea's taking on a social life of its own."[68] In such a case the social scientist's duty would lie primarily in taking these social effects as data and working from there, "just as describing the effects of the Counter Reformation upon Italian and Spanish painting always remains history of art."[69]

The comparison with Weber, although restricted to certain general problems of social science, leaves little doubt that Schumpeter did have a genuine social theory, comparable in scope and generality with Weber's. Although its general outlines are clear, Schumpeter nowhere presented it in systematic form, and it is certain that he never had the opportunity to explore fully its many implications. His study of the sociology of imperialism is essentially an application of his postulate of overlapping *geists*,[70] his analysis of social classes an application of his postulate of social leadership.[71] Only in his *Capitalism, Socialism and Democracy* is the range of his social theory allowed relatively full scope. His analysis of democratic practice represents another application of his social leadership principle,[72] while he views democratic ideals, values and attitudes as essentially a product of the capitalist mode of production. Also, as noted above, his sketch of a sociology of the intellectual is another theoretical implication of his postulate of overlapping *geists*. More light is thrown on his theory here than in any other of his works, but the field of his investigation—the future of capitalism and the rise of socialism—is still relatively narrow.

---

[67] Ibid., p. 39.   [68] Ibid., p. 42.

[69] *Economic Development*, p. 59.

[70] "Imperialism thus is atavistic in character . . . it is an element that stems . . . from past rather than present relations of production." *Imperialism*, p. 65.

[71] Ibid., pp. 159 f., 165 f.

[72] *Capitalism, Socialism and Democracy*, pp. 269 ff., 296 f.

The comparison has also emphasized the methodological superiority of Schumpeter's social theory. As Usher shows, this superiority is genuine, and one of Schumpeter's major achievements. However, it must not be understood as depreciating Weber's contribution. Students of Weber are agreed that his method of ideal types had serious inadequacies, that his categories were not free from methodological obscurity and inconsistency, but they are also agreed on the wealth of insights he provided, sometimes because of, sometimes in spite of, his inadequate tools.

In spite of the differences in areas of interest, the theories display notable structural similarities. Both are fundamentally integrations of history and theory, and neither, unlike almost all such theories, implies a unilinear or evolutionary view of the historic process. Moreover, both theories set out from the Marxian interpretation of history; that is, they accept as a starting point a process in which the forms of thought and goals are largely molded by the existing structure of production. In both theories historic change takes place as a consequence of individual human action, sparked by nonhedonist motives, and in both cases (for the entrepreneur at least) the nonhedonist motive is identified as the persistence of a human behavior pattern after its original *raison d'être* has disappeared.

At this point the theories diverge. Weber identifies the behavior pattern in question as the remains of religious belief. Schumpeter attributes it to learned techniques of problem-solving which were formerly useful for economic survival. Moreover, Schumpeter distinguishes between two theoretically different types of economic action—action carried out within the structured process and action which changes the process itself—and thus evolves a postulate of leadership. As a result, Schumpeter has a process model in which change is almost continuous, one which does not depend on extraeconomic elements (although they can be inserted as required), and one which permits him to analyze many of Weber's problems while using fewer postulates.

SECTION FOUR: CONCLUSIONS

Schumpeter always objected to the practice of evaluating economists' contributions in terms of their presumed philosophical backgrounds,[73] and he probably would not have relished the notion of being placed, as Usher placed him, squarely in the idealist tradition. Nevertheless, Usher's approach is in this case fruitful, suggesting as it does the direction taken in the progressive refinement and improvement of analytical tools in the social sciences.

[73] Cf. footnote 79.

The present comparison tends to reinforce Usher's view. Whether Schumpeter and Weber should be placed in the idealistic tradition or not is of less importance than the fact that Weber's social theory shows many of the signs of being a way-station along the road Schumpeter has traveled. And this in turn is of importance primarily because of the possibilities of mutual criticism and fruitful synthesis that it suggests.

Emphasis has been placed, in this study, on the superiority of Schumpeter's dynamic model over Weber's ideal-type static model. Economists and sociologists have long recognized that the relation between static and dynamic models is one of generality only, and not of inherent superiority. The choice is determined by the nature of the problem to be analyzed. And the comparison undertaken here provides some insights on what a process model can and cannot do. From Schumpeter's standpoint, several of Weber's concepts are seen to be special cases of a single conceptual process, and at least one of Weber's problems is seen to be a spurious one, arising from the inadequacies of "ideal-type" tools.[74] On the other hand, Weber's distinction between class and status, which vanishes in Schumpeter's process model, is of vital importance in analyzing social systems which may properly be regarded as stable, and a process model tends to gloss over such distinctions. Moreover, in such a system, Schumpeter's concept of social leadership would not appear at all.[75] The comparison illustrates both the convenience of static models, in making it possible for certain variables to be dropped entirely, as well as the dangers involved if the system under study is actually in process of change.

Economists studying problems of underdeveloped countries have found themselves faced with the absolute necessity of developing a coherent economic sociology, and many have found Weber's categories of considerable help in this task. Schumpeter's dynamic model of social change should be a useful addition to the economist's tool box, if not as the foundation for an economic sociology, at least as a yardstick against which others may be measured. Schumpeter's dedication to the cause of economic science, and his reputation as a jealous guardian of the integrity of economics, remain unchallenged, and his model could provide some assurance that a significant economic variable would not be overlooked, amid the welter of social, political, religious, and psychological elements being examined.

Schumpeter's Method

Schumpeter's theory has often been described as "monolithic", usually with a pejorative connotation. The comparison with Weber has emphasized the bare

[74] Cf. above, footnote 44.　　　　　　　　[75] *Imperialism*, p. 165.

bones of the theory, and it is clearly, if not monolithic, at least very tightly integrated, with the economic interpretation of history at the apex of the structure. However, the comparison has also indicated the spaciousness of the structure. In his whole productive lifetime, Schumpeter was unable to explore the many insights and hypotheses it suggested to him. These considerations suggest a plausible explanation of certain criticisms which have been leveled at him and his work.

Schumpeter's first duty, of course, was to realize as fully as possible the potentials of his own theory. But more than this, he was obliged by the ordinary canons of scientific inquiry to prefer an explanation having more general validity over one designed to fit a set of special circumstances. For example, his theory of the entrepreneur received additional credibility from the fact that it was a special case of a useful theory of social leadership. But, for Schumpeter, methodological principles were guides for his own inquiry, and he refused to use them as sticks to beat down opposing theories. He designed his own analysis ". . . to grip the wheels of received theory. The armor of methodological commentaries I renounce completely."[76] He insisted that economics could develop with only a minimum of assumptions about psychology, and that in his own case "none of the results to which our analysis is intended to lead stands or falls with our 'psychology of the entrepreneur' or could be vitiated by any errors in it."[77] Moreover, although he mentions his "psychology of nonhedonist character," he does not elaborate. Here and in other places, his reluctance to use anything but the minimum of postulational scaffolding actually obscures the full generality of his social theory.

In view of this, it is not surprising that Schumpeter gave the impression of having a "closed system," and even, according to some critics, of having a closed mind. That his social system, at least, was not closed, is indicated by his making provision for "the religious idea's taking on a social life of its own,"[78] and many other examples could be cited. A related criticism, however, is more serious, since it tends to discourage a careful examination of Schumpeter's work. This criticism attributes his approach and conclusions to his ideological bias.

Schumpeter's "Ideology"

In his *Revolution, Evolution and the Economic Order*, Professor Sievers evaluates Schumpeter on the basis of his presumed social philosophy,[79] and finds

---

[76] *Economic Development*, p. 4.   [77] Ibid., p. 90.   [78] *Imperialism*, p. 42.

[79]Schumpeter, of course, regarded his analysis as being consistent with almost any social philosophy. As early as 1914, he had referred to this approach (Gide's treatment of

that Schumpeter's "... system of values ... is not without contradictions."[80] Among these contradictory elements he includes Schumpeter's "narrow conception of reason," his admiration for "will, courage, ambition, glamor and the aristocratic flair for style."[81] He notes that "The entrepreneur was for Schumpeter a hero"[82] and that he was "very warmly disposed" toward the aristocrat.[83] In relation to this, he finds that Schumpeter "... was not sympathetic to democracy ... and he did not understand it," but is surprised "... that he condemned it for its rationalist and romantic elements."[84] Finally, Sievers had considerable difficulty with Schumpeter's analysis of the rootless intellectual. "For a thinker who ostensibly places reason at the heart of his system, Schumpeter shows little respect for the autonomy of intellectual curiosity and the pursuit of learning."[85]

The comparison undertaken here has shown these elements to be technical concepts—tools of analysis—and the contradictions disappear when they are treated as such. Schumpeter's suggestion that the most probable source of bias is in the writer's "prescientific vision" does not prove very useful when applied to his own case, since his central vision of the capitalist process corresponds, almost point for point, with Weber's. Here any bias of selection or emphasis would presumably be shared with Weber. Another critical source of bias occurs, of course, in Schumpeter's introduction of his postulate of entrepreneurial leadership. At this point all of the elements of Schumpeter's semi-aristocratic background could have entered to shape his analytical structure. Yet it was just this postulate that Usher regards as the essential link in his most significant contribution to historical analysis. Consequently this comparison would tend to support Smithies' suggestion of ideological insight, rather than ideological bias.[86]

However, finally, a possible test for bias is suggested by the comparison undertaken in this paper. In Weber's theory are found many of the same elements which have been attributed to Schumpeter's social philosophy. There is a similar emphasis on will and energy, and essentially the same concepts of

the Physiocrats) as "an example of the tendency of so many economists to cling to superficialities and of the predilection for the 'Philosophy' of economics," and notes that "this confusion of two completely different approaches makes it impossible to do justice to the scientific content of a system." Schumpeter, *Economic Doctrine and Method: An Historical Sketch*, trans. R. Aris (New York: Oxford University Press, 1954), p. 47 n.

[80] Allen M. Sievers, *Revolution, Evolution, and the Economic Order* (Englewood Cliffs, N.J.: Prentice-Hall, Inc.), 1962, p. 52.   [81] Ibid., p. 52.   [82] Ibid.

[83] Ibid., p. 38.   [84] Ibid., p. 53.   [85] Ibid., p. 58.

[86] Smithies, op. cit., in *Schumpeter, Social Scientist*, p. 17. This is also consistent with Schumpeter's doctrine "that ideologies *may* contain provable truth up to 100 percent." Schumpeter, "Science and Ideology," *Essays*, p. 273.

glamor (charisma), magic[87] and rationalism. Moreover, we find a somewhat similar analysis of political leadership in democracy, and a similar evaluation of "the coffee house intellectual."[88] Other similarities would include the two writers' views of the "decline of the capitalist mentality,"[89] and of the development of hostility to capitalism by modern bureaucracy.[90] In effect, a comparison of the two writers' conclusions and insights, in such common areas of interest as capitalism, democracy and rationalism, would be valuable, not only in appraising the usefulness of their respective theories, but also in identifying possible bias of observation and selection.

[87] Weber's notion of "magic" is narrower than Schumpeter's. For examples of its use, cf. Bendix, op. cit., pp. 152, 306.

[88] Ibid., p. 443.

[89] Ibid., p. 451.

[90] Ibid., p. 453, n. 7.

4

THE ENTREPRENEUR IN
ECONOMIC CHANGE

Thomas C. Cochran

FOR at least two centuries, during which economists developed theories about their own Western European culture, the lazy avidity of man for pleasure and the laws of operation of reasonably free markets seemed satisfactory basic assumptions. Only when political needs for forced-draft economic development in backward areas turned the attention of economists to growth in strange cultures were the social assumptions that underlay classic theory clearly evident. The more economists labored with the exotic cultures of Asia, Africa, and Latin America, the more impressed they became with both the force and intricacy of social factors. Ten years after the end of World War II some leading economists were ready to admit that "the really fundamental problems of economic development are noneconomic" (Buchanan & Ellis, 1955, p. 9).

MODELS OF ECONOMIC CHANGE

If for purposes of argument we may side with these distinguished economists, their statement implies the need for primarily social models of economic

Reprinted by permission of the author and the publisher from Explorations in Entrepreneurial History (*Summer, 1965*), *pp. 25–37.*

change. This in turn moves economic change from the exclusive realm of the economist or economic historian into that of the general social scientist or historian.

But a model for social change either is conceived so broadly as to be a blunt tool for analysis (for example: "Change occurs when socially relevant new habits are acquired via a learning process"), or in order to provide detail introduces too many variables. In spite of a wide recognition of the importance of social and cultural factors among economists, I know of no one who has attempted a comprehensive general model.

A solution to this dilemma is to try to narrow the scope of the problem by focusing on a particular type of change where historical analogy can be of use. One way to do this is by concentrating on how the variables that seem most essential affect entrepreneurial decisions. If every economic decision were made by a computer into which social and economic factors were fed, or by different individuals, each differently conditioned and differently placed in the social structure, it would be useless to focus on the decision-maker. But fortunately this is not the case. Decisions are normally made in sequence by the same man, who is not a random selection from the human species but is, rather, a representative of a limited group in his culture. Thus the noneconomic social factors come in a definable set of influences operating on the executive.

The Role of the Entrepreneur

As aggregates, managers or executives in a given type of activity represent certain ascertainable levels of education and social status and types of cultural conditioning that produce a roughly definable modal personality. In making their decisions they play social roles anticipated by their associates and other groups in the culture. Therefore, in the modal entrepreneur (and in general the modes seem broad) there is a channel through which diverse, and in themselves intangible, social forces translate their effects into economic action; a point where social factors can be observed and estimated for relative intensities.

To begin with, the executives' inner character is largely conditioned by the type of child-rearing and schooling common to the culture. He receives the traditional admonitions, absorbs the family attitudes of his class, learns the ideologies and conceptual schemes of the society. Latin-American child-rearing, for example, even in the most advanced countries, tends to produce quite different characters from that of the United States (Landry, 1959, pp. 238 ff.). Similarly, American child-rearing and schooling before about 1920 produced differently conditioned individuals than did that of the 1920s and 1930s. Since this latter difference is of importance to the American business community, it will be well to use this as an illustration.

Middle-class parents of the turn of the century—and important executives have largely middle-class origins—were sure of the Christian moral values and the need for firm guidance and parental authority. A similar atmosphere permeated the school. By the 1920s the new psychology had undermined the old moral principles, up-to-date parents were Freudians or behaviorists, and good schools, public or private, were child- or community-centered (Cremin, 1961). Without going into all the complexities involved, it seems reasonable to suppose that a generation of executives was being trained with fewer fixed values, less secure principles, greater tendencies to be influenced by those around them: in a word, to be good organization men.

Whether this shift has been advantageous to the business community or not, it is probably too early to say, but it has fitted in with the needs of large-scale mass-production to give a particularly co-operative, team-like aspect to American entrepreneurship; one that is in quite striking contrast to the individual- and family-centrism of less industrially advanced areas.

Returning to our model of the entrepreneurial situation, the executive, therefore, plays a social role partly shaped by the modal type of personality that comes from the social conditioning of his generation. While the unusual characters will always depart from the norms, in general invention and innovation will tend to be along lines congenial to the type of conditioning. Anthropologists interested in change support this premise by saying that new items in the culture must be not only physically but also psychologically available. Subjective constructions of the items must be made and these will depend on the value orientations of the culture (Vogt, 1960, p. 25). The rate of change will be a function of the rate of subjective construction. Thus executives in one culture will conceptualize and use a new item, and in another culture, where the item is equally available, they may remain unaware of its existence.

Entrepreneurial roles are defined by the ideas of those important to the success of the actor. In the case of many new pursuits, such as manufacturing in an underdeveloped country, the defining groups, those whom the executive seeks to satisfy, are often not connected with the industrial operation *per se*. A role is established, therefore, that is not necessarily instrumental to the task involved. There is also much operational trial and error. An Argentine manufacturer of the 1920s, for example, wished primarily to become an important family, business, and civic leader, achievements not necessarily functional to his role as an entrepreneur. In operating a pioneer big business he had no guide as to how he should divide his time among production, finance, sales, and government contacts. He could only learn by experience how little working capitaland what amount of time obligations would be safe. But in a well-established corporation, defining groups such as the senior officers or the board have well-formed expectations, and the entrepreneurial role may be said to be closely defined.

It is obvious that the primarily cultural factors operating on the personality of the executive and the defining of his role by those involved must accommodate to some degree to the necessities of the operations to be carried out. But the accommodation does not have to be an efficient one. For example, in West Texas in 1950, industrial risks in new lines such as furniture and other home fittings were relatively safe and offered high rates of return; but the banker role, as defined by both fellow officers and directors, was to loan only on cattle or land, and consequently the role was not efficiently adjusted to the actual needs or opportunities of the situation (Cochran, 1962, pp. 173–174).

This relatively simple framework of an entrepreneurial role defined by the personality of the actor, the expectations of groups with power to sanction deviations from expected behavior, and the operational needs of the function to be performed, subsumes all the social or cultural factors. But obviously, when so much is fitted into so little, each category must and does cover many complications (Jenks, 1949, pp. 108–152).

For example, observation of cultures making the change from agricultural-trading communities to industrial states shows that family obligations are one of the chief dysfunctional elements. But the force of the entrepreneur's feeling of obligation to the members of an extended family is hard to measure. It is easy enough to say that professional middle-management will only arise as this obligation grows weaker, but where are the critical points? How dysfunctional must this holdover from the static agrarian family become before a major alteration will occur in the entrepreneurial role?

It is because such questions, involving a variety of uncontrollable variables, cannot be directly answered by purely theoretical analysis that history becomes useful. The only plausible answers that can be offered have to be in terms of analogies taken from various historic situations. Once the factors are defined, as in the entrepreneurial-role model, it is possible to collect tolerably comparable data for such situations. Whether the facts are collected by economists or historians, whether the time span is two months or twenty years, it is still a historical type of data; it is the record of what appears to have happened in a real situation where the variables could not be controlled to fit a research design. Thus Fayerweather's *The Executive Overseas* (1959), a study based chiefly on intimate observation of a small number of executives in Mexico over a 4-month period, is a history, even though the time-span is short and the data are unconventional.

ENTREPRENEURIAL INTERACTION WITH CHANGE

It is easier to demonstrate the dynamics of the entrepreneurial model by selecting instances from abroad where the pressures of advanced American technology have rapidly penetrated traditional agricultural cultures, but I believe it will be of more interest to American businessmen and economists to select some examples of entrepreneurial interaction with change from our own history, and to ignore events before the nineteenth century. In the last 150 years business executives have participated in three changes that cannot be neglected in any account of how we arrived at where we are: first, the rapid adoption of industrial machinery in the first half of the nineteenth century; second, the rise of professional management in the large corporation, starting in the second half of the century; and third, the spread of mass-production techniques in the twentieth century. In each of these major changes the social factors in American culture operating through the entrepreneur appear to be well marked. The analysis may also be used to answer questions as to why corresponding changes did not occur in other cultures.

Rapid Industrialization

In turning to the first type of change, it is striking that the usual problem of the present-day growth theorist is to account for overly-slow industrial expansion either in some less-advanced area or in the present United States, whereas in studying early nineteenth-century America the problem is to account for unusually rapid industrialization with novel characteristics. The major question is: Why did American entrepreneurs adopt machinery more rapidly than their counterparts in Western Europe? And the most convincing economic answer is because of shortage of labor. Habakkuk (1962) made an extensive analysis of this problem of labor shortage in relation to early American manufacturing methods, and came to the general conclusion that the development of the latter can be deduced from purely economic circumstances. In his arguments he sees certain entrepreneurial characteristics as products of the American economic environment. This is a chicken-egg problem, and my position is that if a modal personality trait exists at a given time it is more realistic to treat it as a cultural factor, regardless of what may have accounted for this trait historically.

While not contradicting any of Habakkuk's economic reasoning, the position taken by Sawyer (1954), that factors of culture and social structure were extremely important in early American manufacturing, seems to offer a more useful explanation, one applicable beyond manufacturing to other fields of entrepreneurial activity.

Using the work of both these scholars, let us see how their conclusions fit our model of entrepreneurial role. The American situation definitely emphasized certain operational needs. Since labor was scarce and valuable there was a greater inducement to plan for its efficient use. This in turn led to greater consciousness of costs and alertness to opportunities for substituting machinery; in other words, to rapid subjective construction of such new items. Habakkuk finds a contrast to England in these respects, and the contrast with Latin America or a nation like Greece would be even more striking.

But American entrepreneurial behavior also depended on different attitudes in such defining groups as fellow managers, customers, and bankers. Innovations within what anthropologists have called the "limits of sameness" met relatively little resistance. That is, if the innovation promised the same general type of product at less cost it was likely to be considered rationally on economic grounds, rather than resisted by both proprietors and labor from disinclination toward change. These matters, of course, are relative. Strassmann (1959) has emphasized early American resistance to risking additional capital. One can only say that comparatively Habakkuk finds British investors still more cautious, and in the nations destined to remain underdeveloped, the resistance was great enough to check almost all large-scale industrial investment.

American customers placed little value on fine craftsmanship—for that they would buy imports. In domestic goods they sought cheapness and utility. There was also a noticeable feeling that expenditure to produce exceptionally long life or permanence in an article was a waste. The migratory American purchaser would often sell his equipment before a move to another locality or replace it by something better.

As far as the general public was concerned the business executive was playing to an appreciative audience. Trade or manufacturing, even on a small scale, carried no social stigma. Financial success could immediately raise the executive to the top level of most American society. This pull of unrestricted opportunity was absent in the more rigid societies which characterized the rest of the civilized world.

These attitudes on the part of defining groups were necessarily reflected in the personality of the entrepreneur. Thus the executives of New England and the Middle States in the first half of the nineteenth century seem to have shared a feeling that work was a duty, and that calling should be carefully selected and vigorously pursued. Child-rearing and education both placed emphasis on the busy, productive individual. Optimism about getting ahead was emphasized in the school texts, and presumably in family conversation (De Charms & Moeller, 1962).

Inadequate though it was, elementary education was probably more widespread in New England and the Middle States than in most Western nations. Governor DeWitt Clinton of New York illustrated a common cultural attitude when he said in 1826: "The first duty of government, and the surest evidence of good government, is the encouragement of education" (quoted in Cubberly, 1919, p. 112). Of executives born between 1790 and 1819 who came to be listed in the *Dictionary of American Biography*, Mills (1945) found a total of 55 per cent with high school education or more, and only 23 per cent with only apprenticeship or a negligible formal education. Of manufacturing executives between 1789 and 1865 whose education is recorded in company histories, Brewer (1962, p. 49) also found 55 per cent with high school or college education and only 7 per cent with no formal education.

There are many characteristics of both the personality of entrepreneurs and the attitudes or expectations of defining groups that appear to be associated with the highly migratory character of the American population. Unfortunately there are few reliable statistics before 1850, but the case studies that exist suggest that the average American moved several times during his life, and that executives were probably more geographically mobile than the average. The elements associated with migration that would increase the efficiency of an entrepreneurial role were: emphasis on self-help as against aid from family status; willingness to co-operate with relative strangers, or impersonality; tolerance of, and adjustment to, strange conditions; and a tendency to innovate in making such adjustments (Lee, 1961). Recent studies have underlined the importance of moderate changes in environment in stimulating new ideas and practices (Barnett, 1953, pp. 87–88, 93).

One recognizes the above list as containing the elements that scholars have associated with successful industrialization. Co-operation and impersonality have been rated as specially important factors (Hirschman, 1958, p. 17). In the 1830s de Tocqueville was impressed with American co-operativeness. Very early, American executives engineered mergers, formed associations to control prices and production, and in general demonstrated a rational ability to put profits ahead of personal rivalries or animosities. This has not been so in other cultures, where pride in family companies has led to complete failure to meet changing market situations rationally (Cochran, 1959, pp. 91, 96). Impersonality, keeping personal friendships apart from business dealings, has led American executives to expect market considerations to govern patronage. There have been, of course, exceptions to this, but in general suppliers are changed for business reasons with a readiness not present in more traditional societies (Sawyer, 1954, pp. 365–366).

From the early nineteenth century on, American executives showed what Hirschman has called the " 'growth,' which comprises not only the desire for economic growth but also the perception of the essential nature of the road leading toward it." (1958, p. 10). On the basis of the rapid and creative subjective construction induced by American conditioning, whatever its original causes, the role of the entrepreneur becomes a major differentiating element in social and economic change. In spite of a level of technological knowledge below that of England, even in 1850, the American entrepreneur introduced a more highly mechanized industrialism and set in motion an upward spiral of labor-saving devices which continued to operate (Sawyer, 1954, pp. 365–366).

The Rise of Professional Management

When we have a longer perspective, it may appear that the second type of entrepreneurially-guided change, the replacing of the owner entrepreneur by the professional executive as the chief managerial type, has been the most important socioeconomic development in American business. The need for readapting the attitudes of certain defining groups, chiefly officers and directors, and altering the role of the chief executives to meet the demands and opportunities of the large, widely-owned corporation inevitably brought about change. Whereas in our first example changes in operations appear to have been accelerated by the peculiar conditioning of American entrepreneurs, in this second example, a change in the methods of business operation gradually altered the role and the personality of the entrepreneur. It should be emphasized, however, that these American executives were peculiarly susceptible to role changes in the direction needed for the functioning of the large corporations.

Between 1850 and 1890, most of the new obligations and opportunities associated with administering other people's money were worked out in the large railroads. In the 1850s, officers and directors saw nothing amiss in being on both sides of a bargain, of selling supplies to the railroad, buying land from the road for resale at a profit, or owning facilities such as bridges or stockyards that the road had to rent. Some of these arrangements had arisen because the early railroads were chronically short of capital, and as conditions became easier after 1865 ethics grew stricter. In the best-run companies, by the middle 1880s, the executive role had been defined with a strictness that has not greatly altered since that time. In 1883 Charles E. Perkins, President of the Chicago, Burlington and Quincy Railroad, wrote to one of his top executives: "The smallest kind of an interest in a coal mine would be objectionable." Officers should not "make money out of side shows." (Cochran, 1953, p. 436).

As important as the improvement in ethics, essential to the continued attraction of capital, was the development of modern systems of big business management. Advancement on the basis of ability, security of tenure, delegation of authority, decentralization of operations, open but orderly channels of communication, and managerial co-operation for company welfare may all seem at first glance to be inevitable adjustments to the problem of size. But anyone who has studied the functioning of large organizations in other cultures knows this is not so. Until very recent years the biggest electrical machinery manufacturing firm in Latin America failed, in spite of the services of United States management consultants, to develop these characteristics (Cochran & Reina, 1962, pp. 184–191, 222–225). Delegation of authority, easy communication between levels of management, and co-operation among managers on the same level have all been difficult to achieve in Latin America, and in most other cultures. Even in England and Germany there is more difficulty in these respects than in the United States.

The decisive difference appears to be that American executives are reared in the equalitarian atmosphere of an outgoing, pragmatic, democratic society. They are taught from childhood on that co-operation for mutual benefit is good, and the type of individualism they develop does not stand in the way of easy relations with their peers.

This latter point is of particular importance. As the result of rather elaborate analyses of United States individualism in comparison to that of Latin America, some basically important differences appear. Fayerweather (1959, pp. 12–17, 194–195) calls Mexican executives "individualistic" in personality and Americans "group-oriented." To the former he attaches the characteristics of: distrust in the relations of managers with their superiors; hostility in relations with their peers; and a sense of separation in their relations with subordinates. To the group-oriented personality he attributes confidence and fellow-feeling in relations with superiors and peers, and a sense of union with subordinates. Research at the University of Pennsylvania has indicated that so-called American individualism is a matter of standing up for one's rights in the group or against government or other external encroachment, in contrast to the more subjective, inward-looking individualism of Latin Americans.[1]

[1] For Latin American traits see Cochran (1959), pp. 122–125.

The Latin type of personality, shared to some degree by entrepreneurs in most under-developed areas, has made it much more difficult to create efficient managerial structures for expanding business; or viewed another way, has tended to put a ceiling on corporate expansion at the level where one man or a small family group can give personal attention to the details of operation. In contrast to Latin distrust of fellow executives, the British missions sent between 1949 and 1952 to observe American manufacturing methods issued reports such as: "Among the executives we met, we encountered . . . a readiness to encourage and pass on knowledge to juniors" (Sawyer, 1954, p. 365). The United States attitudes have accelerated change through expansion, mergers, diversification of products, and decentralization (Chandler, 1962).

Mass-Production Techniques

Economists tend to see the third major change, the rapid spread of advanced mass-production techniques, as a function of both the state of technology and the size of the American domestic market. Since by 1900 the United States had more and wealthier customers than either England or Germany, it developed larger-scale processes and bigger companies. But social historians are impressed by additional factors.

To begin with, American culture as expressed in law and government demanded efforts to maintain the ideal of competition. The interpretation of restraint of trade by the courts and by both state and national antitrust laws deprived medium-sized businesses of the ability to protect their positions by legal agreements or cartels. This led to mergers into larger units which were judged legal as long as they did not try to, or threaten to, monopolize the trade. The bigger units resulting from this social pressure would perhaps have led in any case to a more intensive search for economies of scale than seems to have been pursued elsewhere. In addition to these exogenous forces that altered the operational demands of the entrepreneurial role, the personality characteristics noted in early American manufacturers persisted. The English missions of the mid-twentieth century reported that productivity

. . . is part of the American way of life, an article of faith as much as a matter of economics . . . Americans believe it is their mission to lead the world in productive efficiency.

"Cost-consciousness" . . . does not simply mean cutting costs. . . . It also means not missing opportunities.

American managements look continually towards the future. They base their decisions on an intelligent anticipation of trends rather than wait until the pressure of current events forces them to make the decisions (Sawyer, 1954, p. 365).

Henry Ford, generally credited with being the most dramatic adapter of new mass-production techniques in the twentieth century, shows interesting contrasts to the man who, more nearly than any other, was his counterpart in Argentina. Ford was literally obsessed by machinery (or, in more formal language, oriented toward change in mechanical items). His subjective constructions were in terms of new machines and processes (Nevins, 1954, pp. 49 ff.). Although each of his major innovations—the Model T, the power-driven continuous assembly line, and the five-dollar minimum wage—can readily be attributed to the ideas of subordinates, Ford saw his entrepreneurial role in terms of these achievements. On the other hand, Torcuato Di Tella, who introduced household electric refrigeration and other electrical machinery to Argentina, saw his role in much broader terms, and delegated most of the purely technological work to trusted subordinates. In other words, Ford represented the classic American drives for mechanization and efficiency, Di Tella the Latin interests in the all-around social man who would be family leader, business leader, intellectual, and patron of the arts. Both were extremely "driven" individuals, but Ford had the singleness of purpose so usual to American entrepreneurial personality, Di Tella the more diffused ambitions of men of Latin and many other cultures.

SOCIAL STRUCTURE AND CHANGE

So far, little has been said about elements of social structure, as distinct from values, that may negate change. Most such elements are associated with rigidities. Their existence, however, is usually manifest in the conditioning of the modal entrepreneurial personality. An aristocratic social structure like nineteenth-century England, for example, made becoming an aristocrat a more attractive goal for the successful entrepreneur than continued expansion of his business. This structure tended to produce a cutoff point in expansion similar to that imposed by the limits of direct personal or family control.

Aside from caste or status lines *per se*, some cultures are more static and ceremonial than others. While these conditions might be traced back to geographical and economic circumstances, at any specific time they are given parts of the situation. Fear of change by the power elite, for example, may be based on low energy and resources, but it comes to exist as a separate factor.

CONCLUSIONS

My general position, as distinct from the specific application of role theory, is summed up in technical language by psychologists De Charms and Moeller. They say: "We propose that motivation, or cultural orientation be conceived as an intervening variable standing between antecedent environmental factors associated with economic and political changes and consequent behavior resulting in cultural changes such as technological growth. . . . Thus two cultures undergoing similar economic or political change may react quite differently due to intervening variables of values, child rearing practices, and motives." (1962, p. 142).

The concepts of entrepreneurial role offer ways of defining and organizing these "intervening variables." But unfortunately, neither this nor other current systems can quantify the variables so that additions or subtractions can be made in the measurable terms of land, labor, capital, or market price. One cannot speak of units or doses of personality or values. For problems of change over time where the variables are numerous and nonquantifiable there seems no substitute for historical analogy applied to carefully defined situations. Location of social variables in terms of more or less, or below or above some norm, or as correlates of other variables is frequently possible. These operations do not lead to equations but rather to propositions stating probable relationships. The statement that limits are placed on motivation for achievement by "too large discrepancies between expectations and results," which "may develop an avoidance motive as far as achievement is concerned" (McClelland, Atkinson, Clark, & Lowell, 1953, p. 65), or Vogt's proposition that "the importance of value orientation in shaping the direction of change is proportional to the amount of economic and technological control a society has achieved" (1960, p. 26), are examples of useful but nonquantifiable relationships. They are, however, of the same degree of specificity as such economic maxims as "the larger the market the greater the division of labor."

Role theory allows for change by the deviant action of an individual, but the emphasis in my discussion has been on change as the interaction of modal types of personality with the culturally conditioned expectations of defining groups and the operational needs of situations. Exogenous changes in population, resources, technology, consumer demand, or merely what Hurst (1963, pp. 80–81) has called "cumulative institutional drift," all seem most likely to impinge first on the role structure by creating new operational needs; but the entrepreneurial response to these needs may be either successful innovation or dogged continuance of a dysfunctional way of doing things. The response will depend on variables of personality and culture, which, as we have seen, are predictable within certain limits.

There is no theoretical reason why important innovation in role behavior could not arise from inner-conditioning independently of all immediate exogenous factors. It is merely the bias of my historical observation that I think such instances rare. It may be, for example, that the particular innovations credited to Ford would only have been prompted in the precise year by such a uniquely conditioned character, but over a twenty-year span the exact timing seems relatively unimportant. The given innovations or superior ones usually seem to be in process of introduction by several executives. A general theory for relating economic and other social factors to change should deal with normal responses of functional groups to at least partially repetitive situations. From this standpoint a model of entrepreneurial role is a useful device.

REFERENCES

Barnett, H. G. *Innovation: the strategy of economic development.* New Haven: Yale Univ. Press, 1953.

Brewer, T. B. The formative period of 140 manufacturing companies, 1789–1929. Unpublished doctoral dissertation, University of Pennsylvania, 1962 (Microfilm).

Buchanan, N. S., & Ellis, H. S. *Approaches to economic development.* New York: Twentieth Century Fund, 1955.

Chandler, A. D. *Structure and strategy.* Cambridge, Mass.: MIT Press, 1962.

Cochran, T. C. *Railroad leaders, 1845–1890.* Cambridge, Mass.: Harvard Univ. Press, 1953.

Cochran, T. C. *The Puerto Rico businessman.* Philadelphia: Univ. of Pennsylvania Press, 1959.

Cochran, T. C. *The American business system.* New York: Torchbooks, 1962.

Cochran, T. C., & Reina, R. E. *Entrepreneurship in Argentine culture.* Philadelphia: Univ. of Pennsylvania Press, 1962.

Cremin, L. A. *The transformation of the school.* New York: Knopf, 1961.

Cubberly, E. P. *Public education in the United States.* Boston: Houghton Mifflin, 1919.

De Charms, R., & Moeller, H. H. Values expressed in American children's readers, 1800–1950. *J. abnorm. soc. psychol.,* 1962, 64, 136–142.

Fayerweather, J. *The executive overseas.* Syracuse, N.Y.: Syracuse Univ. Press, 1959.

Habakkuk, H. J. *American and British technology in the 19th century.* Cambridge, England: Cambridge Univ. Press, 1962.

Hirschman, A. E. *The strategy of economic development.* New Haven: Yale Univ. Press, 1958.

Hurst, W. *Law and the social process.* Ann Arbor: Univ. of Michigan Press, 1963.

Jenks, L. H. *Change and the entrepreneur.* Cambridge, Mass.: Harvard Univ. Press, 1949.

Landry, D. *Tropical childhood.* Chapel Hill: Univ. of North Carolina Press, 1959.

Lee, E. S. The Turner thesis re-examined. *Amer. Quart.,* 1961, 13, 77–83.

McClelland, D. C., Atkinson, J. W., Clark, R. A., & Lowell, E. L. *The achievement motive.* New York: Appleton-Century-Crofts, 1953.

Mills, C. W. The American business elite: a collective portrait. *J. econ. hist.*, 1945, 5 (suppl.).

Nevins, A. *Ford.* New York: Scribner's, 1954.

Sawyer, J. E. The social basis of the American system of manufacturing. *J. econ. hist.*, 1954, 14, 361–379.

Strassmann, W. P. *Risk and technological innovation.* Ithaca, N.Y.: Cornell Univ. Press, 1959.

Vogt, E. Z. On the concepts of structure and process in cultural anthropology. *Amer. anthropol.*, 1960, 62, 18–33.

5

THE ACHIEVEMENT MOTIVE
IN ECONOMIC GROWTH

David C. McClelland

Cıvılızatıons rise and fall; cultures grow episodically and
sometimes in quite diverse fields. For example, the people of the Italian peninsula
at the time of Ancient Rome produced a great civilization of law, politics and
military conquest, and during the Renaissance, a great civilization of art, music,
letters and science. What accounts for such cultural flowerings? Some theorists
stress the importance of climate; others feel that the right amount of challenge
from the environment, including its psychic effects, is crucial; still others
find it hard to conceive of any general explanation and must be content with
the notion that a particular culture happens to hit on a happy mode of self-
expression which is pursued until it becomes over-specialized and sterile.

My concern is not with all culture growth, but specifically with economic
growth, for the problem of why some countries develop rapidly in the economic
sphere at certain times and not others, is in itself of great interest. Rapid economic growth has usually been explained in terms of "external" factors—
favorable opportunities for trade, unusual natural resources, or conquests that

This paper represents a summary of a book entitled The Achieving Society, *published by
D. Van Nostrand, Princeton, New Jersey, in 1961, and is reprinted from* Proceedings of the
XIV Int. Congress of Applied Psychology (*Copenhagen, 1961*). *Munskgaard, pp. 60–80, with
permission of the author and the publisher.*

have opened up new markets or produced internal political stability. In the present case however, the emphasis is reversed: it is on *internal* factors, the human values and motives that lead man to exploit opportunities, to take advantage of favorable trade conditions; in short, to shape his own destiny.

Of course, all people have always, to a certain extent, been interested in human motivation. What is different about the psychologist's interest today is that he tries to define his subject very precisely and, like all scientists, to find a way to measure it. Whatever else one thinks of Freud and the other psycho-analysts, they performed one extremely important service for psychology: they persuaded us that we cannot rely on what people *say* about their motives to determine what those motives really are. Freud showed that people's "obvious" motives did not in fact turn out to be the real motives for their often strange behavior, but that those motives could be discovered instead, by the analysis of fantasy or other imaginative material. Psychoanalysis taught us then, that we can learn a great deal about people's motives from observing what they are spontaneously concerned about in their dreams and waking fantasies.

Ten or twelve years ago the research group in America with which I was connected decided to see what it could learn about human motivation by objec-tively coding what people spontaneously thought about in their waking fantasies. Eventually, we isolated several inner concerns or motives, which if present in great frequency in a person's fantasies, would tell something about how he would behave in many other areas of life. Chief among these motives was what we called the need for Achievement: a desire to do well, not so much for the sake of social recognition or prestige, but for the sake of an inner feeling of personal accomplishment. Our early studies showed that people who were "high" in this motive tend to work harder at certain tasks, to learn faster, to do their best work when it counts for the record and not when special incentives such as money prizes are introduced, to choose experts rather than friends as working partners, etc. The results of these studies raised another question: what would happen in a society where there was a concentration of people with a high need for Achievement?

Several kinds of preliminary research into the relation of economic growth to *n* Achievement in societies were conducted. (We use the term *n* Achievement as an abbreviation for need for Achievement and to refer to our particular method of measuring achievement motivation; this measuring is done by counting the number of references to "doing a good job" in imaginative material like stories, letters, etc.). First, historical studies were done in which the amount of Achievement imagery in imaginative literary documents of other eras was compared with the level of economic growth during the relevant periods. For instance, we found, as we had predicted, that the most Achievement content occurred in literary documents during the century before the climax of economic development in Athenian Greece. We also discovered that in England between 1400–1800, the *n* Achievement level based on sea captains' letters, dramas and street ballads, rose twice—each time, a generation or two before waves of accelerated economic growth.

A study of preliterate cultures was also carried out, by comparing the number of full-time "business entrepreneurs" among the adults in several such cultures with each culture's level of *n* Achievement as reflected in folk-tale content. Of nineteen cultures whose folk-tales were high in *n* Achievement, seventy-four per cent contained some entrepreneurs, whereas only thirty-five per cent of twenty cultures classified as low in *n* Achievement contained any entrepreneurs at all.

But what about modern nations? Can we estimate their level of *n* Achievement and relate it to their economic development? In order to apply the research method we had developed to modern nations, we needed a literary document that would be equally representative of the motivational levels of people in countries as different as India, Japan, Portugal, Germany, the U.S. and Italy. We decided to use children's "readers" because they use the same kind of brief story to teach children how to read in all modern countries. Furthermore, the stories are imaginative, and if chosen from the earliest grades, are not often influenced by temporary political events. So, we collected readers for the second, third and fourth grades from every country where they could be found for two periods—roughly centering around 1925 and 1950. Some 1300 stories were translated, shuffled and then coded for *n* Achievement. In all, there were twenty-one stories from each of twenty-three countries around 1925, and from thirty-nine countries around 1950.

For a measure of economic development, we relied on the amount of electricity produced in each country, since the units of measurement are the same all over the world, the figures are available from the 1920's on, and electricity is the form of energy which is essential to modern economic development. The actual gain in electricity produced between 1925 and 1950 was compared with the expected gain, and each country classified as gaining more or less rapidly than would have been expected on the basis of its production in 1925.

The correlation between *n* Achievement level in the children's readers in 1925 and growth in electrical output between 1925 and 1950 as compared with expectation, is .53, which is highly significant statistically. To check this result, we computed the equation for gains in electrical output between 1952–1958 as a function of the level in 1952. Table 1 shows the level of each country compared with predictions from its initial level in 1952, and classified by high and low n Achievement in 1950. Again we found that n Achievement levels predicted which countries would produce more or less rapidly than expected. This finding is more striking than the earlier one because many Communist and underdeveloped countries were included. Apparently, n Achievement is a precursor of economic growth not only under a free enterprise system, but also where business is controlled and fostered largely by the state. In a century dominated by economic determinism both in Communist and Western thought, it is startling to find concrete evidence for psychological determinism, for psychological developments which precede and presumably cause economic changes.

Two other examples from our research findings are intriguing evidence of the influence of psychological factors on economic development. First, we found that adults not only flavor their stories for young children with the achievement concerns they feel, but also with their ideas about how people should be "controlled" or made to conform in their relations to others. In countries which had developed more rapidly economically, children's stories tended to emphasize *reliance on the opinion of particular others* rather than on tradition, for guidance in how to behave toward others. That is, in these countries, *public opinion*—what particular others think—had become a major source of guidance for the individual. Tradition may insist that people go on behaving in ways that are no longer appropriate in a changed social and economic order, but public opinion is basically more flexible and can be used by authorities to inform large numbers of people of the need for new ways of doing things. Generally speaking then, public opinion becomes a guide for social behavior in countries where the mass media—the press, radio, etc.—are best developed, and these are the countries that tend to be "overachievers" economically.

A second example is not directly concerned with economic development, but rather with the means of achieving it. We found that every major dictatorial regime which came to power between the 1920s and 1950s, except possibly one (Portugal), was foreshadowed by a particular motive pattern in its stories for children:[1] namely, a low need for Affiliation (little interest in friendly relationships with people) and a high need for Power (need to control and influence others). On the other hand, very few countries which did not have

---

[1] The German readers showed this pattern before Hitler, the Japanese readers before Tojo, the Argentine readers before Peron, the Spanish readers before Franco, the South African readers before the present authoritarian government in South Africa, etc.

TABLE 5-1

Rate of growth in electrical output (1952–1958) and national *n* Achievement levels in 1950

National n Achievement levels (1950)[b]		Above expectation		National n Achievement levels (1950)	Below expectation
				Deviations from expected growth rate[a] in standard score units	
High n Ach	3.62	Turkey	1.38		
	2.71	India[e]	1.12		
	2.38	Australia	.42		
	2.33	Israel	1.18		
	2.33	Spain	.01		
	2.29	Pakistan[d]	2.75		
	2.29	Greece	1.18	3.38 Argentina	− .56
	2.29	Canada	.06	2.71 Lebanon	− .67
	2.24	Bulgaria	1.37	2.38 France	− .24
	2.24	U.S.A.	.47	2.33 U. So. Africa	− .06
	2.14	West Germany	.53	2.29 Ireland	− .41
	2.10	U.S.S.R.	1.62	2.14 Tunisia	− 1.87
	2.10	Portugal	.76	2.10 Syria	− .25
Low n Ach	1.95	Iraq	.29	2.05 New Zealand	− .29
	1.86	Austria	.38	1.86 Uruguay	− .75
	1.67	U.K.	.17	1.81 Hungary	− .62
	1.57	Mexico	.12	1.71 Norway	− .77
	.86	Poland	1.26	1.62 Sweden	− .64
				1.52 Finland	− .08
				1.48 Netherlands	− .15
				1.33 Italy	− .57
				1.29 Japan	− .04
				1.20 Switzerland[e]	− 1.92
				1.19 Chile	− 1.81
				1.05 Denmark	− .89
				.57 Algeria	− .83
				.43 Belgium	− 1.65

Correlation of *n* Achievement level (1950) × deviations from expected growth rate = .43, p < .01

[a] The estimates are computed from regression equations based on the monthly average electrical production figures, in millions of Kwh. for 1952 and 1958, from United Nations, *Monthly Bulletin of Statistics*, January, 1960, and Statistical Papers, Series J, *World Energy Supplies*, 1951–1954 and 1955–1958.
[b] Based on 21 Children's stories from 2nd, 3rd, and 4th grade readers in each country
[c] Based on 6 Hindi, 7 Telegu, 8 Tamil stories.
[d] Based on 12 Urdu aud 11 Bengali stories.
[e] Based on 21 German Swiss stories, mean = .91; 21 French Swiss stories, mean = 1.71; overall mean obtained by weighting German mean double to give approximately proportionate representation to the two main ethnic population groups.

dictatorships showed this motive combination. We seem to have stumbled on a psychological index of ruthlessness—the desire to influence people (*n* Power) unchecked by a sufficient concern for their welfare (*n* Affiliation).[2]

[2] German readers of today show this pattern just as they did in 1925. Let us hope that this is one case where a social science generalization will not be confirmed by the appearance of a totalitarian regime in Germany in the next ten years.

But to return to the motive which is our main theme, how does *n* Achievement lead to more rapid economic development? Why should it lead to economic development rather than military or artistic development? The link between the concentration of a particular type of human concern in a population and economic growth, is the business entrepreneur. I am not using the term "entrepreneur" in the sense of "capitalist"—I am using it without any connotation of ownership; an entrepreneur is simply someone who *exercises control over production* that is not just for personal consumption. Thus a steel plant manager in Russia is as much an "entrepreneur" in this sense as one in the U.S.

Joseph Schumpeter drew the attention of economists to the importance of "heroic" entrepreneurs in creating industrialization in the Western world. They were the ones who put firms together and created means of production where there had been none before; they often collected the resources, organized a means of production to combine the resources into a new product, and sold the product. Nearly all economists—not only Marx but also Western Classical economists—assumed for many years that these men were activated primarily by the "profit motive." Recently, however, economic historians have been studying the lives of such entrepreneurs and finding (often to their surprise) that many of them seem not to have been interested in making money for its own sake.

In psychological terms at least, Marx's picture of the profit-driven exploiter of workers seems to be slightly out of focus. If these men had been interested primarily in money, many more of them would have quit working as soon as they had made all the money they could possibly have used, and would have stopped risking it in further entrepreneurial ventures. But in fact, many came from religious sects which prohibited the enjoyment of wealth in any of the ways so successfully cultivated (for example) by the European nobility. Instead, consciously at least, they often continued to be greatly concerned with expanding their businesses, with getting a greater share of the market, with "conquering brute nature," or even with altruistic schemes for bettering the lot of mankind or bringing about the Kingdom of God on earth more quickly. Such goals have often been called hypocritical but we can see that they need not actually have been so, if we view these men as having been motivated by a desire for *achievement* rather than for *money*. This new assumption includes the possibility that they were interested in money because it provided a ready, quantitative index of how much they had achieved, by their efforts in one year for example. Desire to achieve can never be satisfied by money, but estimates of profitability in money terms can provide concrete knowledge of how well one is doing one's job.

To find evidence that the major motive of business entrepreneurs of the past was their high *n* Achievement, we checked to see whether individuals with high *n* Achievement behave like entrepreneurs. But what does it mean to "behave like an entrepreneur"? How do entrepreneurs behave differently from other people? Our investigations revealed that one of the defining characteristics of an entrepreneur is *taking moderate risk*, often through innovation. A person who adds up a column of figures is not an entrepreneur—he is simply following established rules. Rather, an example of an entrepreneur is a man who decides to add a new line to his business; he cannot know in advance whether his decision will be correct, yet he does not feel as if he were a gambler placing some money on the turn of a card. Knowledge, judgment and skill go into his decision, and if he has made a successful move, he can certainly get a sense of personal achievement. Thus people with high *n* Achievement who behave in an entrepreneurial way seek out and perform better in situations where there is moderate risk of failure which can presumably be reduced by increased effort or skill.

An illustration of this kind of behavior in people with high *n* Achievement is as follows: we have found that college students with high *n* Achievement choose to play games of skill where there is a moderate risk of failure. For instance, when the students were given a wire ring and told that they could stand at any distance they chose in trying to throw it over a peg, those with high *n* Achievement took *calculated risks*, that is, they tended to stand at middle distances from the peg, at points where the chances of success or failure were moderate. However, the students with low *n* Achievement showed no particular preference for any position, and often stood in the extreme positions—either very close to the peg where they were sure to get the ring over it, or very far away where they were almost certain not to. In this way they act like many people in underdeveloped countries who behave very traditionally economically but who also love to indulge in lotteries—risking a little to make a lot on a very long shot.

We have shown that people high in *n* Achievement who behave in an entrepreneurial way do not work harder than other people at routine tasks or at tasks which are accomplished simply by using the accepted, correct, traditional method. They seek out and work harder at tasks that involve a real challenge, that is, a moderate degree of risk. On the other hand, they avoid gambling situations because even if they win, they get no sense of personal achievement since winning is the result of luck, not skill. They prefer to take *personal responsibility* for their decisions and they want the outcome to depend on their own skill or ability. The following study illustrates this preference.

Business School and College students were asked to play a game in which they could choose between making two kinds of decisions: some which involved doing a task such as solving a personnel problem or a problem in business math, and others which involved simply rolling dice to see what the outcome would be. The students who were high in *n* Achievement chose the entrepreneurial alternative: that is, to do the task and be personally responsible for the result of a decision—rather than to roll the dice which they obviously could not control.

In addition to taking *personal responsibility* for decisions involving *moderate risk*, the entrepreneur also likes a job that gives him accurate knowledge of the results of his decisions. Growth in sales, output or profit margins ordinarily tells him whether he has made a correct choice or not. It is in this sense that profit appears to be a measure of success. This kind of behavior is also illustrated by the college students playing the ring toss game. When the students were asked to say how much money they thought should be awarded for successful throws from increasing distances, the money awarded by those with high and low *n* Achievement was about the same for positions near the peg. But as the task grew more difficult, the amounts awarded by students with high *n* Achievement rose more rapidly than those awarded by students with low *n* Achievement. In believing that greater success should be recognized by greater reward (money return) the students with high *n* Achievement appear to behave just as they should if they are to be society's successful entrepreneurs.

To summarize: we have found that entrepreneurial behavior is exhibited by people who are high in *n* Achievement in (1) their desire to take personal responsibility for decisions, (2) their preference for decisions involving a moderate degree of risk, and (3) their interest in concrete knowledge of the results of decisions.

In our search for further evidence that the major motive of business entrepreneurs of the past was their high *n* Achievement, we undertook many studies which dealt with the question: do *modern* business executives in different parts of the world in fact have higher *n* Achievement than other people of roughly the same status? Let us look at two of these studies.

1. In a mobile society where an occupational position is somewhat dependent on performance (rather than on family or political connections), managers, executives or entrepreneurs should have higher *n* Achievement than men in other comparable occupations. So we decided to compare average *n* Achievement levels among business leaders and professional groups, using a standard set of six pictures representing men in a variety of common but ambiguous situations; these were: an older man talking to a younger one in an office (which suggests a law office); a man in his shirt sleeves sitting at a drafting

board with a photograph of a woman and children in the background; several men talking around a conference table; a man working at a desk in a business office alone; a "father" talking to his son in a rural setting; and an obviously satisfied man relaxing in an easy chair, possibly in an airplane.

A question of considerable interest is whether managers have higher n Achievement not only in a highly developed country like the United States, but also in less highly developed countries, or in a Communist country that does not rely on the free enterprise system. One might easily assume that in underdeveloped countries, the odds against business success are so great that an entrepreneur must be a real Schumpeterian "hero" to get ahead. Or, cultural relativists might argue that the motivation required for business success is different in every country, depending on the structure of the business enterprise. Such considerations led us to make the comparison not only in an economically advanced country, the United States, but also in a moderately developed country, Italy (both in the more developed North and in the less developed South), in an underdeveloped country, Turkey, and in a Communist country, Poland. The results, shown in Table 2, are extremely interesting: the managers were higher in n Achievement than the professionals in every country except Turkey.

In the United States, a very careful comparison was made at the General Electric Company. A group of unit managers was compared with a group of staff specialists of the same position level, age, educational background and length of service. The specialists were professionals in function though not exactly in the same sense as the professionals tested in other countries who were lawyers, doctors, teachers, etc. The managers scored significantly higher in n Achievement. Furthermore, the higher n Achievement level is not limited to managers in the General Electric Company; a group of middle level managers from many different U.S. companies tested at the Harvard Business School scored even higher than the G.E. personnel.

Both in the North and South of Italy, managers scored higher than professionals and the differences between managers and professionals was even greater than in the U.S. But since the Italian professionals who were tested were an average of about six years younger than the businessmen, might not the age difference somehow account for the difference in n Achievement levels? If we consider only the medical students in the professional group—who were an average of only three years younger—the businessmen's average n Achievement scores are still higher. In addition, smaller samples of businessmen and professionals, matched for age and social status of parents, were drawn from the larger populations, and still the managers scored significantly higher in n Achievement than did the professionals.

TABLE 5-2

Average *n* Achievement scores of managers and professionals in the United States, Italy, Turkey and Poland

		Managers	Professionals	Difference (Mgrs.–Prof.)	P
United States	N	31[a]	31[a]		
Mean age		42.1	42.7		
Mean *n* Achievement score		6.74	4.77	1.97	<.025 pd
	SD	4.49	4.54		
Italy	N	68[b]	107[c]		
Mean age		27.6	21.7		
Mean *n* Achievement score		4.18	2.31	1.87	<.01 pd
	SD	4.13	4.31		
Turkey	N	17[d]	48[e]		
Mean age		33.1	27.2		
Mean *n* Achievement score		1.76	3.52	– 1.76	NS
	SD	3.99	5.81		
Poland	N	31[f]	48[g]		
Mean age		35.9	27.2		
Mean *n* Achievement score		6.58	4.85	1.73	<.10 pd
	SD	5.22	4.98		

[a] Matched pairs of unit managers and specialists of same position level, age, educational background and length of service from the General Electric Company.   See Behavior Research Service, 1960.

[b] 41 junior managers from various Italian companies attending an IPSOA management training course in Torino (North Italy), 27 attending a similar course at ISIDA in Palermo (South Italy).

[c] 56 students of law, medicine, and theology from Torino and 51 of law and medicine from Palermo.

[d] Junior managers employed in private companies attending the Middle Management training programs of the Institute of Business Administration of the University of Istanbul (Bradburn, 1960).

[e] Students in the pedagogy program of the Gazi Institute, a higher teacher training college in Ankara (Bradburn, 1960).

[f] Managers from various Polish firms tested through the kind assistance of Dr. M. Choynowski, director of the psychometric laboratory, U. of Warsaw.

[g] Priests and educators also tested through the courtesy of Dr. Choynowski.

In Poland, the pattern is the same as it is in such capitalist countries as the United States and Italy: managers are higher in *n* Achievement than professionals. Even though the job of a manager in a Communist society differs in some respects from an equivalent job in a capitalist society, the jobs seem to be similar enough to require the same type of motivation. As a matter of fact, our finding fits in well with the theory that the Soviet executive is in fact under many of the same pressures to produce as his American counterpart. Apparently, ownership of the means of production is not crucial to people with high *n* Achievement.

The results in Turkey are interesting because they reverse the general trend. Does this suggest that business managers in an underdeveloped country like Turkey do not need to have higher *n* Achievement than professionals? Such a possibility might make us doubt our theory, *if we did not have some other* evidence, as follows. A group of leading Turkish businessmen scored significantly higher in *n* Achievement than the much less successful middle managers whose scores are shown in the table. Thus, apparently in Turkey too, *n* Achievement is associated with business success, and there is no reason to believe that *n* Achievement is not as well suited to the entrepreneurial role in underdeveloped countries as it is elsewhere. The low *n* Achievement among the younger Turkish managers seems to have resulted from poor recruitment of younger people: those with higher *n* Achievement are attracted to teaching rather than business.

2. To escape the complexities of modern business organizations and the way they define occupational roles or reward their incumbents, it is possible to seek out a "pure case": the small-time business entrepreneur who has little or nothing to work with but his own skills. It is here that we should see the effects of higher *n* Achievement most clearly, uncomplicated by organizational factors, differential access to managerial jobs, etc.

Some fascinating data from potential small-time entrepreneurs in a rural village in Orissa Province, India, have been collected. A number of mechanics trainees were tested for *n* Achievement. Over a year later, the experimenter checked to see which of them had made use of their training so as to function more or less as independent artisans in work related to it (i.e., as mechanics, carpenters, masons, etc.) As shown by Table 3, the men with high *n* Achievement showed more entrepreneurial spirit and less involvement in the traditional cultivation of the soil than did those with low *n* Achievement. Three of the four men with the highest scores run very active shops for such a backward rural setting. The fourth may well do the same eventually, if he goes to work in a nearby town as he is thinking of doing: mobility is one of the characteristics of people with high *n* Achievement. The six men with the lowest scores are not engaged in anything like full-time work related to their training. Two of them are in school and may turn out to be active later, but it is wise not to predict it since further schooling can be an alternative to entrepreneurial activity, particularly for people with low *n* Achievement.

Jageswar is classified with the "more entrepreneurial" group although he is not in business at all in the classical sense, because he is behaving like an entrepreneur—fulfilling the entrepreneurial role—even though he does not occupy an entrepreneurial status. He could be called an "untapped manpower resource" as far as the economy is concerned, except for his indirect contribution to the income and development of his family's land.

Note that the men in Class "B" at the bottom of the table cannot be considered "failures" except possibly for Dhaneswar. Kama, for instance, who is busy with the local agricultural cooperative, is a useful and valuable member of his community. The point is only that his low *n* Achievement does not fit him well for entrepreneurial craft activities involving constructions that provide

TABLE 5-3

Subsequent employment of Indian village mechanics trainees varying in *n* Achievement (graphic)[a]

A. Employed more or less fully in work related to construction

Name	n Ach score[b]	Description of employment 12–18 months later
Parmanand	23	Does cycle welding, diesel work, soldering, masonry; take; orders from government agencies (e.g., cement hume pipes)s owns no land.
Chungilal	16	Has set up shop in his village, taken on assistant, invested in considerable supply of lumber for future work, makes doors, door frames, loom parts.
Trilochen	16	Has been in charge of construction of several houses in his village, will build weeders for the cultivators during monsoon; when such work unavailable, supports himself by silver-smithing.
Chandra	13	Full time making bullock cart wheels for sale (expensive items locally); more demand than he can fill.
Chaitanya	13	Small backward village does not provide many jobs but has repaired pumps, helped on construction of school building.
Khadia	11	Full time carpenter's helper, fair pay.
Panika	10	Earns fair income from cot making and loom repairs, also engages in cultivation and priestly duties.
Premanand	9	Full time work as assistant in shop of Barpali Village Service; also helps village carpenter.
Pandaba	7	Takes housebuilding, carpentry jobs whenever he can get them, has specialized in doors and windows, cultivates for lack of demand for furniture, etc.
Average	13.1	7 out of 9 high in *n* Achievement.

B. Not employed more or less fully in work related to construction

Dhansingh	16	Most of the time busy cultivating, has made plows for his family, doors for several houses, is considering getting a carpentry or masonry job in nearby towns.
Kasinath	13	Comes from a family of carpenters, but generally does more agricultural work than others in the family. Takes carpentry jobs when available.
Jageswar	10	Only child of well-to-do, landed family. Has constructed clothes closet, plow, brick cattle feeding trough, latrines, for use of own family.

[a] (After Fraser, 1961)
[b] Since the trainees were not literate, it was necessary to use a performance measure of *n* Achievement based on graphic expression desribed fully in McClelland (1961).

Name	n Ach score	Description of employment 12–18 months later
Kama	7	Too busy with local agricultural co-operative to do much carpentry.
Chaturbhuj	5	Worked as a clerk, now studying blacksmithing.
Bipin	5	Studying carpentry in government school.
Dhaneswar	5	Tried carpentry at low pay, left, has been out of work for some month, supported by brothers.
Dadhi	4	Main occupation is cultivation, but when time permits he does private carpentry and masonry jobs.
Kartikeswar	1	Full time cultivation; aside from building and repairing own tools (as do most other cultivators) has not used his training at all.
Surendra	—13	Has done no work related to his training; currently a dyer for a local weaving organization.
Average	5.3	3 out of 10 high in n Achievement.

p < .05 pd that higher n Achievement is associated with greater occupational activity related to construction.

concrete knowledge of results. He undoubtedly has other motives that fit him well for the work he is doing.

The study shows that n Achievement fits people for entrepreneurial jobs, particularly those jobs which give concrete knowledge of results (represented here by the construction activities of mechanics, masonry, etc.). One wonders what would happen if men like the first four in the table were given financial and technical assistance to expand their businesses, and if Dhansingh were helped to get started in town. Certainly, such people would be most likely to make the best use of outside help and to contribute to the economic development of this backward area.

How can the level of n Achievement in a country be raised? What the agencies charged with speeding economic development can perhaps realize and consciously promote is that an achievement-oriented ideology is absolutely essential to economic development. This ideology should be spread not only in business and governmental circles, but also throughout the nation. If people's motives are what influence the speed with which the economic machine operates, then to increase the speed, one must influence those motives or the factors that create them.

Promoting an achievement-oriented ideology means, first of all, that parents must be encouraged to set high standards for their children. Secondly, it ought to mean increasing the rights of women, both legally and socially, so that they can begin to weaken the effect of paternal authoritarianism, which, we have found, prevents the development of self-reliant achievement thinking in children. It should be realized that while men in underdeveloped countries can come in contact with new achievement-oriented values and standards through their work, women, who play a major role in rearing the next generation, may be left almost untouched by such influences. If the sons are to have high *n* Achievement, the mothers must be reached. Furthermore, it is difficult to think of a single country that has developed substantially and rapidly over a long period of time, in which women have not been freed somewhat from their traditional role to play a more powerful one in society—especially as part of the working force.

To try to raise *n* Achievement levels in the next generation is very important, but most economic planners, while accepting such an objective as desirable, want to known what can be done now—in the next five or ten years. Business and government in underdeveloped countries can immediately promote economic development by fostering achievement-oriented ways of thinking. Such *ways of thinking about problems* can be "taught" in training courses like the one you are now involved in: this kind of course can provide an individual with the means that will allow *him* to change *his own motivation* if he wants to do so.

6

HOW ECONOMIC GROWTH BEGINS:
A THEORY OF SOCIAL CHANGE

Everett E. Hagen

THIS paper proposes a theory of how a "traditional" society becomes one in which continuing technical progress (hence continuing rise in per capita production and income) is occurring. I shall define a traditional state of society in the following section. The hypotheses which I present to explain the change from this state to one of continuing technological progress may be relevant also to the analysis of other types of social change.

The theory does not suggest some one key factor as causing social change independently of other forces. Rather, it presents a general model of society, and deals with interrelationships among elements of the physical environment, social structure, personality, and culture. This does not imply a thesis that almost anything may cause something, so that one must remain eclectic and confused. Rather, certain factors seem of especial importance in initiating change, but their influence can be understood only by tracing interrelationships through the society. It is implied that general system analysis is a fruitful path to advance in societal theory. Since presented in brief compass, the model is necessarily presented rather starkly here.[1]

Reprinted by permission of the author and the publisher from Journal of Social Issues (*January, 1963*), *pp. 20–34.*

[1] The model is present at greater length in E. E. Hagen, *On The Theory of Social Change* (Homewood, Illinois: Dorsey Press, 1962). This paper is in essence an abstract of various chapters of that book.

The purely economic theories of barriers which explain the absence of growth seem inadequate. The assumption that the income of entire populations is too low to make saving easy; that markets in low-income countries are too small to induce investment; that costly lumps of expenditure for transport facilities, power plants, etc., which low-income countries cannot provide, are a requisite to growth—these and related theories are internally consistent but seem without great relevance to reality. Empirical study of low-income societies demonstrates that the supposed conditions and requirements do not in fact exist or are not of great importance.

Neither are the differences among nations with respect to growth explained by differences in the degree of contact with the West. Contact with the technical knowledge of the West is a requisite for growth, but forces quite independent of the degree of contact determine whether a nation uses that knowledge. The most spectacular example of this fact is that among the four great Asian nations, Indonesia and India had the most contact with the West during the period 1600–1900, China had an intermediate amount, and Japan the least. Moreover, Indonesia and India experienced the most Western investment, China an intermediate amount, and Japan none whatever until her economic growth was already well under way. Yet among the four countries Japan began to develop first, and has developed rapidly; Indonesia is the laggard; and if China solves her agricultural problem her growth will probably be faster than that of India.

These facts suggest some hypotheses which a theory of growth should not emphasize. Certain other facts give more positive indications of the elements with which a plausible theory must deal.

Economic growth has everywhere occurred interwoven with political and social change. Lipset and Coleman have demonstrated the correlation between economic change and the transition from authoritarian to "competitive" politics in Asia, Africa, and Latin America, and the same relationship is found in every country elsewhere that has entered upon economic growth.[2] The timing is such that it is clear that the economic growth does not occur first and cause the political-social change. Rather, the two are mutually dependent. Whatever the forces for change may be, they impinge on every aspect of human behavior. A theory of the transition to economic growth which does not simultaneously

---

[2] S. Lipset, "Some Social Requisites of Democracy: Economic Development and Political Legitimacy," *American Political Science Review*, Vol. 53 (March, 1959); G. A. Almond, J. S. Coleman et al., *The Politics of the Developing Areas* (Princeton: University Press, 1960). Adapting their method slightly, I used it in "A Framework for Analyzing Economic and Political Change," in R. Asher and others, *Development of the Emerging Countries: An Agenda for Research* (Washington, D.C.: Brookings Institution, 1962).

explain political change, or explains it merely as a consequence of the economic change, is thus suspect.

One last consideration will serve to lead up to the exposition of the model. It is this: the concept is rather widely held in the West that the present low-income societies can advance technically simply by imitating the technical methods already developed in the West. That concept is ethnocentric and incorrect. Mere imitation is impossible. A productive enterprise or process in the West depends for its efficiency on its position in a technical complex of facilities for supplies, services, transportation, and communication, and on a complex of economic, legal, and other social institutions. The management methods which work well within the plant and in its relationships to other units, depend on a complex of attitudes toward interpersonal relationships which are not closely paralleled by attitudes elsewhere. When the process is lifted out of its complex, to adapt it so that it will function in an underdeveloped economy requires technical and especially social and cultural creativity of a high order.

Requirements for the transition to economic growth, then, are (a) fairly widespread creativity—problem-solving ability, and a tendency to use it— and (b) attitudes toward manual-technical labor and the physical world such that the creative energies are channeled into innovation in the technology of production rather than in the technology of art, war, philosophy, politics, or other fields. I believe that exploration of these facets of the process of economic growth is a useful approach to a theory of social change.

What is in point is not widespread genius but a high degree of creativity in few individuals and a moderately high level in a larger number. I shall suggest reasons to believe that the traditional state of a society is associated with a rather low level of creativity among the members of the society. Further, the persons in traditional society who are in position to innovate are the elite—perhaps the lower elite, but certainly not the peasants and urban menials. It is well known that being concerned with tools, machinery, and in general physical processes seems demeaning to the elite and is repugnant to them. It seems to me that a theory of economic growth must give considerable attention to the forces which change those two aspects of personality.

SECTION ONE: THE STABILITY OF TRADITIONAL SOCIETY

When I refer to a traditional society I have in mind a traditional agricultural society, for while there have also been traditional hunting and fishing societies and traditional pastoral societies,[3] they can hardly accumulate many artifacts and hence continuing technical progress is hardly possible in them. A traditional agricultural society is of course one in which things are done in traditional ways, but two other characteristics which have been typical of the world's traditional societies and turn out to be essential qualities of the type are also worthy of note here.

First, the social structure is hierarchical and authoritarian in all of its aspects —economic, political, religious. The existence of an authoritarian hierarchy does not refer merely to a large mass who were submissive and to a small class who rule. Rather, every individual in a traditional hierarchy except perhaps for one or a few at the very apex is submissive to authoritarian decisions above him, and in turn exercises authority on persons below him. And this is true even of the lowliest peasant, who as he grows older and becomes a husband, a father, and an elder in his village, becomes increasingly an authority in some aspects of his social relations.

Secondly, one's status in the society is, with little qualification, inherited. One does not earn it; one is born to it. The families of the politically dominating groups, who usually also are economically powerful landed groups, provide the officers of the armed forces and the professional classes as well as the political leaders. Lesser elites also perpetuate their status, though with somewhat greater mobility.

These characteristics of the society as well as its techniques of production are traditional and change very slowly. While the model of a completely unchanging traditional society is a construct, an ideal type, it is sufficiently relevant to reality to be useful. From the beginning of agriculture in the world until say 1600 the traditional state of society persisted everywhere except that occasionally, here and there, there was a bursting out of the traditional mode for a few hundred years, than a lapse back into it, sometimes at the original technical level, sometimes at a higher one. The present-day transition to economic growth is such a bursting out. We must ask, Why has the traditional state of society been so persistent? and then, Why have the bursts of change occurred? Or at least, Why have the modern bursts of change occurred?

One condition sometimes suggested as an answer to the first question is that the instruments of power were in the hands of the elite. The traditional authoritarian hierarchical state persisted, it is suggested, because the elite kept the simple folk in subjection by force. This explanation seems inadequate. It is possible for a small group to keep an unwilling ninety-seven per cent of a

---

[3] Industrial societies will probably also become traditional in time, which is to say that technical progress will come to an end, at least for a time.

society in subjection by force for a decade or two, or perhaps for a generation or two, though if the subjection persists even this long one must ask whether it really was entirely unpleasing. But that the masses were kept in subjection primarily by force for many centuries seems improbable. The authoritarian hierarchical traditional social structure must have persisted because submitting to authority above one, as well as exercising authority, was satisfying, and secondly because the conditions of life re-created personalities, generation after generation, in which it continued to be so.

Creative and Uncreative Personality

To suggest probable reasons why authoritarian social structure was satisfying, let me digress to discuss certain aspects of personality.

Many elite individuals in traditional societies are prevented from using their energies effectively in economic development by their repugnance to being concerned with the grubby material aspects of life. The repugnance includes being concerned with the details of running a business effectively, as well as performing manual-technical labor—"getting their hands dirty." Often the repugnance is largely unconscious; the individuals concerned often deny it, because it does not occur to them that any middle- or upper-class person anywhere would have any more favorable attitude toward engaging in such activity than they have. Why does this attitude exist?

It is deep-rooted. I would explain it as follows. Every person in any society who holds or gains privileged position in life must justify it to himself, in order to be comfortable. If he has gained it by his abilities, justification is easy. The person who gains it by the accident of birth is forced to feel that it is due him because he is essentially superior to the simple folk. Typically, the elite individual in traditional societies feels that his innate superiority consists in being more refined than the simple folk. One evidence of his greater refinement is that he does not like the grubby attention to the material details of life which is one of their distinguishing characteristics. However this attitude may have developed historically, once it exists the elite child acquires it from infancy on by perceiving the words, the attitudes, the tone of voice of his elders. By the time he is six or eight years old, it is deeply bred into his personality.

This attitude alone would not contribute to the lack of innovation in social and political fields. Presence of a low level of creativity, however, would help to explain absence of innovation in these fields as well as in techniques of production.

The explanation of a low level of creativity and justification for the assertion that it exists are more complex.

One component of creativity is intelligence, and intelligence is in part due to biological characteristics. However, although individuals differ greatly in inherited intellectual capacity, the best evidence suggests no reason to assume any appreciable average difference in this respect between the individuals of traditional societies and those of other societies. There are varying degrees of innate intelligence in both. Persons in traditional societies are not less creative because they are less intelligent.

A more relevant component is certain attitudes. In formal psychological terms, I would suggest as characteristics central to creativity high need (for) achievement, high need autonomy, high need order (though this needs further definition), and a sense of the phenomena about one as forming a system which is conceptually comprehensible, rather than merely being arbitrary external bundles.

A person who has high need achievement feels a sense of increased pleasure (or quite possibly a lessening of chronic anxiety, which is the same thing) when he faces a problem or notes a new and irregular phenomenon in a field of interest to him; by the pleasure he anticipates in using his capacities he is drawn to use his energies to understand and master the situation. A person with high need autonomy takes for granted that when he has explored a situation in an area of interest to him, his evaluation of it is satisfactory. He does not think he "knows it all"; he seeks ideas; but when he has thus gained a perspective he assumes that his discriminations and evaluations are good; he feels no anxiety about whether the judgments of other persons differ from his. He does not rebel against the conventional view for the sake of rebelling, but neither does he accept it because it is generally accepted. In Rogers' phrase, the "locus of evaluative judgment is within him."[4]

A person with high need autonomy and also high need order, in the sense in which I use that phrase here, tolerates disorder without discomfort, because sensing that the world is an orderly place, he knows that within the disorder there is complex and satisfying order, and he is willing to tolerate the disorder, and in fact even enjoys it somewhat, until the greater order shall suggest itself to him. Such a person is alert to phenomena which contradict his previous assumptions about the scheme of things, for he assumes that he will be able to perceive the order implicit in them and thus gain an enlarged understanding of the world. In Poincaré's terms, he has a "capacity to be surprised"; in Rogers', "openness to experience."[5]

---

[4] H. H. Anderson, ed., *Creativity and Its Cultivation* (New York: Harper & Bros., 1959), p. 76.

[5] Poincaré's phrase is quoted by Erich Fromm in H. H. Anderson, op. cit., p. 48; Rogers' is at ibid., p. 75.

These characteristics are not fully independent of each other. In technical jargon, they may not be orthogonal. This categorization of personality therefore does not quite go to the roots of things. But it will do for my present purpose.

This personality complex may be contrasted with one which for the moment I shall term merely uncreative. It includes low need achievement and need autonomy, high need dependence, high need submission-dominance, and a sense of the world as consisting of arbitrary forces.

If an individual does not trust his own capacity to analyze problems, then when he faces a problem, anxiety rises in him. He anticipates failure, and avoids problems. He will find comfort in the consensus of a group (not on a majority decision opposed by a minority, for this involves a clash of judgment and the necessity of choosing between the two judgments). He will find it comfortable to rely on authority for guidance—the authority of older men or of the appropriate person in the hierarchy of authority and status which is always found in a traditional society. He will enjoy having a position of authority himself; one reason for this is that if he must make a decision, he can give it the sanction of his authority; persons below him, if they in turn find it comfortable to rely on authority, will not question his decision, and he does not need to feel anxiety lest analysis of it would prove it to have been wrong. It is right because a person with the proper authority made it.

A person with such needs will avoid noting phenomena that do not meet his preconceptions, for their existence presents a problem. In any event, since he senses the world as consisting mainly of arbitrary forces, an unexpected phenomenon provides no clue to him. It is simply a possible source of failure or danger.

I shall suggest below that the experiences in infancy and childhood which give a person this perception of the world inculcate rage and need aggression in him, but also fear of his own need aggression, and therefore anxiety in any situation within his group in which power relationships are not clearly defined and conflict leading to aggressiveness might occur. Hence he likes a clearly defined structure of hierarchical authority, in which it is obviously proper for him to submit to someone above him or give orders to persons below him, without clash of judgment. In addition, his need aggression also causes him to feel pleasure in dominating those below him—his children, his juniors, his social inferiors.

Thus there are dual reasons why the authoritarian hierarchy is satisfying. It is appropriate to give this personality type not merely the negative label "uncreative" but also the positive one "authoritarian."[6]

[6] It is not congruent in all respects with the one portrayed by Adorno and associates in *The Authoritarian Personality.*

While it is evident that these two personality types exist, to this point it is purely an assumption that authoritarian personality is typical in traditional societies. One reason for thinking that this is true is that this hypothesis explains many things about traditional societies which otherwise are puzzling. It explains, for example, why many persons in traditional societies not only follow traditional methods, but seem to cling almost compulsively to them, even though to an outsider trial of a new method seems so clearly to their advantage. It explains why the method of decision of local problems in so many traditional societies is by consensus of the village elders, through a long process of finding a least-common-denominator solution on which all can agree, rather than by majority vote. It explains, too, why authoritarian social and political systems have persisted in such societies for such long periods.

That a hypothesis explains a number of phenomena which are otherwise puzzling is strong reason for accepting it. However, there is also more direct reason for believing that authoritarian personality is unusually prevalent in traditional societies. This reason lies in the existence of some evidence that childhood environment and childhood training in traditional societies are of the kind which tend to produce such personality.

Perhaps the factor which is most important in determining whether childhood environment will be such as to cause the formation of creative personality or such as to cause the formation of authoritarian personality is the opinions of the parents concerning the nature of infants and children. Suppose that the parents take for granted that infants are organisms which, while delicate and in need of protection for a time, have great potentials; organisms which as they unfold will develop capacity for understanding and managing life. A mother who regards this as an axiomatic fact of life will if she is sensible take precautions to keep her child's explorations of the world around him from causing harm or alarm to him, but she will let him explore his world and will watch with interest and pleasure as his muscular capacities develop, his range of activity expands, and he accomplishes in endless succession the hundreds of new achievements which occur during infancy and childhood.

His repeated use of his new physiological capacities, as they unfold, is from his viewpoint problem solving—intensely interesting problem solving. Assume that it is successful because his mother has taken safeguards so that he will not fall out of his crib, cut himself, break the glassware, fall down stairs, etc., and because his mother offers advice and restraint when necessary. Assume, however, that his venturings do not meet repeated restraint, because his mother trusts his developing capacities and does not check his every step. Then he will repeatedly feel joy at his own successful problem solving and pleasure in his mother's pleasure. There will be deeply built into him the pattern that initiative is rewarded, that his judgment is adequate, that solving problems is fun.

If his mother wants him to be self-reliant, presses him to do things as soon as his capacities have developed, usually refuses to let him lapse into babyhood after he has gained capacities, and shows displeasure when he does not do things for himself, then the stimulus of her displeasure when he does not show initiative will be combined with that of her pleasure when he does so. I have mentioned only his mother. During the first year or more of his life, her attitude is the most important one in his life; after that the attitude of his father (and also that of his siblings) toward his behavior will also be important.

Suppose, alternatively, that the child's parents have as a part of their personalities the judgment that children are fragile organisms without much innate potential capacity to understand or manage the world. Then during the first two years or so of life the mother is apt to treat the child over-solicitously, and to shield him somewhat anxiously from harm. In doing so, unintentionally she also keeps the child from using his unfolding initiative. The use of initiative comes to alarm him, because it alarms her. Then, after these first few years of life, when the parents think the child is old enough to be trained, parents with the view that children are without much potential inner capacity train the child by a continual stream of commands and instructions concerning what is good to do and not good to do, the proper relationships to them and to others, and in general how he should live. Exercise of initiative on his part frequently brings alarm and displeasure and hence causes him anxiety. He can avoid anxiety only by passively obeying the instructions of these powerful persons so important in his life. The instructions will often seem arbitrary to him, and the repeated frustration of his initiative will create anger in him. He will repress it, but this does not mean that it disappears.

The practices and attitudes of older siblings and playmates who have been brought up under the same influences will provide models which in various ways will reinforce the same lesson.

The impact of these parental attitudes on the child may be reinforced by certain related attitudes of the parents. The existence of any child restricts the freedom of his parents, and interferes with their relations to each other. Moreover, the child exerts a will independent of theirs, and they are not always sure that they can control him. If the parents, especially the mother, are relaxed confident people, they will not be disturbed by these problems. Suppose, however, that they are somewhat anxious persons who feel that they themselves do not understand the world (as they are apt to feel if their own childhood was like that which I have just described). Then their child may repeatedly make them anxious, and unconsciously they may hate him for causing them anxiety and also interfering with their freedom. The child is sure to sense their hostility; it will both make him more afraid to venture and increase his pleasure in venting his frustration by controlling someone below him later in life.

Exposure to the one or the other of these parental attitudes will have an impact on the child through infancy and childhood, but for brevity I shall mention specifically only the most conspicuous manifestation, that during the "period of infantile genitality," which usually occupies about the fourth and fifth years of life. At this age a boy knows that he is a male, like his father, and that he will become big, like his father, and he begins to wonder whether he can successfully rival his father. Specifically, he becomes a rival of his father for his mother's attentions. If his father and mother are perceptive and understanding persons, they will accept him into their fellowship and let him gain an adequate degree of the feminine attention he needs. However, without anxiety or arbitrariness, they will teach him that he can postpone his demands when the circumstances require it, and need not feel anxiety at the postponement. He will learn, as before, that one's initiative must be judicious, and he will also reinforce powerfully the earlier lesson that the exercise of his initiative is safe and brings pleasure.

If the father is weak and the mother is not arbitrary and somewhat rejecting, the son may gain his mother's attentions not because his parents understand his needs and meet them but because his father gives up at the boy's aggressive persistence. In this case too the son will learn that initiative is successful, though he will learn it with overtones of anxiety.

Suppose, however, that the parents doubt their own ability to manage problems, and, having no faith in the capacities of children, regard the boy's initiative as a danger rather than a valuable attribute. Then they will be disturbed by the boy's emerging rivalry with his father during the period of infantile sexuality, will resent the boy's encroachment, and will "put the boy in his place." The experience will reinforce the anxiety and alarm that the boy felt earlier at the exercise of initiative. It will also reinforce the anger that the boy felt earlier at his parents' arbitrary restrictions, and since he cannot vent his anger at his parents, there is apt to build up in him an unformed desire to exercise arbitrary authority himself, and lord it over someone under him, later in life—just as the college freshman humiliated by hazing at the hands of sophomores often waits his turn to vent his humiliation on the new freshmen the next year.

The impact of the one or other type of parental personality on girls during this period is not quite parallel to that on boys, because of the different sexual role which girls have already learned. The differences will not be discussed here.

In these ways, creative or authoritarian personality is formed. There are many other aspects to the process, and many other aspects of authoritarian and creative personalities, which cannot be discussed here.[7] This brief discussion will, I hope, give the general flavor of both the personality types and the process which forms them.

I think that the reader may already have realized that the parental attitudes which tend to create authoritarian personality in the children are themselves components of authoritarian personality in the parents. That is, persons in whom authoritarian personality was created by the circumstances of their childhoods are apt to have such a view of life that they will in turn create an environment which will cause authoritarian personalities to appear in their children. The type, like most other personality types, tends to be self-perpetuating.

It is of great importance, then, that the scattered evidence which is available suggests that precisely the sort of childhood environment and training sketched above as conducive to the emergence of authoritarian personality is the sort prevalent in traditional societies. Fairly intensive sketches of childhood environment in Burma by Hazel Hitson[8] and in Java by Hildred Geertz,[9] and more fragmentary sketches relating to many Latin societies, indicate that in all of these cases childhood environment is precisely of this type. These sketches refer primarily to the simple folk, but there is some empirical evidence to suggest that they are true of personality and childhood environment among the elite as well.

And there is even more convincing evidence that various of the conspicuous characteristics of authoritarian personality are present in many traditional societies in Latin America and Asia. Though our knowledge concerning African countries is more limited, they are probably present in those countries as well. Hence it seems likely that a low level of creativity is also characteristic of such societies.

Presumably this personality type developed initially because the everyday phenomena of the physical world were bewildering to unscientific man. Convinced of his inability to fathom the world, man began to protect his children jealously when they were infants and then train them minutely in the way in

---

[7] For example, models are important in personality formation, and it is of interest to ask where the son of a weak father obtains models of successful behavior. There are several possibilities. This and other complexities must be passed over here.

[8] "Family Patterns and Paranoidal Personality Structure in Boston and Burma" (Ph.D. dissertation, Radcliffe College, April, 1959).

[9] *The Javanese Family* (New York: Free Press of Glencoe, Inc., 1955) and "The Vocabulary of Emotion: A Study of Javanese Socialization Processes," *Psychiatry*, Vol. XXII August, 1959), pp. 225–237.

which they should behave to be safe. And so authoritarian personality appeared and perpetuated itself. Repugnance to concerning oneself with the humble material matters of life and with manual-technical labor also appeared among the elite, in the way sketched earlier in this essay, and tended to perpetuate itself.

SECTION TWO: SOCIAL CHANGE

How, then, did social change ever occur? and technological progress and economic development ever begin?

agricultural

Study of a number of countries in which there has occurred a transition from a traditional state to continuing economic development suggests that an important factor initiating change was some historical shift which caused some group or groups of the lesser elite, who previously had had a respected and valued place in the social hierarchy, to feel that they no longer were respected and valued. This derogation in some societies consisted of explicit indication of contempt for the functions or position of the lesser elite, in others of behavior by a new higher elite which seemed immoral, unmanly, or irreligious to the groups below them, and thus indicated contempt for the moral standards of the lesser elite.

I shall omit the example of England, which is complex and difficult to mention briefly, and shall refer briefly to highlights of three other examples. In the 1650s the Tsar of Russia and Patriarch of Moscow, to attain diplomatic ends by adopting Greek practices, ordered certain changes in the ritual of the Orthodox church which the faithful felt to be heretical and to endanger their souls. There followed conflict and persecution, in waves of varying severity, even down to 1900. The Old Believers, who were the victims of this withdrawal of respect for their status in the society, were prominent in economic development in Russia in the nineteenth century. Concerning the twentieth I have no information.

In Japan the feudal group known as the Tokugawa, who gained national power in 1600, imposed a peace which deprived the samurai of their traditional function; imposed rigid distinctions among social classes which had the effect of relegating the so-called "wealthy peasants," descendants of the lesser elite, to the rank of peasant; and to some extent demeaned other feudal groups, the so-called outer clans. It was the lesser samurai and wealthy peasants, apparently especially of the outer clans, who were the innovators in Japan's industrial revolution.

In Colombia, in the 1530s the Spanish settled on a high plateau around Bogotá and in the valleys around Cali and Medellín. Through historical developments I shall not sketch, during the next two centuries the settlers of the other two areas came to look down on those in Antioquia, the valley around Medellín. The social friction continues to the present; and the Antioqueños have been the leaders in economic innovation out of all proportion to their numbers in the population.

I shall call such events "withdrawal of status respect" from the group no longer accorded its old place. It is important to note that the situation is one in which a group of the elite once had full status respect and later lost it. What are the results? Let me speculate concerning them.

I suggest that among the adults of the first generation so affected, the reaction is anger and anxiety. Their children, however, seeing that their parents' role in life causes anxiety, do not find it a fully satisfying model. Alternative roles are in general not open to them, and so they respond by repressing somewhat within themselves their parents' values—by ceasing to have *any* role values with the same clarity and intensity their parents did. The process, I suggest, is cumulative in successive generations, and in the second or third or fourth generation there appears pronounced "normlessness," shiftlessness, anomie, or, in Merton's term, retreatism. It can be observed, for example, in Negroes of the southern United States, American Indians on any reservation, first and second generation immigrants, and colonial subjects.[10] Historical records suggest that it also characterized the Antioqueños, the samurai, and the Old Believers.

There is reason to suspect that retreatism affects men more than women because of the differences between the normal social roles of the sexes. After several generations, then, there will appear men who are retreatist and weak, but women who are less so. The women will probably feel some pity for their children's lot in life, and will cherish them tenderly. But, reacting to the ineffectiveness of their husbands, the women will have an intense desire that their sons shall be more effective, and will respond with delight to each achievement in infancy and boyhood. During the period of infantile sexuality, the boy will win in the rivalry with his father, both because his initiative pleases his mother and because his father is weak.

Obviously not all home environments in some generation of a group of the lesser elite from whom status respect has been withdrawn will be like this, but it is plausible to believe that some such environment will appear occasionally, or even fairly often. Some combinations and intensities of such maternal attitudes,

[10] In groups who are not of the lower elite, but instead are of the "simple folk," the later reaction may be not creative innovation but violent social revolt. For lack of space, that branch of the theory cannot be expounded here.

combined with weakness in the father, provide an almost ideal environment for the formation of an anxious driving type of creativity.

Where a considerable degree of creativity is inculcated, but the anxiety is great, a variant type of individual may appear, one who gives himself security by being traditional and authoritarian in most aspects of his behavior, and then dares to be bold and creative in some other aspect. Henry Ford was such a person, as was J. Pierpont Morgan. And this type has been important in economic development in Japan, the Soviet Union, and Germany.

Thus, I suggest, there gradually emerges a group of individuals, creative, alienated from traditional values, driven by a gnawing burning drive to prove themselves (to themselves, as well as to their fellows), seeking for an area in which to do so, preferably an area in which they can gain power, and preferably also one in which in some symbolic way they can vent their rage at the elites who have caused their troubles. Moreover, their (perhaps unconscious) rage at the group disparaging them will cause them to turn against some of the values of the group disparaging them. The fact that the disparaging group, in the cases cited above, was traditional, is one of the reasons why the disparaged group rejected traditional values and turned to innovation.

What they turn to will be determined in part by the models they find during their childhood somewhere in their history or their folklore or the tales their elders tell them of the life around them, and in part by the objective opportunities of the world around them. In the modern world, to few socially rebellious groups of traditional societies will any other road to power, recognition, and proof to oneself of one's ability seem as inviting as economic prowess, and creative individuals in most such groups will become economic innovators. In the cases of England, Japan, and Colombia, which I have examined in some detail, such groups have provided a disproportionate share of the leaders in the transition to economic growth.

A word is in point concerning the complexity of the situation in colonial societies. Here there has been rather harsh withdrawal of status respect, but by invading groups from the West who became colonial conquerors. These groups have not traditional but "modern" values toward manual-technical work. The tendency of disparaged groups to reject the values of the disparaging group may cause them to reject engaging their energies in the occupations of the conquerors. Thus even though they desire to gain symbols of economic power, an additional emotional block is put in the way of the indigenous elite becoming effective industrialists. This fact may explain some of the ambivalence and erratic behavior sometimes manifested.

The theory some of whose central points have been sketched so briefly above proceeds in broad sweeps, and of course is subject to a corresponding margin of error. It seems plausible to me because it is internally consistent and because it explains many aspects of social, political, and economic behavior in low-income countries for which no other very logical explanation seems available.

If it is correct it does not follow that economic growth will succeed only where certain rather special historical conditions have existed. For the forces of modern history have caused social tensions among the social classes of low-income societies themselves, by virtue of which some degree of withdrawal of status respect has existed among the indigenous social classes of almost all of them, and what values various groups are alienated from or drawn to is confused and uncertain. However, innovational personality is clearly appearing, in varying degree. The drive for security, self-reassurance, and power will surely lead many innovational individuals to technological innovation, though frequently within social forms differing from those of the West.

7

A MACROSOCIOLOGICAL INTERPRETATION OF ENTREPRENEURSHIP

Frank W. Young

It is difficult to deny that entrepreneurship is a matter of individuals when much of the historical scholarship about the phenomenon consists of the biographies of extraordinary businessmen and when more abstract formulation is typically couched in terms applied to individuals, such as ability to make new combinations, managerial skill, perception of opportunity, risk taking, inventiveness, or, more recently, achievement motivation. In what may be called the "mediation model" of entrepreneurial activity these attributes show up in individuals as a result of particular family backgrounds, experiences as members of certain kinds of groups, and as a reflection of general cultural values. However, these personality characteristics are not simply a pale reflection of these antecedent conditions; they constitute an independent causal factor, mediating between structural factors and consequent economic growth. This model has much to recommend it, and it seems to make a place for all the diverse factors that are thought to influence economic development. However, its comprehensiveness and explanatory power are more apparent than real, as a contrast with what may be called a macrosociological explanation will reveal.

As theory goes, the psychogenic mediation model is untidy. In the first place, there is little or no agreement on the basic conceptual character of the intervening personality characteristics. Moreover, the antecedent conditions may be ascetic Protestantism, status withdrawal, or the laundry list of factors that McClelland[1] gives, and there is a similar vagueness with regard to how the entrepreneurs affect their environment: some do so directly through their technological or organizational innovations that diffuse to the wider society, whereas others form groups that compete for positions of more general influence. Nevertheless, there is one point on which there is general agreement. The thing to be explained is a group-level phenomenon. Whatever else it may be, economic development involves a reorganization of productive resources. Whether one thinks of it in institutional terms, as the development of new forms such as modern capitalism, or whether one conceives of it as the succession of "leading sectors," it is an organizational phenomenon, that is, it is coordination of individual effort and not simply the operation of parallel psychological tendencies.

Psychogenic interpretations do not explain what needs to be explained, which is the appearance of a new kind of organization. Without exception they are mute on the question of how individual tendencies, special abilities, unusual motivation, or perception of particular opportunities are transformed into the emergent property that is social organization. Neither do they explain why, during certain periods in history, entrepreneurs seem to cluster in particular activities, such as textiles, railroading, or electronics. They do not deal with the apparent fact—although it needs careful research—that entrepreneurs are often involved in political or religious pursuits that are not obviously relevant to their business success, and more generally, that they are located with high frequency in subgroups that have a religious or ethnic character. Insofar as the social contexts of entrepreneurial activity are recognized by the mediation model, they are considered among a number of antecedent factors. This approach automatically denies the possibility that the apparent individual-level characteristic may in fact be an inseparable component of a group structure, one that combines the industrial, religious, and individual aspects in the tightly coordinated pattern.

A second major difficulty with the psychogenic interpretation of entrepreneurship is that its postulated causal sequence requires at least two generations and yet economic development often occurs more rapidly than that. In commenting, for example, on the rapid development of Germany between 1925 and 1950, McClelland[2] suggests that the absence of so many fathers during the two wars might have provided just the right family structure for generating achieve-

[1] David C. McClelland, *The Achieving Society* (Princeton, N.J.: D. Van Nostrand Co., 1961), p. 438.   [2] Ibid., p. 406.

ment motivation in the younger generation. Such an "absent father" pattern may explain Germany's economic success after 1945, but the *ad hoc* character of this explanation is exposed when one remembers that Great Britain—where many fathers were also absent—had considerable economic difficulties after 1945. Indeed, the problem of timing that is inherent in psychogenic explanation reveals a deeper flaw: its capacity for ignoring events of a macrostructural nature that any ordinary observer would admit as probably having a great effect, and indeed, must have had an effect if such a massive transformation as economic development took place. The obvious fact in all these cited cases and in many more is reactive nationalism. It seems much more plausible to assume that the spurts of development in Germany were reactions to setbacks in national power and after 1945, the continuing Soviet threat. Threats such as these may mobilize energy, prompt new institutional forms, and eliminate or streamline traditional structures with the result—although it is not the only one and does not always happen—that economic development spurts ahead.

The example of reactive nationalism raises the possibility that what evidence that has been accumulated for a correlation between, say, high achievement motivation and economic development has been misinterpreted. McClelland's content analysis of children's school books for the purpose of scoring the presence of themes of striving and goal-directed activity may have only tapped the degree to which the rhetoric of national progress has permeated the mass media. McClelland himself is forced to consider this possibility in his discussion of the lack of correlation between achievement motivation as shown by school books and as measured in individuals:

> The reader stress on achievement may represent something more like "national aspirations" . . . what people are concerned about for public consumption may not be the same as they are spontaneously concerned about in writing stories privately, yet it is the "public concerns" that may be diagnostic of public achievements, as in economic development.[3]

The reinterpretation of the individual-level entrepreneurial characteristics as the "underside" of a group-level pattern points the direction that a more thoroughgoing structural interpretation can take. Instead of looking at individuals, one must find clusters: ethnic communities, occupational groups, or politically oriented factions. Naturally, not all of these will qualify as entrepreneurial groups, for to do so they must show a certain reactiveness or solidarity, defined as the degree to which the members create, maintain, and project a

[3] Ibid., p. 79.

coherent definition of their situation. Such groups typically seize upon the rhetoric of religion or politics as a vehicle for expressing their deviant view of the world. The most important aspect of this group-level definition of the entrepreneurial phenomenon is that it prompts us to see that the entrepreneur does not typically work his miracles single-handedly. He is simply the most visible member from an economic point of view of what is typically a cluster of families whose activity is mutually reinforcing and coordinated by a coherent outlook on the world.

It is a curious fact that in the literature on entrepreneurship and economic development, the theoretical emphasis on psychological motivation exists alongside extensive description of and stress on the importance of reactive subgroups. Weber's initial interest in the institutionalized aspects of Protestantism are even more accentuated in his less well known later essay "The Protestant Sects and the Spirit of Capitalism."[4] Hagen's series of vignettes is typical of later scholarship that consistently takes account of subgroup patterns.[5] When it comes, though, to isolating the crucial causal factor, even those writers who are sensitive to structural patterns have recourse to psychological motivation. Yet, a group-level explanation deals more adequately and more directly with the very psychological tendencies that they feel they cannot do without.

The frequent minority status of solidary groups suggests one element of the explanation of what are usually labelled psychological tendencies. They lack relative centrality with respect to the dominant system; that is, the social identity of the subgroup is in question. At the national level, examples readily come to mind: Israel with respect to the surrounding Arab states, Taiwan with respect to mainland China and the rest of the world, Pakistan after Partition, and Japan and the United States at various points in history as both fought to gain acceptance in a world that had expanded far beyond its original European base but without agreement as to how it should be ordered. Similarly, one could name many reactive subgroups, from the Calvinists in Geneva to the white settlers in Rhodesia, whose social identity is either not well accepted or else has been called into question.

However, not all groups with low relative centrality develop solidarity, since only those with relatively high differentiation have the capacity to react. Differentiation is defined as the diversity, as opposed to the coherence, of the social meanings maintained by the group, and is empirically shown by the range

---

[4] Max Weber, "The Protestant Sects and The Spirit of Capitalism" in *From Max Weber: Essays in Sociology*, eds. H. H. Gerth and C. Wright Mills (New York: Oxford University Press, 1946), pp. 302–322.

[5] Everett E. Hagen, *On The Theory of Social Change* (Homewood, Illinois: The Dorsey Press, 1962)

of occupations and institutions, familiar as "the social division of labor." As a formal proposition, we may state that solidarity is generated by a high differentiation/relative centrality ratio.[6] That is, when a group has a high degree of institutional and occupational diversity relative to its acceptance as a participant group in the larger society, it tends to intensify its internal communication with the result that a unified definition of the situation emerges. In the course of the defensive deliberation that members of such subgroups engage in as they attempt to understand their predicament and to improve their symbolic position in the larger structure, they must find ways of thinking that will allow mutual understanding despite the differences in occupation and family status. The "transformation codes" that are developed under such pressure are usually drawn from the available theological or political rhetoric and become the distinctive ideology of the subgroup. However, such pressures also bear on economic factors; some members of solidary groups excel at combining resources, labor, capital, etc., in new ways and they become the entrepreneurs.

Intercommunication despite social differences may account for one small but interesting finding that Hagen reports. The overall pattern of responses to the Thematic Apperception Test by a group of twenty entrepreneurs in Medellín, Columbia, showed a tendency to describe the situation in the pictures as a problem to be solved, an awareness that pragmatic effort was required, confidence in their own ability to solve the problem, and "a tendency to take the viewpoint of each individual in turn and analyze the situation as he might see it before suggesting an outcome."[7] These are precisely the characteristics that one would expect in the context of a reactive subgroup. The constant knowledge that the group was vulnerable would eliminate any tendencies toward fantasy or indefensible kinds of problem solving; one dose of ridicule or an open attack has a sobering effect on the deliberations of any group. Moreover, it generates the tight social control that the outside world sees as asceticism. Most of all, such long-term vulnerability motivates all numbers of a subgroup to a constant search for opportunities that will improve the group's position without bringing it into conflict with other groups. Thus, there is a tendency to go into business in places where business activity is relatively open to newcomers, and once in business, to remain independent except for the depersonalized and cautious transactions that must be made.

[6] For a more detailed and extensive statement, see Frank W. Young, "A Proposal for Cooperative Cross-Cultural Research on Intervillage Systems," *Human Organization*, Vol. 25 (Spring, 1966), pp. 46–50. A related analysis of countries is Ruth C. Young, "A Structural Approach to Development," *Journal of Developing Areas*, II (April, 1968), pp. 363–376.

[7] Hagen, op. cit., p. 368.

Thus, the concept of solidarity implies many accepted entrepreneurial functions. Given a group bent on finding a suitable reformulation of its outlook on the world, it is likely that recombination of economic factors, higher standards of labor, the search for new resources, technology, markets, and a more disciplined management of money and time will emerge as part of this effort. However, the assumption that a subgroup is the locus of entrepreneurial effort also resolves certain other economic problems. The initial capital can be obtained from members of the subgroup because of the mutual trust among them or, if it is sought from outside sources, it is more readily obtained because the group's general reputation supports the borrower. Similarly, particular businessmen can obtain advice and assistance from other group members; in new areas of business activity, specialized expertise cannot be hired because it does not exist as a separate role, but knowledge and thought on problems can be pooled if a network of free intercommunication exists. Finally, the group in which a particular business is embedded may even supply the initial market for a product. Acceptance of a new product or service is something of an act of faith under the best of circumstances, so if a sympathetic group is available to take the first step and perhaps even sustain the enterprise until the product is perfected, dealings with a more critical out-group market are simplified.

The sociogenic explanation of solidarity structures, as they may now be called, is reminiscent of and was probably influenced by Hagen's hypothesis that "withdrawal of status respect" from a group results, ultimately, in a high frequency of "creative personalities."[8] But the differences in the two hypotheses are considerable. The solidarity hypotheses uses two variables, in combination, where Hagen postulates simply loss of prestige. Consequently, the solidarity hypothesis is better able to deal with those groups, such as the despised traders of Modjokuto that Geertz[9] describes, or even Hagen's own Antioqueños, who appear never to have been accorded much prestige that could be withdrawn. Also, it sidesteps the considerable operational problems in measuring prestige, dependent as it is on social perception, a notoriously slippery phenomenon. The most fundamental difference, however, is that the psychological reactions, although present in the sociogenic explanation, are not considered to be independent causal factors. The reactions merely describe individuals as they participate in the intensified defensive intercommunication that occurs when a group is under the structural pressures described. Thus, in the solidarity hypothesis, the range of characteristics that go to make up entrepreneurial activity

[8] Hagen, op. cit., pp. 185 ff.
[9] Clifford Geertz, "Social Change and Economic Modernization in Two Indonesian Towns: A Case in Point," in Hagen, op. cit., pp. 385–410.

are generated directly, and there is no need for a succession of changes in family structure, over generations, to bring them about. This ability of the solidarity explanation to overcome the long and awkward time lag required by psychogenic explanations is important because it makes for a more parsimonious explanation and clear-cut empirical tests. Also, it reveals a possible negation of Hagen's interpretation. In his descriptions of the several cases of outstanding entrepreneurial success, and especially that of Antioquia, he notes that the group lacks respect long after it has developed its entrepreneurs. "Condescension existed, [and] it persists today."[10] Thus, his crucial social determinant is still operating, and according to the theory, it should be producing enraged, frustrated men who then begin the several generations of family disorganization that finally results in creative personalities. But Hagen does not mention these unhappy men. On the contrary, his picture of the present-day Antioqueños suggests that such men do not exist, for if they did, they would contrast sharply with the successful entrepreneurs and would thus figure in any account of the social structure.

Further illustration of the solidarity hypothesis is provided by Clifford Geertz's analysis of the locus of entrepreneurial activity in two Indonesian towns. His article, which appears in Hagen's book but seems out of place because it is not interpreted and perhaps cannot be interpreted in terms of Hagen's theory, can, however, be handled by the solidarity hypothesis. The subgroups that supplied the entrepreneurs for the two towns are the traders of Modjokuto and the aristocrats of Tabanan, and both, according to Geertz's summary, are inclined to see themselves as "the main vehicle of religious and moral excellence within a generally wayward, unenlightened, or heedless community."[11] Geertz has already noted that these entrepreneurs come from clearly demarcated subgroups and that both groups have a history of contact with other villages and towns, suggesting that their level of differentiation was relatively high. Then he goes on to state what for the solidarity hypothesis is the decisive antecedent condition: "In prewar Modjokuto the town's traders were a self-contained, set-apart, rather despised group; today they are becoming integrated into a broad and generalized middle class within an uncertainly urbanized structure. In prewar Tabanan the aristocrats were the unquestioned political and cultural elite of the region; today their position is increasingly threatened by the growth of a universalistic civil bureaucracy and the populist sentiments of nationalist ideology."[12] Thus, the traders, although they are increasing their relative

---

[10] Hagen, op. cit., p. 376.   [11] Geertz, op. cit., p. 406.
[12] Ibid. See also his more extended account in *Peddlers and Princes* (Chicago: University of Chicago Press, 1963).

centrality, are probably still disadvantaged as compared to their higher differentiation. The ruling families of Tabanan, in contrast, are losing their position, but the analytic pattern is the same: there is a differentiation/relative centrality discrepancy that generates solidarity.

An obvious question at this point is how do groups come to be in the discrepant structural position required by the hypothesis? Although the proposition is such that a shift in either differentiation or relative centrality could bring about the hypothesized structural bind, there are two main types of events that tend to place groups in the discrepant situation. These two events are migrations and regional expansions. Migrations work to lower the relative centrality of a subgroup because it usually ends up in a peripheral position, whether it moves to the edge of a new structure, as in the case of migrating groups to Latin American cities, or away from an old structure, as in the case of the American colonists. Regional expansions amount to an alternate mode of subgroup migration, much as a glacier carries a rock along and deposits it in some distant place; but such shifts may also be considered as the context in which increases of differentiation occur. In general, subgroups develop the level of differentiation that their regional location permits; so if a group is urban in origin, it is likely to be more differentiated than one from a rural area, and similarly even a rural group from a European country is likely to be more differentiated than a rural group from a less developed country. Hagen's list of four situations that may result in withdrawal of status respect includes migration, and he adds to that conquest, denigration of valued symbols, and inconsistency of status symbols.[13] The last two determinants seem merely to rephrase the idea already contained in withdrawal of status respect. Much of the underlying meaning is better captured by the notion of regional expansions with their accompanying rearrangements of subgroup memberships.

A consideration of the interplay between a subgroup and its incorporating region leads to almost infinite complexities, but one aspect of it must be mentioned for a full understanding of how the concept of solidary structure can replace, or at least enlarge, that of entrepreneurship. If solidarity is defined as the degree to which activities, beliefs, and even artifacts are coordinated into a coherent outlook on the world, it is clear that any group, whether it is a nation, a region, or a smaller subgroup, can show solidarity. The term "reactive nationalism" has already been used as a synonym for national-level solidarity. A similar term, "reactive ethnicity," might serve for many smaller groups. What is suggested is the possibility of a nesting series of solidary structures which, under certain conditions, operate as a kind of social "chain reaction." Indeed, the

[13] Hagen, op. cit., pp. 188 ff.

concept of solidarity can even be applied to individuals, and thus the macro-sociological interpretation can find a place for individual innovators,[14] although in general, they are better thought of as catalysts and specialized loaders of particular subgroups, which are here taken to be the typical loci of entre-preneurial activity. Also, it should not be supposed that the direction of influence is necessarily from the bottom up. From a macrosociological perspective, it is more reasonable to suppose that the highest system level, which in recent times would be nations, is most subject to the structural strains that produce solidarity. In turn, these solidary nations are more likely to experience a reshuffling of their internal regional structure, with the result that subgroups are dislocated all down the line, many developing solidarity.[15]

Such a process of successive solidarity formation may account for Pakistan's spurt of economic development since 1947. As Gustav Papanek suggests, there probably were new investment opportunities,[16] but the more fundamental causal determinant, as his critic Frederic Shorter proposes and as a macrosociological perspective requires, is the national mobilization that in turn made it possible for subgroup solidarity to appear. In fact, the theory says that a solidary group is required if the entrepreneurs are to perceive or create the investment oppor-tunities. If this interpretation is correct, Pakistan should also show a higher level of "entrepreneurial activity" in areas other than business: local government, education, scientific research and the like.

In addition to the possibility that entrepreneurial activity, now viewed as an aspect of the activity of reactive subsystems, may show up at many different system levels, the macrosociological perspective broadens the problem in another way. The definition of solidarity does not specify the content of the subgroup's view of the world, so long as it shows a high degree of focus. Thus, entrepreneurial activity is not simply a characteristic of businessmen. It shows up in all walks of life, from the theological innovators of the last century who opened up a great new "market" with their recombinations of old ideas in Christ-ianity, to present-day research or educational "entrepreneurs," who are actively finding or creating new publics. In short, the world is full of entrepreneurial

[14] For those relatively few cases where an individual operates apart from a group—perhaps creating his own—it is useful to construe his activity as a one-man solidarity move-ment. Then the differentiation/relative centrality ratio should apply as before. There is scattered comment in the literature to the effect that a distant or absent father (low relative centrality?) in conjunction with a warm supportive mother (leading to differentiation?) often results in "creative personalities." A recent citation is David C. McClelland and David G. Winter, *Motivating Economic Achievement* (New York: The Free Press, 1969), p. 281.

[15] Compare Hagen, op. cit., p. 193, for a similar conception.

[16] Gustav Papanek, "The Development of Entrepreneurship," *American Economic Review*, Supplement (May, 1962), pp. 46–66.

activity; only stagnant systems lack reactive subgroups of some sort. Such a widening of the concept of entrepreneurial activity forces the economist to return to fundamentals in his analysis of the relationship of profit to the motivation of such innovators. As Benjamin Higgins points out in criticizing what he considers McClelland's lack of understanding of the economist's conception of profit, money is only an index of the businessmen's efficiency in the market and the status rewards therefrom.[17] So abstracted, the concept of profit applies to the work of the research scientist, the ghetto educator, or even the religious leader fomenting a new sect movement. Although they may call it "professional recognition" or "doing one's duty in the eyes of God," it is still a quest for profit in its fundamental sense. But at this point the solidarity hypothesis calls attention to the large element of social perception in this abstracted notion of profit. If one rejects the concrete monetary indicator, as one must when dealing with activities other than business, then the group's social perception of its efficiency and status is clearly dependent on consensual validation. So profit is fundamentally social. But where does the particular criterion originate? Are status criteria generally available in society? Not according to the reactive subsystem hypothesis. Rather, the formulation of some calculus of group progress is an intrinsic component of solidarity. By definition, it is the tightly coordinated activity and beliefs of a group, and such a focus is reflected in the use of concepts such as profit, prestige, religious duty, and the like. Such a concept of group progress is an example of the transformation codes that develop in solidarity groups, and the greater the solidarity, the more seriously they are taken.

It may be, however, that the approach to measurement and analysis that comes out of the macrosociological perspective will in the long run be its most attractive feature, because changes in methodology do not at first require radical revision of many types of theoretical perspectives. Preliminary work shows that it is in fact possible to measure the degree to which groups show a coherent or focused structure. It is possible to code the qualitative features of such groups: institutionalized modes of coordinated activity, stereotyped phrases that function as transformation codes, "central symbols" such as dress, a well known town of origin, or the business enterprise itself, and of course, leadership, particularly in its more charismatic manifestations. Such qualitative features can be combined by procedures such as factor analysis or Guttman scaling into continuous variables which can then be handled according to standard correlational procedures. Inasmuch as the initial qualitative data are just the sort that is reported

[17] Benjamin Higgins, *Economic Development*, 2nd ed. (New York: Norton & Co., 1968), p. 248.

by economic historians, there seems no reason in principle why samples cannot be assembled of, say, industries or businesses. If the many business biographies mentioned in the beginning of this essay contain more general information on the nature of the firm, as many of them must, then they can serve as a valuable initial data base for the study of entrepreneurial activity at the group level. The very facts that make the individual-level interpretation of entrepreneurship so plausible may in the end be the means of justifying a radically different view.

8

VALUES AND BEHAVIOR IN ECONOMIC DEVELOPMENT

John H. Kunkel

THE PROBLEM

Recent theories of economic development and social change have assigned prominent roles to individuals as savers of capital, entrepreneurs, and consumers with rising expectations.[1] Such emphasis is new and has created new problems; in the past most theories of economic development and social change disregarded the individual or treated him as a constant, and those theories which did indicate the importance of social structure or political climate for industrialization usually did not seriously investigate these social prerequisites. When, however, the individual is given a prominent role in a theory of economic development, two problems arise which must be adequately solved if the theory is to be useful in explaining or predicting change.

(1) What are the determinants of human behavior? This question is important because, in the last analysis, it is not the individual, unique person who

Reprinted with permission of the author and the publisher from Economic Development and Cultural Change *(April, 1965), pp. 257-277.*

[1] For example, Everett E. Hagen, *On the Theory of Social Change* (Homewood: Dorsey Press, 1962); Don Martindale, *Social Life and Cultural Change* (Princeton: Van Nostrand, 1962); David C. McClelland, *The Achieving Society* (Princeton: Van Nostrand, 1961).

is important in the process of economic development, but rather the actions in which he engages.

(2) What is the relationship between the individual and the societal context? This is an important problem, since human beings are always found in groups and are influenced by them as much as they influence the groups to which they belong.

If theories of social change and industrialization do not answer these two questions, they cannot assign prominent roles to individuals—acting either singly or in groups—and thus are forced to concern themselves largely with abstractions, such as social climate, since concrete social phenomena cannot be investigated without reference to their observable and measurable components —individuals and their actions.

The analysis of human activities in terms of these two questions involves specific conceptions of behavior, or models of man. Any causal analysis depends on and is limited by these conceptions and models, and any shortcomings or inadequacies of the model will result in incorrect or inadequate analyses. In order to assure the adequacy and validity of the concepts and models used in the analysis of behavior, their components and interrelations should be unambiguously defined, their referents should be specifically stated, and competent independent observers should be able to assess the validity of the model and test the principles involved on the basis of objective, replicable procedures, against all available data.

If these criteria for the evaluation of concepts and models are not met, the incorrect concepts and inadequate models likely to arise will result in invalid answers to the questions of what the determinants of behavior are and what the relationship between the individual and the social environment is. Since planned social change, or any action designated to further economic development, is based, ultimately, on a model of human behavior, it is important that the model be valid so that policies to which it gives rise and actions based upon it have at least a chance of being successful. Any concerted action designed to further economic development, if based on an incorrect conception of human behavior and its determinants, cannot but result in failure.

There are, today, various models of man and the determinants of his behavior, since every psychological "school" gives rise to its own model of man, with its own set of characteristics, underlying postulates, and principles governing behavior. While there are many models, however, there are enough similarities so that they may be considered as falling into two major categories, provisionally labeled "psychodynamic" and "behavioral" approaches. Generally speaking, the psychodynamic models assign causal properties to various components of man's internal state, such as values and need dispositions, and it is this type of model which is commonly utilized in the analysis of the social prerequisites of economic development.[2] Unfortunately, it is difficult for these models to account for rapid changes occurring in a short span of time, for example, in Vicos, Peru,[3] and Pakistan,[4] since they usually assume that values and personalities change only very slowly, over the generations. The inability to handle all data, the questions which have been raised concerning the validity of many psychodynamic concepts and principles,[5] and the unresolved controversy surrounding the roles of social structures and personality in economic development, have necessitated the search for alternatives. One alternative, a model based on principles formulated in experimental psychology, will be presented in some detail; it is one of several utilizing the behavioral approach to the explanation of human activities.

A BEHAVIORAL MODEL

According to the behavioral model here presented, man's internal state is beyond the scope of presently available means of measurement and objective analysis, and knowledge of it is largely unnecessary for the explanation and prediction of behavior. The model is concerned, instead, with the overtly expressed activities of individuals and their relations to the previously and presently surrounding social structures and physical conditions.

An individual's behavior patterns are shaped (established by means of operant conditioning procedures involving the differential reinforcement of activities) after they have been performed. That is, not all possible but only certain activities judged desirable by a society or group are positively reinforced,

[2] For example, Eliezer B. Ayal, "Value Systems and Economic Development in Japan and Thailand," *Journal of Social Issues*, XXIX, No. 1 (January, 1963), pp. 35–51; Ralph Braibanti and Joseph J. Spengler, eds., *Tradition, Values, and Socio-Economic Development* (Durham: Duke University Press, 1961); Hagen, op. cit.; McClelland, op. cit.

[3] Richard N. Adams et al., *Social Change in Latin America Today* (New York: Harper, 1960), pp. 78–106.

[4] Gustav F. Papanek, "The Development of Entrepreneurship," *American Economic Review*, LII, No. 2 (May, 1962), pp. 46–58. The problem of the role of social and economic structures in economic development is discussed both by Papanek and by Hagen in comments following the article.

[5] For example John H. Kunkel, "Psychological Factors in the Analysis of Economic Development," *Journal of Social Issues*, XIX, No. 1 (January, 1963), pp. 68–87.

others are not, and still others may be punished. By positively reinforcing an activity after it has been performed the probability of repetition is increased, and if such reinforcement is frequent and intermittent the probability approaches certainty. The principles of operant conditioning, and the causal chains and principles which underly the determination of behavior, are based on experimental analyses carried out in laboratories, performed under carefully controlled conditions and subjected to replication and validation procedures involving objective, verifiable measurements. This approach to human behavior includes the following basic ideas:[6]

(1) Behavior (R) is maintained or weakened by a reinforcing (S^r) or aversive (S^a) stimulus which follows it. More accurately, the presentation of reinforcing stimuli (loosely speaking, rewards) increases the probability that a behavior pattern will be repeated, whereas the presentation of an aversive stimulus (loosely speaking, punishment) decreases the probability that the behavior pattern will be repeated in the future. These contingencies may be visualized in terms of the following diagram:[7]

	Reinforcing stimulus S^r	Aversive stimulus S^a
Presented	(positive) reinforcement	punishment
Withdrawn	punishment	(negative) reinforcement

(2) The absence of reinforcement or punishment (S^0) also decreases the probability that the activity will be repeated, and over time the extinction of behavior is the ultimate result.

(3) When a reinforcing stimulus is presented after an activity has been performed in a certain context (*e.g.*, telling a joke in a group of men), the

[6] The following summary of principles and procedures is based on Arthur J. Bachrach, ed., *Experimental Foundations of Clinical Psychology* (New York: Basic Books, 1962), esp. Ch. 6 by Murray Sidman, "Operant Techniques." The works of B. F. Skinner, *Cumulative Record* (New York: Appleton-Century-Crofts, 1959), and *Science and Human Behavior* (New York: Macmillan, 1953), have also been consulted.

[7] This diagram illustrates the various ways in which the presentation and withdrawal of positively reinforcing and aversive stimuli affect behavior. From James G. Holland and B. F. Skinner, *The Analysis of Behavior* (New York: McGraw-Hill, 1961), p. 245.

behavior will be emitted again in the same context, or a specific aspect of it, even without immediate reinforcement. Those characteristics of the context in whose presence a behavior pattern was reintroduced, called discriminative or controlling stimuli (S^D), eventually come to control the behavior under consideration; that is, the probability of their being followed by the behavior pattern increases. If another aspect of the context, when present, does not result in the reinforcement of an activity (*e.g.*, telling the same joke in mixed company), then the activity will not occur again in the presence of that aspect of the context (S^Δ). It should now be clear that the creation of discriminative stimuli depends on the reinforcing stimuli present, and thus a close association between S^r and S^D, and S^a or S^0 and S^Δ exists in all cases.

(4) The schedule of presentation of any S^r is important since the smoothness of behavior and its maintenance are dependent upon it. If positive reinforcement is continuous, behavior is easily maintained while the reinforcement lasts, but upon termination of rewards extinction proceeds very quickly. If positive reinforcement is intermittent or discontinuous, behavior will be equally well maintained, and after the termination of such reinforcement extinction will be quite slow. The shaping of behavior is usually best accomplished with an initially continuous schedule of reinforcement.

(5) Constant stimuli (SSc) form the larger context of any situation, beyond the discriminating stimuli, and usually do not affect behavior directly, although their alteration may result in changes in the behavior patterns under analysis.

(6) The effectiveness of any reinforcing stimulus for the shaping of behavior and its maintenance depends on the state variables (SV) which are an organism's characteristics of deprivation and satiation. They may be primary (*i.e.*, largely physiological) or secondary (*i.e.*, largely learned), such as, for example, the culturally determined emphasis on popularity.

(7) Behavioral elements are usually combined into patterns, *e.g.*, preparing a cup of coffee, and such patterns are usually parts of more complex chains in which one's own behavior or others' reactions come to be reinforcing and discriminative stimuli "tying together" large numbers of behavior patterns.

The social context of an individual, including his family, the various groups to which he belongs, and the society of which he is a part, plays an important part in the shaping and maintaining of his behavior. The normative structure of the immediate and wider social context determines:

(*a*) which behavior patterns of the thousands available to the individual will be followed by rewards, by punishment, or by no specific consequences—(R);

(*b*) the specific circumstances under which behavior patterns will be followed by rewards, by punishment, or by no specific consequences—(S^D and S^Δ);

(*c*) the nature of the reinforcers, including the amount, definition, and propriety—(S^r and S^a);

(*d*) the schedule of reinforcement;

(*e*) the state variables, especially the secondary—(SV).

FIGURE 8-1　A Behavioral Model of Man

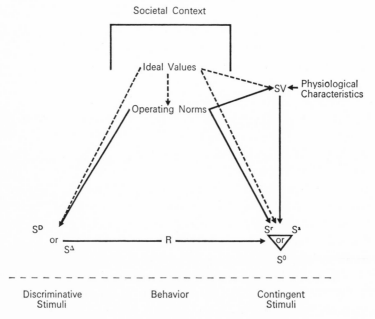

Glossary of Important Terms:
R　=any activity
S^r　=reinforcing stimulus (loosely speaking, rewards)
S^a　=aversive stimulus (loosely speaking, punishment)
S^0　=absence of any consequences
S^D　=stimulus in whose presence R has been reinforced
S^Δ　=stimulus in whose presence R has not been reinforced
SV　=state variables (i.e. conditions of deprivation and satiation)
Ideal Values=theoretical determinants of state variables, discriminative
　　　　　　and contingent stimuli
Operating Norms=actual determinants of state variables, discriminative
　　　　　　and contingent stimuli

The relationship between the individual and the societal context, together with the wider determinants of behavior, can now be stated in the form of the "behavioral model"[8] on p. 156.

From the foregoing the optimum societal characteristics for the efficient shaping of human behavior are apparent:

(1) Reinforcement should be consistent; that is, norms should be universally applicable and accepted within a society, with only a few known, accepted, and institutionalized exceptions (*e.g.*, Shamans).

(2) Positive and negative sanctions should be attached to all norms and should be enforced in such a way that the reinforcing stimuli can be immediately presented.

(3) Discriminative stimuli should be firmly established; that is, the normative structure of a society must cover all behavior under the various circumstances within the society's purview and be made up of elements which form a consistent, coherent system.

According to the behavioral model, the determinants of an individual's activities are to be found largely in the conditioning procedures—both deliberate and accidental—to which he has been subjected in the past, and in the sets of reinforcing and discriminative stimuli which have become part of his behavioral chains and are part of the present social context. The relationship between the social environment and the individual is reciprocal; the social context of an individual creates particular secondary deprivations, a particular reinforcement on a specific schedule, and the associated controlling stimuli which are the essential elements of the operant conditioning process. An individual manipulates the social context with his behavior, deprivations are reduced or noxious stimuli are eliminated or avoided, and new S^D's for further activities may thereby be established (chaining).

The result of these events and procedures is personality, considered as the totality of behavior patterns in the individual's repertoire, which he has acquired as a consequence of his often unique experiences and as a member of several groups and of his society. Personality, thus, does not determine behavior, but IS

---

[8] This model is based in part on the operant conditioning paradigm presented by I. Goldiamond in his chapter on "Perception" in Bachrach, op. cit., p. 295.

behavior.[9] There is no need to postulate attitudes, values, or needs in order to explain and predict behavior. These concepts are useful only in describing behavior since they turn out to be, upon close examination, shorthand terms for rather complicated behavior chains and probabilities of behavior which make up the daily life of man. This is not to say that the behavioral approach denies the existence of man's internal state or depreciates the human spirit—it simply does not make use of these concepts in the analysis of behavior because their ambiguities so far outweigh any advantages that their use cannot at present be justified.

APPLICATIONS OF THE BEHAVIORAL MODEL

In the literature on economic development which has grown up within the last decade, the explanations and determinants of human behavior have usually been assumed to be one or another characteristic—or set of elements—of an individual's internal state.[10] From this assumption it follows that if behavior is to be altered, the characteristics of the internal state must be changed first. A list of psychological prerequisites of economic development, for example, the propensity to save, rising expectations, and the motivation to work in factories, has been proposed, and the conclusion is drawn that only if the content of men's minds, their values and attitudes, are changed, can behavior patterns conducive to economic development—for example, risk-taking—come into being. This point of view is illustrated in Spengler's thesis that "the state of a people's politico-economic development, together with its rate and direction, depends largely upon what is in the minds of its members, and above all upon the content of the minds of its elites, which reflects in part, as do all civilizations, the conceptions men form of the universe."[11] In addition to psychological prerequisites there are assumed to be social prerequisites, characteristics of groups or nations which must exist if economic development is to occur, or which must

[9] This conception of personality is based on Robert W. Lundin, *Personality, An Experimental Approach* (New York: Macmillan, 1961). Similar ideas are found in J. Milton Yinger, "Research Implications of a Field View of Personality," *American Journal of Sociology*, LXVIII, No. 5 (March, 1963), pp. 580–592. For the application of a slightly different behavioral model of man to sociological analysis in general, see Franz Adler, "A Unit Concept for Sociology," *American Journal of Sociology*, LXV, No. 4 (January, 1960), pp. 356–364.

[10] See, for example, Ayal, op. cit.; Braibanti and Spengler, op. cit.; Hagen, op. cit.; and McClelland, op. cit.

[11] Braibanti and Spengler, op. cit., p. 4.

come into being along with industrialization. On the national level social prerequisites are usually considered in terms of political climate, social circumstances, or economic atmosphere.[12] Unfortunately, however, the social and psychological prerequisites of economic development are usually not well defined and are difficult to put into measurable terms. A more important problem is that no methods of changing values, attitudes, and personality are known at present, and thus the analysis of economic development in terms of social and psychological prerequisites never develops beyond the level of description and enumeration.

From the previous discussion it is apparent that concern with values, attitudes, and most other psychological prerequisites as causes of behavior rests on a fundamental misconception of human behavior and the disregard of basic psychological principles discovered in the experimental analysis of behavior. To change man's activities one need not concern oneself with altering values; one needs to change only certain elements of the operant conditioning context of which all men at all times are an integral part. According to the behavioral model, the psychological prerequisites of economic development are certain behavior patterns, whereas the social prerequisites are the determinants of the reinforcing and discriminative stimuli by means of which desired behavior patterns are shaped and maintained.

Individual and group values, attitudes, and personalities have been utilized in the analysis of economic development with little attention to the meaning of these concepts. Definitions of these terms, based on the behavioral model of man, will be presented as an alternative, and the utility of these conceptions will be evaluated in terms of four cases of economic development.

Values

Values have been variously defined as "goals which are objects of inclusive attitudes,"[13] "a conception, explicit or implicit, distinctive of an individual or characteristic of a group, of the desirable which influences the selection from available modes, means, and ends of action" (p. 395),[14] or "that aspect of

---

[12] For example, Clark Kerr et al., *Industrialism and Industrial Man* (Cambridge: Harvard University Press, 1960); Gerald M. Meier and Robert E. Baldwin, *Economic Development, Theory, History and Policy* (New York: John Wiley, 1957); Walt W. Rostow, *The Stages of Economic Growth* (Cambridge: Cambridge University Press, 1960).

[13] Theodore M. Newcomb, *Social Psychology* (New York: Dryden Press, 1950), p. 130.

[14] This and the following quotations are from Clyde Kluckhohn, "Values and Value-Orientations in the Theory of Action," in Talcott Parsons and Edward A. Shils, eds., *Toward A General Theory of Action* (Cambridge: Harvard University Press, 1951).

motivation which is referable to standards, personal or cultural, that do not arise solely out of immediate tensions or immediate situations" (p. 425). The term value "implies a code or standard . . . which organizes a system of action" (p. 430) which the individual has internalized, and which has thus become part of a person's internal state. A complex set of values forms a value orientation which has been defined as "a generalized and organized conception, influencing behavior, of nature, of man's place in it, of man's relation to man, and of the desirable and undesirable as they may relate to man-environment and inter-human relations" (p. 411). In studies not explicitly concerned with the elucidation of concepts, the definitions of value are usually more vague, such as the conception of a value system as "the syndrome of general rules, sanctions, and goals underlying the activities of a society."[15]

In everyday life the confusion of meanings may be overlooked, but in any serious attempt to explain and predict behavior a concept such as value presents severe limitations since it must be inferred from behavior. The inferences made, however, cannot be validated with presently available means, since there are no ways of defining or measuring values independent of inferences based on behavior. This makes possible the capricious use of reaction-formation, a procedure which may be used to support any theory by either taking phenomena at face value or considering them in terms of their opposites; as a consequence any theory can be supported by any data. Whether such inferred characteristics can be considered as causes of behavior, useful in the prediction of human activities, is quite doubtful.

A way of eliminating the difficulties encountered with the definition and measurement of values is based on the simple question of how one knows what a man's values are. Knowledge of a man's values is based either on observations of his activities or on his verbal statements that he values, for example, honesty. But what are the dimensions of the value of honesty? One may say that a man values honesty highly, and that this value he has internalized determines his behavior. But what are the referents for this statement? In reality one is saying something about certain activities and nothing else. When one speaks of a man's values, or when one infers his value orientation, one is in actuality only summarizing certain features of many of his activities in shorthand form. One is abstracting, from a great variety of behavior patterns, certain manifestations or elements called "honest" or "honesty" in a society. One is able to predict to some extent a man's behavior on the basis of his past activities in a particular situation, but one is not thereby saying anything about the causes of human behavior.

[15] Ayal, op. cit., p. 35.

According to the behavioral model, a man acts honestly if honesty leads to success, for example, in terms of reducing deprivations or avoiding noxious consequences. The causes of the behavior called honest, then, are to be found in the conditioning history of the individual, in the course of which he has learned that particular behavior patterns, namely, those defined by his society as honest, are usually rewarded, whereas their opposites usually are not. Along this line of reasoning Homans has defined value as "the degree of reinforcement and punishment [a person] gets from [behavior]."[16] A better conception of value, emphasizing the individual's experiences of the past and expectations of the future within the dynamic social context, would be the following:

(1) *From the point of view of the observer*—The probability that a particular behavior pattern will occur in an individual under certain circumstances. When we say, then, that honesty is a strongly held value, a well internalized value, or that it is deeply ingrained in an individual or a group, we mean simply that the probability of the occurrence of particular behavior patterns is great; conversely, if a value is lightly held, the probability of the occurrence of a behavior pattern is small.

(2) *From the point of view of the individual*—A value is the perceived set of probabilities that certain events will occur—rewards will be obtained—if certain activities are performed under specific circumstances. When a person, then, is said to value honesty, it means that he believes that behavior patterns regarded as honest by his society will be rewarded. These rewards may exist on earth or be conceived as being found only in heaven; if the latter, he may act "irrationally" from the point of view of others.

In either case the individual's values are based on previous experiences on the part of himself or of groups to which he belongs and include as integral parts his conceptions of the determinants of the operating reinforcing and discriminative stimuli. Values, then, are to be considered as summary expressions of an individual's or a group's conditioning history. From the point of view of society, values are the standards which ideally determine which behavior patterns will be rewarded, punished, or disregarded under specific circumstances. The problem that verbal standards are often different from those which are actually operating may be solved by calling the verbal standards the "values" of a society, and those standards which actually are operating the "norms" of a society; this usage will be followed throughout the paper.

[16] George C. Homans, *Social Behavior, Its Elementary Forms* (New York: Harcourt, Brace, and World, 1961), p. 40. Adler defines values in an even more strictly behavioral fashion; according to him, "for the purposes of sociological scientific discourse, values and actions may safely be treated as identical." Franz Adler, "The Value Concept in Sociology," *American Journal of Sociology*, LXII, No. 3 (November, 1956), pp. 272–279.

According to the behavioral model, then, the concept value as used in daily life and in much scientific discussion in the fields of anthropology and sociology has at least four distinct meanings:

(1) The probability that a behavior pattern will occur;

(2) The probability that a behavior pattern will be reinforced;

(3) The ideal standards of behavior verbally expressed in a society;

(4) The actual standards which in reality determine differential reinforcement.

Since it is usually not clear which meaning is used at any particular time, it is best to disregard all meanings except the third, and to consider the first two simply in terms of probability. The definitions of values quoted above are seen to contain many of the elements of the conception of value based on the behavioral model. The differences lie mainly in the strictness of the definition, the amount of necessary inferences, and the fact that values cannot be considered as causes of behavior. The term value orientation, for example, refers to nothing more than the often complicated set of probabilities that a system of behavior patterns and chains has been or will be reinforced, and thus will occur with great frequency under the proper conditions.

Attitudes

Allport has defined attitude as "a mental and neural state of readiness, organized through experience, exerting a directive or dynamic influence upon the individual's response to all objects and situations with which it is related."[17] Newcomb admits that the concept of attitude is nothing more than a theoretical device referring to "the state of readiness for motive arousal. It is the individual's susceptibility to stimulation capable of arousing the motive in him. . . . Attitudes thus represent persistent, general orientations of the individual toward his environment."[18]

Such conceptions of attitude present great difficulties to the student of economic development since "states of readiness" cannot be inferred with

[17] Quoted by Kluckhohn, op. cit., p. 423.
[18] Newcomb, op. cit., pp. 118–119.

certainty and depend, ultimately, on actual activities for validation. It is, furthermore, doubtful whether the determination of human behavior can be assigned to "theoretical devices."

The problem of what an attitude really is can again be approached best by asking what the referents of the term are. How do we know what a person's attitudes are? We learn by observing his behavior or by asking him directly, and we usually will not be content with his word but try to observe his actions. We say that a person has a particular attitude toward an object, person, event, or someone's actions, if he behaves in specified ways toward the object and if his behavior is consistent and persists over time. A "negative attitude" toward saving, for example, refers to certain elements of behavior which are common in his actions towards money, banks, and goods. Attitude, thus, is simply a shorthand term for certain abstracted characteristics common to a number of behavior patterns which are frequently repeated whenever certain conditions prevail.[19] Attitudes are to be considered as summary measures of behavior, a convenient labeling of actions, and not as causes of any activity. Once we know what the common elements of a large group of activities are, we can better predict the behavior of a person when his behavior pattern falls into the same group, or when he is exposed to the appropriate discriminative stimulus, but we can say nothing about the causes of his actions.

Personality

Another important term which appears in discussions of economic development is personality, conceived by Hagen as the "complex of qualities other than purely bodily ones which determine how an individual will behave in any given situation."[20] Newcomb defines this elusive term as "the individual's organization of predispositions to behavior. . . . That which 'holds together' all his motive patterns—that which determines that all his behavior, both attitudinal and expressive, shall be just what it is."[21] Thus personality is considered to be the totality of values, attitudes, needs, and motivations of an individual and is equivalent to the individual's internal state itself. The difficulty with the concept of personality lies in the fact that "personality is something that must be inferred from facts. Hence, in actual practice, the personality is an abstract formulation composed by the psychologist."[22]

[19] This conception is based in part on personal communications with I. Goldiamond.
[20] Hagen, op. cit., p. 99.
[21] Newcomb, op. cit., p. 344.
[22] Clyde Kluckhohn and Henry A. Murray, *Personality in Nature, Society, and Culture* (New York: Knopf, 1953), p. 6.

The definition of this concept can be made more specific by considering the referents of personality: how do we know what the personality of a man is? Again the answer is his behavior—only by looking at his activities can we know his personality. A "pleasant personality," for example, on close examination turns out to be no more than a set of behavior patterns which is similar to our own or which we judge to be pleasant on the basis of some standard. The problem of the referent of personality has been implicitly recognized by some writers, for example Parsons and Shils, who define personality as "the organized system of the orientation and motivation of action of an individual actor"[23] and then again as simply the "relatively ordered system of resultant actions in one actor."

In the behavioral model, personality is defined as the set of behavior patterns which an individual has acquired under the special circumstances of his development and as a member of his society and the several groups to which he belongs. Personality, then, is not inferred from behavior or considered to be a cause of it, but rather IS the sum of a man's activities which show some durability. Just as in the psychodynamic model the term personality includes all of a person's values and attitudes, so it includes, in the behavioral model, the behavior of individuals and the probabilities that various patterns of behavior will occur under specific circumstances. Changes in personality, then, do not refer to changes in the internal components of this entity, but rather to the altered behavior patterns themselves and the changed probabilities of their expression based on the altered reinforcement contingencies and circumstances of the social enrironment. The determinants of change, then, are not to be sought in alterations of a man's values or attitudes, but rather in the changes of the social context which determines the perceived and actual probabilities of reinforcement in terms of which the individual acts, *i.e.*, the reinforcing stimuli, their schedules, and the associated discriminative stimuli which are provided by a society and the various groups to which the individual at all times belongs.

An important component of personality formation is the process of internalization. The importance assigned to the process, however, has not resulted in a general understanding of it; as Kluckhohn says, "most acquired or derived drives are dependent upon group values which the individual has somehow interiorized as part of himself."[24] According to the behavioral model, the internalization or interiorization of values refers to the learning of various sets of probabilities that certain behavior under specific circumstances will be rewarded or punished. This is not to imply that the individual is necessarily able to

---

[23] This and the following quotations are from Parsons and Shils, op. cit., pp. 7 and 38.
[24] Kluckhohn, op. cit., p. 429.

explicitly state these probabilities or their determinants. Internalization, or the learning of probabilities and discriminative stimuli, is the result of communication and experience and depends upon the consistency of reinforcement, the number of occasions on which particular behavior patterns have been rewarded under specific circumstances, and on the reinforcement schedule in effect during the learning process.

Summary View of These Concepts

Values, attitudes, personality, and the process of internalization are terms whose major function in everyday life is to communicate probabilities and descriptions of behavior. The statement that someone has a pleasant personality, that his values of honesty have been well internalized, and that he never lets his attitude toward success interfere with these values, serves the major purpose of increasing the chance that an observer's predictions of his behavior will be accurate. Certainly we have a better idea of how a person will act than if we had no access to the statement. But although we can predict with some confidence how the person will act under certain circumstances, we cannot say *why* the person behaves in the particular way he does.

Concepts such as values are useful in the language of everyday life but cannot be considered as explanations of behavior since these terms have, as their ultimate referents, the present behavior of individuals and nothing else. In behavioral terms, any differences among these concepts are essentially differences in the abstractions made, in the point of view of the observer, and in the temporal context of the individual's activities. If one is interested in the description of behavior these concepts may be used, but if one is engaged in any causal analysis it is not necessary that these concepts be part of it or that they be considered as part of any causal nexus.

The contribution of the sociologist to the analysis of economic development involves the study of the interrelation and reciprocal influence of human behavior and the social context, the study of the structure of the social context, and the analysis of the changes in the social context which are necessary to create behavior patterns conducive to industrialization. Any sociological analysis will be inadequate as long as poorly defined concepts are given great weight as integral parts of causal chains when, in fact, these concepts refer to the "end products" of such chains. The essential characteristics of attitude, value, and personality may best be summarized in terms of the probability that a particular behavior pattern will occur, under certain conditions of deprivation and discrimination, based on the conditioning history of the individual. From the point of view of the individual, these concepts all include the perceived probability that a particular action, under certain conditions, will be reinforced by the social and physical environment. The specific task of the sociologist, then, includes the analysis of such sets of probabilities and of their origin and determinants and the study of ways to maintain or alter them.

The psychological and social prerequisites of economic development cannot be established by changing the values, attitudes, or personalities of people in underdeveloped countries, as has so often and so eloquently been argued in recent years. In fact, to say that values, attitudes, and personalities must be changed is to say nothing more than that changes in behavior patterns must occur. There is no disagreement on this point—but the question is: how can these changes be brought about? The belief that values, attitudes, and personality determine behavior, that behavior will change once attitudes or values are altered, and that one must consequently concentrate on the alteration of these, besides being meaningless, leads into blind alleys of theory and action. This is so because there is no generally recognized definition of these terms which includes elements other than behavior or inferences based upon it, since the components of these terms are often unclear (*e.g.*, state of readiness) and since there are no generally recognized procedures for altering what are said to be a person's values or personality.

The behavioral approach, emphasizing the shaping of behavior by means of differential reinforcement and punishment, opens a way not only to the testable explanation and prediction of behavior, but also to its alteration. The behavioral model of man leads to the conclusion that, if behavior is to be changed, changes must first occur in the reinforcing stimuli, in their presentation and schedule, and in the discriminative stimuli. This can be accomplished only through the alteration of those aspects of the social context which influence these components of the conditioning process. Changes in character, rather than being the prerequisite of economic development, are to be considered as concomitants and consequences, insofar as economic development means, for the average individual, changed reinforcers, changed schedules, and new behavior patterns, newly reinforced, under new circumstances. The problem of economic development, then, is not the alteration of character or certain elements of it, but the change of those selected aspects of a man's social environment which are relevant to the learning of new behavior. Analytical emphasis on the role of economic and industrial elites in underdeveloped countries rests on the fact that the necessary changes in the social environment would be difficult to produce for the population as a whole but are, in effect, produced by the social structure itself for a small number of persons.

The recent emphasis placed on the role of individuals in economic development has raised the question of the role of social structures in the process.[25] The efficacy of the "structural approach" to economic development is explicitly recognized by the behavioral model of man, in that a person's activities at any moment are not only the consequences of a long conditioning history, but are also influenced by the immediately surrounding social context which maintains or alters the probabilities of behavior patterns established in the past and is largely responsible for the shaping of new patterns. The behavioral model of man, then, reconciles the "individualistic" and the "structural" approaches to economic development by recognizing the effects on behavior of both the past and the present societal context.

The difficulties encountered when values, attitudes, and personalities are considered as causal factors, and the advantages of considering these concepts from the behavioral point of view, will now be represented.

EXAMPLES OF BEHAVIORAL ANALYSIS

Indian Values and Economic Development

The uncertainties which surround the meaning and measurement of value as a causal factor are well illustrated in the recent discussion concerning the role of Indian values in the process of industrialization. The question which faces the social scientist is: are Hindu values detrimental or conducive to India's economic development?

India's spiritualism, philosophy of renunciation, and asceticism, which especially in the eyes of Western observers present almost insurmountable obstacles to economic development, turn out to be quite different in reality than any deductions based on scriptures. As Singer points out, Indians in their everyday activities are as materialistically oriented as Western men; "this-worldly asceticism" is quite widespread; and the philosophy of renunciation is just that; a philosophy to which most men pay lip service, perhaps an ideal, but an ideal which attracts few practitioners in everyday life. In Singer's words, "the Indian

[25] Papanek, op. cit., emphasizes the importance of social and economic structures rather than personality change. Hagen, in discussing the article, points out that "new personality may not cause a conspicuous change in behavior until it has burst through external barriers. Where institutional change suddenly eliminates former barriers and creates new economic opportunities, a slow budding process may suddenly burst into bloom" (p. 60).

world view encompasses both material and spiritual values, and these can be found in the behavior of the ordinary Indian existing side by side and in functional interdependence. . . . Overspecialization on the spiritual, the sacred, and the life-denying [is] to be found [mainly] in the interpretations of some Western scholars."[26]

The backwardness and stagnation of India's economic system thus cannot be explained in terms of other-worldly religious values. As Singer and Srinivas point out, Indian peasants are eminently practical in their approach to the physical and social world. Why then the backwardness? Because of social and political institutions, such as the caste system, say Srinivas and Lambert. In fact, "it is possible that popular interpretations or misinterpretations of *maya*, *samsara*, and *karma* were the aftermath of defeat—rather than its cause."[27] Karve, too, mentions that it is "not necessary to go into the early economic and social history of industrially developed nations to show that the tempo of work is more often the reflection of opportunities of progress than a prime cause."[28] After all, Christianity, too, is quite other-worldly, and glorifies poverty and humility, but this does not mean that men's lives revolve around these poles. As Singer points out:

A society dominated by a philosophy of renunciation need not be a society of ascetics. In India, ascetics and holy men have never constituted more than a tiny fraction of the population. There have always been a sufficient number of householders willing and able to do the world's work. And while the ideals of asceticism may indirectly influence the general population, not all of these influences oppose social reform and economic development.[29]

The reasoning of many Western observers of India seems to be as follows: the sacred literature of India contains certain values which are internalized by the people who then act in accordance with these values, and thus India is economically stagnant, and there is little hope of economic growth. This reasoning is based on a number of inferences and assumptions which have not yet been supported by evidence obtained by replicable procedures based on objective

[26] Milton Singer, "Cultural Values in India's Economic Development," *The Annals*, CCCV (May, 1956), p. 83. See also Richard D. Lambert, "Social and Psychological Determinants of Savings and Investments in Developing Societies," in Bert F. Hoselitz and Wilbert E. Moore, eds., *Industrialization and Society* (Den Haag: UNESCO, 1963).

[27] M. N. Srinivas, "A Note on Mr. Goheen's Note," *Economic Development and Cultural Change*, VII, No. 1 (October, 1958), p. 6.

[28] D. G. Carve, "Comments," *Economic Development and Cultural Change*, VII, No. 1 (October, 1958), p. 7.

[29] Milton Singer, "Postscript," *Economic Development and Cultural Change*, VII, No. 1 (October, 1958), p. 11.

criteria of measurement. The major assumptions are that the sacred literature contains a particular set of values and no other; that this set is internalized by a majority of the population; that the values internalized by the Indians are precisely those which the Westerner "sees" in the sacred literature; that men's actions are a function of internalized values; and that the immediate circumstances in which the individual finds himself play a rather insignificant role in the determination of his behavior.

It is apparent from Singer's work, however, that the values "contained" in the Bhagavad-Gita, for example, are merely interpretations of words which men choose to make; Westerners interpret the work as "teaching" certain values, whereas Gandhi thought that quite different values were being "taught." The interesting question which remains is: what values *are* contained in the Bhagavad-Gita; and have we any means of discovering which values *are* taught?

The controversy centering on the suitability of Indian values for economic development leads to the conclusion that, as long as definitions of values are vague, as long as proof of their existence and criteria for their measurement are absent, and as long as it is impossible to determine with any certainty the role played by values in the determination of behavior, it is better to disregard the concept of value in the analysis of human behavior. This conclusion is justified not only by the difficulties encountered in the use of the concept, but also by the fact that the concept, as ordinarily conceived, is not necessary in the explanation and prediction of behavior. This point will be elaborated in the following sections.

The Argentine Value Orientation and Economic Development

In a recent work Fillol hypothesizes that "the basically passive, apathetic value-orientation profile of the Argentine society must be regarded as the *critical* factor limiting the possibilities of steady, long-run economic development" (p. 3).[30] From this it follows that "only a transformation of Argentina's value-orientation profile towards higher degrees of activity can insure that economic gains achieved during one period will not be wiped out in a following one by social and political dislocations" (p. 110).

The starting point of Fillol's analysis is that actions are determined by personality and the environment. Personality, in turn, is considered as consisting of value orientations and a need structure. These elements are interrelated, for "in the process of personality formation, needs which have been acquired help

[30] This and the following quotations are from Tomas R. Fillol, *Social Factors in Economic Development, The Argentine Case* (Cambridge: MIT Press, 1961).

to determine value orientations, and acquired value orientations help to determine needs" (p. 7). A society's basic personality type, which helps to determine the behavior of groups, is ascertained "by defining those dominant value orientations shared by the bulk of the society's members as a result of the early experiences which they have had in common" (p. 6).

Fillol's description of the Argentine value orientation is nothing more than a description of behavior and a listing of particular abstractions which are useful in tying together various disparate elements of action. These abstracted elements of descriptions of behavior (*e.g.*, suspiciousness) are assumed to be causal factors, but there is no indication that they are anything more than abstractions of current behavior. One of the basic conclusions of the study, that the Argentine "value orientation profile is inimical to the emergence of social relationships which would enable individuals to act concertedly in the pursuit of common goals" (p. 22), means nothing more than that the abstracted elements of a number of behavior patterns are incompatible with cooperation. Nothing has been said regarding causes, and to the extent to which causal qualities are assigned to simply descriptive abstractions, there is no way to break the vicious circle—or the circular argument—of cause and effect.

The insecure foundation of Fillol's argument is especially apparent in his discussion of needs. Need aggression, for example, is defined as "a characteristic of the individual's personality which makes [him] feel satisfaction from the act of being aggressive in thought or action, from attacking others and overcoming real or imaginary opposition forcefully" (p. 23). Such a need shows itself in various actions—*i.e.*, is inferred from behavior—and receives theoretical underpinning from psychodynamic theories which have yet to be validated. If the theories are not supported by behavioral data, reaction formation is assumed to have taken place—for no other reason than that the data do not fit the theory. An Argentinian's "apathy is actually a means of suppressing his need aggression, a cover for the anxiety and intense rage which must arise in a society built on authoritarian values" (p. 24). What objectively validated proof is there for the existence of a great variety of needs, the repression of some and the expression of others, and for the statement that anxiety and rage *must* be created in certain societies? If such necessity follows from a theory, and if such theory must be supported by the capriciously applied concept of reaction-formation, it is perhaps better to investigate alternative means of analysis.

The behavioral model of man permits a much simpler explanation of the Argentine data, based on principles validated by often repeated experiments under controlled conditions. There is no necessity to refer to explanatory fictions such as need structures and value orientations or basic personality types. Fillol himself acknowledges repeatedly that an individual's previous experiences are of great importance. Early experiences result in value orientations, some needs are culturally transmitted, and thus personality (a combination of the two) is also the result of the socialization process.

Value orientations and needs are unnecessary and cumbersome abstractions of behavior which may be made but play no role in explaining behavior since they *are* aspects of behavior. Men learn to be suspicious, to be fatalistic (that is, to behave in ways defined as fatalistic), or to concern themselves only with the present, just as they learn to behave in opposite fashion. It all depends on what behavior patterns are reinforced and on what chains are slowly established over the years. There is, then, no need to postulate an intervening variable (such as value orientation) which explains nothing and only clutters up the analysis. Fillol's and especially Hagen's elaborate analysis of why people do not engage in manual labor rests, for example, on status and self-conceptions, feelings of superiority, and justification of individual worth.[31] According to the behavioral model, manual labor is not engaged in because it is followed by aversive reinforcers, for example derision, and because in the past the peasant who worked hard often lost the fruits of his labor. It would follow that, if the circumstances of work were altered, manual labor would occur more frequently; as we shall see, this is precisely what happens.

The fact that the concepts used by Fillol in his analysis of the Argentine problem are useless not only in the explanation of behavior but also in the manipulation of it—as in deliberately altering work habits—is illustrated in the discussion of how to change the behavior of individuals. Fillol's suggestions for the solution of Argentina's problem are essentially concerned with changes in the presently operating reinforcers and controlling stimuli.[32] New incentives for both workers and managers, worker participation in management, explanations of decisions to those affected by them, the encouragement of cooperation, and the hands-off attitude of government are all aspects of attempts to shape new behavior patterns through a new system of differential reinforcement. Fillol's theoretical foundation for proposing the above changes—that parental rage will no longer be directed against children, and that therefore children will be less authoritarian and will thus bring about, in two or three generations, value orientations in harmony with economic development—is irrelevant and is based, in any case, on incorrect conceptions of man and the determinants of his activities. At the very least, the relationship between managerial policy changes and alterations in needs and value orientations is not spelled out, and the process

---

[31] Fillol, op. cit., pp. 16–17; Hagen, op. cit., pp. 76–81.
[32] Fillol, op. cit., Ch. 6.

of the formation of values is not clear at all. It seems, indeed, that Fillol, in the last section of his work, pays verbal tribute to his earlier concepts but disregards them in his concrete descriptions of possible solutions—which is the logical fate of explanatory fiction in the face of reality. The behavioral analysis of the Argentine situation would have arrived at the same specific recommendations for the amelioration of the problem—the changing of behavior patterns—as did Fillol; the behavioral alternative would have been simpler, based on validated principles and relying on a minimum of inferences.

Values and Change in the Peruvian Andes

In 1952 the Indian community of Vicos was in a highly disorganized state, "positions of responsibility in public affairs were lacking, . . . adequate leadership did not develop, and almost no public services were maintained" (p. 80).[33] In addition, "cooperation within the community was the exception rather than the rule, and resistance to the outside world was high. Attitudes toward life were static and pessimistic" (p. 81), and the tenor of life had not changed much since the arrival of the Spaniards three hundred years earlier. Agriculture was based on the motto "plant and pray," and Indian peasants usually worked slowly and produced little more than the barest minimum of basic necessities.

In order to change this situation, the determinants of behavior have to be ascertained, and alterations in them would be the first step in any project of change. Instead of altering the personality and attitudes of the Indians, however, Holmberg and his associates (there never were more than two advisors on the hacienda) began a broad and integrated approach to the problem of development, involving economics and technology, nutrition and health, education and social organization.

Holmberg did not assume that behavior is determined by childhood experiences converted into a largely unchangeable personality and value orientation which can be altered only over the generations. Rather than involve himself in the manipulation of the internal state of the Indians, for example, their values, he analyzed the contemporary circumstances of Vicos life and proceeded to change these. Up to 1952 the fate of the Indian had depended almost completely on the whims of the patron, who made all decisions and left Indian officials with only religious tasks to perform. If the context of the Indian's existence could be changed—if the reinforcement contingencies could be altered—behavior would

---

[33] This and the following quotations are from Allan R. Holmberg, "Changing Community Attitudes and Values in Peru," in Richard N. Adams et al., *Social Change in Latin America Today* (New York: Harper, 1960).

be altered too. Holmberg and his associates assumed that "in the area of economic activity positive steps could be and were taken, for the desire to improve the community's livelihood existed, at least in a dormant state" (p. 84). The reason for this desire being dormant was to be found in the labor setup of the hacienda, for the Indian "is not willing to labor long and well under all conditions. In most instances he will do so only when he is working for himself or within his own culture. When working outside this framework, under conditions in which he is held in disrespect and generally receives little in the way of reward, he usually tries to get by with as little effort as he can" (p. 85). Furthermore, it was assumed that help given by outsiders should not involve unilateral activities— the villagers themselves should be involved in all projects; a "welfare approach [would not] lead to a solid type of environment, rooted in the desires and responsibilities of the community itself" (p. 85).

In terms of concrete action, the worst abuses of the hacienda system, for example, unpaid maid service to the patron, were eliminated easily. Work for the patron began to be paid for. New agricultural methods and fertilizer were introduced, through a system of loans to Indians, and peasants were allowed to keep what they produced. Power was gradually transferred to the Indian leaders of the community; weekly meetings were held, decisions were discussed, and gradually more and more important responsibilities were given to Indians —to make decisions, carry them out, and be responsible for the success and failure of Indian activities. Education, which had not before been a goal, became one when the quality of teachers improved, when children were no longer used for maid and gardening service, and when a school lunch program was instituted. Later on, the ability to read and the knowledge of the outside world gained through education became sufficient reinforcers in themselves to make the school program a success.

The results of the Vicos project are indicated by the transfer of the hacienda to the Indian community in 1957, when the Indians gained complete control over the workings of the hacienda. Holmberg's conclusions are significant in their optimism based on experience: "The process of modernization within this long-isolated population can take place without the loss of certain fundamental and positive values that are deeply ingrained in Indian society: respect for work, frugality, and cooperation. . . . If granted respect, the Indian will give respect. If allowed to share in the making of decisions, he will take responsibility and pride in making and carrying them out. The fundamental problem of the sierra is largely a problem in human relations" (p. 97).

The success of the Cornell–Peru project was due not to the alteration of Indian behavior (*e.g.*, working hard) by means of a prior change in attitudes or values, but rather to changes in the reinforcing stimuli (*e.g.*, the ending of exploitation and the instituting of wage labor), thus altering the behavior preceding them. Holmberg's model of human behavior was, implicitly, the behavioral one and not the psychodynamic model, for he set about changing the environment of Indian life. Although he used such terms as dormant desires for improving one's livelihood, ingrained values of work, or values regarding education, he operated on the basis of an essentially behavioral frame of reference. This is especially notable in his discussion of education, which is almost a model of planned change based on the behavioral approach. As soon as educational experiences were no longer aversive (*e.g.*, poor teachers who used students as servants), more students came and learned more, and when reinforcing stimuli were added (*e.g.*, the school lunch program), the educational process became a fully accepted value within the community, based partly, of course, on the success of students in the intellectual and vocational subjects taught. Values, then, seem to be easily created in the right circumstances—which follows logically from the behavioral model of man. The "problem of human relations" in the sierra consists, essentially, of the aversive reinforcers provided by the mestizo and white social environment. As long as Indian initiative and labor are not rewarded, and as long as the Indian's attempts to better his position are followed by punishment (confiscation and derision), the problem of the sierra as described by Holmberg and others will remain.

The experience of Vicos does not fit readily into the internalist model of behavior. Were men's actions determined by personalities and values, largely created during youth, any changes in a community would be slow in coming about since changes in values and personality, especially in adults, are considered to take a long time if they can be produced at all. The fact that fundamental changes in the activities of the people of Vicos occurred in a five-year period— changes so radical that the Indians within five years were able to efficiently operate the hacienda by themselves, creating a surplus where for decades little more than basic necessities had been produced—shows either that internal states are unimportant in determining the behavior of man, or that these internal states can be easily and swiftly manipulated by alterations in the social environment. The behavioral approach, which holds that human activities are largely the result of operant conditioning procedures which are intimately tied to the social environment, finds support in the success of the Vicos project, whereas the project confronts the psychodynamic position with important questions which can be answered only by proposing fundamental changes in the conception of internal states and their relation to behavior.

Achievement Motivation and Economic Development

McClelland and his associates have investigated the hypothesis that one aspect of man's internal state, the need for achievement, is largely responsible for economic development. "A society with a generally high level of n-Achievement will produce more energetic entrepreneurs who, in turn, produce more rapid economic development" (p. 205).[34] Need for achievement is one of a constellation of needs which characterizes man and determines much of human behavior and is created largely during childhood. The sources of high need achievement are "early mastery training . . . provided it does not reflect generalized restrictiveness, authoritarianism, or rejection by parents" (p. 345), and the " 'amplitude of affective change' associated with the achievement situation" (p. 352). Mothers who are more actively involved in what their sons are doing are also likely to create high n-Achievement in them. The best environment for high n-Achievement consists of "reasonably high standards of excellence imposed at a time when the son can attain them, a willingness to let him attain them without interference, and real emotional pleasure in his achievements short of overprotection and indulgence" (p. 356). Conversely, "one of the ways in which the child can develop low n-Achievement is through having careless or indulgent parents who do not expect great things from him" (p. 351). The same effect is produced if achievement is expected too early, so that the child is not physiologically able to be successful.

The evidence for the existence of the achievement motive is the verbal, artistic, or active behavior of children and adults and the literature of nations. Children who build high towers, students in whose stories based on TAT pictures there is much "achievement imagery," and the "achievement imagery" found in plays, novels, and grammar school readers of ancient and modern nations are all considered to be reflections of need for achievement. McClelland's data support the hypothesis, for economic development (variously defined depending on the information available) usually follows those periods of history in which the need achievement of a nation is found to be high.

Two questions regarding need achievement must be asked. How valid are the inferences made, and what evidence—not based on inferences—exists for such an aspect of man's internal state? From McClelland's work it appears that there is no way to check on the validity of inferences except through other inferences; the high reliability of the scorers of stories, and the great consistency which various observers show in determining the degree of n-Achievement in various phenomena, simply indicate that observers, once trained, make the same

[34] This and the following quotations are from McClelland, op. cit.

inferences or, more accurately, are able to categorize stories, pieces of art, etc., with high consistency. This, however, does not validate the instrument and does not prove that n-Achievement exists. Need for achievement, it is apparent, is a theoretical construct, a characteristic common in the verbal and actual behavior of many individuals and groups. It is a hypothetical causal factor which is, in reality, nothing more than an abstraction of concrete behavior.

The behavioral analysis of McClelland's data leads to the following conclusions, based on the behavioral model of man and involving no characteristics of a postulated internal state.

Need for achievement is an abstracted characteristic common to various types of behavior, indicating achievement direction or striving for success. Like other activities, striving behavior, as the common element may be called, is shaped by means of differential reinforcement. The characteristics of child-rearing methods which create high need-achievement sons are equivalent to the positive reinforcement of striving behavior. Parental standards which are high, and the "amplitude of affective change," indicate that only certain behavior patterns—those which come up to the parental standards—are rewarded, through hugging and kissing, for example, while others are not. Conversely, careless parents who expect little of their children do not reward their children consistently for being successful, in part because there is no parental standard or definition of success. Indulgent parents, who reward a child often, even when he does not do well or come up to parental expectations, do not by their actions shape striving behavior. Finally, if too much is expected of children too early, the continual failure of their efforts results in aversive stimuli, e.g., failure, being associated with attempts at achievement so that striving behavior is effectively punished or at least not followed by rewards to such an extent that striving behavior is either never shaped or soon extinguished.

If striving is consistently rewarded, then those conditions under which it was rewarded, if present again, will in all probability be followed by the previously rewarded striving behavior. If a large variety of such behavior patterns is reinforced, a large response class is created, which will result in striving behavior being exhibited whenever the appropriate stimuli can be created by parents and other aspects of the social environment, resulting in a large stimulus class, including such initially neutral stimuli as TAT tests. It should be noted here that "striving behavior" is an abstracted element of many different behavior patterns and does not refer to a complete chain, e.g., the writing of a story as such. It refers, rather, to those elements of behavior which, if present, make it highly probable that the end result of the chain will be a particular state of the environment (in relation to the individual) defined by the society as success or achievement. The shaping of striving behavior is difficult and complicated since only certain specific aspects and not all elements of a pattern or chain are reinforced. To the extent to which striving behavior is rewarded, discriminative stimuli are established which control future striving. These discriminative stimuli, again simply certain aspects of particular circumstances and characteristics of the environment, are not to be considered as being inherent in any situation. They are, rather, elements which the individual considers to be associated with a high probability of reinforcement of certain behavior patterns, based on his previous experiences in similar situations.

If striving behavior is not reinforced, especially by one's parents, no corresponding discriminative stimuli are created, and thus no "signals" are established in the environment to indicate high probability of reinforcement if particular behavior patterns are exhibited. Thus, when striving potential exists for some people in a particular characteristic of the social and physical environment, this need not be true for all. The striving potential of a situation is a product of the conditioning history of the individuals who come into contact with the situation and are aware of it. In the case of Vicos, for example, one would hypothesize, in McClelland's terms, low n-Achievement before Holmberg arrived on the scene, and high n-Achievement afterwards, the changes being due to the rewarding of success in agriculture, education, etc.

McClelland's data, then, can be easily explained in behavioral terms without the use of assumptions concerning man's internal state, such as the existence and creation of needs. If it is true that striving behavior, like any other, is shaped through differential reinforcement, there is no reason why an internal state, characterized in part by a constellation of needs, should have to be postulated as an essential element in the analysis of economic development.

IMPLICATIONS OF THE BEHAVIORAL MODEL

According to the behavioral model of man, the characteristics of a person's internal state have no place in the study of psychological prerequisites of economic development. Instead, concern with the behavioral prerequisites themselves and their shaping and maintenance is required, and this includes, as an integral part of any analysis, the study of the structure of the social system which plays a major role in the shaping process.

Among the behavioral prerequisites of economic development are the saving of money, the investment of savings, risk-taking, economic innovation, the ability to wait for returns on investments, abandoning the land, selling one's labor, working in factories, buying food products, hiring people on the basis of competence rather than affinity, etc. All of these are requirements involving individuals, whose counterpart on the societal level are rationality, functional specificity, a stable government, etc.[35] According to the behavioral model, such societal characteristics are to be considered as the context within which the shaping process occurs and in terms of which behavior patterns are created and maintained. The behavioral model, then, while it reduces the importance of some psychological (i.e., internal) characteristics as determinants of behavior, emphasizes the role of societal characteristics; it places the analysis of societal prerequisites of economic development within the framework of psychological processes and principles which operate in the creation and maintenance of behavior. In the interest of clarity, then, it would be best to either consider the "psychological prerequisites" of economic development in terms of behavior, or to speak simply of "behavioral prerequisites," since the analysis of industrialization centers not around man's internal state but rather around his behavior and its determinants.

As long as man's activities are considered to be a function of values or personality, little attention need be directed to the immediately surrounding social environment, since it is not so much the present social structure as that of the past which is most involved in the formation of values and personality. The delineation of societal prerequisites of economic development, according to this view, can accomplish no more than prepare the ground for industrialization years, if not decades, in the future. However, as soon as behavior is considered to be a function largely of the surrounding social structure, both past *and* present, which affects behavior through the continuously operating determination of reinforcing and discriminative stimuli, the present social system takes on great importance. The behavioral prerequisites of economic development can be created only through alterations in the social structure, or certain elements of it, viewed broadly and including the economic system of a society.

Because of the interrelation of behavior chains, stimulus generalization, and the existence of generalized reinforcers such as money, it is unlikely that one behavior pattern can be shaped or changed without affecting other components of an individual's repertoire. In general, it may be expected that a considerable number of interrelated chains must be taken into consideration when the shaping

[35] For a discussion of societal prerequisites of economic development, see Bert F. Hoselitz, *Sociological Aspects of Economic Growth* (Glencoe: Free Press, 1960), esp. Ch. 3; and Marion J. Levy, Jr., *The Structure of Society* (Princeton: Princeton University Press, 1952), esp. Ch. 4.

of even a small number of new behavior patterns is contemplated. In order to establish the behavioral prerequisites of economic development, therefore, much of a man's life is subjected to alterations. An illustration of this point is seen in Holmberg's attempt to change the conditions of the Vicos Indians; only a "total approach" had a chance of bringing about the desired changes.

A scheme of steps and procedures which might be drawn up on the basis of operant principles cannot be considered as a guaranteed method of instituting change, however, since much of the context of a community, or the structure of a society, is usually beyond the control of action-oriented anthropologists. The smaller the planner's control over the relevant aspects of the social environment (*e.g.*, various reinforcers), the greater the difficulty of shaping new behavior patterns, the longer it will take, and the greater the chance of failure. The behavioral model of man, then, may be considered not only as a tool for the alteration of behavior, but also as part of the explanation of communities' resistance to change.[36]

The analysis of economic development, within the framework of the behavioral and societal prerequisites outlined above, does not lead to the pessimistic conclusions which are apparent in many studies concerned with the psychological requirements of the process of industrialization. There is no need to wait for a number of generations for the creation of new values and personalities. Alterations in the societal environment, sometimes even minute elements of it, constitute the first step in planned action, behavioral changes will follow, and both will be reflected in changes in man's internal state as conceived and measured by today's clinical psychologists.

There is no foundation, on theoretical grounds, for the pessimistic outlook concerning the capacity of underdeveloped countries to industrialize in a short period of time. Pessimistic conclusions regarding the time necessary for the preparation of the right psychological conditions for economic development are based, essentially, on an incorrect conception of man and on the disregard of principles of behavior formation and maintenance derived from experimental psychology. This is not to imply that the tasks ahead will be easy. But whereas the alteration of man's internal state presents insuperable obstacles and is,

---

[36] A good example of many which have appeared in anthropological literature is found in William R. Bascom and Melville J. Herskovits, *Continuity and Change in African Cultures* (Chicago: University of Chicago Press, 1959). The British were unsuccessful in their attempts to introduce economic and social changes into the Pakot tribe, for example, because they had no effective control over any of the important reinforcers. The problems discussed in Edward H. Spicer, ed., *Human Problems in Technological Change* (New York: Russell Sage Foundation, 1952), also provide illustrations of the necessity of having control over reinforcers in order to bring about lasting change.

essentially, beyond the reach of man's present knowledge and power, various selected elements of the societal environment are amenable to change today, thereby making possible the shaping of behavior patterns necessary for economic development. Such procedures involve difficulties, but these are due in large part to the small amount of control which can presently be exerted over the relevant aspects of the societal environment. Since usually only a few aspects of the societal environment can be altered, present efforts to create behavioral prerequisites must begin on a small scale. This is no easy task, but it is a possible one.

PART

II

9

n ACHIEVEMENT AND ECONOMIC GROWTH:
A CRITICAL APPRAISAL

Sayre P. Schatz

DAVID C. McCLELLAND has developed an eye-catching theory of economic growth centering around the concept of n Achievement (the need for achievement). n Achievement is a specific type of motivation involving "a strong 'inner concern' with achievement."[1] Persons with high n Achievement have a particularly strong drive to do well in situations in which the individual expects to be evaluated in terms of standards of excellence.

Simply stated, McClelland's hypothesis is "that a society with a generally high level of n Achievement will produce more energetic entrepreneurs who, in turn, produce more rapid economic development."[2] This theory has aroused respectful interest among economists. Reviewers greeted it as a remarkable and significant piece of work even when they had serious reservations.[3]

Reprinted by permission of the author and the publisher from Quarterly Journal of Economics (May, 1965), pp. 234-241.

[1] David C. McClelland, *The Achieving Society* (Princeton, N.J.: Van Nostrand, 1961), p. 43.

[2] Ibid., p. 205.

[3] George Katona calls the book a "solid achievement." He believes that "the manifold data presented must be viewed as strongly supporting his major hypothesis," and states: "Future studies of economic development cannot disregard what has been presented by McClelland." *American Economic Review*, LII (June, 1962), pp. 582–583. Walter A. Weiss-

Benjamin Higgins devoted seven pages of his general book on development to an unhurried exposition of McClelland's theory.[4] Those associated with *Economic Development and Cultural Change* have evidently been impressed, viz., the favorable opinion of the acting editor (Hoselitz) mentioned below, the twelve-page review article by Eisenstadt mentioned in footnote 3 here, and articles maintaining that English economic growth during the sixteenth to eighteenth centuries and Spanish economic growth during the fourteenth to eighteenth centuries resulted from prior increases in the average level of *n* Achievement.[5] Others working near the boundaries of the traditional disciplines have also been impressed.[6]

A number of economists, and others, have felt that McClelland's theory calls for a re-orientation of our thinking about economic development. Hoselitz tends to accept McClelland's basic thesis[7] and to move on to the questions, what forces in society tend to bring about a greater frequency of high *n* Achievement and what policies can be employed to stimulate these forces. Thomas C. Cochran argues that entrepreneurship and economic growth depend to a substantial degree on personality and cultural factors and, citing McClelland, he says that patterns of child-rearing, education, and family life largely determine the cultural and the personality patterns "favorable or unfavorable to entre-

---

kopf, though critical, felt that the book was a "magnificent attempt" involving an "awe-inspiring amount of effort, research, collaboration . . . data-gathering, experimental, and statistical techniques . . ." *Journal of Political Economy*, LXX (June, 1962), p. 311. S. N. Eisenstadt concluded that the book was a "very stimulating and important work which anybody interested . . . in the . . . problem of economic development cannot ignore." S. N. Eisenstadt, "Need for Achievement," *Economic Development and Cultural Change*, XI (July, 1963), p. 431.

[4] Benjamin Higgins, *Economic Development: Principles, Problems, and Policies* (New York: Norton, 1959).

[5] Norman N. Bradburn and David E. Berlew, "Need for Achievement and English Industrial Growth," *Economic Development and Cultural Change*, X (October, 1961), pp. 8–20, and Juan B. Cortés, S.J., "The Achievement Motive in the Spanish Economy Between the 13th and 18th Centuries," *Economic Development and Cultural Change*, IX (January, 1961), pp. 144–163.

[6] "This is an amazing book. It is so broad in scope, so ambitious in objective, so ingenious in technique and so full of correlations and tests of significance that few will escape a feeling of awe as they set out to read it." Charles J. Erasmus, review in *American Anthropologist*, Vol. 64 (June, 1962), p. 622. See also Thomas W. Shea, Jr., "Barriers to Economic Development in Traditional Societies: Malabar, A Case Study," *Journal of Economic History*, XIX (December, 1959), pp. 506–507.

[7] He believes that the book "makes such a strong case" for the central hypothesis that "few will be able to deny the power of McClelland's case and none will be able to adduce convincing evidence to refute the assertion that *n* Achievement is one of the principal factors in economic growth." Bert F. Hoselitz, review in *The American Journal of Sociology*, LXVIII (July, 1962), p. 130.

preneurship and economic growth."[8] M. Brewster Smith discusses "the effect of an American study sojourn . . . on arousing in foreign students higher levels of the achievement motivation that David McClelland holds to be the central ingredient of the entrepreneurial spirit and an important precondition of economic growth."[9] John Powelson, advising on American aid programs, states that capital, technical assistance and education are not enough. "There is still a missing element, or elements, related to what . . . David McClelland has dubbed '*n*-ach' or 'need for achievement'." He finds McClelland "sufficiently convincing to have an impact on United States educational assistance" and believes that instances in which education in developing economies failed to accomplish much may be due to lack of *n* Achievement.[10]

In this critical piece, I will assume that McClelland's measures of *n* Achievement are valid and reliable.[11] I will not consider any of the criticisms that the psychologist might make; I will make only the criticisms of the economist. As a matter of fact I will examine only one—although the central—aspect of his economic analysis: his purported relationship between *n* Achievement and economic growth. In general terms, it is my belief that McClelland, like many other scholars, has become so attached to his own hypothesis that he has unconsciously selected and used data in a way designed to *support* rather than *test* his theory. A straightforward analysis of his own data does not support his hypothesis.

I will make five specific criticisms of McClelland's hypothesis regarding the relationship between *n* Achievement and economic growth.

(1) The first concerns the data he has chosen to emphasize. Although it is axiomatic among economists that the growth of national product is the best index of economic growth, McClelland finds reasons for rejecting national

---

[8] Thomas C. Cochran, "Cultural Factors in Economic Growth," *Journal of Economic History*, XX (December, 1960), p. 519.

[9] In Don C. Piper and Taylor Cole (eds.), *Post-primary Education and Political and Economic Development* (Durham, N. C., Duke University Press, 1964), pp. 68–69.

[10] John P. Powelson, "Educational Assistance, Economic Development, and United States Foreign Policy" (pp. 128–152), in Piper and Cole, op. cit., pp. 140–144. In the sentence quoted, Powelson links McClelland with E. E. Hagen.

[11] *n* Achievement is ideally measured by the frequency of occurrence of achievement-related ideas, *i.e.*, thoughts and fantasies which in some way reflect a concern with achievement. McClelland attempts to get at this in a wide variety of ways, ranging from careful psychological tests ("a simple count of the number of such achievement-related ideas in stories written under normal testing conditions" (p. 43), to quantifying the degree to which designs on ancient Greek vases approximated certain ways of "doodling" that were characteristic of subjects with high *n* Achievement (pp. 124–125). At a national level, he measures *n* Achievement primarily by the frequency of achievement-related ideas in school books used by second to fourth grade children (pp. 70 ff.).

product in favor of the generation of electricity.[12] While electrical output is sometimes used as one indicator of growth, it may not be coincidental that McClelland's data show that *n* Achievement has a much higher correlation with the growth of kilowatt hours (.53) than with the growth of national product (.25). Particularly in view of the fact that in an earlier essay McClelland accepted income as the best measure of economic growth,[13] one may be permitted to suspect that his choice might have been different if the correlations were reversed.

In like fashion, McClelland explicitly points out that "78 per cent of the countries above the mean in *n* Achievement in 1925 were 'over-achievers' [*i.e.*, had a high rate of growth during the next 25 years] so far as electrical output is concerned, as compared with only 25 per cent below the mean in *n* Achievement . . ."[14] He neglects however, to mention the fact[15] that only 44 per cent of the countries above the mean in *n* Achievement in 1925 were "over-achievers" so far as *national product* was concerned during the subsequent twenty-five years, while 57 per cent of the countries with lower than average *n* Achievement showed high national product growth. These latter figures suggest, if anything, that high *n* Achievement tends to cause a lower rate of economic growth!

TABLE 9-1

Comparison of *n* Achievement in 1952 and Growth of National Income, 1925–1950, 22 Countries

n *Achievement level*	*High Growth*	*Low Growth*
Above mean	44%	56%
Below mean	57%	43%

(2) The second criticism concerns the way McClelland has worked with his data. When one examines even the electrical output data in a fairly straightforward way, the results are not convincing. Whether dealing with national product or electric power, he employs an unusual method of measuring growth. He has rejected the use of percentage increases as a measure. However, the reason he gives for doing so—that "the lower the initial level, the more likely it is that the percentage increase will be larger"[16]—is simply not applicable. The

---

[12] McClelland, op. cit., pp. 82–85.

[13] "The best measure of the economic prosperity of a country is probably something like income per capita . . . ." "The Use of Measures of Human Motivation in the Study of Society" in John W. Atkinson (ed.), *Motives in Fantasy, Action, and Society* (Princeton, N.J.: Van Nostrand, 1958), p. 534.

[14] McClelland, op. cit., p. 93.

[15] Calculated by this writer from McClelland's data, ibid. p. 90.

[16] Ibid., p. 88.

fact is that poor countries have generally shown *lower* percentage rates of growth rather than higher ones. Furthermore, in justifying this rejection, McClelland presents the startling thesis that percentage rates of growth of national product are not significant "because the denominators are all expressed in terms of local currencies . . . one cannot help wondering how much of the fact that Japan has twice as high a rate of growth as France is due to the fact that Japanese income is expressed in yen, and French income in much more numerous francs."[17] Presumably, then, if we express British gross national product in shillings instead of pounds or American output in cents instead of dollars, this would lower the percentage rates of growth of GNP.

Instead, McClelland uses as his index of economic growth variations around a regression equation relating *n* Achievement to national product or to electric power. If actual growth is greater than that indicated by the regression equation, this is interpreted as a high rate of growth, and vice versa.[18] This works out in such a way, *e.g.*, that if Bulgaria's national product grew more than 37.5 per cent during the 1925–50 period, McClelland would call this a high rate of growth while if the United States' national product grew less than 45.0 per cent, he would consider it a low rate of growth.

If we use percentage increases as a measure of growth, and if we again assess the significance of *n* Achievement by relating above average *n* Achievement to above average growth, the electric power data do not provide adequate support for McClelland's thesis.

Table 9–2 lists the twenty-two countries for which McClelland has 1925 or 1929 and 1950 figures for both *n* Achievement and electric power output. It shows McClelland's figures for *n* Achievement and the percentage increases, calculated from McClelland's data, in electricity output.

We find (Table 9–3) that of the nine countries having above average *n* Achievement in 1925, five (56 per cent) had higher than average rates of growth while four (44 per cent) had below average rates of growth.[19] Five (39 per cent) of the countries having below average *n* Achievement had high rates of growth, while eight (61 per cent) had slower than average rates of

[17] Ibid., p. 88.

[18] The regression equations are, for national income, predicted gain = .484 initial level − 13.8, and for electricity output, predicted gain = 1.01 initial level + 147.

[19] Those with above average rates of growth were Sweden, Britain, Australia, Ireland and Denmark; those with below average growth rates were United States, Canada, Austria and Argentina. The average rate of growth of electricity output is represented by the unweighted mean of the percentage increases for each country; thus each country is given equal weight. This is parallel to McClelland's method of calculating mean *n* Achievement. The final results of Tables 9–3 and 9–4 would not be much different, however, if a weighted mean of the increases in electricity output were used.

growth.[20] Thus, even when electrical output figures are used McClelland's case is not convincing.

(3) A crucial facet of McClelland's theory is that n Achievement and economic growth are not merely related but that n Achievement is causal; high n Achievement comes first and causes subsequent rapid economic growth.

TABLE 9-2

n Achievement and Electricity Output 22 Countries

Countries	n Achievement in 1925	n Achievement in 1950	Percentage Increase in Electricity Output, 1929 to 1950
Sweden	2.19	1.62	218.13%
United States	1.90	2.24	166.11%
New Zealand	1.48	2.05	230.58%
Canada	2.67	2.29	122.10%
Britain	2.10	1.67	314.49%
Australia	2.81	2.38	223.12%
Finland	1.24	1.52	208.64%
Union of South Africa	1.05	2.33	223.64%
Ireland	3.19	2.29	851.52%
Denmark	2.00	1.05	227.85%
Norway	1.33	1.71	90.63%
Netherlands	.29	1.48	150.00%
Austria	1.57	1.86	136.84%
Hungary	1.29	1.81	214.00%
Chile	· 1.29	1.19	129.38%
Greece	.38	2.29	305.56%
France	.81	2.38	108.99%
Argentina	1.86	3.38	114.29%
Uruguay	1.48	1.86	120.00%
Spain	.81	2.33	110.28%
Belgium	1.00	.43	97.23%
Germany	1.38	2.14	94.74%
Total	34.12	42.30	
Unweighted mean	1.55	1.92	202.64

TABLE 9-3

Comparison of 1925 *n* Achievement and Percentage Growth of Electrical Output, 1929–1950, 22 Countries

n Achievement level	Above Average Growth	Below Average Growth
Above mean	5	4
Below mean	5	8

[20] The five with faster than average growth rates were New Zealand, Finland, Union of South Africa, Hungary and Greece; the eight with slower than average growth rates were Norway, Netherlands, Chile, France, Uruguay, Spain, Belgium and Germany.

McClelland's main support for this contention comes from his comparison of 1929–50 electrical output growth (as he defines it) to 1950 as well as to 1925 *n* Achievement figures. He finds that the correlation between 1950 *n* Achievement and economic growth is an insignificant .03 compared with the highly significant .53 correlation between 1925 *n* Achievement and growth during the 1929–50 period. Since *n* Achievement correlated with subsequent but not prior growth, this supports his thesis that high *n* Achievement is a cause rather than a result of high growth.

However, if we once again rely on percentage increases as a measure of growth and then compare above average *n* Achievement and above average growth we find little support for this hypothesis. We see (Table 9–4) that

TABLE 9-4

Comparison of 1950 *n* Achievement and Percentage Growth of Electrical Output, 1929–1950, 22 Countries

n *Achievement* level	*Above Average* Growth	*Below Average* Growth
Above mean	5	6
Below mean	5	6

higher than average rates of growth were experienced by five out of the eleven countries which were above the mean in *n* Achievement in 1950[21] as compared with five out of the nine countries which were above the mean in *n* Achievement in 1925 (Table 9–3). It makes little difference whether we compare growth with *n* Achievement at the beginning of the growth period or with *n* Achievement at the end of the growth period.

(4) McClelland repeatedly argues that deficiencies in his samples, and the unreliable nature of his data make his results *more* rather than less convincing. Concerning *n* Achievement and electrical output, e.g., he states that ". . . the relationship is surprisingly high . . . considering the short range nature of the electrical output figures and possible sampling errors in the selection of children's stories . . ."[22] Shortly afterward he says that "the estimates of *n* Achievement level, or of economic gains for that matter may be *unrepresentative . . . for particular countries*. The fact that the relationship is substantial and significant, *despite such errors*, is all the more reason to take it seriously . . ."[23] Does this suggest, then, that the worse the data one has to support a hypothesis, the stronger is the hypothesis?

[21] These five were New Zealand, Australia, Union of South Africa, Ireland and Greece. The other six countries with above average *n* Achievement in 1950 but below average growth rates were United States, Canada, France, Argentina, Spain and Germany.

[22] McClelland, op. cit., p. 99.

[23] Ibid., p. 101. Italics in the original.

(5) His findings regarding *n* Achievement in various countries conflict with what economists know, or think they know, about economic growth. In the countries for which he has data for both years he finds little correlation between the relative *n* Achievement levels in 1925 and in 1950.[24] This appears to be a serious blow to his entire hypothesis. The countries which were experiencing a high rate of secular economic growth in the 1920's are generally the same ones which experienced a high rate of economic growth in the 1950's, and vice versa.

McClelland also finds that *n* Achievement in the poor countries in 1950 is significantly higher than in the rich countries. His explanation is that "many of the backward countries realize their backwardness and are now motivated to close the gap between themselves and the more industrially developed countries."[25] This finding about *n* Achievement and therefore entrepreneurial ability certainly contradicts the general impression of economists about relative entrepreneurial capacity in poor and rich countries. Moreover, since McClelland has argued that his data reflect *n* Achievement of the vigorous adults of each society and that his 1950 *n* Achievement figures "are correlated with economic growth in the very near future or practically simultaneously,"[26] this would lead us to expect that the less developed economies, since 1950 at least, should have grown more rapidly than the advanced economies. This has certainly not been the case, nor are there many economists who expect that it will be the case in the near future.

Furthermore, evidently without realizing it, McClelland later presents a quite contradictory hypothesis about *n* Achievement and the level of economic development. When his figures show high *n* Achievement in the United States, lower *n* Achievement in Italy, and still lower *n* Achievement in Turkey, he blandly indicates that this is to be expected because it "agrees with the level of development of those countries . . ."[27]

Crossing the conventional boundaries of the social science disciplines is a salutary practice. If economists are to take McClelland's hypothesis seriously, however, it must have sturdier and more objective support than McClelland has managed to provide.

[24] McClelland, op. cit., 99.   [25] Ibid., p. 102.   [26] Ibid., p. 102.   [27] Ibid., p. 287.

10

THE TRANSITION IN COLOMBIA

Everett E. Hagen

ALTHOUGH the economic growth of Colombia during the past forty years has gone largely unnoticed by the world at large, one could count on one's fingers, possibly on the fingers of one hand, the countries of the world whose rate of increase in per capita income during this period has been greater. That rise has continued in spite of governmental mismanagement and resulting foreign exchange problems during several years of the 1950's.

In area and population Colombia is the third largest country of South America. Its area is about one seventh that of the United States; its population in 1960 was some 14,000,000. The country's per capita gross national product in 1957 was 1,066 pesos, equivalent in purchasing power to perhaps $265 or more.[1] Thirty years earlier, in the mid-1920's, it was only one half as great. This

Reprinted by permission of the author and the publisher from On the Theory of Social Change, *Dorsey Press, Evanston 1962, chap. 15.*

[1] This figure is derived by use of the 1957 free market rate of exchange of four pesos equal to one dollar. Estimates of Colombian economists suggest that, since the purchasing power of the peso in 1957 for capital and consumer goods and services used in Colombia was higher than 25 cents, the dollar figure equivalent in purchasing power to 1,066 pesos should be more than $265. At the rate of exchange prevailing early in 1961, per capita income in dollars would be computed at less than one third as much, or say $80; but the specific

is the earliest date for which a comprehensive estimate of output and income in Colombia has been made, but partial estimates make clear that 30 years earlier still it was even lower.[2] As I shall note in more detail later, industrial production had been rising fairly rapidly since at least the turn of the century,[3] and agricultural production had been increasing markedly since at least the 1870's.

This economic growth has occurred in three areas barred from the outside world and from each other by rugged mountain ranges and on a humid tropical lowland. One could hardly pick a less likely place in Latin America

conditions which cause that rate make it invalid as a measure of the relative purchasing power of the peso and the dollar.

[2] The earliest year for which an estimate of gross national product in Colombia has been made is 1925. The Economic Commission for Latin America has estimated that from 1925 to 1953 the gross product of Colombia increased at an average rate of 4.6 per cent per year. Since the average annual rate of population growth was 2.1 per cent, output per capita increased at an average rate of 2.4 per cent. Per capita output rose by 5.2 per cent per year during 1925–29, 2.0 per cent even during the depression years 1930–38, 0 per cent during the war years 1939–44, when both exports of commodities and imports of supplies were especially severely curtailed for lack of shipping, and 3.6 per cent during 1945–53. The rate from 1953 to 1960 averaged about 2 per cent. (United Nations Economic Commission for Latin America, *Analyses and Projections of Economic Development, III. The Economic Development of Colombia*, Geneva, 1957. [E/CN.12/365/Rev.1] Section I, chap. i.)

[3] Many of the leading industrial companies of today, or their predecessors, are listed in the *Anuario Ilustrado de Bogotá y Registro Mercantil de Colombia*, issued in Bogotá in 1921. Of the manufacturing companies listed on the Bogotá stock exchange (Bolsa de Bogotá, S.A.) in 1947, certainly one third and perhaps one half were the companies or the legal successors to companies which were flourishing before 1920. An appreciable number existed before 1900.

If any date should symbolize the beginning of modern industry in Colombia it might be 1901 or 1906. In 1901 a modern sugar refinery began to operate at the La Manuelita plantation near the town of Palmira in the Valley, after more than 1,800 mules and oxen had been employed for some three years in hauling the machinery from Buenaventura over the roadless Cordillera Occidental to the Valley. (According to Phanor J. Eder, in the biography of James M. Eder, *El Fundador: Santiago M. Eder* [Bogotá: Ltda., 1959].) American engineers, laying a pipeline in 1957, on one stretch of which even then they had to haul in pipe and equipment by muleback, uncovered one of the large cogwheels which had been lost en route at some time between 1898 and 1901. In 1906 a modern textile mill began to operate in Antioquia, the machinery for which, transported up the Magdalena by boat and then to Antioquia by mule, had arrived in such shape that it is said in Antioquia that it was built in the repair shops of Medellín. Ex-president Pedro Nel Ospina, exiled in the war of 1899–1902, had decided then to construct in Antioquia a textile mill like one he observed in Mexico. In the financial crisis of 1904 his enterprise became bankrupt. The factory was opened by F. Restrepo y Compañía in 1906. In 1908 a more modern factory, the Compañía Colombiana de Tejidos, which had benefited from Restrepo's experience with technical problems, began operations. This company, known as Coltejer, is now, after several consolidations and great prosperity in World War II, one of the largest manufacturing corporations in Latin America. However, these are symbolic rather than logically significant dates. The development of industry, in Colombia or elsewhere, was a gradually accelerating process.

unless it is Bolivia. Colombia's economic progress is therefore doubly impressive. Why did it occur?

THE SETTING

The Land and the People

Colombia is the northwestern-most country of South America, its coastline interrupted by the Isthmus of Panama. The eastern half of the country's area, the extensive transmontane undeveloped grasslands known as the *llanos*, contains less than 2 per cent of the country's population.[4] It may be neglected for our purposes. In the western half of the country three rugged fingers of the Andes, the western, central, and eastern Cordilleras, thrust northward from Ecuador. The central and western ones taper down and disappear 150 miles or so short of the Atlantic, but the eastern one continues aggressively to the ocean. Between the central and eastern ranges, the Magdalena River runs the length of the country to the Atlantic. The Cauca River flows down through the valley west of the central range, joining the Magdalena perhaps 125 miles from the ocean.

In the eastern Cordillera there lies a high plateau, called the Sabana, some 400 miles south of the Atlantic. On it stands the capital city of Bogotá, at an altitude of 8,500 feet. The two other most important cities lie in the valley of the Cauca, Cali some 150 miles southwest of Bogotá and Medellín some 150 miles northwest, so that the three form an equilateral triangle. Cali lies at an altitude of 3,000 feet and Medellín at 5,000. The area around Cali is known as the Valley of the Cauca, or simply the Valley (Valle); that around Medellín as Antioquia. Between the two, hills and ridges only less rugged than the Cordilleras cross the Cauca Valley and create a formidable barrier to north-south travel.

The three cities have grown rapidly during the last century. In 1960 the population of Bogotá plus its many suburbs was one million or more, and that of Medellín and Cali may be estimated very roughly at 500,000 each. The fourth city in size, Barranquilla, at the mouth of the Magdalena River, is somewhat smaller. Between Barranquilla and the other cities lie the hot swampy lowlands of the lower Magdalena and then the mountains. It is difficult to overemphasize how removed Bogotá, Medellín, and Cali were from the world and from each other until airlines and improved surface routes over the mountains opened up access in the 1920's. Until some time after 1900 every pound of material which

[4] According to the 1951 census.

came into any of the three was carried over the mountains on the backs of animals or men; no vehicle could traverse the mountain paths.

Ethnically, except for a handful of non-Spanish immigrants, Colombians are of Spanish, Indian, and Negro blood. The proportion of the population with Negro blood is greater in some parts of Antioquia and the Valley and on some parts of the Atlantic and Pacific coasts than elsewhere. The census of 1918, the last to inquire concerning ancestry, indicated 33 per cent of the population of white, 52 per cent of mixed, and 15 per cent of Indian or Negro blood. The percentage given for pure white blood is undoubtedly considerably exaggerated.

Formally the entire country is Roman Catholic in religion, though in the villages there is a noticeable tendency to identify some saints with pre-Christian gods or guardian spirits. The handful of non-Catholic Christian congregations minister largely to foreigners.

Historical Background

Spaniards first landed on the Atlantic coast of what is now Colombia in 1500. Between 1530 and 1540 they discovered the Sabana, the Valley, and Antioquia, conquered the Indian tribes in each, and established settlements. In all three regions the Spaniards were seeking gold and silver. Here and there throughout Colombia they found gold and silver deposits, a few of them of some size, but on the Sabana and in the Valley they found none. Yet they remained because of the fertility of the soil and the attractiveness of the environment.

Under the decrees of the king each conqueror was permitted to occupy an area of land and to take a number of Indians under his guardianship and require work from them, in return for which he was to assure their material welfare and to confer upon them the benefit of Christianity. In practice, and in spite of occasional rulings to the contrary from Spain, the lands became the property in fee simple of the individual Spanish families, and the Indians became slaves. On the Sabana the land grants were large and the Indian tribes peaceable and skilled in agriculture, and the conquerors soon became landed gentry. In the Valley a similar development occurred except that the rolling land was less suitable for farming and the settlers specialized in cattle raising. Yet here and in fertile lands nearby they found it profitable to produce other food as well as meat for export over the western Cordillera to the miners working in the jungles along the Pacific coast and in Antioquia. In Antioquia a number of small gold and silver deposits were found, and attention centered more than elsewhere on the quest for wealth in gold mining. The Indians in Antioquia were gatherers, not cultivators, and did not learn to farm well.

During the first 50 years after the conquest, and to a lesser degree until the beginning of the seventeenth century, two or three areas in Antioquia yielded considerable wealth in gold; but as the gold was laced throughout the rock or lay in a lean mixture in river bed sands, much cheap labor was required to extract it. The methods of extraction were primitive ones learned from the Indians, and only the Indians knew how to do some of the aqueduct building required. Through depletion both of the richest gold-bearing rock and of the labor supply, by about 1630 gold production had passed its peak. From the mid-seventeenth century until almost 1900 it continued barely on a subsistence basis, and it was increasingly the descendants of the conquerors, who termed themselves Spaniards, who did the mining, often with pick and hammer and hand screening of the crushed ore or the sands. The most prosperous communities of the region after the beginning of the seventeenth century seem to have been Medellín and Rionegro, which benefited not from the mining itself but from the trade by which the miners were supplied.

Spain's economic control of her colonies in the New World followed the usual mercantilist pattern. Trade was permitted only with the mother country, and on both sales to and purchases from the colony taxes were levied which greatly burdened the producers in the colony.

Politically the dominance of the home government was complete. Not only did the colonists have neither representation in Spain nor formal voice in the administration of the colony;[5] in addition, when in Spain they had neither the freedom of movement nor the full right to hold property which a native of Spain possessed, and socially they were looked on as inferior. In part their exclusion from important political offices may have been because it was known that many of the original immigrant adventurers had been of the lowest Spanish classes, economically and socially, and in part because it was suspected (correctly) that many or most of them were in part of Indian or slave blood; but it was also motivated by a desire to maintain the authority of the crown and hold centrifugal tendencies in check.[6] In any event, resentment at social and political discrimination festered in the colonists. In the New World persons of local birth who could claim pure Spanish blood looked with contempt on the mestizos or "men of color"—contempt the fervor of which may perhaps have been proportionate to the dubiousness of their own blood claim.[7]

[5] Though some individuals who could claim pure Spanish blood were appointed to administrative posts.

[6] I am indebted to William P. Glade for this suggestion as well as for refinement of several points below.

[7] Today Colombians insist a little too forcefully that there are no discriminations in Colombia on the basis of colour. There are no such legal distinctions, but the persons one

In 1810 the colonials of Spanish blood on the Sabana rose up in a movement for reform, then a demand for autonomy. It was harshly put down. During the decade that followed, disturbances and demands rose in several waves, but within the small Spanish group troops loyal to the motherland were able to quell the revolts. Then at the end of the decade, after previously leading two unsuccessful attempts at independence, Bolivar called on the mestizos to rise against the Spaniards. Under this call and the magnetic leadership of Bolivar, the revolution succeeded; in 1819 the leaders of New Granada declared their independence, and thereafter they successfully defended it. But the hopes of the mestizos were not fulfilled; the creoles dominated political life. They called the new republic Grancolombia. But there was little cohesion among the various regions of Grancolombia. In 1830 Ecuador and Venezuela seceded,[8] and throughout the remainder of the nineteenth century, or until 1902, differences within Colombia erupted in a series of civil wars.

ECONOMIC CHANGE: THE HISTORICAL RECORD

The Gradual Expansion of Agriculture and Manufacturing

One of the impressive facts revealed by a detailed study of Colombian economic history is the gradualness of the appearance of technological progress.[9] To identify any given date as marking its beginning would be as absurd as to identify any given point on an exponential curve as the point at which it begins to rise rapidly. Because specific information concerning the early stages of economic growth is rarely available, it seems useful to narrate that for Colombia in some detail.

During the eighteenth century little economic change is recorded: It is a plausible speculation, though only a speculation, that with the increasing percentage of persons of European blood in the population aggregate output rose more rapidly than did total population. In the nineteenth century, and

---

meets at the country club tend to be of light skin while those carrying burdens on the street are dark. In at least one recent instance cited to me it was impossible to promote a dark-skinned factory worker over others because two valued lighter ones in the group he would have directed would have resigned.

[8] Colombia included Panama until the secession of Panama in 1903 fostered by President Theodore Roosevelt.

[9] My information concerning economic change before 1900 is mainly from Luis Ospina Vásquez' basic work, *Industria y Protección en Colombia, 1810–1930* (Bogotá: Editorial Santafé, 1955).

especially after independence, economic change became slightly more noticeable. The production of unrefined brown cake sugar known as *panela* grew in
importance, and, although this growth may have been mainly a displacement
of even more primitive sugar production in the home, the change probably
increased productivity and income. More important, coffee cultivation, which
was known in the first years of the republic in valleys near Venezuela, spread to
Antioquia, then to the slopes on the edge of the Sabana, and finally to the department of Caldas, geographically within the Valley, but peopled with Antioqueños, and became the nation's largest industry. After 1880 coffee cultivation
increased rapidly in Antioquia and Caldas.[10]

New industries gradually arose in the nineteenth century and contributed
to the rise in per capita income. Early in the century the textile industry of the
Sabana had been injured by the import of foreign fabrics, but the records of
1830–60 indicate a proliferation on the Sabana of consumer goods industries.[11]
During the next decade or two production of china and additional textiles
began. Steam-powered wheat mills were established. Gas lighting was introduced into Bogotá in 1876.

Meanwhile heavier industry had also been appearing. Early in the nineteenth
century an improved gunpowder plant replaced or augmented primitive
establishments. At some time after 1810 iron mining methods were improved
in three mining areas, with foreign technicians and in part with English capital,
and an iron refining plant was established. These enterprises struggled along
throughout the century. At some time after 1830 the refinery installed a blast
furnace. At about the same time production of some chemicals began.[12] The
first commercial bank in Colombia, a branch of an English bank, was established
in Bogotá in 1865. Within a year or two the first bank owned by Colombians,
the Banco de Bogotá, was opened. After 1875 iron processing developed further.
The Sabana felt a sense of great progress as the century drew to a close, and in
1899 an industrial exposition at Bogotá celebrated that progress.

Industrial activity was more impressive on the Sabana than anywhere else

[10] By 1913 Antioquia and Caldas together produced 36 per cent of Colombia's growing
output of coffee, and by 1940, 50 per cent.

[11] Handicraft and cottage enterprises were numerous, and slightly larger establishments, using newer machine methods, began to produce beer, hats, pottery, porcelain,
matches, flour, glass and crystal, paper, and cloth. The paper factory lasted only some 25
years; the glass and crystal plant collapsed after a time, to be revived later. Between 1890
and 1900 a modern brewery, a bottlemaking plant, a new pottery plant, new textile plants,
a tannery, and a salt manufactory appeared.

[12] A sulphuric acid plant failed after some years; it was the first of several during the
remainder of the century, each failing for lack of demand and being succeeded after some
time by another.

in Colombia during the nineteenth century. At the other end of the scale, the Valley continued with very little industry. The region's economy rested largely on general agriculture, the raising of cattle, and the production of sugar and later of coffee.[13]

In Antioquia industry was of intermediate importance. Early in the century the main industries other than agriculture and mining seem to have been production of hats and beer. (A steam engine was first used in mining not long after 1800.) Then, during the last half of the century, economic growth in Antioquia, though starting behind that of the Sabana, seems to show greater vigor. By the 1860's breweries with advanced methods and various other small consumer goods enterprises existed, and during the 1870's and 1880's many others appeared.[14] In the 1870's textile plants began to appear. By the end of the 1880's small plants with machine looms had appeared here and there among the many handloom establishments, though socks were still woven by hand of jute and sisal. Unlike earlier iron works, one established in 1864 survived and 20 years later entered upon production of simple mining and agricultural machinery and especially machinery used in coffee processing. By the end of the century production of this machinery was a flourishing industry in itself.

Of the 42 commercial banks which existed in Colombia in 1881, 12 were in Cundinamarca, 11 in Antioquia, and from one to five in each of seven other regions.[15]

This incomplete listing of consumer goods industries which developed in Colombia during the nineteenth century indicates the trend of events. As in all early development, the picture includes overoptimism, many false starts, and failures together with steady expansion. From Ospina Vásquez' account one gets the impression that the false starts and failures were more frequent in Cundinamarca than in Antioquia—that even in the last half of the nineteenth century business entrepreneurs in Antioquia were less wishful and more capable in their judgments or in their execution of projects, though equally bold. This impression, however, may result from a difference in the extent of the information available to Ospina Vásquez rather than from a difference in reality.

Even in the absence of data concerning aggregate production in the

[13] Even toward the end of the century, apart from handicraft industries, cottage industries processing agricultural produce, the woolen and Panama hat industry, and the ubiquitous breweries, the only industry in the Valley mentioned in Ospina Vásquez' account is a textile industry specializing in the production of flannel cloth.

[14] A cacao mill, a pottery industry, production of ceramics, half-peasant, half-capitalist in method, and the tanning of hides and making of shoes by primitive methods are reported in the 1860's. By the 1880's, improved tanneries had been opened, and shoes, cigars, cigarettes, and chocolates had become products of some importance.

[15] Camacho Roldán, *Escritos Varios, Segunda Serie* (Bogotá: Librería Colombiana, 1893).

economy it seems fairly certain that per capita income was increasing steadily (with interruptions during the civil wars) during the last four or five decades of the century, and quite possibly earlier as well.

The Development of Transportation

During this period of gradually accelerating economic growth, transportation facilities were remarkably primitive. Before 1850, except in the immediate vicinity of cities, all "roads" apparently were pack trails which only a single beast of burden might traverse. Items too large or heavy to be packed by mule[16] were transported on poles between mule backs or human backs. Extremely heavy ones were drawn up mountainsides by block and tackle. Coffee, sugar, machinery, pianos, even the first locomotives—everything was carried in this fashion out to the rivers or in from the rivers.

Indeed, even trails were not everywhere present. The first "mule road" from Cali over the Cordillera Occidental toward the Pacific was not completed until 1866.[17] In the 1850's there occurred a flurry of building of wagon roads around Bogotá (and perhaps, if one had the local histories, around other cities as well). In the 1870's railroad construction began. Between 1872 and 1880 eight railroads were built, extending a few miles in one direction or another from major cities or closing the first few miles of a link between some city and the Magdalena River. They were built by the national government, by the states, or by individuals with governmental financial aid. By 1890 four had failed financially and had ceased to operate,[18] but the early lines on the Sabana, in Antioquia, and carrying freight for the first leg of the journey from the Magdalena to the one region or the other were successful.[19] The rapid development of coffee cultivation in Antioquia and Caldas came only when railroad and truck transportation to the Magdalena was possible.

Even by 1912 there were only 1,000 kilometers of railroad track in

[16] Each mule carried two packs weighing not more than 70 kilograms or about 155 pounds.

[17] And the first mule road from Cali to the important Valley town of Palmira was not completed until 1869. Phanor J. Eder, *El Fundador: Santiago M. Eder.* James (Santiago) M. Eder was a leading force in the construction of both.

[18] Camacho Roldán, *Notas de Viaje* (Bogotá: Librería Colombiana, 1890).

[19] Of the four railroad stretches which survived of the first eight built, one ran from Bogotá toward the edge of the Sabana, one from Medellín northeastward toward the Cordillera Central, and one from Puerto Berrío on the Magdalena toward Antioquia. My historical information is not specific enough to be certain which other road survived.

The first locomotive to be used in Antioquia, which was carried across the Cordillera Central by a gang of from 30 to 50 men, is still on display in Medellín. It is shorter than the smallest American automobile of the 1950's before the advent of the compact car.

Colombia, and it was divided among 14 separate lines, of which the longest was 135.7 kilometers.[20]

Not long after 1900 a wagon road of a sort was completed from Bogotá over the mountains rimming the Sabana down to Puerto Salgar on the Magdalena; thereafter goods were drawn to Bogotá by teams of two, four, or six pairs of oxen.[21] The first wheeled transportation to Medellín from the outside world became possible in 1909, when a yard-gauge railroad was completed from Puerto Berrio on the Magdalena to a point on the Cordillera Central, whence a 27-kilometer road over the ridge joined the section of the railroad running from Medellín.[22]

Not until 1929 was a tunnel completed which achieved a railroad connection direct from Medellín to the river; not until some time in the 1930's did a road over the Cordillera Central permit motor transport into and out of Antioquia to the east and south; and not until 1958 was a railroad connection from Medellín to Bogotá (other than by a long loop to the South) completed.

Cali was similarly mountain-locked until the completion of the railroad from Buenaventura on the Pacific, over the Cordillera Occidental, to Cali in 1914. This plus completion of the Panama Canal in 1915 suddenly made transport between Cali and the eastern United States coast and Europe almost miraculously easy. A motor road from Cali to Bogotá was completed in 1928, and one from Cali to Medellín in 1940 or 1941. The last link of a railroad between Cali and Medellín was completed in 1942. No railroad traverses the mountain ranges between Cali and Bogotá even today. A road across the mountain from Cali to Bogotá was completed in 1928, but even now it is still cheaper for most freight to use a combined road-railroad route—by railroad northeast to the town of Armenia, then across the Cordillera by truck, then by railroad on to Bogotá.

The Twentieth Century

After 1900, while transportation facilities were still primitive, heavier industry began to expand. The first modern sugar refinery began production in

[20] René Roger, *La Colombie économique* (Paris: Librairie de la Société du Recueil Sirey et Librairie R. Roger et F. Chernovez, 1914).

[21] But Puerto Salgar was on the upper reach of the Magdalena, above a rapids, and almost dry during the dry season. Above the rapids all goods had to move by small boat and then be hauled by road or rail around the rapids.

[22] From Medellín one could then travel to Bogotá by taking a train to the pass, a cart across the pass, train to Puerto Berrio, boat up the river to La Dorada, railroad around the rapids above La Dorada, smaller river boat to Girardot, 1-yard gauge railroad up to Facatativa on the edge of the Sabana, and 1-meter railroad to Bogotá. With luck, the trip (now one hour by DC-3) could be completed in the greatly improved time of six days; with bad luck, it required twice that time.

1901 (in the Valley), the first modern textile plant in 1906 (in Antioquia), and the first major cement plant in 1909 (on the Sabana). One after another, others appeared. Then the stream became a widening tide. Small metallurgical plants increased their output; production of simple agricultural and mining machinery increased in importance. New glass plants were established. Electric light and power plants became numerous and prosperous. Production of pharmaceuticals began. The industrial system became able to manage the construction of larger and larger, more and more demanding structures.

Agriculture steadily declined in relative importance, though its output continued to increase in amount, and manufacturing and tertiary industries steadily and rapidly increased in both absolute and relative importance. Data for 1925, 1945, and 1953 are presented in the table below.

TABLE 10-1

Columbia: Growth and Composition of Production of Goods and Services

	Composition of the Product by Activities			Average Rates of Growth	
	1925	1945	1953	1925–53	1946–53
Total	100.0	100.0	100.0	4.6	5.9
Agricultural and livestock	58.8	47.0	36.9	2.9	2.7
Mining	1.5	3.7	3.7	8.1	5.7
Manufacturing	7.6	13.4	17.2	7.7	9.2
Artisan industry	2.9	3.1	3.8	5.6	8.4
Construction	2.6	6.1	4.8	7.0	2.7
Transport	2.3	4.2	7.4	9.1	13.7
Energy, communications, and public utilities	0.4	0.7	1.2	8.7	12.7
Government	5.7	5.5	6.9	5.4	8.9
Trade, finance, and services	8.7	10.2	12.9	6.1	9.0
Personal income from rentals	9.5	6.1	5.2	2.3	3.8

Source: ECLA, *The Economic Development of Colombia*, Table 3, p. 16.

Bloodless though the statistics are, detailed estimates by the Economic Commisssion for Latin America tell the story from the 1920's on impressively. Industrial growth continued during the 1930's after falling in 1930 and 1931. During earlier periods of foreign exchange shortage Colombia was able neither to produce substitutes for the finished products whose importation was cut off nor to cope with the shortage of imported industrial components, and her domestic industrial production probably fell rather than rose; but by the 1930's Colombian entrepreneurs had gained enough technical versatility so that absence of imports provided an opportunity rather than a handicap, and industrial expansion continued.

Since World War II, industrialization has been occurring within agriculture. In the hot lands little above sea level stretching from the middle reaches of the

Magdalena between Bogotá and Medellín down to the Atlantic, Colombian entrepreneurs have established large-scale mechanized production of rice and other tropical crops and large cattle ranches. The cattle are of breeds, some imported and some developed in Colombia, which are suited to the hot humid climate. Large unused areas remain; the taming of the hot lowland jungles is continuing. Growth in this sector of the Colombian economy is as important in some ways as the continuing industrial expansion.[23] Technological progress is now so deeply rooted in Colombian behavior patterns that it is a thoroughly safe assumption that economic growth will continue indefinitely.

WHY DID GROWTH BEGIN?

Not for the Economic Reasons Conventionally Advanced

One thing is clear: Economic growth in Colombia did not begin for the economic reasons conventionally cited as causes of such growth.

Foreign companies or individuals did not provide capital and thereby break a bottleneck. Foreign investment in Colombia before World War II was minimal; before World War I it was almost negligible. While there were a few earlier investments, in the main foreign capital began flowing into Colombia only after economic growth was firmly implanted and the expanding market attracted foreign enterprises.[24]

Contacts with foreign goods and technology were not greater in Colombia than elsewhere where growth has been slower in starting. On the contrary, as I have noted, the Sabana, the Valley, and Antioquia, where growth has centered, were extremely difficult of access until well into the twentieth century. Moreover, the seedbed of growth was Antioquia, which in turn had far less opportunity for contact with Europe and other American countries than did Bogotá, the national capital.

Growth did not wait upon the development of an infrastructure, or social overhead capital, to use the economic terms, which created a national market or otherwise laid a base for progress. The extremely primitive state of transportation until growth was under way has been sketched. Transportation, communication, and power facilities all developed in response to the demands created by

---

[23] Perhaps next will come expansion onto the *llanos*, but difficult problems of transportation, or the establishment of a largely self-contained economy on those eastern grasslands, must be solved before development there can proceed.

[24] Concerning earlier United States investment, see J. Fred Rippy, *The Capitalists and the Colombians* (New York: Vanguard Press, 1931).

growing production rather than as prior steps which laid the basis for it. (As they developed, they in turn stimulated further advance.) Production until say 1910, except for primary commodities, was for small regional markets, not for a national market. It is possible that the protection provided by transportation difficulties stimulated rather than hampered early industrialization. Even today production of cement, steel products, and other heavy products is for regional markets limited by transportation costs.

Thus growth began in spite of the supposed economic barriers, not because those barriers were removed.

The Antioqueños

The proximate answer to the question why growth began is: Because of the enterprise of the Antioqueños.

It is a Colombian national myth that virtually all of the nation's important industrial enterprises are run by Antioqueños. "If they did not found them," it is said, "they own them now." "The only person a Turco can't outsmart in a business deal," I was told so often that it is clear that this is a stock statement, "is an Antioqueño." The facts do not support these extreme versions of the myth. Capable and effective entrepreneurs have arisen in every region of the country. Yet the predominance of Antioqueños is impressive.

From the 1956 Census of Industry[25] I obtained lists of all nonfinancial private business concerns in Cundinamarca, in Antioquia, and in the Valley employing more than 100 workers. I then asked informed individuals to identify the founders of these enterprises by nationality, and, if Colombian, regional origin. This was done hurriedly shortly before my departure from

TABLE 10-2

Origins of Founders of Larger Enterprises in Cundinamarca, Antioquia, and the Valle del Cauca

Number of Enterprises with More Than 100 Workers in 1956
Founded by Individuals from:

Department	Antio-quia	Cundi-na-marca	Valle del Cauca	Other Regions	Persons of "For-eign" Origin	Subsidi-aries of Foreign-Com-panies	No In-forma-tion	Total
Antioquia	45	1	0	0	5	1	6	58
Valle del Cauca	17	2	8	1	9	7	0	44
Cundinamarca	13	17	0	6	15	1	7	59
Totals	75	20	8	7	29	9	13	161

[25] República de Colombia, Departmento Administrativo Nacional de Estadística, *Directoria industrial (Provisional), 1956* (Bogotá, 1957).

Colombia, but I believe that the margin of error is not great. The results of the survey are presented in Table 10-2. The classification included as Antioqueños entrepreneurs from Caldas of Antioqueño stock.

Of the 148 enterprises concerning which information was obtained, 110, or just under three fourths, were founded by persons referred to as "Old Colombians." Nine, of which at least seven were founded after World War II, are subsidiaries of foreign companies, and 29 were founded by individuals of families termed "foreign" in Colombia. Almost all of the 29 are older companies founded by individuals of non-Spanish stock who had settled in Colombia but whose families are still termed "foreign." Of the 26 identified by origin, 10 were from the Middle East, six were identified as Jewish without other designation of nationality, and the other 10 were Italian, German, French, Dutch, and Russian. The persistence of the label of "foreign" is indicated by the fact that one of the firms so identified (the largest) is Cervecería Bavaria, a major national brewery founded before 1900 by German families which have been Colombian since that time.[26] In general these 29 companies are of the second rank in size and importance, 24 of them in textiles or food products. With due recognition of their role, the relative unimportance of foreign entrepreneurship as a focal point of economic growth and capital and the importance of entrepreneurship of Old Colombians are facts of the Colombian record.

Among the 110 enterprises founded by Old Colombians, 75, or 68 per cent, were founded by Antioqueños. In 1905, a pertinent year for this comparison, the population of Antioquia and Caldas constituted somewhat less than 40 per cent of the population of Antioquia, the Valley, and Cundinamarca.[27] The percentage of individuals of Antioqueño ancestry to the total population was probably slightly higher. Assuming that it was 40 per cent, that per cent of the population provided more than two thirds of the entrepreneurs of large companies, while the remaining 60 per cent provided less than one third. In proportion to population, more than three times as many Antioqueños became entrepreneurs as Old Colombians of non-Antioqueño stock.[28]

Waiving historical precision to make a point vividly, it might be said that if the Bogotanos, in their more favorable economic environment, had been as

[26] But the Eder family, of Russian stock, a generation farther back, was termed Colombian. All the other families termed Colombian were of Spanish stock.

[27] Because I do not have complete data from the 1905 census, this estimate is imprecise. I estimate that the percentage was between 38 and 39. In 1951 the population of Antioquia and Caldas constituted 49.1 per cent of that of the three departments, a result primarily of the rapid rate of natural increase among Antioqueños.

[28] Because some persons may have been termed Antioqueños who are of mixed regional origin, these data may overstate the facts. However, with due allowance for a margin of error, the evidence is impressive.

effective entrepreneurs as the Antioqueños, rapid economic growth in Colombia would have begun half a century sooner than it did, or around 1850; whereas if the Antioqueños had been no more effective entrepreneurs than the Bogotanos or Caleños, rapid economic development would not have begun until half a century later than it did, or around 1950.

Such a statement is subject to misinterpretation. It is an important fact of Colombian history that effective economic innovators arose in every region of the country. There is no difference in kind among regions, but only one of degree. But the difference in degree is so great that it must be concluded that factors at work in Antioquia were not present elsewhere or were much weaker elsewhere. It is of interest to sort out the facts of history to try to decide what those factors were.

Until some time in the nineteenth century Antioquia was the poorest of the regions of Colombia. The romance attached to silver and gold should not mislead one. "Instead of representing the wealth of the Crown," wrote Padre Joaquín de Finestrad in 1783, "the mines seem to have been responsible for the notable backwardness in certain provinces. Antioquia, which is paved with gold, is the poorest and most miserable of all."[29] In 1808 an Antioqueño observer, José Manuel Restrepo, wrote of the mines in Antioquia, "Those in operation today are poor and only make enough profit to keep their owners alive."[30] Until the end of the colonial period (or through the first quarter of the nineteenth century) observers "were struck by the general backwardness, illiteracy, and poverty of the province."[31] Then some change gradually became manifest. It was noticeable by mid-century and conspicuous a generation later. In 1883 the German traveler Ferdinand von Schenck wrote:

There are probably few places of similar size in South American where as many important fortunes are concentrated as in Medellín. The number of families considered as rich is considerable, but with few exceptions they appear so unassuming that their wealth, won mostly by trade and mining, and less commonly through farming and stock-raising, is not apparent. Even the middle classes or artisans are well situated.[32]

[29] *El Vasalle Instruído*, quoted by Rufina Gutiérrez, *Monografías* (2 vols.; Bogotá, 1920–21), Vol. 1, p. 413. I in turn have this quotation, not from Gutiérrez, but from James J. Parsons, *Antioqueño Colonization in Western Colombia* (Ibero-Americana: 32) (Berkeley and Los Angeles: University of California Press, 1949), p. 55.

[30] José Manuel Restrepo, "Ensayo sobre la Geografía: Producciones, Industria y Población de la Provincia de Antioquia en el Nuevo Reino de Granada," in Francisco José de Caldas (ed.), *Seminario del Nuevo Reino de Granada* (Bogotá, 1808–10). Reprinted in 3 vols. (Bogotá, 1942), Vol. I, p. 257, quoted by Parsons, *Antioqueño Colonization*, p. 55.

[31] Ibid., p. 5.

[32] Ferdinand von Schenck, "Reisen in Antioquia," *Petermanns Mitteilungen*, Vol. XXIX 1883), p. 89, quoted in ibid., p. 6.

During the last half of the nineteenth century the energies which led to these results were exerted mainly in Antioquia. In the twentieth century they sought new outlets throughout the nation.[33]

Why this burst of creative activity in business and technology by the people of one region?[34]

WHY THE ANTIOQUEÑOS?

Not Because of Economic Advantages

The reason does not lie in economic advantage—a larger market, greater access to technical knowledge abroad, better natural resources, greater capital. On the first two of these four counts, a great advantage lay with the people of the Sabana, and they probably had an advantage with respect to the other two as well. The population of the Sabana, throughout both the colonial era and the nineteenth century, was considerably larger than that of Antioquia. The Sabana had the best land and the most prosperous agriculture in Colombia throughout the colonial period. Next most prosperous was agriculture in the Valley and the regions south of it. Per capita income in both must have been higher than in Antioquia. The market available on the Sabana was much the largest in Colombia, one reason why the first attempts at development of industry, during the first half of the nineteenth century, were there.

Further, during the colonial period and the nineteenth century (and indeed with some qualification up to the present) Bogotá was the main point of Colombian contact with Europe and the foreign world in general. Before independence it had been the most important administrative seat. After independence it became the nation's capital. Foreign diplomats, such representatives

[33] When I asked a taxicab driver in Cartagena, on the Atlantic seacoast, whether there were Antioqueños there, he replied, "De aqui a China, Antioqueños." ("From here to China, Antioqueños.")

[34] The economic rejuvenation of Antioquia is sometimes attributed to the reforms directed by the royal inspector Juan Antonio Mon y Verlarde during his three-year turn of duty in the province in 1784–87 (or possibly 1785–88). He reformed governmental administration, directed the establishment of new agricultural towns, provided bounties for the introduction of new crops, enforced vagrancy laws while simultaneously providing opportunities to work in the new towns, and so on. However, we may reasonably distrust a thesis which assumes that reforms in external institutions over a three-year period fundamentally alter the nature of the people and account for their creativity over the following 175 years.

of the sciences and arts as visited Colombia,[35] and foreign businessmen seeking to establish trade or looking for a new area in which to establish themselves came first of all to Bogotá. Until the late nineteenth century many more families on the Sabana than elsewhere were wealthy enough and sufficiently interested in culture and the foreign world to send their sons and daughters abroad. Through contacts with Peru and Ecuador, the Valley had more lines of communication with the outside world. Of the three regions, Antioquia was the most isolated.

The only natural resource to be noted in Antioquia other than the gold is a number of small waterfalls. These indeed provided the occasion for the location of several textile mills at the turn of the century, but they were of no importance in the subsequent development of the mills. Greater falls, though probably fewer in number, exist on and at the edge of the Sabana.

Creative Personality

One is led to the conclusion that the difference between Antioqueños and others lay not in the external conditions but in the people. And as soon as one considers this possibility, convincing evidence appears.

First, differences appear in psychological tests in which a number of Colombian business and community leaders courteously agreed to participate. The successful economic innovators of Antioquia in 1957 were so different in personality structure from a group of equally prominent community leaders elsewhere in Colombia who were interviewed and studied that they may be thought of as a different breed of men. The differences are discussed in a monograph being written by my colleague, Dr. Louis C. Schaw. Since that monograph is not yet available, let me summarize some of them.

The group of entrepreneurs studied in Antioquia are a group of some twenty businessmen in Medellín whose careers stamp them as effective innovators, entrepreneurs of the Schumpeterian type. Not all are among the wealthiest men in the community; some are men in mid-career who started as poor men and whose wealth today, relative to Medellín innovators in general, is only moderate. The contrasting group is a group of community leaders in Popayán, a city with a present population of some 60,000 which was a cultural and political center in colonial days and the nineteenth century, and which now lives in the past, rather defensively spurning the "crass materialism" of such cities as Medellín.

[35] See Jesús María Henao and Gerardo Arrubla, *History of Columbia*, trans. and ed. J. Fred Rippy (Chapel Hill, N.C.: University of North Carolina Press, 1938), *passim.* Bogotá's rival in this respect was not Medellín but Popayán.

One of the psychological instruments used in analyzing these men was the "thematic apperception test" or "TAT," in which simple pictures are shown to the individual one at a time. In the series usually used, one picture is of a young man and an older one; another of a young man and woman; another of a group of men around a table; and so on. Others are less commonplace. Concerning each, the respondent is asked to use his imagination to tell out of what situation the scene pictured arose, what the individuals in the pictures are thinking and feeling, and what the outcome of the situation will be.[36] In the process he tells much of his own attitudes toward life, for no interpretations of the pictures come to his mind so readily as ones which arise out of his own view of the world.

Some simple aspects of the differences between the two groups are as follows. The responses of the Medellín innovators typically embodied: (a) a perception of a situation as a problem to be solved, (b) awareness that to be solved a problem must be worked at (absence of any fantasy of magic success), (c) confidence in their ability to solve it (though sometimes tension and anxiety are also present), (d) a tendency to take the viewpoint of each individual in turn and analyze the situation as he might see it before suggesting an outcome, rather than to adopt a formula identification with any one type of character—with the old versus the young, the young versus the old, and so on. In the terms used in previous chapters, they manifested high need autonomy, need achievement, and need order; had a keen sense of the realities of a situation; saw the world as manageable with good judgment and hard work. The Popayán leaders gave intellectually more complex responses. They associated a picture with something in literature or the arts, philosophized about the ways of youth, were led into speculation about the course of history—but tended to see no problems in the situations pictured. Or, if they saw problems, they had formula solutions for them ("the old know best; he should listen to his father"), or visualized success without any suggestion that it would entail effort and pain. Frequently they gave the impression of running away from the possibility that they might be facing a problem, as though it made them uneasy; they veered away to some peripheral aspect of the picture. They found it easy to turn to fantasy or reverie not closely connected with reality. They showed low need autonomy, achievement, and order; saw the world as not manageable, one's position as given. These differences of course were matters of degree; there was a range of response within each group with regard to various elements. If the responses were shuffled, without identification, a person examining them would not unerringly separate all of those from Medellín and all of those from Popayán

[36] He is asked, that is, to tell what themes he perceives in each picture. Hence the name of the test.

correctly. Nevertheless, the net differences between the groups were striking.[37]

It should be emphasized that what is portrayed is not a difference in personality between all Antioqueños and all Popayanese or other Colombians. The Antioqueños selected were those most apt to have creative personalities. So, however, were the Popayanese, for they were community leaders. There are undoubtedly creative individuals, some of whom have turned their talents to problems of technology and some elsewhere, in every region of Colombia. What is suggested, however, is that the incidence of creative personality is probably much higher among Antioqueños than elsewhere, and that this is an important cause of their greater entrepreneurial success. [38]

Not surprisingly, along with this creativity goes an attitude that any man worth his salt will get into business for himself—"get his own feet wet"—and make his way. A prominent Medellín executive stated that when he came home from college in the 1930's and took a salaried job with a large corporation his action in becoming merely a hired hand was looked upon with raised eyebrows. Many other individuals confirmed the prevalence of such an attitude.

There probably is also a regional difference in the attitude toward manual-technical work, though here my evidence is merely impressionistic. An industrialist in Bogotá, hiring ten college graduates, put them at operating jobs in his factory for training. Within a year eight had resigned. Underlying the avowed reasons, he felt, were attitudes on the part of the individuals or their families that the jobs demeaned them. (The two who remained, interestingly, were of lower-income families.) "If they had been Antioqueños," he said, only half jokingly, "all of them, having learned the processes, would have resigned within the first year—in order to start their own competing businesses." And the head of an enterprise with operations in four centers in Colombia, himself neutral so far as regional affiliation is concerned, told me that the learning time for office and clerical detail is clearly somewhat shorter in Antioquia than elsewhere.

Finally, there is a feeling in Medellín that effective work is a social duty. I did not sense this feeling equally in Cali or Bogotá. It is felt by many Antioqueños that the man who fails to put his capital at work productively in business is somehow lacking in the best qualities and is failing in a duty to the community.

[37] Professor William E. Henry, a distinguished analyst of thematic apperception tests, said jokingly when he examined the responses of the two groups to the test, "Of course you made these up, but you didn't need to exaggerate the contrast so sharply."

[38] An alternative explanation may be that creativity is randomly distributed everywhere but that more of the creative Antioqueños chose to exert their talents in problems of business and technology. There is no evidence in Colombian history, however, that in other regions an equal share of the population was creative in other fields.

"He neither uses his axe nor lends it" is the Antioqueño phrase of disapproval. And, while the entrepreneurs in all regions are pious Catholics, both Dr. Schaw and I thought we sensed a difference in religious attitude. We thought we sensed a feeling in Medellín, not paralleled in the same degree elsewhere, of a personal involvement with the deity[39] and a feeling that to achieve is a personal moral duty. In short, we thought we found among Antioqueños the "Puritan ethic."[40]

Associated with the personality differences among regions is a difference in procreative behavior. During the past 35 years population growth in Colombia as a whole has been rapid—slightly more than 2 per cent per year, almost altogether from natural increases. The increase in the fraction of the total population which Antioqueños constitute is such that natural increase among them must have been at least 0.5 per cent per year faster than among other Colombians, and census data and estimates for periods extending back to 1870 suggest an earlier differential of at least 1 per cent per year.[41] I have no suggestion to make concerning the relationship of this greater vigor of population growth to other personality characteristics; it may be observed, however, that more rapid population growth in an innovating group than in the rest of a society has been remarked on by various writers, and that psychologists have commented on the association observed in a number of individuals between creativity and sexual vigor.[42]

Perhaps the innovative activity is also related in some way to need aggression. It may be that Antioqueños are characterized by higher need aggression than the Colombians of other regions, or that they are less afraid of their need aggression and release it more freely in overt activity. However, beyond the general considerations relating some degree of need aggression to economic innovation, . . . there seems little to add.

Having asserted that these differences in personality exist, we must attempt to find why they exist. If there is a personality difference, what is its source?

[39] Some other Colombians have an image of Antioqueños as "always praying."

[40] Parsons notes a regional difference in religious attitude, though with what authority I do not know since his stay in Colombia was limited to six months and apparently was spent almost entirely in Antioquia. "In piety and devoutness," he states, "the Antioqueños are far ahead of other Colombian ethnic groups, for the Catholic faith is embraced by them with the conscientious passion of their forefathers." *Antioqueño Colonization*, p. 6.

[41] The statement is based on a comparison of data for the population of Colombia as a whole in República de Colombia, Departamento Administrativo Nacional de Estadística, *Anuario General de Estadística, Colombia, 1956* (Bogotá, 1957), with the estimates of Antioqueño population in Parsons, *Antioqueño Colonization*, p. 103.

[42] Though there is no clear evidence concerning whether in general greater sexual activity is associated with greater creativity.

Ethnic Differences

Contrary to one popular fancy, the source of personality differences does not lie in the degree of Jewish blood. Neither early nor later immigrants to the region were in any unique degree Jews.

Concerning later immigration there is no dispute, but the legend dies hard in Colombia that the sixteenth- and seventeenth-century immigrants to Antioquia were Spanish Jews who forged records of Christian blood to obtain permission to migrate. Dr. Emilio Robledo of Medellín has done a scholarly job of evaluating the legend.[43] The assertion first appears in print, so far as Robledo could determine, in a volume published in 1803 by a Franciscan priest who had taught in Antioquia for a time. But neither early histories nor the voluminous primary materials in archives in Medellín and Bogotá contain any suggestion of this origin of Antioqueños. And although the Inquisition tribunal which held forth at Cartagena for some two centuries found Jews elsewhere in Colombia— 68 of its total 767 sentences were against Jews—it found none in Antioquia.

The legend gained wide circulation in the nineteenth century. It was spread among others by the noted Colombian Jewish author, Jorge Isaacs, who was proud of it. It probably owes the credence given it today to its convenience. Bogotano businessmen, for example, look down on their aggressive competitors from Antioquia and at the same time take pride in their own pure Spanish Catholicism. When they say of the Antioqueños, "They are *New Christians*, you know," they are at the same time condescending toward them and explaining away the lesser frequency of effectiveness in business activity among Bogotanos.

The other variant of the defensive explanation given for Antioqueño business success is that the Antioqueños are of Basque origin. The Basques, being rugged individualists who have survived in a spare and rugged mountain environment, are presumed to have qualities conducive to achievement in business. This explanation has a better claim to credence. Whether or not the ethnic difference is an explanation of the difference in economic prowess, some difference with respect to Basque blood may exist.

Data presented in Appendix 2 . . . indicate that, while only some 15 per cent of those families in Medellín listed in the city telephone directory bear Basque names, between 20 and 25 per cent of the executives and directors of industrial enterprises in Antioquia do.

[43] He narrates the results of his study in a preface to Gabriel Arango Mejía, *Geneologías de Antioquia y Caldas* (2d ed.; Medellín, Colombia: Imprenta Editorial Medellín, 1942), Vol. I.

These facts are not entirely conclusive evidence that persons of Basque blood have been more successful entrepreneurs than have others; subscribers to telephones are not necessarily representative of the entire population, and there are also other possible sources of error (noted in the Appendix).

There is no obvious reason, however, why these sources of error should result in an upward distortion of the proportion of Basque names. Hence the evidence is suggestive that persons of Basque descent in Antioquia tend to achieve business executive status to a greater degree than persons of non-Basque Spanish descent. This does not necessarily demonstrate a regional difference in entrepreneurship within Colombia, for we do not know what fraction of individuals in other regions are of Basque blood and how well they have fared in business careers. However, the argument—often advanced in Colombia—that the Basques, living in mountain mining country, tended to select Antioquia as a destination to a greater than random degree is a plausible one. One must therefore conclude that Basque ancestry in Antioquia may be associated in some degree with the economic success of Antioqueños.

If it is, there is no reason to assume that the greater propensity for business success is biologically inherited. It is much more apt to be inherited culturally. The people of the Basque provinces have long been looked down upon, or at least have been looked upon as different and a little odd, by many other Spaniards. They are rugged hard-working mountain people who have preserved a cultural separateness. These personality characteristics may have been transmitted in Colombia over many generations.

However, even if true, that circumstance hardly seems sufficient to explain the differential entrepreneurial achievement of Antioqueños. The extra margin of entrepreneurship among Antioqueños is much greater than that attributable to Basque ancestry. Of course the Basque example could have motivated all other Antioqueños to more vigorous and judicious entrepreneurship, though why it should have increased their judiciousness is hard to see. With due allowance for the possible influence of Basque blood, some other causal factors must be important.

Mining Experience as a Cause

Is it possible that their careers as petty miners prepared the Antioqueños to be industrialists? It seems reasonable to suppose that to some degree it did.

I have noted that from some time in the first half of the seventeenth century the Spaniards themselves were by force of necessity workers in the mines. If we take 1850 as the date when the process of economic growth had its early beginnings, we may say that for three centuries previously Antioqueños had been managing the mines and for two centuries had been working in them with their own hands. The *conquistadores* had come to New Granada with the fantasy of of being lords of creation who would make their fortunes romantically and rule over their own little kingdoms. Even though things did not work out just as they had hoped, many of them made this fantasy come true on the Sabana and in the Valley. It may be supposed that, determined to bury their humble past, those who had been of working-class origin turned all the more zealously and haughtily to the values of landedness and gentility. This is a familiar phenomenon.

But in Antioquia that life slipped away from them, and they had to work again with their hands, with tools, at dirty work. There is reason to think that at first they yielded to apathy; but by six or eight generations the need to believe in the worth of the occupation to which one and one's ancestors have voluntarily devoted their lives asserted itself, and the Antioqueños found value in their labor.

The fact that large risks were involved in mining forced a bit of social invention which is of some importance. To the traditional Spaniards, family ties were of great importance, and the logical unit of economic activity was the family. However, a single mining venture might take all the family capital, and by risking it in a single venture one might lose it all and leave the family destitute. Therefore the very regard for the family which is at the base of the family relations elsewhere forced the Antioqueños to divide the risks of mining ventures among a number of families.

Thus there arose in Antioquia a special form of business association, permitted for a mining venture but for no other type of business operation. When a prospector had filed a claim, he might organize a company with 24 shares and invite participation. As the company needed added funds, the shareholders (presumably by majority vote among them) could be called upon to contribute equal added amounts, without limit. If one was unable to do so, reorganization ensued. Legal liability to creditors was limited, as in the modern corporation. In practice, however, it was compulsory for shareholders to contribute equally sums needed to pay the debts of a venture which failed. The essential effect was that a majority of stockholders could decide when to call a halt to a failing venture and divide the losses among them.

At the present time even in Antioquia business corporations tend to be family firms; and in even the largest corporations instances in which the top executives are not closely related by blood are uncommon. But there are more such instances in Antioquia than elsewhere in Colombia; Antioquia has escaped to a greater degree from the identity of family structure and business structure than have the people of other regions of Colombia. The necessity of spreading the risk of mining ventures may be the major explanation of this fact.

One of the essential features of entrepreneurial talent is the ability to assess business risks judiciously. Perhaps engaging in mining ventures gave the Antioqueños experience and judgment in business risk-taking. This point should not be stressed unduly, however, for entering on a prospecting and mining venture often partook more of the nature of gambling than of rational assessment of risks. The companion argument that their mining experience gave the Antioqueños familiarity with machinery and mechanical operations probably has more merit. Perhaps apart from the higher valuation of work with their hands and with machines, their experience in mining gave them more skill, confidence, and judgment in assessing and conducting mechanical operations.

However, only 40 per cent of the gold mined in New Granada was mined in Antioquia.[44] Perhaps within Colombia alone as much gold was mined elsewhere as in Antioquia. In addition, silver mining and mining of other metals was carried on in various regions other than Antioquia in significant amounts. If mining experience were the major influence, it should have produced a relatively larger number of entrepreneurs from the other mining areas. Yet the mining experience of the Antioqueños is certainly one of the causal factors.

Trading and Economic Development

Another possible explanation lies in regional differences at the time of the decline, early in the twentieth century, of large-scale trading in Colombia.

I have noted that until after 1900 the process of getting goods to the Sabana, Antioquia, and the Valley was expensive and risky. In addition to overcoming physical transportation difficulties, the trader had to establish contacts with traders and sources of finance in London, Paris, New York, or other centers, and to manage the necessary financial accounting and negotiations. For an individual or firm in a Colombian city, far from the foreign financial and industrial centers and without internationally recognized *bona fides*, these processes were not simple. Individuals who possessed both the necessary capacities and ability or luck in carrying on the physical processes of exporting or importing possessed a natural monopoly of importance.

[44] The total gold production of New Granada up to 1886 has been estimated at $639 million (U.S.) in value, of which about $255 million had come from Antioquia. Vincente Restrepo, *A Study of the Gold and Silver Mines of Colombia*, trans. C. W. Fisher (New York: Colombian Consulate, 1886), cited in Parsons, *Antioqueño Colonization*, pp. 58–59.

For each family which made a fortune, small or large, in foreign trade there were apparently several who lost the capital they invested. At the turn of the twentieth century there were in each of the three main cities a few families who were doing exceedingly well in trade and whose income and wealth, relative to that of the other families around them and also by most absolute scales, were considerable.[45] A substantial volume of coffee was exported from Medellín, and imports were correspondingly large.

The risks in the trade were great, but for firms that could master them the margin of profit was also great. Then, between 1900 and 1915, improvements in transportation tremendously reduced both the cost and the risk of importing and exporting. In reaction, what did the trading families do?

According to accounts given me in the three cities, the differences in the opportunities open to them are important in explaining their reactions. In Bogotá families who had made fortunes of some size in trading and now foresaw reduced opportunities in that field automatically did one or both of two things. If their sons were so minded, they educated them for the professions. Whether or not they did this, they invested their money in land and entered into the landed elite. The professions and life as a member of the landed gentry were the two social positions of highest status, and by instinctive reaction they turned to them.

In Cali the reactions were more diverse. Two of the families which were prominent in trade at the end of the century are now prominent in finance or industry in Cali. (One was already more in industry than in trade.) One, the Menotti family, has left Colombia. (Gian-Carlo Menotti is a son.) Others have to some degree disintegrated. While perhaps some of the trading money has gone into the cattle business, there has been no general reversion to the land comparable to that in Bogotá.

But in Medellín, it is said, money which had been made in trade flowed into industry because these alternative opportunities were lacking. There were neither cattle ranches nor landed estates to acquire; there was no landed gentry with the social prestige of that on the Sabana. Neither was there a humanistic cultural *milieu* in which the professions were of quite as high status. Hence, lacking these alternatives, the families with money appraised the opportunities around them and went into industry.

[45] In Cali, the leading individuals of which this was true included a German named Bomer (perhaps Bohmer), Pedro Pablo Caicedo, Henry J. Eder, Gregorio Gonzalez, Fidel Lalinde, Ulpiano Lloreda, Benito López, and perhaps others. In Antioquia the four most important trading firms were perhaps Alejandro Echavarría e Hijos, Pablo Lalinde y Compañía, Lazaro Mejía y Compañía (or, Lazaro Mejía e Hijos), and Hijos de Fernando Restrepo. I do not have a corresponding list for Bogotá. A little later other families came to prominence who are now prominent in both cities.

Such an explanation does not explain enough. Industry was not developed in any of the three regions merely by the trading families. The rise of industry had begun both in Antioquia and on the Sabana before the decline of the large trading margins occurred. The tendency to enter the professions existed in Bogotá before the turn of the century. Further, the phenomenon to be explained is not simply the greater entry of Antioqueños into industry but also their greater business acumen, entrepreneurial foresight, and organizational skill. The availability of capital from trade probably accelerated the later growth of industry in Antioquia and is one strand in the explanation we are seeking, but other, sturdier strands remain to be located.

SOCIAL TENSIONS

There remains for consideration an influence affecting personality in Antioquia which is less tangible, less obvious to common sense than those so far discussed above, but which seems of peculiar importance. This is the impact of withdrawal from Antioqueños of respect for their status in the society.

As I have attempted to show above, the Antioqueños, like the settlers in other regions, came from Spanish stock. In Spain they had been of equal status with the immigrants to other regions, and they looked upon themselves as of equal worth in the new land. But they were not looked upon as equals by Colombians of the other regions.

Economically, throughout the colonial period and into the era of independence, they were looked upon as backward; and clearly in fact they were less successful than their fellows in other regions. They were also looked upon by the Bogotanos, the Caleños, and the inhabitants of Popayán as socially inferior, In view of the traditional values of those groups, it is obvious that they would look with some scorn or at least condescension on a group who worked as menials. Perhaps the greater number of Basques among them provided an added reason for condescension toward them. In any event, condescension existed.

It persists today. When the Bogotano of today says, "They are New Christians, you know," he is expressing condescension (and rage at their success) which is like that felt by a New Englander of 1875 at a prosperous gauche Chicagoan (the Antioqueños probably were gauche too) or by an Englishman of the eighteenth century at any American. The sense of this attitude which one gets in Bogotá (or Cartagena, or Popayán) does not depend merely on such verbal comments. It is manifested in tone and attitude in almost any luncheon conversation about business progress in Colombia.

The disparagement is not merely a defensive reaction to the greater economic success of the Antioqueños. It existed before that success was achieved. The pervasiveness in the nineteenth century of the legend that Antioqueños are of Jewish origin was probably a rationalization of the attitude felt then that they were different, that is, alien, and therefore inferior; it certainly is evidence of such an attitude.

Politically and socially Antioquia was a backwater. In a history of Colombia which stresses political events, like that by Henao and Arrubla, one finds Antioquia rarely mentioned in the account of the nineteenth century. Political events took place in Bogotá, Popayán, the Valley, Cartagena, and to a lesser extent Pasto and Santa Marta. Antioquia did not enter conspicuously; it did not count. When technical experts were sent to New Granada to suggest improvements in the mines, they did not visit Antioquia. Schools or scientific institutes were established by the Spanish government of the colonial administration at Bogotá, Popayán, and Cartagena, but not at Medellín.[46] When armies from Antioquia joined in the nation's civil wars, they were markedly less successful than armies from other regions. Apparently they did not fight with fervor. Antioquia was regarded as so much outside the stream of things that in mid-century a political leader exiled in the bitter civil strife or who fled for his personal safety went to Antioquia—as though that were an alien territory which did not count in the rivalry.

In all probability, the Colombians of the Sabana, the Valley, and elsewhere in the nineteenth century were not self-conscious about an attitude that the Antioqueños were of inferior worth (as many of them are self-conscious today); it was just that, as they perceived the world, the Antioqueños were inferior just as the grass is green and the rain wet.

If this sort of social relationship had been the traditional one, and the relative social status taken as a fact of life by both parties to it, then it might have been merely an aspect of a stable social structure, as serfdom and other differences in social level were in the feudal system and the caste system in India. The Antioqueños, however, did not think of themselves as inferior. Today they are as conscious of the attitudes of many other Colombians toward them as an outsider is, and they smart under them. Undoubtedly they did so in the nineteenth and eighteenth centuries. I suggest that this tension, by its effect on family environment, caused changes in personality (in needs, values, and world cognition) conducive to creativity. I suggest, too, that as these changes in personality proceeded, the Antioqueños sought restlessly to prove their worth and,

[46] See Henao and Arrubla, *History of Colombia*. The Antioqueños themselves early established a university at Medellín, but that is a different matter.

in the world of the nineteenth and twentieth centuries, found what they sought in economic prowess. In other eras they would have found it in some other type of activity, but the availability of advanced techniques to those who sought them out, the importance of economic power, their economic experience, the noneffectiveness in the Colombian setting of channels such as military or political activity, and the probable aversion they had acquired to aping the humanistic-intellectual activities of their disparagers combined to channel their energies into economic activity.

Over a series of generations the Antioqueños seem to have passed through a period of apathy or retreatism and then become creative. Colombian accounts imply that the Antioqueños in colonial times were shiftless, reckless, gambling, bawdy—all characteristics which may be associated with retreatism as I have defined it. The entire sequence of historical events is consistent with the hypothesis that the Antioqueños reacted gradually over a period of several centuries to withdrawal of status respect, and that this reaction and its impact on their personalities form an important strand in the explanation of the economic growth of Colombia.[47]

I have noted in earlier chapters that a group which rejects traditional symbols of status which it does not possess and cannot attain, and by the yardsticks of which it has been denied the status it feels due it, apparently never rejects them entirely. Even while it suppresses them and overlays them with new values such as the worth of hard work in erstwhile menial occupations, it yet retains also a melancholy longing to attain the old symbols of status for further self-reassurance. So it has been with the Antioqueños. They have turned to business prowess, but when they have attained economic success they replant one foot on the land which their ancestors abandoned by force of necessity. Thus one will find that almost every successful Antioqueño (among those with whom I became acquainted there were no exceptions), whether in Antioquia or elsewhere, has purchased an estate, small or large, in the country and thinks of that estate as his home or his "second home." If his career is elsewhere than in Antioquia, preferably his *pied-à-terre* is back in Antioquia.

CONCLUSION

These, then, are possible strands in the web of causation which led to Antioqueño leadership in economic innovation. Their activity in this field has more

[47] A far more detailed study of Colombian social history than I have been able to make, to test this hypothesis more comprehensively, would be of interest.

than sufficient causes; it is, in the terminology of logic, overdetermined. Perhaps a higher incidence of Basque blood in Antioquia than elsewhere contributed. Perhaps the mining experience of Antioqueños, even in the absence of other factors, would have caused them to be leaders in economic growth. Perhaps the differences between the opportunities most open to them and those open to the traders of other regions when the opportunities for profit in international trade shrank at the beginning of the twentieth century would have been sufficient. Probably withdrawal of status respect would have been sufficient. No doubt, the combination of these factors explains their predominance in economic entrepreneurship.

APPENDIX 1
NEED AGGRESSION IN COLOMBIA

Even though its relationship to economic growth is not clear, need aggression in Colombia is so conspicuous that it should be noted.

It would be rash to refer to the brutal treatment of the indigenous population by the Spanish conquerors as evidence of unusually high need aggression, for indigenous populations which were uncivilized by European standards have been treated brutally by virtually every conquering group. However, unrestrained need aggression is apparent historically both in the civil wars which were so conspicuous in the nation's history from its independence in 1819 until 1902 and in some political behavior since that time. No decade, and hardly any four-year period, from 1819 to 1902 was free from minor or major civil wars, 70 of which in all are recorded. The political differences which were the ostensible causes of civil strife were never great enough to account for the repeated blood-letting except by a people whose need aggression was almost uncontrollable. An estimate generally accepted in Colombia is that in the last great conflict of 1899–1902 some 100,000 persons were killed;[48] and an American authority presents an estimate, which I cannot trace to another source, that in the late 1870's, 80,000 were killed.[49] The 1899–1902 figure is 2.5 per cent of the total population of that time, or one person of every 40 men, women, and children in the country. The estimate of deaths 20 years earlier is a slightly larger percentage of the population. Deaths in the four-year American Civil War were a considerably smaller fraction of the population (about 2 per cent). These are only two of the most spectacular in a series of bloody chapters. They are not chapters in a closed book. It is estimated that rural violence in Colombia during the past 13 years has apparently taken more lives than the civil war at the end of the century. It was exacerbated in 1948 when political violence flared and some leaders of the party in power encouraged

[48] See, for example, Henao and Arrubla, *History of Colombia*, p. 519.
[49] J. Fred Rippy, *The Capitalists and the Colombians*, p. 23. He gives the date of war as 1879. This is in error, and renders the estimate doubtful.

bands of peasant thugs to seize the lands of political opponents, but its continuing level, even in 1961, is not explained by the aftermath of those incidents.[50]

The high need aggression is manifested less spectacularly today in urban traffic, in the national beauty contests, and in the prostitution rate. Traffic at major urban intersections is rigidly controlled—so rigidly controlled that one senses awareness of a special need for control. Elsewhere it reflects a sort of tense, proud warfare between driver and pedestrian. In the annual beauty contest the candidates are not, as in the United States, young women of lower or lower-middle income classes who among other attractions see the contest as a path to a possible luxurious future, but include daughters of the most influential "recently arrived" families—though not of the "old" society. Regional excitement is intense. During the several weeks before the national contest late in 1957 the leading metropolitan daily newspapers devoted an average of more than two full pages daily to the contest. Judges for the national contest are brought in from abroad, presumably because no Colombian would be thought to be impartial. When the national champion ("winner" is not an adequate term) came home to Medellín in the 1957 contest, the expectant crowd milled about the main street in a burst of aggressive release which included a degree of drunkenness, rowdyism, destruction of property, and minor brutality by police attempting to control the most extreme individuals. In Bogotá the automobile carrying the national and regional champions was unable to make its way through a similar crowd to reach a social occasion in the elite section of the city; one of the girls fled into a drugstore, minus one shoe and in fear for her person, while, according to newspaper reports, the crowd stripped hub caps, rear-view mirror, and one headlight from the automobile bearing her.

Licensed prostitution is a more regular outlet for the same need aggression, one tolerated by the arbiters of community morals presumably in an attempt to keep sexual aggression from bursting out of bounds elsewhere. Prostitution is said to be greater in Antioquia than in other regions. Licensed prostitution has been increasing there. In 1930 there was one registered prostitute in the city of Medellín for every 50 males of all ages. In 1946 the number had increased to 4,260, or one for every 30 males of all ages,[51] and I was told by a responsible informant that in 1957 the number was about 12,000, or one to every 24 or 25 males (say one to every 12 to 15 males old enough to be patrons) in metropolitan Medellín.

In noting this I would not suggest that need aggression is higher in Colombia than in other Latin countries. Manifestations of high need aggression in most or all Latin countries are frequently recorded in descriptions of those countries. Neither would I assert that need aggression is higher than in non-Latin Western countries; all that can safely be asserted is that the manifestations are different.[52] Whatever the relative facts may

[50] *New York Times*, February 14, 1961.

[51] *El Colombiano* (Medellín), January 18, 1947, quoted in Parsons, *Antiqueño Coloniza-tion*, p. 108.

[52] Perhaps North Americans are as high in need aggression but because of greater guilt about it release it in less overt ways, for example, in watching the portrayal of brutality in

be, it is worthwhile to record that the personality mix out of which the economic and political innovations of recent generations have arisen includes high need aggression which manifests itself in various active ways.

This need aggression in Colombia is probably a result of social tensions that affect the environment in the home. I do not know whether it contributes to or retards economic growth, but because some reader may be more perceptive than I in sensing its significance I record it here.

APPENDIX 2
BASQUE ANCESTRY AMONG
ANTIOQUEÑO ENTREPRENEURS

The evidence that persons of Basque blood in Antioquia may be business entrepreneurs in relatively larger numbers than persons of other Spanish blood derives from a notable genealogical volume by Gabriel Arango Mejía, *Geneologías de Antioquia y Caldas,* Vol. I.

This opus lists the names of all the families mentioned in the earlier records of Antioquia and Caldas (excepting perhaps some for whom Arango could not obtain information) and traces them to their Spanish origins. It is the work of most of the lifetime of a man, freed of the necessity of earning a living by the earlier success of his family, who turned instead to this particular piece of scholarship.

Clearly many of the genealogical facts stated in the volume are open to question. It is known that some early migrants to the new world bought their family papers, for example, to conceal prison records which would have caused them to be denied permission to join the *conquistadores*. But it is reasonable to assume that in such cases the individual was apt to assume a name from his section of Spain, so that the practice, however rare or common it may have been, probably does not greatly distort the analysis of the regional origins of Antioqueño families.

On this assumption, I had a research worker tabulate all of the surnames listed in the 1957 Medellín telephone directory into three groups: Spanish names listed in the genealogy, Spanish names not listed in the genealogy,[53] and non-Spanish names. Almost 97 per cent of the names listed were of Spanish origin, and of the Spanish names more than 70 per cent appear in the genealogy. The Spanish names shown in the genealogy were then tabulated according to the region in Spain from which they originated.

The same procedure was then followed for the chief executive officer (*presidente* or

---

Western and detective stories on television. However, the probable presence in Colombia of a greater degree of authoritarianism in child training makes me suspect that the level of need aggression, insofar as this can be isolated in personality, may be greater than in the United States (or Canada).

[53] With this group were also included names which according to the genealogy were native to more than one region of Spain, so that from the name it was not possible to assign a Medellín family to one or another region.

TABLE 10-3
Origin of Medellín Surnames[a]

Spanish Region of Origin	Families Listed in Telephone Directory		National Association of Industrialists										FENALCO: President or Owner[b]		ACOPI: President or Owner[c]	
			Presidents		Presidents: Mother's Family		Principal Directors		Alternate Directors							
	No.	%	No.	%	No.	%	No.	%	No.	%	No.	%	No.	%
Vasconia	1,700	10.4	14	11.1	14	13.5	30	13.0	40	17.8	33	9.9	16	11.9
Andalucia	2,298	14.1	12	9.5	15	14.4	18	7.8	24	10.7	42	12.7	12	8.9
Asturias	2,283	14.0	13	10.6	11	10.6	29	12.6	25	11.1	50	15.1	23	17.0
Castilla	3,355	20.5	16	12.7	15	14.4	28	12.1	34	15.1	63	19.1	23	17.0
Extremadura	1,255	7.7	7	5.5	10	9.6	9	3.9	11	4.9	20	6.5	7	5.2
Aragon							2	0.9			7	2.1		
Navarra							1	0.4	1	0.4				
Galicia	80	0.5	1	0.8							2	0.6		
Region not identified	4,813	29.4	25	19.8	21	20.2	54	23.4	50	22.2	73	22.3	32	23.8
Not Spanish	567	3.5	38	30.1	18	17.3	60	26.0	40	17.8	39	11.8	22	16.3
Total	16,351	100.1	126	100.1	104	100.0	231	100.1	225	100.0	329	100.1	135	100.1

Memoranda:

1. Names of Vasconia origin as percentage of Spanish names:

	10.8		15.9		16.3		17.5		21.6		11.4		14.2

2. Names of Vasconia origin as percentage of Spanish names whose regional origins are indentified:

	15.5		22.2		21.5		25.6		29.6		15.2		19.8

[a] Father's family, except for "Presidents: Mother's Family" columns.
[b] FENALCO = National Federation of Commercial Companies.
[c] ACOPI = Association of Small Industrialists.

gerente)[54] and the principal and alternate directors of all companies in Medellín which were members of the National Association of Industrialists (Asociación Nacional de Industriales) in 1957; the president or owner of each company which was a member of the National Federation of Commercial Companies (Federación Nacional de Comerciantes); and the president or owner of each company which was a member of the Association of Small Industrialists (ACOPI, or Asociación Colombiana de Pequeños Industriales).[55]

The terms "principal" and "alternate" director require explanation. The "regular" members of boards of directors are termed "principal directors." In all or almost all companies, for each principal director there is an alternate who serves as a member of the board of directors at any meeting which the corresponding principal director is not able to attend.

It should be noted also that, as in other countries of Spanish culture, every individual has two surnames, that of his father (which is written first, following his given name) and that of his mother (which is written last). The maternal surname is the family name of the mother's father. Most though not all individuals use both names. Thus Gabriel Arango Mejía, author of the genealogy, is the son of a man whose surname was Arango and of a mother whose surname was Mejía. He would customarily be referred to by his father's surname, that is, as Señor Arango. In the study of regional origins the maternal surname of chief executives of the National Association of Industrialists was checked as well as the paternal surname. The results are shown separately.[56]

The results of the research are shown in Table 10-3.

The figures which probably are of most interest are those of the second memorandum line at the bottom of the table. Among persons bearing Spanish names whose region of origin in Spain is known a much higher percentage are from the Basque country in every executive group than in the population at large.

The differences are so large that obviously they are statistically significant. That is, they could hardly have come about by chance.[57] It is not equally certain that they reflect a greater tendency for persons of Basque blood than persons of other Spanish blood to be successful as business executives. There are a number of possible sources of error. Perhaps the persons bearing certain surnames in Medellín are not in fact the descendants of persons of the same names in the genealogy. Or subscribers to telephones in Medellín may not be

[54] As in United States companies, there is some ambiguity concerning the title of the chief executive officer. In some companies the president of the company may be the chief executive; in others, the general manager (or *gerente*). The name used in the tabulation was that of the individual who, according to the knowledge of officials at the National Association of Industrialists in Medellín, was in fact the chief executive.

[55] For this study I am indebted to the very capable and conscientious work of Juan Be Londoño B.

[56] The names of many families are identical. Each name was counted as many times as it appears in the directory except for the elimination of duplication between office and residential listings.

[57] The possible sources of error in the analysis are sufficient so that deriving precise numerical measures of significance by applying standard statistical procedures does not seem justified.

representative of the entire Medellín population; possibly some distortion is involved here. Possibly for some historical reason persons in Spain buying false family names purchased names from one region to a greater extent than from other regions. But there is no obvious reason to assume that these possible sources of error would have a greater tendency to bias the results so as to increase the percentage of Basque ancestry shown among executives relative to that in the population as a whole.[58]

Perhaps one final fact should be noted. In 1951 the estimated population of the Basque provinces was only 3.7 per cent of that of all Spain. If the same ratio prevailed in the sixteenth and seventeenth centuries, persons from the Basque provinces either migrated selectively to Antioquia or formed a much higher percentage of all migrants to New Granada than they did of the Spanish population. However, the difference in the rate of population growth in the new environment and that in the old may in any case have been so great that population ratios now are no guide to those 300 or 400 years ago.

[58] A surprising percentage of the executives, especially of the presidents and principal directors of the larger industrial firms, bear non-Spanish names. Presumably this large foreign representation among executives is due in part to the need of larger Colombian firms for foreign capital and financial connections. To get them, they admitted foreign representation into their management.

11

FAMILY STRUCTURE, MIGRATION, AND THE ENTREPRENEUR

Leonard Kasdan

T HE problem of entrepreneurship has been one of the central interests of economic theorists since the industrial revolution. Discussions of the entrepreneur in such theory tended to a large extent to focus upon the basis of entrepreneurship. This argument is typified by Schumpeter's criticism of Marx's handling of the problem of primitive accumulation; Schumpeter argues against the rejection by Marx of superior intelligence and energy as explanatory factors in entrepreneurial success.

> Nobody who looks at historical and contemporaneous fact with anything like an un-biased mind can fail to observe that this children's tale, while far from telling the whole truth yet tells a good deal of it. Supernormal intelligence and energy account for industrial success and in particular for the *founding* of industrial positions in nine cases out of ten.[1]

Aside from reiterating the importance of such factors, he adds no information

Reprinted by permission of the author and publisher from Comparative Studies in Society and History, *VII, 4 (1965), pp. 345-357.*

[1] Joseph A. Schumpeter, *Capitalism, Socialism and Democracy* (New York and Evanston, 1962).

explaining how such people are recruited to entrepreneurial activity, or telling us if energy and intelligence are all that characterize such individuals.

Recent years have seen the examination of the question of entrepreneurship come to the fore again, albeit in a somewhat different form. The more recent discussion rather than assuming that entrepreneurs are more intelligent and energetic, has focused upon the social and psychological corollaries of entrepreneurship. This paper concerns itself with aspects of the more recent discussion.

PART ONE

One of the by-products of the current interest in economic development has been the attempt to relate the personality characteristics which typify entrepreneurs to the social groups with which they have affiliations. One of these attempts has been made by Everett Hagen in his book *On the Theory of Social Change*.[2] Hagen raises certain questions about this relationship which the present paper will seek to clarify. This will be done by primarily examining one problem, the Basque contribution to the economic development of Colombia, with reference being made to some other comparative data where relevant. Although Hagen's argument in no way depends exclusively upon this one case, I believe that an examination of it can be useful in helping to refine the general treatment of such problems.

One of Hagen's primary concerns is to ". . . state something about the nature of the functional relationships between elements of social structure and elements of personality which need to be introduced into models of society."[3] He stresses the fact that personality develops and changes throughout the life of the individual, and he does not make the mistake of equating single factors, such as toilet training, with the complex and continuing process of socialization. There are, however, areas in which I believe his analysis is open to criticism. First, there is too little attention paid to social structural features which modify the manner in which socialization impinges upon different members of the same society. Secondly, the model he uses of a traditional (peasant) society is overly static and social structure is seen as deriving from psychological phenomena. The reasons for these statements will become clearer after the analysis of the particular case.

In a chapter entitled, "The Transition in Colombia",[4] Hagen analyzes the

---

[2] Everett Hagen, *On the Theory of Social Change* (Homewood, Illinois, 1962).
[3] Ibid., p. 5 and passim.   [4] Ibid., pp. 353–384.

basis for Colombia's autonomous economic growth, growth largely independent of outside support or stimulation. One of the problems he raises deals with the disproportionate contribution made by the region of Antioquia and its citizens (Antioqueños). He points out that "politically and socially Antioquia was a backwater."[5] Other Colombians considered the Antioqueños inferior. Hagen examines various stereotypic explanations for the alleged inferiority, as well as the stereotypes which seek to explain the success of the Antioqueños.[6] He disposes of the argument that Jewish descent is responsible for their characteristics, but has less success with another argument based upon ethnic differences—that of the Basque origin of the Antioqueños.

In an appendix entitled, "Basque Ancestry among Antioqueño Entrepreneurs," Hagen marshalls evidence which demonstrates that persons with identifiable Basque surnames may be represented in the entrepreneur group in greater proportion than other people of Spanish descent.[7]

> Among persons bearing Spanish names whose region of origin in Spain is known a much higher percentage are from the Basque country in every executive group than in the population at large.[8]

Thus:

> One must therefore conclude that Basque ancestry in Antioquia may be associated in some degree with the economic success of Antioqueños.[9]

Furthermore, if the ratio of Basques to immigrants from other areas of Spain was the same in the past as at present in Antioquia, there must have been a higher percentage of migration of Basques to this area than of other Spaniards. There are today 15.7 per cent persons with Basque names and yet the Basques represent only 3.7 per cent of the population of Spain today.[10]

As Hagen himself points out[11] contemporary proportions may be no index of proportion in the past, or of rates of growth in the country of immigration. If the more recent patterns are examined as possible sources of information they prove to be of little help in explaining the role of Basques. Kulischer points out that:

> The afore-mentioned contrast between interior Spain and the coast had been created by an earlier migratory current connected with Spain's past expansion by way of the sea.

[5] Ibid., p. 377.   [6] Ibid., p. 371–372.
[7] The figures are 15.5 per cent in the population at large versus 22.2 per cent among executives.   [8] Ibid., pp. 380–383.   [9] Ibid., p. 372.
[10] Ibid., Table 15–3, pp. 382–383.   [11] Ibid., p. 383.

The population flocked to the coasts, whence in former times a fleet of conquerors and colonists departed and where later simple emigrants embarked for overseas countries.[12]

In general the coastal and port provinces (of which the Basque provinces are a part) show the highest rate of emigration per thousand of population with the northern provinces sending most of their emigrants to the Americas and those of the south sending most of theirs to N. Africa. The fact that the Galician provinces of La Coruña and Pontevedra have led all other provinces in number of emigrants per thousand of population (e.g., 13.3 and 12.7 per cent in 1885–86 according to Vicens[13]) and yet are represented by only 0.5 per cent of Hagen's Colombian sample, while Vasconia with a much lower rate (2.7 per cent according to Vicens) has 10.4 per cent of his sample would indicate that selective migration of Basques to Colombia may well have been of some importance. This, however, does not explain the disproportionate contribution the Basques make as entrepreneurs in proportion to their representation in the Colombian population. The data are not available for an answer in quantitative terms even if it were possible to give such an answer. Thus we must look to qualitative factors for a possible explanation.

Hagen rejects biological arguments, and suggests a cultural explanation instead.

The people of the Basque provinces have long been looked down upon, or at least have been looked upon as different and a little odd, by many other Spaniards. They are rugged hard-working mountain people who have preserved a cultural separateness. These personality characteristics may have been transmitted in Colombia over many generations.[14]

However, the rugged, hard-working, culturally separate nature of these mountain people does not constitute a set of characteristics which make for entrepreneurial skills. Quite the contrary, these characteristics are conservative traits which are hard to associate with risk-taking and change. Basque society fully meets the criteria of a traditional peasant society as Hagen characterizes it.[15] The settlement pattern consists of nucleated villages with few houses; religion is a primary integrating force; there is family cultivation with specialists working at their specialties only on a part-time basis; production is through the use of hand tools; mobilization of labor beyond the family is on a communal basis. Hagen argues that such a society ". . . in short tends to be custom-bound,

---

[12] Eugene Kulischer, *Europe on the Move* (New York, 1948), p. 227.

[13] Jaime Vicens-Vives, *Historia Social y Económica de España y América*, Vol. 2, Book 2 (Barcelona, 1959), p. 256.   [14] Hagen, op. cit., p. 372.   [15] Ibid., pp. 61–74.

hierarchical ascriptive and unproductive."[16] It is hard to see why this combination of features should lead to the creation of entrepreneurs among the Basques when it stultifies such activities in other peasant societies. The Basques in fact are a classic example of a peasant group which has used every means to resist change, including force. This is brought out quite clearly if one looks at their role in Spanish history since the eighteenth century.

Thus the question of the contribution of the Basques to the entrepreneurial pool of Antioquia is still unresolved. I believe that this question can at least partially be answered by an examination of the institutional pattern which impinged upon the prospective emigrants, particularly the Basque family system. I will attempt to demonstrate that migration from the traditional community was selective and that this selectivity operated in such a manner as to maximize the chances for entrepreneurial personality types to emigrate to places like Antioquia. This analysis will also suggest a possible explanation as to why the Basque immigrants make proportionately a larger contribution in entrepreneurship than do other Spanish immigrants. Some theoretical implications of this analysis will be discussed.

PART TWO

The rural Basques differ from most Spaniards not only in language and customs, but also the typical ecology in which the great majority of their farms are found is different. The Basques are a typical wet area group as contrasted with the more usual Spanish agricultural areas which tend to be dry. These differences are brought out clearly in the table below where the corollaries of adequate rainfall in the Basque areas are contrasted with those which accompany an arid ecology.

TABLE 11-1
The Contrast between Dry and Wet Spain[17]

Wet Spain	Dry Spain
1. Intensive agriculture	1. Extensive agriculture
2. Polyculture (with one money crop in recent times)	2. Monoculture
3. Subsistence farming primarily	3. Primarily market oriented
4. Small holding (minifundia)	4. Large holdings (latifundia)
5. Long-term, well protected leases	5. Short-term, unprotected leases
6. Family and reciprocal communal labor	6. Hired labor

[16] Ibid., pp. 55–56.

[17] For a province by province analysis see Gerald Brennan, *The Spanish Labyrinth* (Cambridge, 1960), pp. 87–130.

Thus the Basques are seen to be a good example of the kind of European peasantry which is oriented towards independent family farming. Ideology, social organization and economic organization all reflect this fact.

The basic unit of the Basque rural community is the family farm (*casario*), which is ideally a self-sufficient unit,[18] producing enough to support its residents and only marginally dependent upon the money economy for most of its needs. A concomitant of this type of economic unit is a strongly land-centered value system, which has the perpetuation of the casario as its most salient feature. One could fairly say that a large part of custom and of Basque customary law is oriented towards the realization of this value.

If we examine the typical social composition of a casario we can see how the central value of perpetuation of the casario is reflected in its social organization. Caro[19] mentions five groups of people found in a typical casario. These are: a wedded couple (the elders), a younger couple (the heir and his or her spouse), unmarried children of the heir, one or two relatives of the above (commonly unmarried children of the elders, *i.e.*, brothers or sisters of the heir), servants (usually no more than two, who are celibate). There are other factors which lend further support to the central value of self-sufficiency and inviolability of the casario through time. Unmarried residents may make no claims of inheritance upon it. Both rules of inheritance and rules of marriage buttress the inviolability of the casario. In general, inheritance is by male primogeniture, with patrilocal residence. Where deviations from this primary rule occur, the determining principle is perpetuation of the casario as an undivided unit. The variations which occur are actually flexible ways of achieving this primary goal. The following brief examination of these variations will lend support to Dovring's argument that:

> Most rules on indivisibility of farms have as their underlying practical reasons the economic danger in treating parts of an agricultural enterprise as the mere sum of objects which can at any time be disposed of one by one. Other considerations such as fiscal interests, or the special concerns of families or a familistic society at large are, regarded closely, mainly consequences of this general principle.[20]

The *casario* being inviolable, without consent of the heir-to-be, the problem facing each farm family is the choice of an heir. It is here that we find a great deal of variation which can be summarized in relation to particular local,

---

[18] Since the middle of the nineteenth century there has been a decrease in the degree of self-sufficiency.

[19] Julio Caro, *Los Vascos* (Madrid, 1949), p. 275.

[20] Folke Dovring, *Land and Labour in Europe 1900–1950* (The Hague, 1956), p. 158.

ecological, social, and economic conditions. The easiest way of proceeding is to take, as a point of departure, the system of marriage, for as in almost all peasant communities it represents and reflects the realities of economic life in an easily analyzable form.

The main problem in marriage, from the Basque point of view, is to assure the inviolability of the patrimony, the general rule being that inheritance is patrilineal with this reflected in patrilocal residence. However, in cases where there are no males to inherit, a man may marry the daughter of such a family and eventually come to be head of the family.[21] This is the most general and widespread occurrence.

There are also cases in which there is absolute primogeniture, regardless of the sex of the heir,[22] accompanied by a rule which prevents a male heir marrying a female heir, which in turn would challenge the inviolability of the *casario* by presenting an either/or choice relative to residence. In such a case an heir marries a junior member of another house who is of course not an heir.[23] Another variation is that the heir may be freely chosen regardless of sex or sequence of birth. This is done by the parents or else by an informally constituted family council. This practice seems to be very limited in its distribution.

In some Pyrenean valleys of Navarre, male youths regularly become *indianos*, i.e., emigrate at an early age to the Americas, leaving their sisters behind *para casa* as heirs to the natal houses. The sisters will then marry returned *indianos* while their brothers return years later, presumably with an accumulated store of capital, and marry in the same vicinity women left *para casa* by their brothers. There are also areas in which strict primogeniture by the oldest daughter prevails.[24] Caro says that these are found widely scattered all over France and Spain but gives no explanation for them except that they meet local conditions.

One factor which can be seen both as a correlate of such latitude of choices and also as a necessary condition is that the male and female roles relative to power are not nearly so rigidly distinguishable here as in the rest of Spain. There is much more participation by women and weight given to them in decision making than where other conditions prevail. Caro, quoting from Jacques de Bela, notes that the women are in the same position as the men with regard to the management of the farm and "thus men and women work in the same way."[25] This fact is further reflected in the inscriptions over the doorways of houses which mention both the husband's and the wife's names as "master

---

[21] Caro, op. cit., p. 277.   [22] Ibid.

[23] Phillippe Veyrin, *Les Basques: de Labourde, de Soule et Basse-Navarre* (Grenoble, 1947).

[24] Caro, op. cit., pp. 277–278.   [25] Ibid., p. 278.

and mistress of this house," and results in the partners in a marriage being conceptualized as "companions in matrimony," an intensification of the Catholic conception.

The inevitable situation resulting from these practices is the existence of a large group of individuals whom the casario cannot support and who therefore have no claim upon it. What happens to these redundant individuals is as important to the viability of this social system as the rules of inheritance or marriage. If institutionalized mechanisms were not developed, the continuation of the system would be placed in jeopardy by the pressures generated by the presence of a disinherited and disaffected population which, because of a low demand for outside labor, could not be employed locally. The history of anarchism in Andalucia bears testimony to how explosive a force a chronic labor surplus can be.

The traditional solutions for non-heirs are as follows:

1. Some are given payment in cash which they are expected to use in building an independent income, usually outside of the local community.

2. Some become *indianos*, immigrants to the New World, who will in theory return with fortunes made there.

3. Being highly orthodox Catholics, many Basques join religious orders or pursue other ecclesiastical careers.

4. A very small number may remain in their natal communities as artisans or shepherds.

5. Some become sailors, and today many are absorbed into industry, just as in the distant past many were absorbed into the armies of the reconquest and/or in the interior colonization attendant upon the expulsion of the Moors.

6. A small number remain celibate within their own casarios.

Sufficient ethnographic information has now been presented so that I can return to the initial problem involving the prominent role of individuals of Basque extraction in the rapid development of Antioquia.

PART THREE

It should be obvious from the above discussion that a significant number of individuals in each farm-born generation are forced out of the local community. Non-heirs must choose one of the avenues listed above as a solution to their problems. With the exception of that small minority who come from areas where free choice prevails, they will be made aware of their alternatives early in life, and will develop different attitudes and personality characteristics than their sibling (in most cases a first-born son) who has his status as an heir defined by birth order. The latter group inherit their statuses and have only to be trained to play a well-defined traditional role. Non-heirs, on the other hand, must choose among a large number of alternatives and have no way of predicting the outcome of their choices. Thus most non-heirs are forced into situations which give status only for achievement on the basis of individual initiative.[26]

Thus people choosing the alternative of most interest here, emigration, would constitute a group resulting from a highly selective process. They would be particular individuals within the farm family, who have been inculcated throughout their childhood with the necessity of making their own way when mature. Among these individuals those most willing to strike out on their own and sacrifice the assured security of a celibate existence in the home or church would become emigrants. Thus the Basque population which emigrated to Antioquia was probably highly biased in the direction of entrepreneurial personality types and their disproportionate contribution there should not be surprising. Carefully gathered genealogical data, if available, could conclusively test this point.

There remains one more question to be answered. If we grant that there has been selective migration of Basques to the New World, why do not all Spaniards who immigrate make equal contributions—since they too may be selectively chosen? The answer to this lies in different inheritance patterns, and differences in the structure of the local Spanish community outside of the Basque country. These differences may result in a much lower selectivity for entrepreneurial types because of the presence of an institutional structure which would not provide the necessary type of socialization for them.

Equal inheritance among offsprings is the rule in almost all of Spain outside of the Basque provinces. Thus subdividing a farm, while it may leave some

---

[26] Those who choose the Church, or to remain celibate members of their own households, would tend to be individuals who want a well-defined institutional framework and are willing to accept it at the sacrifice of possibly much greater, although less sure, rewards outside.

individuals with little, does not disinherit them completely or deny to any special group the basis for status within the local community. Equally important, there would not be the anticipatory socialization pushing one towards independent risk-taking which would accompany the situation of primogeniture. By this is meant the fact that a non-heir among the Basques would very early in life have the differences in status between himself and that of an heir made very clear. He would see disinherited siblings leave, or if he had none of his own who had left, he would have seen the disinherited of other casarios leaving. He might also have come into contact with some who had left, made their fortunes, and returned sufficiently prosperous to buy the high status which the inheritance system denied them. In contrast to this, in a system of equal inheritance, the necessity of achieving status through unsupported individual effort, would not be emphasized until after the death of the father and no well-defined roles such as that of a second son would exist. If we add to these conditions the fact that in most of Spain the structure of agriculture and of the local community is such that many individuals can remain as part of a local agricultural proletariat (a thing impossible in the Basque areas) working for wages, we have another important differentiating factor.

From the foregoing discussion we see that Hagen has tended to make it more difficult to answer the question of the origin of entrepreneurs by his use of an inadequate model of traditional peasant society. From the Basque case it should be clear that two things must be added to the considerations stressed by Hagen. First, since peasant societies are parts of larger more complex wholes, the very fact of incapsulation in the larger unit allows for surplus population to be syphoned outside of the local community.[27] Such channels may in fact be necessary in order for some societies to maintain their cultures in a traditional manner. The second point is a corollary of the first. Generalizations which derive entrepreneurship from the culture of an undifferentiated ethnic group (as Hagen has attempted to do for the Basques) masks the fact that only a very special subgroup within the larger one actually becomes entrepreneurial types.

Hagen develops the concept of status deprivation as molding behavior in such a way that one among several possible outcomes is the creation of personality types which may make significant contributions in entrepreneurial activities.[28] In the case of the Basques the argument that differentness from other Spaniards would lead them to develop status anxieties would be hard

[27] A similar adaptation may be at the root of the boundary maintenance systems of many peasant groups where the land is inadequate for supporting a growing population. Cf. Everett Hughes, *French Canada in Transition* (London, 1946), pp. 20–21, 216.

[28] Hagen, op. cit., 193–194.

to support historically. However, there is little doubt that the disinherited Basques discussed above would in all likelihood have the kinds of anxieties about their personal statuses which might explain their success as entrepreneurs.

PART FOUR

To anticipate any argument that the foregoing analysis applies only to Spain, and not more generally, I will briefly compare the Basque case to two other land-centered traditional social systems, that of the Irish countryside and that of Northern Norway.[29]

Table 11-2 summarizes the ethnographic information on the three societies under discussion. An examination of it shows the basic units to be very similar

TABLE 11-2

Some salient characteristics of Basque, Irish and Norwegian rural society

		Basques	*Norwegians*	*Irish*
1	Economic Unit	Family farm tending towards self-sufficiency.	Family farm tending towards self-sufficiency.	Family farm tending towards self-sufficiency.
2.	Ownership	Individual ownership or equivalent long-term leases. Land in short supply.	Individual ownership. Possibility of home-steading.	Individual ownership. Land in short supply.
3.	Inheritance	Inheritance by primogeniture, with flexibility to meet special conditions.	Heir chosen on retirement of father who has free choice.	Heir chosen on retirement of father who has free choice.
4.	Marriage	Only the heir may marry. Others remain celibate until leaving farm	Mating before marriage. "Understandings".	Delayed marriage and parenthood.
5.	Family	Nuclear family with non-heirs remaining celibate if in residence.	Nuclear family with offspring of unmarried daughters.	Nuclear family with non-heirs leaving with their portion after succession.
6.	Population	Population surplus	Population surplus.	Population surplus.
7.	Personality Characteristics	Character traditionalistic, conservative except for non-heirs.	Independent enterprising character. Non-enterprising individuals become hired hands or crofters.	Traditionalistic, conservative.

[29] This is greatly facilitated by the fact that the basic comparative data on Ireland and Norway have been summarized in a form particularly useful for the interests of concern here. George K. Park, "Sons and Lovers: Characterological Requisites of the Roles in a Peasant Society," *Ethnology*, 1 (4): 412–424, Oct. 1962. Professor G. P. Murdock suggested this comparison to me.

in formal composition. In all three cases there is a land-based peasantry living on relatively self-sufficient farms of family size. Thus they all share the problem of transferring the farm as an undivided unit, as well as the corollary problem of coping with surplus population in the form of non-heirs.

If we look further, however, we find that the basically similar units in the three societies do not show uniformity in the structural and ideological solutions to the problem of persistence. The problems of marriage and succession are treated in radically different ways with the expectable differences in character and personality as a result.

The Irish and Norwegian family farm systems have a degree of indeterminacy as to succession which is absent where primogeniture is practiced. In the case of the Irish farm, free choice of an heir made at a very late age from the viewpoint of the ultimate heir and his siblings, delays marriage and ties individuals so closely to home that there is no possibility of the children becoming socialized to independent action. This is best exemplified in the term "boy" being applied to grown men still dependent upon their fathers. All of the children of a farm are in this sense in a state of dependence which is in many ways a prolongation of childhood.

The situation in the Norwegian countryside is quite different despite the fact that free choice prevails here as well. For a person to become an heir takes initiative, and in fact the inculcation of independence at an early age is a characteristic feature of rural Norwegian child-rearing practice.[30] The father has to choose an heir who will maintain the farm, but in distinction to both the Irish and Basque cases he has the problem of holding his grown sons on the farm. An adventurous son may leave to homestead on his own before the succession has been decided. Or alternatively he may go to sea. On the other hand a son who wants to be chosen as an heir must demonstrate not only his farming abilities but his ability to produce a family who will help him work the farm. Thus in the Norwegian system of the "understanding" a young man might have children by a young woman of another farm and legitimize the attachment with marriage upon taking over his father's farm.[31]

If we focus upon the results of these three systems of succession some interesting and suggestive considerations emerge with reference to enrepreneurship. In terms of anticipatory socialization, there are some interesting contrasts. If we consider the Basques and the Irish, we see that non-heirs among the Basques know the range of alternatives open to them at an early age and have only to focus on their particular choice. The Irish countryman's

[30] George K. Park, personal communication.
[31] George K. Park, op. cit., pp. 417–419.

situation is quite similar to those in the parts of Spain where equal inheritance is the rule, although a much greater proportion of the Irish have been forced to emigrate. Like the immigrants from the non-Basque areas of Spain the Irish are not noted for entrepreneurial activity but rather, as in the U.S., most have gravitated to manual labor despite the advantage of not having had to learn a new language. This is of course quite consistent with the kind of socialization which prevails, given the rural Irish succession system.

The Norwegians represent a distinct contrast to both Basques and Irish. As with the Irish, free choice of an heir is the rule. In contrast to the Irish, however, this does not result in a delayed age of mating and marriage nor in the degree of dependence of children upon their father. Independence is valued and positively sanctioned. In contrast to the Basques, entrepreneurial types are not forced to emigrate but may very well fulfil their goals through competition for a farm or by homesteading. The small number of Norwegian entrepreneurs in the U.S., as compared to farmers, may be due to the fact that farming was an occupation which provided an outlet for these characteristics in rural Norway as well as in the U.S. Thus Norwegian immigrants with entrepreneurial skills may have applied them to pioneering on the land rather than in commerce or industry.

IMPLICATIONS

The focusing of attention on previously neglected underdeveloped areas has had the salutary effect of bringing into question many of the basic assumptions about motivation and economic behavior which have been essential parts of European-oriented development theories. Because such theories have been found to be weakest in their assumptions of a psychological nature, there has been a tendency to focus on this area to the neglect of intervening institutions. There has been a tendency to accept psychological analyses of personality as largely a product of child-rearing practices to the neglect of institutional factors which may influence such practices. Socialization influences adult behavior, but how one is socialized is limited and influenced by the institutional arrangements of his society. Institutional factors may cause peoples socialized by the same practices to have quite different personalities.

Assuming that the same set of parents do not use radically different child-rearing practices on heirs and non-heirs, the Basque case would suggest that perceptions of individuals treated in similar ways may well vary according to their position in the social structure[32] as well as varying with the way in which a social structure selects for a "character" structure congruent with its persistence.[33] To look only at the child-rearing practices and the resulting personality in terms of entrepreneurial contributions may be to seriously over-simplify the issue. To take a particular ethnic and/or religious group and look at its contributions as an undifferentiated group may in fact interfere with psychological explanations of entrepreneurship. One cannot assume that whole populations, whether Parsees, Jews, Jains, Samurai, etc., can be treated as undifferentiated groups. There may be, as in the Basque instance, important divisions within each group between those who become entrepreneurs and those who do not. Holding differences in ability and opportunity constant, generalizations based upon characteristics of the whole population may be of little use in answering the question of the social origins of entrepreneurs.

One indication of the inadequacy of child-rearing practices as causal factors can be seen in the policy recommendations which result when these variables are taken as primary. They are frequently utopian in nature, suggesting that radical change can only be brought about through changes in motivation, and that these in turn must be inculcated through child-rearing practices. The advocates of such views are forced to admit that these variables are not easily accessible to manipulation by administrative decision and thus an impasse is reached.[34] A possible way out of this dilemma may be through concentrating more upon institutional factors as the key variables. If it can be shown that such practices can be modified by changes in institutional patterns (e.g., changes in inheritance rules or in the division of labor) which are accessible to administrative modification, the social scientist as well as the administrator will be left with more practical policy alternatives than purely psychological arguments would leave them.

In conclusion I would like to stress that the position taken here is not an appeal for the abandonment of the search for broad generalizations and the substitution of an approach which would treat each case as unique. It is rather

[32] It might seem reasonable to assume that birth order determines differences in personality. The most recent evidence on this is largely negative. See Ralph Turner, "Some Family Determinants of Ambition," *Sociology and Social Research*, 46: pp. 397–411 (July, 1962), and also Leonard Weller, "The Relationship of Birth Order to Anxiety," *Sociometry*, 25: pp. 415–417 (December, 1962).

[33] Park, op. cit., pp. 422–423, makes a similar point in discussing "character" as a sociologically significant variable in understanding peasant societies.

[34] Charles Erasmus, review of David McClelland, *The Achieving Society* in *American Anthropologist*, 64: p. 624 (June, 1962).

an appeal which joins that of Charles Erasmus in calling [35] for a move further from the psychological pole of social psychological research toward the sociological pole. The Basque example has been used to illustrate how social factors can be used in such analysis.

[35] Ibid., p. 625.

12

THE ORIGINS OF ENTREPRENEURSHIP
IN MEIJI JAPAN

Johannes Hirschmeier

PART ONE

THE Meiji Restoration brought about a new evaluation of the government and its role in the life of the nation. During the feudal era, the bakufu officials were feared but hardly admired, and few talented and ambitious men were attracted into official service. The Restoration carried the government from the margin of attention into the center of everyone's interest. Everything that was great and exciting in these years, the restoration of the emperor, the unification of the country, the abolition of feudal privileges, the beginnings of modern industry, all had been wrought by the Meiji officials. The light radiated again from the imperial precincts, and those who wanted to stay in the light had to move to the center and become officials, or at least associate with them. By way of contrast, the rest of the population appeared to be all the more backward. There is small wonder that the officials were idolized and the common man counted for little at this time. This *kanson minpi* attitude (awe for the official, contempt for the crowd) was but the other side of the coin of the astounding Meiji achievements.

Few people expected any initiative or contributions to progress from the

Abridged from the author's book of the same title, published by Harvard University Press (Cambridge, Mass., 1964). Reprinted with permission of the author and the publisher.

private business sector, which still seemed so backward and which had disappointed hopes so often during the first Meiji years. The great industrial enterprises, the large and centrally located factories, had been established by officials; now the private sector was expected to accept guidance gratefully and humbly. Indeed, the bowed head and passive obedience to government officials had been the chief traits of the *shōnin* all through the Tokugawa period. The populace had no other image of a businessman than the one represented by the former merchant class, and that class, during the first decade of the Meiji era, was not only leaning nostalgically backward, but had become disorganized, unreliable, and prone to pursue profits in total disregard of the public interest.

In the early years of the Meiji, two new types of businessmen emerged in the private sector: the *seishō* (political merchants), who rode on the crest of government favors and used every opportunity to amass fortunes for themselves, glorying meanwhile in official titles and patriotic slogans; and the many second-rate businessmen or industrialists who had neither experience nor capital but only enthusiasm. We find the latter chiefly among the founders of national banks and also in cotton spinning in its first period. But neither of these two types could be counted upon to build a viable and independent sector of the modern economy. The private sector needed a progressive business group that would develop its own initiative with less reliance upon government coaching and government subsidies.

The Entrepreneur, A New Status

In the last decades of the Tokugawa period, the merchants had, through the back door of daimyo lending, purchase of samurai titles, and land reclamations, managed to break down at least part of the social prejudice against their lowly status. The Meiji Restoration had practically wiped out those gains. Business needed a complete rehabilitation of its status if it was to succeed in the establishment of a strong private sector. The public as well as would-be entrepreneurs had to be impressed with the fact that modern business was not only beneficial to the country, but was as vital as the work of the Meiji government itself. Only by restoring the social status of private business, or rather by establishing it for the first time, could a healthy growth of private industry be guaranteed.

The need to create a new image of business, and to make the businessman confident of his own worth, was clearly perceived, and the task was taken on by a small group inside and outside of the business sector. A conspicuous contribution to the eventual rehabilitation of business pursuits and the creation of new status for the entrepreneur was made by two men: Fukuzawa and Shibusawa, the one an educator, the other an entrepreneur.

Fukuzawa Yukichi (1835–1905), the founder of Japan's first modern college, the Keiō Gijuku, had been for a few years following the Restoration closely associated with the government: he was a close friend of Ōkuma Shigenobu, one of the leading government officials. He had been one of the brain trust that promoted the *bummei kaika* and had been chiefly responsible for shaping the new educational policy; the graduates of his school entered government service. But when Ōkuma was ousted from the government in 1881, Fukuzawa also severed his ties to the regime and became one of the most outspoken enemies of government control over economic and cultural life. Although he had stressed modern business rationality in the education of his students, he now steered his graduates almost exclusively into the private business sector. Thus Fukuzawa's Keiō Gijuku and the Imperial University came to deviate widely in their educational policies: the former represented Western liberal thought and stressed individualism, in the tradition of John Stuart Mill; the latter was a state institution, working for the state, educating officials, and maintaining more of the feudal Confucian mentality.

Mori Arinori, the Minister of Education, shared with Fukuzawa an admiration for Western ideas and methods, but he wanted college education to serve primarily the purposes of bureaucracy. Officials, not businessmen, were to be educated in the state universities, in pursuit not of the English but of the Prussian example. Fukuzawa often gave expression to his aversion to the prevailing *kanson minpi* mentality and insisted that his graduates ought to stand on their own feet and spurn government connections. The prevailing bureaucratism became an object of his scorn, as the following shows: "The schools are officially licensed, sermons and moral preachings are licensed, cattle raising, sericulture, and indeed, eight out of every ten enterprises are connected with the government . . . the flattering of the official, the awe and idolization of the official, is ugly and unbearable."

The Keiō students were trained for private enterprise, while the graduates of the Imperial University regarded private business as degrading. When Shibusawa on one occasion asked a few graduates of the Imperial University to join the Tokyo Gas Company, they answered typically that they did not intend to "descend to the level of the common people." Fukuzawa taught his students to respect business pursuits, and he himself presented an example: he insisted that he taught "for money" and demanded that the tuition fees be paid into his hands, something unheard of for a samurai-teacher. By tradition, teaching was an honorable occupation and teachers were given presents, wrapped in special paper. Since almost all of Fukuzawa's students were samurai, he had to fight their deep-rooted contempt for business.

A frequently recurring theme in his writings was the stress on a new business rationality. His "merchants of the *bummei kaika*" were to take pride in their occupation if it was "for profit and for Japan." In his opinion, only educated and independent businessmen could build up the economy of the country. Fukuzawa insisted on education as a prerequisite for modern business because without learning a merchant could neither understand the problems inherent in the new business activities nor find social respectability. Fukuzawa urged his students to enter business and not the government because, at a time when everybody was rushing into administrative positions, pioneers were needed in industry and trade.

Fukuzawa's influence was by no means confined to his Keiō Gijuku; it reached the entire population through his numerous writings. His most successful book was *Gakumon no susume* (An exhortation to learning), which in the five years between 1872 and 1876 reached the record sale of 3.4 million copies in seventeen editions. In this book Fukuzawa forcefully propounded a new pragmatism and assailed the traditional views on learning, business, and status. Learning was to be emancipated from its theoretical bias and put into the service of daily life, notably of business; it was to open the way to social and economic success. Self-respect ought not to depend on status but on learning and business achievement. Other of his books contained similar views. In *Seiyō jijō* (Conditions in the West) he described life in Western societies, with its stress on the respectability and rationality of business. At a time when newspapers and books were still scarce, Fukuzawa's books with their many editions must have exercised a tremendous influence on the public mind. By 1897 the total sales of his books and pamphlets had reached about ten million.

The immediate effects of Fukuzawa's pragmatic approach were, of course, most evident in the Keiō Gijuku. The school became the chief supplier of the leading Meiji business managers and entrepreneurs. The Mitsubishi and Mitsui zaibatsu in particular drew heavily on Fukuzawa's graduates to fill top positions in their enterprises. Fukuzawa's connections with Mitsubishi were particularly close, and people used to say the Mitsubishi Company was run by Iwasaki's money and Fukuzawa's men.

Shibusawa Eiichi (1840–1931), perhaps the outstanding entrepreneur of Japanese modern history, through his knowledge and moral leadership most decisively influenced the course of private industry in the crucial stage of its development. Like Fukuzawa, Shibusawa insisted upon joint-stock enterprises and upon independence from the government. He himself resigned his respected position in the Ministry of Finance in order to work as a leader in establishing a viable private sector.

The son of a rich farmer in Musashino province, Shibusawa acquired some early experience in business dealings, but had leisure enough to become an ardent sonnō jōi partisan; he even entered into a plan with a few others to overthrow the bakufu. After the failure of this scheme he entered the service of the Tokugawa and gained the confidence of the last shogun. He was chosen to accompany the shogun's younger brother, as his financial manager, to the World Exhibition in Paris in 1867. In France Shibusawa absorbed his new experiences with intelligence and zeal. Three things in particular made a lasting impression on him. First, he saw the ease and liberty with which businessmen moved in the highest social circles and were accepted as equals. Second, he realized that large industrial ventures and other vast projects could only be realized on the basis of joint-stock operations. Finally, he was introduced by a friend, the banker Flury-Herald, to the technicalities of the modern banking system.

After his return to Japan in 1869, Shibusawa was called by Ōkuma to serve in the Ministry of Finance; he accepted on condition that he might resign at any time to work as a private businessman. During his four years in the Ministry of Finance, Shibusawa is said to have been the man chiefly responsible for the tax reform and the monetary reorganization. Although at the age of thirty-four he had become second in command in the Ministry of Finance, he resigned his post in 1873.

Shibusawa had not yet left the ministry when he was elected general superintendent of the newly established First National Bank (later the Dai Ichi), a joint enterprise with capital mainly from Mitsui and Ono. In 1875, after the downfall of Ono, he was unanimously elected president of the bank, which became the headquarters from which he coordinated and directed many of the newly emerging business and industrial enterprises. Shibusawa had not only spurned a career in the Ministry of Finance. He also refused extremely tempting offers from the private sector: Minomura Rizaemon wanted him as his own successor as manager of the entire Mitsui combine, the largest enterprise in Japan; and Iwasaki invited him to become a partner in the powerful Mitsubishi zaibatsu. Shibusawa firmly declined both offers in order to remain free for the work of promoting modern industry in general.

One of Shibusawa's chief concerns was the spread of the joint-stock form of enterprise. The traditional merchants shunned the pooling of capital for a common purpose, and the new strongmen of industry and finance, such as Iwasaki, sought their own aggrandizement and built up private empires. Shibusawa was strongly opposed to both types; he chided the old-fashioned merchants, and he fought Iwasaki's dictatorial monopoly tooth and nail by organizing a powerful rival shipping company. For Shibusawa the common good, the progress of the country's economy, was more important than personal gain and power, and he demonstrated this unselfish attitude time and again in organizing new joint enterprises from which he could expect little or no gain. He felt that the company form of enterprise was necessary not only in order to gather sufficient capital for large-scale ventures, but also because the capital owners were still too uneducated and immature for modern business management. The company form of enterprise made it possible to entrust direction and management to capable and progressive men, whether or not they had capital of their own. Shibusawa himself had become president of the Dai Ichi Bank because of his capabilities alone, and he in turn chose the managers for his own numerous enterprises on the same basis.

Shibusawa, like Fukuzawa, was most emphatic about the need for education in the conduct of large-scale enterprises, and in this he wanted his businessmen to be radically different from the Tokugawa merchants. According to Shibusawa, a modern businessman had to be able to evaluate trends and to understand the consequences of his plans and actions, for his own enterprise and also for the whole country; this could only be accomplished by means of a thorough education. He was so insistent upon learning as a prerequisite for his type of entrepreneur that he refused assistance and cooperation to those who failed to qualify. Suzuki Tōsaburō, the pioneer in sugar refining, recalled with bitterness that he had been refused a loan by Shibusawa on grounds of insufficient education.

In 1874 Shibusawa, together with Mori Arinori, planned the establishment of the first business school in Japan, which developed into Hitotsubashi University. Under his presidency, the Jitsugyō no Nihonsha (Japanese association of enterprise) published a periodical to bring business knowledge and ideas to those who could not attend a school. As president of the Tokyo Chamber of Commerce and of the Bankers' Association, both of which he founded in 1878, he exercised his leadership to form the new business attitudes. The ever-recurring theme in his many speeches was the necessity for the modern entrepreneur to be different from the old merchant in terms of education, standards of honesty, and dedication to the public good, while at the same time maintaining his independence from the government.

Shibusawa was not content to be the recognized leader in the top echelons of the Meiji industrial, banking, and business communities. He also wanted to extend his influence over the younger generation. In his own house he gathered a group of business students who became known by the name Ryūmonsha (lit., "dragon door club"). They published a periodical, the *Ryūmon zasshi* (Ryūmon periodical), one of the first in Japan to be dedicated to economic matters. In it were propagated the basic tenets of Shibusawa's business ideology, which was essentially the same as Fukuzawa's. In one article Shibusawa was compared to the famous warlord of the eleventh century, Minamoto Yoshiie. "Just as the samurai gathered behind Minamoto to follow him into the battle of war, so now the younger generation gathers around Shibusawa to follow him into the battle of enterprise, as merchants of the modern kind."

Shibusawa's leadership in raising educational standards, and consequently the efficiency and the self-respect of the new business community, was imitated by many of the pioneering entrepreneurs of his time. Among the fifty entrepreneurs selected for discussion in Part Four, nine built schools at their own expense. Godai Tomoatsu established a private school in Osaka for the education of the children of merchants in order to break down their conservative business attitudes. The first three subjects taught there were accounting, economics, and arithmetic. The rapidly increasing number of students made enlargement of the school necessary within a few years. Iwasaki, who was probably the most successful of all Meiji entrepreneurs, acted differently from Shibusawa in many ways, especially in so far as government connections and political machinations were concerned, but he agreed with him completely with respect to a thorough education. And Toyokawa Ryōhei, himself a Keiō man, made his most valuable contribution to Iwasaki's Mitsubishi company by scouting for talented college graduates and bringing them into that zaibatsu.

Independence from the government and freedom from bureaucratism were very difficult to achieve in reality. As much as Fukuzawa insisted that private enterprise should be built "for profit and for the sake of Japan," the first thirty years posed such tremendous problems in terms of technology, organization, and, especially, capital supply that the ideal so much admired in Britain and the United States was almost unattainable. Shibusawa, however, took energetic steps in the direction of independence. He frequently scored the group of political merchants who made hay from government contracts and boasted of their titles and privileges, and he asserted that his basic motive in giving up his own government post was his desire to fill the vacuum of leadership in private enterprise.

Godai Tomoatsu also exchanged a government post for an entrepreneurial career in Osaka, although in his case political opposition was behind the move. He later received large favors from the Meiji government. Yet when he handed in his resignation, he told his friend Ōkubo: "There is no lack of able men in the imperial government; therefore I may now resign and descend to the level of the common people. I intend to promote henceforth the general state of business and industry, and to work for the prosperity of the people's enterprise. In this way I shall also be contributing to the prosperity and strength of the country and the nation." This statement at least reveals the sorely felt need to boost private initiative, even if actions would not or could not always be in step with such pronouncements. For the time being, the private entrepreneur was not only a scarce commodity, but he enjoyed neither adequate capital backing nor social prestige. As Shibusawa once put it, he was like the tools in the kitchen, very useful but earning little attention as compared to the showpieces in the living room—meaning the officials.

At the bottom of the widespread contempt for private business was the persistence of popular opinion concerning low business ethics and standards of honesty. The prevalence of the attitude stems from the fact that the disorder in the business world since the opening of the ports aggravated the situation and brought the merchants' reputation to an all-time low. Shibusawa and his associates had to prove to the public that they were totally different from the speculators in the port cities or the monopoly traders of old. In order to stress this difference, Shibusawa went so far as to coin a new word for his type of businessman: the name *shōnin* (merchant) was to be replaced by *jitsugyōka* (entrepreneur, lit., "a man who undertakes a real task"). He defined a *jitsugyōka* as "someone who works with honesty for the establishment of industry." In his mind honesty and industrial enterprise were linked. When he once heard a graduate of the Imperial University remark at a banquet that in business matters "a lie must sometimes also be considered as a way," he scolded the man in public and insisted that a businessman should go so far as to "vow to the Gods and to Buddha never to tell a lie." Other men followed Shibusawa's lead in fighting for the honor of the businessman. Ōtani Kahei, a tea exporter of Yokohama, is probably best known for his untiring efforts to stamp out cheating and unreliability within the trade association.

Indeed, Shibusawa did succeed in creating a new self-respect among the entrepreneurs of the Meiji period; they used the new word *jitsugyōka* with pride and eventually came to be highly respected by the people. A large part of his achievement must undoubtedly be attributed to the *bummei kaika* mentality and to effective support by the government. But the leadership of Fukuzawa and Shibusawa and of a few similarly minded men was most crucial to the formation of the new status for private entrepreneurs.

As much as Shibusawa planned and founded new industrial undertakings, as generously as he encouraged and supported the closely knit group of pioneering Meiji entrepreneurs in any work that would promote industrial progress, he seemed little interested in building an industrial and financial empire of his own. Although he could unquestionably have become a zaibatsu builder much like Iwasaki, Ōkura, or Yasuda, he did not strive for this type of power. The man who was connected with over six hundred enterprises by way of presidential or advisory positions often left control to others as soon as the enterprise was firmly established. Although he was president of the Dai Ichi Bank from 1875 to his retirement in 1916, his family owned no more than 4 per cent of the bank's stock by 1926. Shibusawa was a man of cooperation; he wanted to serve the common cause, the cause of the country and of the business world.

Shibusawa's dedication was molded by his Confucian background. He used to carry the Analects of Confucius in his pocket and knew large parts of it by heart, quoting Confucius frequently in his speeches. In his Confucian outlook he differed from Fukuzawa whose thinking was molded by the English liberal school. Confucian ethics during the Tokugawa period had been an instrument to preserve the status quo. Shibusawa set out, in his own words, "to manage business enterprise using the Analects of Confucius." It may be that it was precisely this fusion of the best of Japanese tradition with the most progressive ideas and methods of the West that gave Shibusawa his influence on the Japanese business world. But in a sense Shibusawa was a cross between a businessman and a government official. He never tired of proclaiming the need for self-respect in business for profit, but he acted half of the time like a Meiji government official, worrying and working on problems of economic and educational policy, of domestic and international politics. His thousands of speeches and addresses do not sound at all like those of a private businessman. . . .

PART TWO

It was auspicious for Meiji Japan that, at a time when the government could not continue its initial building program, private entrepreneurs continued the task with almost the same bold perspective that is so characteristic of government planners. The long time horizon of the Meiji entrepreneurs is a fact, but it too calls for an explanation. One has been mentioned already: the entrepreneurs' faith in progress, their sense of being pioneers in a new era, and their optimism with respect to the new technology. However, I think that there were two more important, noneconomic, motives.

The Noncapitalist Mentality

Shibusawa wrote and spoke frequently about the ideal entrepreneur. He had to be, above all, a man with a keen sense of responsibility for the welfare of society. "While pursuing one's own advantage one should be also mindful of the opportunity for others. As one wishes to achieve one's own welfare and happiness, one has also the duty to exert oneself for the state and for society." Shibusawa's business attitudes, while progressive in many ways, were hardly touched by the spirit of capitalism as it existed in the utilitarian and individualistic forms of the eighteenth-century philosophers and economists. Shibusawa's thinking was, of course, not identical with that of most of the other entrepreneurs. But, to a lesser degree, the whole status-conscious group of pioneering industrialists and foreign-trade merchants shared his outlook.

If we compare this keen sense of social responsibility with the spirit of capitalism in the West, we may say that the basic difference probably lies in divergent concepts of the relation between the individual and society. Capitalism in the West emerged through a gradual but fundamental shift in the value system. The individual, his worth and his welfare in worldly terms, moved into the central position so long reserved for the group, for society and the common good. This trend started as far back as Nominalism, which challenged the validity of universal concepts. The direction became clearer in the growth of the natural sciences, where men rejected all interference by the established religious authority with the individual's quest for objective truth. Humanism and the Renaissance were powerful movements forward toward this emancipation of the individual and of the establishment of a worldly value system. Protestantism sanctioned the supremacy of the individual by rejecting the mediation of a social authority—the Church—between God and the individual.

We need only translate this new concept of the individual into economic and purely secular terms, and we have "the economic man," who considers the achievement of material welfare as the ultimate rationale and reward for his work. "Man is dominated by the making of money, by acquisition as the ultimate purpose of life." According to this capitalist creed, society and its welfare will be taken care of by automatic forces, by an invisible hand that will coordinate self-centered pursuits with the common good.

This evolution of the spirit of capitalism, as it appeared in much eighteenth-century thought, did not proceed in a smooth fashion. Rather, when the problem of man's relation to the world and to worldly activity was seen in a new light and given a new answer, that answer was at its best a religious one. The spirit of capitalism was for a time carried by a very strong religious movement which purposely set itself apart from the tradition of medieval Christianity. Puritanism discovered its task in this world in terms of material pursuits and gave it a religious sanction. There is probably no contradiction between Max Weber's thesis that the spirit of capitalism owed its victory to the Puritans and the view that it had been prepared gradually by a shift toward the individual and toward secular values. Puritanism idealized what had previously been regarded as a lapse from spiritual concerns. Weber's term "worldly asceticism" pinpoints this mentality. What had been chided before as unworthy became now a calling by God: to do business, to accumulate, and to lose no time at it. This religiously conceived version of the spirit of capitalism, and not its selfish and materialistic basis, became the powerful urge that could drive men toward entrepreneurial endeavors in the face of great risk and sacrifice.

There seems to exist a parallel between this Western evolution and what happened to entrepreneurs in Meiji Japan. First there had been the well-established official contempt for business, maintained ostentatiously by the samurai and supported by Confucian ethics. Then came the breakdown of the Tokugawa political and economic system, and with it the disdain for material accumulation. But we do not find a smooth line of change toward a hedonistic and individualistic kind of capitalism. A new element appeared that resembled, in its function, the mentality of the Puritans. It was nothing religious, not a calling by God; it was rather a calling by the nation, by the emperor. The direction was that of service to the country in terms of worldly success. But one's very success would be a sign of having fulfilled a noble duty. Iwasaki and Ōkura, in their quest for self-assertion, were singularly obsessed with the thought of fighting for an ideal and not just for private gains. Theirs was not a belief in the "invisible hand" that would take care of society—they were men for whom business was a sacred duty. There is a similarity between the Puritan drive to accumulate and that of the Meiji pioneers: the one was backed by a faith in God, the other by a faith in the Nation. It is even possible to discover a certain parallel, however different the two men may be otherwise, between Benjamin Franklin, who preached thrift while quoting the Bible, and Shibusawa Eiichi, who preached business ethics while quoting the Analects of Confucius.

But a basic difference remains between the Puritan version of the capitalist and the type represented by Shibusawa and his school of thought. Western capitalism was ultimately individualistic; its religious sanction was individual perfection, a manifestation of one's own salvation, a problem of God and I. The Confucian version of Shibusawa stressed Society and I, the State and I, and thus demanded the subordination of the individual to the common good. This may account for a number of seeming contradictions in Japan's economic development. We encounter in Meiji Japan and later starvation wages, but not an anonymous employer-laborer relationship with hiring and firing according to the dictates of "economic rationality." We find that talented men were attracted to business, but only to those branches that were clearly recognized as in the service of the community; they had to be *jitsugyōka*, not *shōnin*. We find a ruthless drive for power and money, with a "survival of the fittest" as in Western capitalism, but then these same "fittest" assumed a role of service and worked for public objectives.

The community-centered thinking that was largely preserved by the union of Confucian traditions and Western influences can perhaps account in part for the extended time horizons of many Meiji entrepreneurs. When these men so obviously discounted present sacrifices in favor of the future success of their enterprises, the enterprise assumed a function similar to that of the family, the community, or for that matter, the merchant store. The individual—entrepreneur as well as worker—was but a part of and had to serve the higher unit, the enterprise, and work for *its* success. This is quite similar to the attitude displayed by the merchants with respect to their family businesses. But the remarkable difference was this: the merchants served their house traditions—with them the time horizon was stretched to the past—while the modern entrepreneurs applied the long view to the future. In any case, the element of time lent a nonindividualistic character to economic pursuits.

It is open to question whether an unrestrained bourgeois type of capitalism can work at all beneficially for economic development in any latecomer country. The task does not so much constitute a challenge for individuals as for society as a whole. It requires cooperation and sacrifices from the community, and responsible leadership in both the government and the private sector. In times of smooth and continuous development, the pursuit of each individual's welfare as the primary goal of activity may not reveal its inherent dangers. But whenever crises and extraordinary tasks appear, society cannot rely on an invisible hand, on an "automatic harmony" between social and private benefits. A conscious coordination of the two, and even subordination of private advantage to society's needs, is then called for. The swift and energetic modernization of the Meiji economy owed a great deal to the continuance of this kind of noncapitalist mentality among its best entrepreneurs; these men were characterized by a blend of Confucian ethics, patriotism, and faith in Western technology.

National Awakening

Nationalism unquestionably constitutes one of the most dynamic elements in the economic growth of many modern underdeveloped countries. Industrialization and a new sense of national purpose usually go together and thrive on patriotism as their common powerful motive. The determined leaders of a nation's elite, given the proper objectives, can mobilize immeasurable energies toward social and economic advance. A gradual process of development without these nationalist emotions may be less wasteful as far as capital resources are concerned; but it may evaporate without being able to overcome fast enough the great difficulties of the initial spurt. Nationalism is like a stallion; it may turn the cart upside down and create havoc, especially if the leaders are power-mad. But the same strong stallion, properly harnessed and controlled, may pull the cart of the economy all the way to the top of the hill, something a slow-moving plug horse may not accomplish. In the "new" countries, hostilities toward "oppressor countries" or toward their own former ruling classes are often only a means used to create passionate dedication to a national purpose which requires enormous sacrifices.

The Meiji was an era of national awakening. The cultural, social, and economic life that had been bottled up in the islands of Japan for over two centuries burst forth into a new spring of growth. Many events before and after the Meiji Restoration seem to the casual reader senseless and contradictory. But here was a people rushing forth with sudden energy, aware of both a new greatness and a new challenge. The greatness was epitomized in the restoration of imperial life, accompanied by a sense of national unity and by the equality of all citizens who were to share the blessings of education and progress. . . .

PART THREE

The development of Mitsubishi from its small beginnings as a trading company in Tosa han to the powerful zaibatsu rival of Mitsui rested on two pillars: political connections and the genius of Iwasaki Yatarō (1834–1885). Iwasaki was daring in the extreme, but he was also shrewd in his use of men and especially in securing privileges. To this political merchant *par excellence* can be applied the criticism of a contemporary, who wrote: "These merchants with government connections pile up enormous profits because of their close ties with government officials. They know the laws before they are published, they receive the favorable deals in the sale of government enterprises." But the same man wrote something else that is equally applicable to Iwasaki: "For business ventures Japan needs the spirit of the samurai who are ready to sacrifice their lives for the country. In competition with the foreigners only such a spirit can be successful; that is, a man must think not only of his private good but also of the benefit to the country." In Iwasaki shrewdness and the spirit of the samurai were uniquely blended, and it is difficult to assess the relative strength of his two predominant motives, his drive for power and his patriotic idealism.

Iwasaki began his trading career within the framework of the Tosa han administration. There he learned very early the power of money. Although he belonged to the country samurai, who differed little from the peasants, he came into close contact with the great Tosa reformers and himself became an official. With his accumulated practical experience in trading, he did not find it difficult to exchange the samurai swords for the abacus. When after the Restoration Iwasaki acquired the official Tosa shipping company as his private property, he called it first the Ninety-Ninth Company and later changed the name to Mitsubishi. He assembled his samurai managers and told them to don the "apron of the merchants." They would fully acknowledge the power of money. On the other hand, Iwasaki had been strongly influenced by Yoshida Shōin's patriotic ideas, and he remained essentially a fighter in the samurai fashion; his ambition was to make Japanese shipping competitive with the great foreign lines.

Iwasaki's close association with government officials, notably Ōkuma, made it easy for his enterprise to get huge subsidies and privileges such as no other zaibatsu got. He was considered the champion of Japan's competitive race with the foreign shipping companies. But Iwasaki was also ruthless in building a system of monopolies. In 1880 he started a documentary-bill company with over 3 million yen in capital. The customers of this company were obliged to ship their goods in Mitsubishi bottoms, to insure them with the Mitsubishi Maritime Insurance Company, and to store the freight in Mitsubishi godowns.

Iwasaki's ruthless monopoly practices and his enormous profits created enemies in the government and also among leading businessmen. Shibusawa was one of them. He cooperated with others, notably with Mitsui's Masuda, to break the Mitsubishi monopoly in shipping; their endeavors culminated in the establishment of the Kyōdō Unyu Company in 1883. Ōkuma, Iwasaki's chief protector in the government, had been ousted in 1881, and Iwasaki's enemies among the officials succeeded in granting the Kyōdō Unyu Company a government subsidy—nominally a share subscription—of 2.6 million yen, thus raising the total of this powerful rival's capital to 6 million yen. In the fierce cut-throat competition, principles, personalities, and politics clashed. During the two years of war between the two giant companies, passenger fares between Kobe and

Yokohama dropped from 3.50 yen to 0.25 yen. Iwasaki conducted a rather unfair smear campaign against Shibusawa, charging him with working for foreign interests, while many labeled Iwasaki an enemy of the state.

This was in the last analysis a fight between two diametrically opposed principles: Shibusawa fought for an economic order ruled by cooperation, with joint-stock companies and fair competition. Iwasaki believed that the strong should rule and that monopoly was a good thing because private profits would eventually also benefit the nation: what was good for Mitsubishi was bound to be good for Japan. The war between the two companies ended in 1885. Iwasaki had secretly bought up the majority of the rival company's stock and had secured control in the new amalgamated Nihon Yūsen Company.

Although he concentrated on shipping and connected enterprises, Iwasaki and his associate managers branched out into other new ventures. In 1884 Iwasaki bought the Nagasaki shipyard from the government, which had not been able to make it a going concern. Iwasaki applied for the purchase by pointing out that Russia was just completing her large shipyard in Vladivostok while Nagasaki could barely handle minor repair work. He paid 539,000 yen for the yard; within a few years he had put into it another 6 million yen and had transformed this small repair yard into Japan's largest and most modern shipyard of the period.

Iwasaki also bought the Takashima coal mine—actually not directly from the government—which had been operated at a continued loss, and transformed it into one of Mitsubishi's best assets. He sent his close associate, Kondō Renpei, to Hokkaido to investigate new investment possibilities, especially in mining, and to exploit the untapped natural resources of that northern frontier area. In order to raise capital for this Hokkaido venture, he began his documentary-bill company. Shipping, mining, shipbuilding, and banking were the main branches of Iwasaki's activity, and within twenty years his entrepreneurial efforts had made Mitsubishi the second-ranking zaibatsu in Japan and a dangerous rival to Mitsui.

At the height of Mitsubishi's power, in 1936, the central Mitsubishi Company, which was totally owned by the Isawaki family, had a capital investment of 120 million yen and a net worth of 300–350 million yen. But controlled by, or at least connected with, the company was a huge industrial and financial empire of shipping, shipbuilding, mining, heavy industry, electricity, storehouses, and trading.

Iwasaki was probably the boldest of all Meiji entrepreneurs. His efforts put him into the forefront of Japanese shipping and mining. He himself was not at all modest in assessing his own achievements and his contribution to Japan's economy. On his deathbed in 1885 he claimed before his friends that he was "The Man of the Far East," and he regretted his untimely death because not even a third of his great plans were realized. His quest for power and greatness, combined with samurai patriotism, are reflected in his Mitsubishi family rule: "Do not take up small projects, engage only in large enterprises. Once you begin something, see to it that it becomes a success. Do not engage in speculation. Do business with a patriotic attitude."

Although Iwasaki had gathered associates, all of them samurai—his company was called the "samurai company"—they did not gain prominence as independent business leaders until his death. It was his planning and his decisions that ruled the whole Mitsubishi concern. The first two paragraphs of its "constitution" spell out the dominant position of Iwasaki within the combine:

1. Although this enterprise assumes the name of a company and establishes company structure, in reality it is entirely a family enterprise and differs therefore greatly from a company with joint capital. Therefore, all things that concern the company, praise and blame and all, are entirely up to the president.

2. All profits return to the person of the president and the losses, too, are borne by him alone.

Almost all zaibatsu men shared this dictatorial attitude, although it was most openly expressed by Iwasaki and Yasuda Zenjirō. This trait contrasts strongly with Fukuzawa's democratic principles, although Fukuzawa was close to Iwasaki and supplied Mitsubishi with a number of its most talented men. Shōda Heigorō, one of his closest associates, had been a teacher at Keiō; so had Kondō Renpei, Toyokawa Ryōhei, and Asabuki Eiji. Iwasaki himself built a school to promote business education along Fukuzawa's lines, and his preference for Fukuzawa-trained clerks and managers was proverbial. But he himself retained the mentality of a strong-willed official, and his entrepreneurial talent, ambition, and competitive spirit made of him an unbending and stormy leader. . . .

Yasuda Zenjirō, the Banker

The Yasuda zaibatsu ranked fourth among the empires of finance and industry, and its development from small beginnings was no less spectacular than that of Mitsubishi. Yasuda Zenjirō (1838–1921), who had left home at the age of twenty and gone to Edo to make a living, succeeded so well that when summing up his blessings in 1908, at the age of seventy, he controlled in his empire of finance: eleven banks, with 21.2 million yen in capital; three insurance companies, with 13.3 million; one construction company, with 5.0 million; three railway companies, with 10.63 million; and one electric company, with 1.0 million.

Yasuda was appointed a member of the board of trustees of the Bank of Japan in 1882 and held the post for two years; at one time he was financial agent of the Ministry of Agriculture and Trade. But these official positions were not at all typical for Yasuda. In striking contrast to Iwasaki, Yasuda remained almost entirely independent of government support. His success was due to genius, favorable circumstances, and his insatiable drive to win profits.

Born the son of a poor samurai, Yasuda Zenjirō began his trading career by selling flowers in his native village. He had learned early that money was more powerful than samurai swords, so he went to Edo where, in those days, a daring and clever man could become rich in a short time. Yasuda displayed a remarkable instinct for turning a penny and multiplied his initial five ryo through lending, trading, and exchange manipulations. A few years after the Restoration, he was already a wealthy banker. But even at the height of his success, he remained miserly; on his inspection rounds of factories and on his Tokyo business trips, he would take the early cheap-rate streetcar and carry his lunch.

But this man, who had set out to become rich by ruthlessly exploiting any opportunity, began later to display a remarkable degree of responsibility with respect to the use of his wealth, and thus came to rank among the great Meiji entrepreneurs. He became a tireless advocate of large and modern investments. Although we have good reason to doubt whether he was always motivated by a consideration of the public benefit in his investment decisions, his own large-scale ventures, and especially his financial backing of industrial undertakings, contributed in no small measure to the economic development of Meiji Japan. When a sulphur-mining company to which he had extended large loans continued to operate in the red and could not pay him back, he made a careful study of the technical possibilities and then took over the mine. He invested heavily by installing new machinery, putting up new buildings, and constructing a railway line to the mine site; the mine became a financial success.

With regard to industry and large-scale innovations, Yasuda could at times forget his caution and appear reckless in his drive to have innovations carried out. Yasuda cooperated in many schemes of industrial pioneering with Asano Sōichirō, who was another almost reckless innovator. People used to say that lending to Asano or Amamiya was equivalent to "throwing one's money into a ditch." But Yasuda said that, if it were not for men like Asano, great enterprises would not be undertaken in Japan. He considered Asano as his "general manager" working with his money. Asano, who had founded the Tōyō Shipping Company, once placed an order for three large ships with the Mitsubishi Shipyard in Nagasaki at a total cost of 15 million yen, although he had almost no money in reserve. Even Shibusawa refused to extend a loan to Asano, but Yasuda lent him 7.5 million yen in spite of the great risks that this newly established shipping company faced in its competition with foreign lines and with Mitsubishi.

Toward the end of his life, Yasuda's innovating plans became almost fantastic in scope. He proposed to the Ministry of Railways that he electrify the entire Tōkaidō Railroad extending from Tokyo to Osaka, at an estimated investment of 100 million yen, but his plan was refused. Yasuda became very bitter at this rejection of his great "service to the country." He had mapped out a plan to modernize the entire city of Tokyo and supply through his banks the estimated capital of some 800 million yen. Over this, his last plan, he was assassinated by a fanatic because he would not contribute to the building of a "workers' hotel."

The banker and entrepreneur Yasuda appears to have combined two attitudes not always found together in one man. He was, on the one hand, a pitiless "profit maximizer," especially in the early part of his career, and at times he displayed miserly traits. On the other hand, he had a genuine interest in general economic progress and in the things that would benefit the nation as a whole. Among the conditions essential to the establishment of an enterprise, he demanded, first of all, that "the purpose of the enterprise be good, that is for the public benefit, contributing to the welfare of the people and the progress of society." Probably it is not wrong to attribute his zeal for innovations for the sake of Japan's advancement to his close association with the group of leading entrepreneurs. If this is true, we have here a good example of how a group spirit and status consciousness can influence the actions of men who otherwise might take a very different approach. It is also true, of course, that in such large-scale projects as the modernization of the city of Tokyo, Yasuda would have reaped his fair share of the profits, together with public acclaim for his services.

Yasuda, like Iwasaki, was a dictator within his own banking empire. It was difficult for him to find congenial men to whom he could delegate powers of decision. In this respect the zaibatsu builders were almost all alike. While Iwasaki saw to it that a few of his aides were groomed for independent entrepreneurial positions, the Yasuda concern was considerably handicapped after the death of its founder by the lack of capable managers. . . .

PART FOUR

Fifty Leading Entrepreneurs

The detailed presentation of the zaibatsu builders enabled us to assess, among other things, the relative role of government subsidies and of private initiative and personality in the entrepreneurial process. But it would be misleading to take the few giants of industry and banking as a basis for sweeping generalizations on all aspects of Meiji entrepreneurship. How did the less successful but still important innovators approach their task? This section contains an examination of fifty leading businessmen—all entrepreneurs in the broad sense; from this sampling we may be able to draw valid conclusions about Meiji entrepreneurs in general. . . .

FORMATIVE INFLUENCES

The Older and the Younger Group

The year of birth is given in column 2 [Table 12-1] simply to show the relative ages of the men. But by the same token this column enables us to time the major political and social events occurring during the early life of each entrepreneur. It is believed that most basic attitudes and concepts are fixed during the "formative years" of adolescence and early years of manhood. Not only his parents and the kind of education but also the political events that stir up public emotions may exert a lasting impact on a man's view of life and society. Because of the selected time limits we do not, of course, get much differentiation with respect to age groupings. Roughly, the men all lived through the same turbulent years of the pre-Restoration period, with its uprisings, the controversy over the opening of the ports, and the rallying resistance against the bakufu. They were all influenced by patriotic attitudes; if we try to find differences in this respect, we have to content ourselves with something other than black and white contrasts.

If we call the men born before 1840 the "older group" and those born in 1840 or later the "younger group," we meet a few rather surprising facts. Among the twenty-one entrepreneurs of the older group, we find all the founders of the zaibatsu except one, Asano. . . . Another characteristic of the older men is their tendency to "go it alone," to maintain private ownership, in contrast to the company form so frequently and strongly urged by Shibusawa. A third feature of the older men is their semiofficial approach, characterized by ties with

TABLE 12-1
Survey of Fifty Leading Entrepreneurs in the Early Meiji Era

Name (listed in order of success) (1)	Birth Year (2)	Class (3)	Practical training (4)	City (5)	Entrepreneurial type (6)	Main fields of activity (7)
				Formative Influences (before age 20)		
Shibusawa Eiichi	1840	P	M, P	Tokyo	R	Banking, general industrial pioneering
Iwasaki Yatarō	1834	S	Official, M	Nagasaki, Tok.	R	Shipping, shipbuilding, mining, banking
Ōkura Kihachirō	1835	P	M	Tokyo	R	Trade, mining, heavy industries
Yasuda Zenjirō	1838	S	M	Tokyo	(R)	Banking, promotion of industry
Hirose Saihei	1828	S	Mining	Osaka	CI	Mining, allied fields (Sumitomo)
Asano Sōichirō	1848	S	M	Tokyo	R	Cement, general industrial pioneering
Furukawa Ichibei	1832	M	M	Tokyo, Yok.	CI	Mining
Godai Tomoatsu	1834	S	Official	Nagasaki, Tok.	R	Mining, indigo, general industrial pioneering
Kawasaki Shōzō	1837	M	M	Nagasaki	CI	Shipbuilding, heavy industry
Tanaka Gentarō	1853	P	M	—	R	Banking, pottery, electricity ("Shibusawa of Kyoto")
Matsumoto Jūtarō	1844	P	M	Osaka	R	Banking, railways, promotion of industry in Osaka
Minomura Rizaemon	1821	S	M	Tokyo	(R)	Banking, modernization of Mitsui
Nakamigawa Hikojirō	1854	S	Student, teacher	Tokyo	R	Banking, Mitsui industries, spinning
Ōkawa Heizaburō	1860	S	M	Tokyo	CI	Paper manufacturing, advising in other enterprises
Hara Rokurō	1844	P	Army, student	—	(R)	Banking, general promotion of industry
Kondō Renpei	1848	S	Student	Tokyo	(R)	Shipping, mining (Mitsubishi)
Masuda Takashi	1847	S	M	Tokyo, Yok.	(R)	Trade, mining, general industrial pioneering
Fujita Denzaburō	1842	M	M	—	R	Shipping, railways, general industrial pioneering
Kawasaki Hachiuemon	1837	M	M, official	—	CI	Banking
Yamabe Takeo	1851	P	Student	Tokyo	CI	Cotton spinning
Katakura Kentarō	1849	P	Student, P	Tokyo	CI	Silk spinning
Kinbara Meizen	1832	P	P	—	R	Land improvements, banking, social-welfare schemes
Sakuma Sadaichi	1846	S	Army	Tokyo	CI	Printing, libraries
Okuda Masaka	1847	S	M	—	R	Spinning, banking, railways ("Shibusawa of Nagoya")
Morimura Ichizaemon	1839	M	M	Tokyo	CI	Trade
Ōtani Kahei	1844	P	M	Yokohama	(R)	Trade, banking

Name	Birth	Class	Training	Location	Type	Activities
Toyokawa Ryōhei	1851	S	Student	Osaka, Tok.	CI	Banking (Mitsubishi)
Shōda Heigorō	1847	S	Student, teacher	Tokyo	(R)	Shipping, shipbuilding, other (in Mitsubishi)
Suzuki Tōzaburō	1855	M (?)	M	—	CI	Sugar refining
Kawada Koichirō	1836	S	Official, M	—	(R)	Shipping, banking (Mitsubishi)
Takashima Kazaemon	1832	M	M	Tokyo	R	Railways, gas, land reclamation
Amamiya Keijirō	1846	P	M	Yokohama	R	Trade, mining, railways
Nakano Buei	1838	S	Official	—	R	Railways, general industrial pioneering
Hirano Tomiji	1846	S	Shipbuilding	Tokyo	CI	Shipbuilding
Tanaka Chōbei	1858	M	M	Tokyo	R	Mining, iron casting, gas
Hirose Sukesaburō	1844	M	M	—	R	Banking, railways, newspaper, education
Motoki Shōzō	1824	S	Interpreter	Nagasaki	CI	Type printing
Tanaka Heihachi	1834	?	M	—	(R)	Trade, banking
Magoshi Kyōhei	1844	S	M	Osaka	(R)	Beer brewing, cooperation with industrial pioneers
Nishimura Katsuzō	1836	S	Teacher, M	Nagasaki,Tok.	(R)	Leather, bricks
Kashima Manpei	1822	M	M	Tokyo	CI	Cotton spinning
Abe Taizō	1849	S	Student	Tokyo	CI	Insurance
Doi Michio	1837	S	Student	—	R	Textiles, banking, railways
Tanaka Ichibei	1838	M	M	Osaka	R	Trade, banking, railways, shipping
Hiranuma Senzō	1836	?	M	Tokyo	(R)	Trade, banking
Nakano Goichi	1842	S	Official	Tokyo	(R)	Trade, banking
Yonekura Ippei	1831	P	P	—	CI	Sulphur production, participation in Osaka industries
Wakao Ippei	1820	M	P	Tokyo	CI	Internal tea and rice trade
Imamura Seinosuke	1849	P	M	Yokohama	(R)	Internal trade, railways, electricity
					(R)	Railways, banking, participation in industrial projects
Asabuki Eiji	1849	P	Student	Osaka	(R)	Trade, cotton spinning, general promotion (Mitsui)

Totals

S: 23		M: 30		Tokyo: 27		R: 18
P: 13		Other: 9		Osaka: 6		(R): 16
M: 12		None: 11		Yokohama: 5		CI: 16
Unknown: 2		——		Nagasaki: 5		——
——		50		None: 13		50
50				——		
				56 (doubling counting)		

Notations. Class and training: S, samurai (including physicians); M, merchant; P, peasant. Entrepreneurial type: R, Romantic; (R), semiromantic; CI, classic. These types are defined in text.

the government and the receipt of privileges and commissions from the government.

These three characteristics can probably be explained by the way in which these men entered their entrepreneurial careers. They belonged predominantly to two classes, officials and adventurer-merchants. The officials like Godai, Hara, Motoki, Kawada, and, of course, Iwasaki were naturally inclined to continue the familiar approach, to maintain close political ties to the government and to promote enterprise in the spirit of the *fukoku kyōhei* (wealthy nation, strong army) in which they had grown up in the han administrations. Even in the private wing of the economy, these men remained half officials.

Doi Michio, who abandoned his samurai status prior to the Restoration and moved to Osaka to engage in trade, occupied an official post under Godai which started him off on his business career. Doi retained the official approach all through his life. He became a promoter of modern establishments, cooperated with others, and staged exhibitions to stimulate industrial advance. Examples of this kind are numerous.

Those who made their start as adventurer-merchants usually began in a very rough way, not caring about the government or about anything except money. Men of this type were Ōkura, Yasuda, Tanaka Heihachi, Takashima, Morimura, Hiranuma, Nishimura, and Wakao. But in their dealings these same men began to realize the weakness of Japan's trading position. They then came under the influence of nationalism, which was particularly strong in Tokyo, and so eventually combined their private money-making with public service by carrying out government commissions. Increasingly they turned towards projects that were in the public interest. Almost anyone who had participated in the fears, hopes, and enthusiasms of the Restoration became a patriot in those days, whatever social group he belonged to.

Kashima Manpei was a cotton merchant of Tokyo who established the first private cotton-spinning mill because he thought that this was the only way to drive down the price of calicoes. In the face of a host of difficulties and much resistance, he carried his plan through. He later had machines constructed according to his own designs; they cost him far more than imported ones would have, but he insisted on making Japanese cotton spinning independent of imported machines. Kashima was not only a successful spinner whose mill never had losses, but he was also a bold and politically minded man. He advocated the opening of the ports and carried on business dealings with foreigners at a time when such actions could very well inspire assassinations by fanatics.

Whether merchants or samurai, these men became involved in the political matrix and behaved like officials, and they felt that their own work was almost as important as that of the government leaders. Iwasaki's dictum, "I am the Man of the Far East," and Takashima's remark, "Even if Prince Itō should die, as long as Takashima lives there is no need to worry about the affairs of the country," characterize the strong and prideful political make-up of the men of the older group.

The former adventurer-merchants had amassed their starting capital through boldness and shrewdness in foreign trade or from government commissions. Therefore they needed no joining of capital and remained lone-wolf entrepreneurs who built their own empires of trade and industry. The officials, too, could dispense with the cooperation of shareholders, and to them especially the idea of bowing to majority decisions must have been hard to accept. This probably explains why the older men favored private ownership and why some of them built such large empires for themselves.

The younger group, in contrast, tended more toward the joint-stock form of enterprise, with less reliance on government help. . . . To what extent a genuine turn toward democratic ideas, majority rule, and cooperation were involved is difficult to say. The government became less generous in meting out favors, and the younger men had had little occasion to build up their own capital; so they were forced to depend on the capital of shareholders and on the cooperation of men like Shibusawa, Yasuda, Hara, and Masuda. The Chamber of Commerce and the leadership of Shibusawa welded the men together more firmly as an entrepreneurial group; cooperation in joining capital for large well-planned ventures thus became easier.

Class Origins

Of the fifty men in the table, twenty-three were of samurai origin, thirteen were peasants' sons, twelve were born as merchants; the class origins of the remaining two could not be ascertained. Some qualifications must be introduced here. A few of these attributions could be disputed and changed: for example, one might call Ōkura the son of a peasant or of a merchant, since his father was both, and the same could be said of two or three others; two or three country samurai could also be called peasants, since they differed in almost nothing but name from rich peasants who were commoners. Finally, the physicians, who were usually commoners, are here included in the samurai group because of the samurai-like education, occupation, and social privileges, which made them too unlike merchants and peasants to be grouped among them. Excluding country samurai and physicians, then, we would have seventeen or eighteen clear-cut samurai. . . .

Some students of Meiji business maintain that industrial leadership and innovations were a near monopoly of the samurai class; they cite examples of the innovators within the Mitsui and Mitsubishi zaibatsu and a few others where samurai concentration was most pronounced. Then again we find assertions that merchants predominated as business leaders throughout the Meiji; these statements are based on a survey of those who held prominent positions in the largest businesses, including domestic trading and manufacturing of the traditional type. In the second approach the crucial distinction between innovating (entrepreneurship in the sense used here) and routine business is completely dropped. If such a point conveys anything at all it is that, by the middle of the Meiji, merchants and their capital were still dominant in the traditional sectors of business. This in turn strengthens my conclusions that merchants as a class were the least progressive group of all.

It was mentioned earlier here that the entrepreneurs of peasant origin did not as a rule stay in their villages; they went to the city—usually Tokyo— early in their lives. Only two of the peasants here became entrepreneurs in their villages, Katakura and Kinbara. Katakura used his large landholdings as the financial basis for a silk filature, and Kinbara devoted his energies to land improvements and rural welfare projects. The others, such as Ōkura, Hara, Amamiya, Asabuki, and Shibusawa, left home, resolutely breaking the fetters of village traditions and limitations.

The merchants' sons in the sample similarly broke with family rules and guild restrictions and usually left their fathers' businesses to gain freedom of action. Whether peasants or merchants, they were restless young men, dissatisfied with society and with conditions at home. Of the merchants' sons, Hirose Sukesaburō and Suzuki had traveled and tried various new things before achieving entrepreneurial success; Fujita had been a political adventurer more interested in fighting battles than in his father's lucrative business and sake brewery. Morimura was a poor man but he was disgruntled with the merchants' ways, and in his later career he never tired of scoring the low business morale and ethics of merchants in general. Tanaka Ichibei had rejected the idea of continuing his inherited business as a wholesaler in Osaka and decided to become an entrepreneur of the modern type. Most of the men with merchant backgrounds, then, were anything but the typical *shōnin*. . . .

My conclusion is that class origin was not of decisive importance in molding entrepreneurs. All three groups of samurai, peasant, and merchant descendants in the sample had cut the ties to their previous economic life—the samurai by force of events, the others usually by free choice. Economically, the men had to start all over again, at least insofar as their approaches and places of activity were concerned, although some entered existing enterprises which they either reorganized themselves or which had been modernized by a predecessor.

The surprisingly equal representation of the classes according to numerical strength—the rich peasants as a class being no exception—confirms the conclusion that the socioeconomic forces peculiar to one class were of secondary importance in influencing entrepreneurial careers. The voluntary cutting of ties to the past, which resulted in economic uprootedness, the migration to the centers of foreign influence, indicate that the political and ideological forces at work in Tokugawa society before the Restoration constituted the single most important factor in the making of entrepreneurs. These forces were not confined to any one class; any man who was able to follow the course of events intelligently could be affected. Thus the economic uprootedness and the new start in a new place are only indicators of the dynamics of political and social pressures. The men were not uprooted ideologically, but belonged to the first wave of a general trend. The entrepreneurs were genuine children of the same national ferment that brought forth the Meiji Restoration itself. . . .

Summing up all the formative influences to which the fifty entrepreneurs were exposed, we notice a clear pattern. Neither class origin nor initial capital resources was of decisive importance; what mattered most was the new ideology, the new system of values, that each man had to absorb. If the entrepreneurs were to be innovators and pioneers, they had to be men of the new era, men who believed in the future of the Meiji Restoration. Capital was supplied from various sources, as has been shown in the case of the zaibatsu men. Certain key factors stand out which facilitated the necessary change in ideology or values: original dissatisfaction with conditions at home, which led these men to leave and become economically uprooted; learning, which became a vehicle for the new ideas and an aid in grasping the complexities of the enterprise system; finally, a "center" from which the new ideas radiated and attracted the dissatisfied and the dissenters. The closeness between entrepreneurs and government officials stemmed from their sharing of a common task and a common viewpoint. This made these entrepreneurs sometimes act like officials, and in spite of their "faith in Mill" they were hardly touched by laissez faire and the spirit of capitalism.

13

A RE-EXAMINATION OF ENTREPRENEURSHIP IN MEIJI JAPAN (1868–1912)

Kozo Yamamura

ALONG with many favourable factors which contributed to the rapid economic development of Japan, the unique and important role played by the early Meiji entrepreneurs has been stressed by many students of the Japanese economy. The Meiji entrepreneurs, these economists seem to agree, were "community-centred"[1] and "had a genuine interest in general economic progress and in the things that benefit the nation as a whole."[2] "Almost all leading Japanese entrepreneurs of that time," one recent article observed, "cooperated with the government. Both strongly desired to establish a wealthy, powerful country which would ward off a feared colonization by Western powers."[3] The predominant view of existing literature, both in English and Japanese, appears to be that the Meiji entrepreneurs possessed

Reprinted by permission of the author and the publisher from Economic History Review, *XXI (February, 1968), pp. 148–158.*

[1] This phrase was coined by Gustav Ranis in his "The Community-Centered Entrepreneur in Japanese Development," *Explorations in Entrepreneurial History*, VIII (1955). For the definition of the term see a quotation above in the text on the following page.

[2] Johannes Hirschmeier, *The Origins of Entrepreneurship in Meiji Japan* (Cambridge, Mass., 1964), p. 232. This quote applies to Zenjiro Yasuda whom this article discusses.

[3] Kazuo Noda, "Japan's Industrialization and Entrepreneurship," *Research in Applied Social Science*, VII (Tokyo, 1964), p. 24.

unusual degrees of patriotism, *shikon shōsai* (the soul of the samurai with business acumen),[4] and profits could be a "by-product"[5] of their activities.

Among the sources in English, Ranis's work is an outstanding example of this view. He wrote:

> Somewhere between [the extreme Schumpeterian auto-centered entrepreneur and the caricature of the government official—with very few intense desires of any kind] lies the community-centered entrepreneur who seeks to accumulate wealth or power for the community by his individual action; as a by-product he may and very likely will accumulate wealth or power for himself. The motivation is quasi-tribal, to further the ends of the community; the individual seeks to grow, not so much in the reflexion of his wealth, a private good, as in the prestige of the cohesive unit, a social good.[6]

More recently Hirschmeier supported this view when he observed that:

> After the opening of the ports, the Japanese people were shocked into a realization of their own backwardness, which had been concealed from them by the closed-door policy and by the official contempt for the western barbarians. . . . The "New Deal in emotions" had indeed taken hold of the nation, and it is the major explanation for the irrational, non-capitalist, dynamic and romantic approach of the pioneering entrepreneurs.[7]

Among the Japanese scholars, Horie and Tsuchiya are leading proponents of this view. Horie reiterated that "the former *chōnin* (merchant) class, especially the wealthy *chōnin* were passive" while "the samurai class possessed strong entrepreneurial spirit" which was the product of their training, ability to cope with hardships, and selfless dedication. In Horie's view the samurai class, therefore,

---

[4] One Japanese source wrote of *shikon shōsai* as follows: "The samurai class was also the dedicated class. This meant that, in the process of modernization, strong revere-the-officials and scorn-the-public ((*kanson mimpi*) and scorn-the-merchants (*senshō*) attitudes were deeply rooted among the leaders of this modernization. The theory of *shikon shōsai* was advanced to make the full use of the samurai's educated and moral backgrounds in achieving *fukoku* (enrichment of the nation)."—Yoshio Sakata, *Shikon Shōsai* (*The Spirit of the Samurai and Business Acumen*) (Tokyo, 1964), pp. 139–140.

[5] See quotation from Ranis above.

[6] Ranis, op. cit., p. 81. George B. Sansom, a well-known student of Japan, also wrote that: "It was these men [samurai], and not the bourgeois, who laid the foundations of a capitalist structure and at the same time developed a political system that bore little resemblance to those which came into force in the advanced industrial countries of western Europe under the influence of a powerful money class."—G. B. Sansom, *The Western World and Japan* (New York, 1951), pp. 110–111. On Sansom's view, Hirschmeier commented that: "He [Sansom] is ready to agree that the samurai played a dominant role in the private sector as well as in the government. *Many present-day students of economic development will be in basic agreement with Sansom's statement.*" (My italics.)—Hirschmeier, op. cit., p. 46.

[7] Hirschmeier, op. cit., p. 289.

was particularly suited "for the advancement of the new nation."[8] Tsuchiya, who wrote nearly a dozen volumes on related topics, repeatedly stated his view with little or no variation. One of his books expressed his theme as follows:

In the case of Japan, the feudalistic samurai or their sons shouldered the leadership role of the Meiji entrepreneurs. Unlike any other nation, the development of capitalism was guided by bureaucrats who were samurai and by business leaders who were also of samurai origin. . . . Thus, the Meiji entrepreneurs were strongly motivated by the semi-feudal spirit of *shikon shōshai*. This, of course, was inevitable.[9]

Notwithstanding the consensus of opinion on the Meiji entrepreneurs, as seen above, the purpose of this article is to argue that the view is a product of deductive theorizing, conveniently suited to a general discussion of the rapid economic development of Japan, but hardly supportable when a closer examination is made of the behaviour, decisions, and motivations of the leading Meiji entrepreneurs. In discussing the rapid transformation of the Japanese economy, these "community-centred" or patriotic Meiji entrepreneurs, it will be argued, played the role analogous to that performed by a theoretical competitor. Just as the actions of a theoretical competitor "explain" the workings of a smoothly functioning market and provide "solutions" for optimum resource allocations and demand-supply equilibria, a "community-centred" Meiji entrepreneur "explains" Japan's response to the Western stimuli and her rapid economic development and provides a set of convenient "solutions" for the problems involved in the emergence of Japan as a modern industrial nation against the background of Tokugawa traditions of rigid class structure and of *bushi-dō* (the way of the samurai).[10] However, a significant difference between these two —the perfect competitor and the "community-centred" entrepreneurs—is that

[8] Yasuzo Horie, *Nihon Shihonshugi no Seiritsu* (*The Formation of Japanese Capitalism*) (Tokyo, 1938), pp. 238–239. Horie's English article, "The Government and Industry in the Early Years of Meiji Era," *Kyoto University Economic Review*, XIV (1939), a condensed version of his book published in Japanese, has been quoted widely by several writers including Ranis in his article cited on p. 144, n. 2.

[9] Takeō Tsuchiya, *Gendai Nihon Keizaishi Kōwa* (*Lectures on Economic History of Modern Japan*) (Tokyo, 1958), p. 53.

[10] The way of the samurai was characterized as follows by a recent Japanese writer: "The samurai, as a member of the ruling class, is responsible not only for the protection of the lives of people, but also for an ethical leadership. Therefore, a samurai, even if he is a mere lower class samurai, must fulfil this responsibility . . . Because he takes on this responsibility, the samurai must build up a personality which commands the respect of the ruled as their example."—T. Sagara, "Bukeshakai no Dōtoku-kyōiku" ("The Moral Education in the World of Samurai"), in T. Furukawa, ed. *Nihon Dōtoku Kyōikushi* (*A History of Japanese Moral Education*) (Tokyo, 1961), pp. 118–122. Quoted from Noda, op. cit., p. 139.

while no one claims ubiquitous existence for the former, the latter have been said to have carried out the entrepreneurial function in Japan.[11]

To show that the "community-centred" entrepreneurs are a product of deductive theorizing, two closely connected points must be made. The first is that the practice of emphasizing the class origin of Meiji entrepreneurs is continued in order to support the current view of "community-centred" entrepreneurs, though it hinders rather than aids the understanding of the entrepreneurial function performed during the crucial years of Japan's economic transformation. The second is that the Meiji entrepreneurs are often revealed as unabashed profit-maximizers (in the ordinary sense of the term), regardless of their class origin, when one examines their deeds rather than their public utterances, and the results rather than the reasons given in the autobiographies for their business decisions.

To show that a close examination of Meiji entrepreneurs does not yield the "image" often attributed to them, the first two sections of this article will present a case study of Zenjiro Yasuda.[12] Instead of many candidates far more suitable for the writer's purpose, this banker was chosen for his "genuine desire to serve the nation" and for the fact that he was one of the most successsful entrepreneurs of the early Meiji years.

The third section will present evidence, to make the two points referred to above, which has been gathered from a available biographies, company and bank histories, and from recent empirically-oriented studies made by Japanese economic historians. Given the scope of the questions involved and the wealth of sources yet unexamined, this article is presented as a suggestion for further exploration into the neglected areas of Japanese economic history.

PART ONE

Zenjiro Yasuda (1838–1912),[13] "the King of Banking," who founded one of the two Zaibatsu which began in the mid-nineteenth century, came from gener-

[11] Ranis, op. cit., p. 81.

[12] With the exception of Oland D. Russel's *The House of Mitsui* (Boston, 1939), there exist virtually no biographies or company histories of Meiji entrepreneurs or firms. Russell's work is highly journalistic as he was interested in telling the story of the Mitsui family rather than Mitsui enterprises or the family members' roles as entrepreneurs. The case study of Yasuda presented here is therefore intended partially to fill this gap, as was also the purpose of my "The Founding of Mitsubishi: A Case Study in Japanese Business History," *Business History Review*, XLI (1967), pp. 141–160.

[13] The standard authoritative biography of Yasuda is Fumio Yano, *Yasuda Zenjiro Den* (*The Biography of Zenjiro Yasusa*) (Tokyo, 1925), written by a personal friend of Yasuda.

ations of peasants.[14] It was his ambitious father who finally bought the share of a *gōshi*[15] (low-ranking country samurai) to become a *chabōzu* (a *han*[16] official who officiates at tea-ceremonies). Though technically a samurai, what a *chabōzu* received from the *han* provided less than an adequate income to the family. To supplement the income, the family farmed, and Zenjiro was found selling flowers on streets, beginning at the age of seven or eight.

Upon finishing six years of schooling at a *terakoya* (temple school), Yasuda —now twelve years old—sold vegetables in Toyama, the *han* capital several miles away from his village. The boy was already very much like the man whom one comes to know shortly. "Not liking to carry empty vegetable baskets,"[17] he bought china in Toyama to sell them in villages on the way home. By doing so he had to carry a heavy load to and from Toyama, but earned more than his fellow pedlars who rested their shoulders on their way home. This was not all. At nights, he copied books to earn a few additional pennies, often sacrificing his sleep. "At the age when most boys wanted time to play, he did not rest if he could earn."[18]

Other sources here used include: Shigeo Oda, *Ningen Yasuda Zenjiro (The Man Zenjiro Yasuda)* (Tokyo, 1953); Denkichi Matsushita, *Zaibatsu Yasuda no Shin-Kenkyū (A New Study on Yasuda Zaibatsu)* (Tokyo, 1937); Toshio Obama, *Yasuda Konzerun Dokuhon (The Yasuda Konzerun Reader)* (Tokyo, 1937); Takeō Tsuchiya, *Zaibatsu o kizuita Hitobito (The Zaibatsu Builders)* (Tokyo, 1955); The Research Association on Japanese Economic History, *Kindai Nippon Jimbutsu Keizaishi (A Biographical Economic History of Modern Japan)* (Tokyo, 1955); Yasuda Gakuen (Yasuda School), *Shō'ō Yasuda Zenjiro Den (A Biography of Shō'ō Zenjiro Yasuda)* (Tokyo, 1958). (*Shō'ō* means an aged pine tree and was an honorific title assumed by Yasuda. During the Meiji era, it was customary for those having achieved some financial, political, or literary status to assume such an honorific title ending with *ō* which means an aged man. Pine tree in Japanese connotes honesty, perseverance, and a straightforward personality.)—Kamekichi Takahashi, *Nippon Zaibatsu no Kaibō (Dissection of the Japanese Zaibatsu)* (Tokyo, 1930); and Aizan Yamaji, *Gendai Kinkenshi (A Contemporary History of the Power of Wealth)* (Tokyo, 1908).

[14] The other founder of a Zaibatsu was Yataro Iwasaki who founded Mitsubishi Zaibatsu, and the subject of my article cited in note 12. The other two of the four Zaibatsu were Sumitomo and Mitsui. Their origins could be traced back to the seventeenth and eighteenth centuries respectively.

[15] The cost of becoming a *gōshi* and a *gōshi's* status varied from *han* to *han*. But it is known that towards the end of the Tokugawa era the purchase of the *gōshi's* status by peasants and merchants became a nation-wide practice. While it is unlikely that quotations for *gōshi* shares remained fixed throughout the Tokugawa period, and it had undoubtedly varied by *han*, one could safely assume that, on the average, 200 *ryo* entitled a non-samurai to use a surname; 500 *ryo* to wear swords; and 1,000 *ryo* entitled him to both. For this information on *gōshi*, I am indebted to Prof. Kazuo Noda of Rikkyo University, Japan. *Ryo* is a monetary unit used in Japan before the Meiji Restoration.

[16] A feudal unit of administration under the control of a *daimyō* (local feudal lord).

[17] Yano, op. cit., p. 105.   [18] Ibid., p. 107.

One reason for his unusual motivation, invariably cited by his biographers and confirmed by Yasuda himself, was an incident which took place when he was still in his early teens. It is said that he and his father were obliged one day, by the custom of the time, to prostrate themselves as a *kago*[19] surrounded by samurai was passing by. Yasuda found to his surprise that the passenger was not a *daimyō*[20] as he had expected, but a rich money-lender from Osaka. Yasuda, who had always disliked prostrating, vowed to himself then that he must become rich. Though one must guard against overemphasizing the impact of such an incident, this object lesson undoubtedly contributed in forming Yasuda's *Weltanschauung*.

Yasuda's anxiety to "amount to something" caused the seventeen-year-old boy to run away from his home to Edo (renamed Tokyo after the Restoration of 1868) where, he had learned from Toyama medicine-pedlars,[21] he must go to become rich. Though this attempt was unsuccessful, as he was lost in the mountains,[22] Yasuda went to Edo three years later with his father's permission and little else. Upon arriving in Edo, he obtained a job as a *detchi* (shopkeeper's helper) with a toy-wholesaler. In a short time so impressed was the wholesaler by Yasuda's "diligence, clean-living and thriftiness,"[23] that he asked the new *detchi* to marry his daughter. Yasuda declined the offer and went to a new job after the three years of contracted service. His next job was with a retailer (dry-fish and seaweed) who was also a money-changer. Again it took very little time for Yasuda to win the complete confidence of his new master. When the contracted three years were up, Yasuda had accumulated six *ryo* and six years of experience. The former was the product of heroic self-denial, saved out of his annual cash wage of two and a half *ryo*,[24] and the latter consisted of a thorough knowledge of both wholesale and retail business and money-changing. The first step to wealth had been completed.

The second step for Yasuda was to become an independent money-changer. With the capital of six *ryo*, his new "shop" consisted of a few rows of coins spread over a discarded sheet of galvanized iron on a busy street corner of

---

[19] A basket-like accommodation carried on the shoulders of two men.

[20] See note 16.

[21] The medicine-pedlars of Toyama were as well known throughout Japan as the Yankee pedlars were in the United States.

[22] Having no permission from his parents, he was unable to obtain a *tegata* (pass) which was required at this time to cross a *han sekisho* (border-gates), situated on more commonly used routes. This accounts for his crossing mountains.—Oda, op. cit., p. 29.

[23] Yano, op. cit., p. 121.

[24] He was expected to defray all minor expenses out of this meagre annual cash income. This meant that he practised an "unusual degree of austerity" in order to achieve this saving. —Obama, op. cit., p. 21. See also Yano, op. cit., pp. 130–131.

Edo. To assure the supply of coins he made rounds of public bath-houses at the crack of dawn, *i.e.* before his competitors could buy small denomination coins collected the night before by these bath-houses. Though the profit margin was thin and his capital small, Yasuda rapidly increased his business as he won the confidence of his customers for his honesty and the superb "touch" he had with them.[25] In two years he had accumulated 25 *ryo* and was ready to open a little store specializing in money-changing and selling dry-fish, seaweed, and sugar on the side.[26]

As was with his "shop," his new venture was an instant success. As the year 1865 opened he began to concentrate on more lucrative money-changing. The prevailing confusion of the monetary system—*han*-notes, various degrees of debased coins, and their counterfeits[27]—afforded Yasuda an opportunity to expand his trade. When many money-changers were closing their businesses during this period of relative lawlessness, Yasuda, though burgled a few times by *rōnin*,[28] kept his store open, continued to do a brisk business, and gradually established his reputation as being one of the most reliable money-changers in Edo.

When the Restoration came in 1868, Yasuda was no longer a small money-changer. He had become well known for his accurate judgement of coins and the complete reliability of his seals.[29] He had also gained handsomely by selling gold coins to foreigners who were taking advantage of the undervalued gold in Japan.[30] The new government offered Yasuda a new opportunity in the form of *dajōkan-satsu* (Privy Councillors' notes) which were issued in large quantity to finance the civil war and to defray the costs of the government.

Dajōkan-satsu had been issued early in 1868, and by April of that year

[25] A vivid account of Yasuda's "ingratiating manner" is given in Yano, op. cit., pp. 133–134.

[26] Matsushita believes that "the 25 *ryo* consisted of a bonus he received from his former employer and the cash he obtained by selling all that he owned" in addition to his savings.— Matsushita, op. cit., p. 11.

[27] According to Takagaki, 1,694 coins and notes of all types were in use at that time.— Torajiro Takagaki, *Kindai Nippon Kinyū-shi* (*A History of Finance in Modern Japan*), Local Banking Association Monograph no. 20 (Tokyo, 1955), p. 28.

[28] A *rōnin* is a masterless samurai. Yano wrote: "In 1867, the Tokugawa regime had lost its power and *rōnin* and undesirables roamed even in Edo [Tokyo]. Robberies were common and . . . money-changers were constantly victimized."—Yano, op. cit., pp. 151–152.

[29] Coins were sorted and sealed for the convenience of customers who, lacking professional ability to judge the value of coins, had to depend on the honesty of money-changers.

[30] While the international silver–gold ratio was 15 : 1, the Japanese ratio was 5 or 6 : 1 during this period.—Shimbun Newspapers, *Nihon no Rekishi* (*A History of Japan*) (Tokyo, 1965), x, pp. 91–92.

limited public acceptance and continued issue had caused them to depreciate up to 40 per cent of their face value. Faced with this difficulty, the new government issued an order that the *dajōkan-satsu* were to be accepted at face value. But even with a provision to punish the disobedient, the order had to be cancelled shortly as the new government soon discovered the futility of defying Gresham's Law.[31] But this experiment was enough to triple Yasuda's fortune. Upon learning of the order several hours ahead of the public, he bought as many *dajōkan-satsu* as he could at the depreciated price and sold them at face value, thereby taking advantage of the short-lived order.[32] This *coup* along with his prospering business made Yasuda a rich man by 1870. His fortune was now the sizeable amount of 5,000 *ryo*, over 800 times the original capital with which he had opened a "shop" on a street corner several years before.[33]

Another opportunity for Yasuda was the issue in 1871 of samurai commutation bonds.[34] These were bonds which the new government gave to former samurai who had, in effect, lost their livelihood by the Restoration. But the disorganized monetary market and the continued issue of non-convertible notes in large quantities by the government caused these bonds to depreciate rapidly. Only several months after the initial issue of these bonds, their market value stood at 70 yen, 30 yen below the par value.[35] Yasuda bought these bonds from impoverished samurai and earned better than a 10 per cent return, in addition to what he earned by speculating on the fluctuating prices of these bonds. As seen by the above examples, the first few years of the new government were extremely profitable for Yasuda. By 1874, he had become one of the leading money-changers in Tokyo.[36]

With financial success and an established reputation, profitable opportunities now presented themselves to Yasuda. The Ministry of Justice selected Yasuda in 1874 as its *goyōkin-gata* (a handler of the official funds). This meant that

[31] This short-lived government order to enforce the circulation of *dajōkan-satsu* at par value was issued on 2 May 1869; violators were to be liable to imprisonment.—Yano, op. cit., pp. 159–160.

[32] Yano wrote: "The record shows that Yasuda's total capital tripled between 1869 and 1870, and I am prepared to credit most of this increase to this operation."—Ibid., p. 160.

[33] Obama, op. cit., pp. 32–33.

[34] These were stipends given to former samurai. For an excellent account of the background, magnitude, and the economic significance of the bonds, see Henry Rosovsky, "Japan's Transition to Economic Growth, 1868–1885," in H. Rosovsky, ed. *Industrialization in Two Systems* (New York, 1966), pp. 123–130.

[35] The initial commutation bonds earned a 7 per cent interest. Thus, given the going interest rate of about 10 per cent, samurai in need of cash were forced to sell these bonds at approximately 70 yen. Yasuda's speculative activities in relation to this bond are described in Oda, op. cit., pp. 56–57.   [36] Yano, op. cit., p. 198.

Yasuda could use nearly 100,000 yen of the Ministry funds for his benefit without paying interest on it.[37] Though Yasuda was obliged to reimburse the Ministry funds on a regular and predetermined schedule, he was free to use the funds any way he saw fit while they were in his possession.

By 1876, Yasuda was employing 16 assistants and his half-yearly net profits exceeded 5,000 yen.[38] Thus in that year, when the Banking Act of 1872 was amended, Yasuda was able, with two other leading money-lenders, to establish the Third National Bank. A few years later, in 1879, when it became possible to establish private banks, Yasuda was wealthy enough to establish the Yasuda Bank and be its sole owner.[39] With these two banks as its foundation, Yasuda's fortune multiplied in a predictable fashion. Unlike the colourful and dramatic life of Iwasaki, the founder of Mitsubishi Zaibatsu,[40] Yasuda rose steadily to become "the king of banking" by a series of shrewdly selected investments, by making full use of cost-free government funds at his disposal,[41] and by sound operation of his increasing number of banks.[42] He uncannily judged the trend of the time, taking risks when they were justified and avoiding popular but risky investments.[43]

He was a constantly calculating, "no-nonsense" banker. Even his closest friends were unable to borrow from him if their investments failed to meet all of Yasuda's requirements.[44] Any amount of extravagant V.I.P. treatment failed to

---

[37] Until the mid-1880's this was a common practice of all branches of the central and local governments in Japan.   [38] Yano, op. cit., p. 219.

[39] For details, see Yasuda Bank, *Yasuda Ginkō 60-nen-shi* (*A 60 Year History of the Yasuda Bank*) (Tokyo, 1940), pp. 44–59.

[40] For the description of the founder of Mitsubishi Zaibatsu, see my article cited in note 12.

[41] Yasuda's cost-free government funds increased as follows (with the year in which he acquired each): The Ministry of Army (1874); Courts and Ward Offices of Tokyo (1874); Tochigi Prefecture (1875); The Ministry of Agriculture and Commerce (1881); The Toyama Prefecture (1883); Hokkaido Administration Agency (1884).—Oda, op. cit., p. 59.

[42] By the end of the Meiji period (1868–1912), Yasuda was in direct control of 15 banks. See also *Yasuda Ginkō 60-nen-shi*, op. cit., pp. 275–276, which has a complete chart of all the banks Yasuda came to control before 1923.

[43] All the biographies of Yasuda make the point that his investments were the kind which "walked on a stone bridge," i.e. were little influenced by short-run trends. Though details cannot be given here, his investments were made, as examples in the following footnotes show, on an unwavering rule of what he considered was "sound". In a word, he was a "conservative" banker. For examples which are demonstrative of his judgement, see Yano, op. cit., pp. 503–515; Oda, op. cit., pp. 167–169; Obama, op. cit., pp. 230–237.

[44] Yano, like many others, cites the case in which one of Yasuda's old friends, who frequently played *go* (a game) with Yasuda, was unable to borrow from Yasuda. Yasuda "refused the request of his friend under circumstances in which all of us would find it impossible to do so."—Yano, op. cit., p. 487.

loosen his purse strings, as the Chinese government discovered to its chagrin.[45] He remained, in spite of his financial success, a penny-pincher. Though his biographers try to explain it as "a residue of his experience in his earlier life,"[46] one of the richest men in Japan was justifiably called "miser" when he rode early-morning trams to take advantage of the "pre-dawn rate" and carried a lunch to business meetings.[47] He was also well known for paying as little as possible to his employees, not because "he might have been thinking in terms of the prices of his early days"[48]—as one biographer suggested—but certainly because of his reluctance to pay not a cent more than absolutely necessary. It is highly unlikely that the shrewd banker was unfamiliar with the price levels of the time.

While the founder of the Mitsubishi Zaibatsu was known for his questionable ethical standards, Yasuda, on the other hand, was a man of a few quiet pleasures. He painted, enjoyed tea-ceremonies, rode horses, and travelled with his family. When elected to the Diet against his will, he refused to serve on the ground that his political involvement might influence his business judgement. He refused to make political contributions of any kind, or for that matter any charitable contribution, even when he would have received the status of nobility in return.[49] In his old age he became a devout Buddhist, and the story of his life was adopted by children's textbooks for an illustration of "frugality." His death was also characteristic. He was murdered by a young man who was incensed by Yasuda's refusal to contribute to the murderer's cause.[50] When he died the richest man in Japan at the age of 84, he controlled 19 banks with total assets of 18 million yen and had a string of large investments in railroads, insurance, real estate, electricity, gas, and many other areas.[51]

[45] In 1902, the Chinese government invited Yasuda to discuss a possible investment (the nature of which is not stated). The dignitaries of the government treated Yasuda as though he were a chief of state. The Chinese officials went so far as to refurbish a hotel where Yasuda stayed. But, "finding the venture too risky for his liking, he coldly refused any assistance to the Chinese government." After all the preparation it had made, the Chinese government which had anticipated at least some investment, found his "strength of will" incomprehensible.—Yano, op. cit., pp. 489–490.

[46] Ibid., p. 457.

[47] Yasuda Gakuen, op. cit., p. 310.

[48] Yano, op. cit., p. 458.

[49] In 1911, the government solicited donations from the wealthiest men in the nation to start a social welfare project. Several who contributed received the rank of *danshaku* (baron). Yasuda "refused in spite of the charge that he was more concerned with holding on to his money than getting social recognition."—Yano, op. cit., p. 511.

[50] The contribution was requested to build a "workers' hotel."

[51] "According to the tax office, Yasuda's income during the past year [1920] was 4,360,000 yen and his total wealth exceeded 100 million yen."—*Kokumin Shimbun* (a daily), dated September 29, 1921, appended in Yasuda Gakuen, op. cit., pp. 263–264. This would

PART TWO

In the standard biographies of Yasuda, one notes that a few "examples" of his "ability to disregard his self-interest" are cited.[52] These examples are to show his patriotism and his "genuine interest in general economic progress," as Hirschmeier put it. Let us examine three "examples" which Yano and Oda cited.

The first "example" is his recommendation to the government to issue bonds to finance the preparations for the Sino-Japanese War. Yasuda, his biographers noted, advised the government to issue the bonds at 5 per cent rather than at 6 per cent because he believed that, "by letting the public know the importance of the bonds in aiding the war effort,"[53] the bonds could be sold at 5 per cent. However, Yasuda's concern for the nation's finance is found to be less than patriotic and selfless when one finds that:

Facing the new bond issue of 30 million yen, the bankers objected to six per cent bonds and refused to cooperate if the bonds were issued at six per cent as the Diet had decided. The main concern of the bankers was that they had already owned a plethora of five per cent bonds issued earlier and feared that, if the six per cent bonds were issued, it would reduce the market price of earlier (five per cent) bonds and create a great confusion in the money market.[54]

Yasuda, who was the leader of these bankers, was the most vigorous in objecting to the proposed bonds.[55] The writer of this quotation was perhaps discreet enough not to mention that the bankers may have feared personal loss more than "confusion" in the money market.

The second example cited to show Yasuda's "vision" to enrich the nation is

---

place Yasuda's private wealth over those of Iwasaki of Mitsubishi and the Mitsui family of the Mitsui Zaibatsu. Yasuda Zaibatsu continued to grow rapidly after his death under his brother and sons. Takahashi and Obama, op. cit., have detailed descriptions of Yasuda Zaibatsu before it was dissolved by the Occupation Forces.

[52] The biographies of Yano and Oda are major ones in this category. If one includes such a biased biography as the one written by Masao Terajima, *Zenjiro Yasuda* (Tokyo, 1938), one could find numerous "examples" of Yasuda's "ideal personal qualities" (p. 3). The examples discussed below in the text are only those recurring in several of his more widely read biographies.

[53] Yano, op. cit., p. 518. Yano, however, noted earlier that "at this time he had an unusually large amount of idle cash on his hands."—Ibid., p. 517.

[54] Yasuda Gakuen, op. cit., p. 178. Though this was written by a group of faculty members at the Yasuda School, careful readers would find that the authors made efforts to present new material which was not included in Yano, op. cit. In my judgement, this book is useful in evaluating Yasuda's actions more objectively.

[55] Yasuda Gakuen, op. cit., p. 178.

Yasuda's interest in the large Tokyo harbour project. The biographers noted in unison that "Yasuda was motivated to bring the wealth to the public."[56] But again Yasuda's motivations must be examined with care when one reads:

Yasuda had been buying real estate around the projected canal areas. He had been planning to be the largest owner of these lots. The eight million yen project was a large one. But he had also planned to use his banks and their branches to stimulate deposit for this purpose. This meant that the planned interest of 8.5 per cent could be divided: 6.2 per cent for the depositors, 1.3 per cent for the costs of this operation and the net earning of 1 per cent. One per cent seems to be a small sum, but it is one per cent of eight million yen.[57]

Though Yasuda was murdered before he could actually put his plan into effect, this "example" shows this writer not Yasuda's "interest in the general economic progress of the nation" but his ability to devote his energy to make a large gain by accumulating small but sure returns, as he had done throughout his life.

The last example involves Yasuda's efforts to save the 130th National Bank "in the spirit of saving the nation"[58] which was preparing for the Russo–Japanese War. This influential bank in Osaka was on the verge of collapse and had asked for emergency aid from the Bank of Japan. The government, then planning to float external and domestic bonds for the war purposes, supplied one million yen to the bank in an effort to avoid possible financial crisis. But the aid was found insufficient, and Yasuda was "soon found trying to save the bank to avert the nationally undesirable consequences."[59]

Claiming that Yasuda did not profit by his efforts, his biographers insist that this was an exception from his constant practice of "saving" failing banks to his profit.[60] Rather, Yasuda in this case, his biographers argued, was attempting to alleviate a possible national crisis. One well-known contemporary writer agreed with his biographers that this was an "exceptional case" in that Yasuda failed to profit,[61] but disagreed sharply with Yasuda's motive:

[56] Yano, op. cit., p. 554.

[57] Yasuda Gakuen, op. cit., p. 258. Both Yano and Oda touched upon the observations contained in this quote. But Yano, for example, stated merely that "this [accumulating deposits at all branches of the Yasuda Bank] would invariably aid the nation's virtuous custom to save."—Yano, op. cit., p. 551; Oda, op. cit., pp. 212–213.

[58] Oda, op. cit., p. 158.

[59] Yasuda Gakuen, op. cit., p. 207.

[60] Oda, op. cit., p. 157.

[61] Oda, however, noted that "After this incident, the 130th National Bank came under the control of Yasuda, and finally . . . in 1923, it was absorbed by the Yasuda Bank."—Ibid., p. 157.

In 1904, in the affair involving the 130th National Bank, many have written that it was Yasuda's scheme to borrow six million yen from the government, interest free. But Yasuda failed in this scheme. It has also been said that he mistreated his subordinates to enrich himself. But there is no reason to denounce him on those grounds. Ours is a time of individual freedom and of free competition and no reason exists for denouncing Yasuda who did everything he could to get ahead in this world.[62]

Observed through these "examples", even Yasuda—the man many writers would agree was far less ruthless than others of his time, *e.g.* Yataro Iwasaki, Sōichiro Asano, or a dozen others[63]—has difficulty in meeting the specifications of the "community-centred entrepreneur" Ranis described. Yasuda's "obsession" or "prime mover" was not "national strength and survival"[64] but the acccumulation of wealth. The energy of his life, it appears to this author, was directed and devoted to making profit not as a "by-product" but as its primary goal.

Reading through Yasuda's biographies (or for that matter the biographies of many other leading Meiji business leaders), Hirschmeier's "irrational, non-capitalistic, dynamic and romantic approach of the pioneering entrepreneurs"[65] can hardly be found. Yasuda was every inch the cold rational capitalist, and his business approach was systematic and wholly unromantic. Neither the few lines excerpted from his writings and compiled for publication a few years before his death[66] nor the contribution he made to the University of Tokyo to build a Yasuda auditorium—an exception to his life-long non-donation policy—make him a "community-centered" or a patriotic entrepreneur any more than the charitable contributions and Sunday-school speeches of John D. Rockefeller make him any less a competitive profit-maximizer.

PART THREE

The implicit theory of those who support the current view of the Meiji entrepreneur is, in effect, that: (a) "Almost all of the leading Meiji business leaders were samurai or quasi-samurai";[67] (b) the *Weltanschauung* of the samurai class is

[62] Yamaji, op. cit., pp. 281–282.   [63] See notes 12 and 70–73, this article.

[64] Ranis, op. cit., p. 81.   [65] Hirschmeier, op. cit., p. 289.

[66] Hirschmeier quoted from Oda only the first part of the so-called business principles which read: "the purpose of the enterprise to be good, that is for the public benefit . . ." The unquoted second part read, "provided that it is profitable."—Hirschmeier, op. cit., p. 232; Oda, op. cit., pp. 139–140.

[67] Takeō Tsuchiya, *Nihon Shihonsjugi no Keieishiteki Kenkyū* (*A Business History Study of Japanese Capitalism*) (Tokyo, 1954), p. 170.

distinct from that of other classes because of the long tradition of the "spirit of the samurai" which was cultivated and preserved by their education and mode of living. The spirit of the samurai was their ability to sacrifice self-interest, be it for his feudal lord (*daimyō*) or for *fukoku* (enrichment of nation, a popular slogan of the Meiji government); thus (*c*) most of the leading Meiji entrepreneurs possessed *shikon shōsai* and were "community-centred."

The dangers of this type of theorizing have been made evident by examining the case of Yasuda. To emphasize or to assume the meaningfulness of class distinction is the common and necessary weakness of the current view. Yasuda technically was a samurai, but his education and the pattern of his daily life differed little from a peasant's, and, moreover, he is not an exception.

Examinations of the biographies of the leading Meiji entrepreneurs whom Hirschmeier classified as "of samurai origin"[68] reveals that in many cases their class origins are at least doubtful and that they are often very marginal samurai, as was Yasuda. Examples can be cited easily. Yataro Iwasaki came from generations of peasant-merchants. He bought a *gōshi* share so that he could obtain a job with a *han* bureaucracy.[69] Both Rempei Kondo and Ryōhei Toyokawa who helped Iwasaki to build the Mitsubishi Zaibatsu and who were leading businessmen in their own rights, were also *heimin* (commoners, i.e. non-samurai) who became marginal samurai. The former was a son of a *han*-doctor who was given a quasi-samurai status and the latter was a son of a *gōshi* who later became a *han*-doctor.[70] Saihei Hirose, the great manager of the House of Sumitomo, is known to have come "from the farm," *i.e.* either of peasant or, at most, of *gōshi* origin.[71] Rizaemon Minomura, who had almost single-handed rebuilt the House of Mitsui, is known "to have come from nowhere" and to have worked as a child. Tsuchiya ventured his opinion that Minomura's father "was a *rōnin*."[72] Sōichiro Asano, who was called a "demon of business" for his ruthless activities in the cement and shipping industries, was selling cloth at the age of 15 when "he would have been going through a ceremony of *genpuku* (to mark his attainment of manhood) had he been a samurai."[73]

These men and others, such as Tomiji Hirano, Takeo Yamabe, and Koiichiro Kawabe,[74] were in fact *chōnin* or at best marginal samurai as in the

[68] Hirschmeier, op. cit. pp. 248–249.   [69] See my article cited in n. 12.

[70] See Kazuo Suehiro, *Kondo Rempei Den oyobi Ikō* (*A Biography of Kondo Rempei and his Writings*) (Tokyo, 1926).

[71] See Kumakichi Uzaki, *Toyokawa Ryōhei* (Tokyo, 1922).

[72] Tsuchiya, *A Business History Study . . .*, op. cit., p. 174.

[73] Tsuchiya, *The Zaibatsu Builders*, op. cit., p. 210.

[74] Bibliographical accounts of these men are found in: Kōkichi Mitani, *Motoki Shōzō to Hirano Tomiji no Shōden* (*Detailed Biographies of Shōzō Motoki and Tomiji Hirano*) (Tokyo,

case of Yasuda. Coming from "very poor families in which there was only one *kimono* for each person,"[75] they rose to become leading entrepreneurs through their willingness to work "for days without sleep"[76] and other qualities similar to those found in Yasuda. In short, biographies of these men show that, however important it may be for the current view, they simply were not the kind of samurai who, with the "spirit of the samurai" and knowledge of Confucian ethics, dedicated themselves to great causes.

A more important point is that the distinction between the samurai class and the *chōnin* class—a distinction which is necessary for the current view—is of highly questionable validity. That the distinction had become unimportant by the late Tokugawa period has been noted often.[77] Horie himself wrote in another part of his book that: "Many samurai had been reduced to supplementing their income by earning wages or by trading,"[78] and Yui, in reviewing Hirschmeier's book, pointed out the fact that "at the end of the Tokugawa period, one finds rich peasants and small scale entrepreneurs in villages who begin to have thoughts and education akin to those of the samurai class, and [class] distinction between the samurai class [and others mentioned above] became indistinguishable."[79] Many writers, Western and Japanese alike, would agree with the view that the class distinction had been, as Hirschmeier put it, "blurred" in the late Tokugawa period.[80]

1923); Toyo Textile Company, *Tōyō Bōseki Nanajunen-shi* (*Seventy Years of Tōyō Textile*) (Tokyo, 1953); Tsuchiya, *The Zaibatsu Builders*, op. cit., pp. 77–78. In this writer's view, biographical sketches of these men mentioned in this and the preceding paragraphs show them like Yasuda in their determined efforts to become successful "entrepreneurs" in the usual sense of the term.

[75] Tsuchiya, *The Zaibatsu Builders*, op. cit., p. 78.

[76] Mitani, op. cit., p. 229.

[77] The weakening of the class structure during the late Tokugawa period and its implication for the Meiji Restoration are, for example, discussed in Takashi Ishii, *Meiji Ishin Ron* (*A Theory of Meiji Restoration*) (Tokyo, 1961), pp. 213–222. Articles Ishii cited in his discussion and the more popularly read Yomiuri Shimbun's *History of Japan*, op. cit., are good sources to appreciate the weakening of the class distinction.

[78] Horie, op. cit., p. 83.

[79] Tsunehiko Yui, "On the Entrepreneurship in Meiji Japan by J. Hirschmeier," *Japan Business History Review*, I (1966), pp. 105–106.

[80] Hirschmeier wrote: "The last decades of the Tokugawa period had done much to blur class distinctions with respect to education, patterns of thinking, and economic activity."—Hirschmeier, op. cit., p. 47. As Hirschmeier clearly stated that "class origin was not of decisive importance in molding entrepreneurs" (ibid., p. 256), it is perhaps not accurate to classify him as a supporter of the current view of the Meiji entrepreneurs in all parts as suggested in the syllogism described earlier. However, in spite of his explicit statement to the contrary, Hirschmeier's work invited such a comment as that by Yui (see note 79). Hirschmeier would, on the other hand, be the first to support the view that the Meiji entrepreneurs were "irrational, non-capitalist, dynamic and romantic" in their approaches.

The importance of rejecting the current view lies more in the fact that it encourages misinterpretations of historical facts rather than in the invalidity of the type of theorizing *per se* as depicted in the syllogism described earlier. A case in point is provided by the interpretations of the development of modern banking in Japan. The available sources—especially those written in Japanese—have long maintained that modern banking in Japan was developed by the samurai class under the guidance of the government (which also was manned by the lower-class samurai). These sources also reiterated that the *chōnin* had to be pressured by the government and that the samurai class had to provide examples for the *chōnin* class to follow.[81] Horie and Tsuchiya were vocal in condemning the lack of interest and ability of the *chōnin* class and, like Hirschmeier, credited the samurai class with the founding of the modern banking system in Japan.[82]

Recent studies, however, have shown that the above view is untenable.[83] The results of the author's own investigation and that of several other Japanese scholars show that the foundation of modern banking in Japan was laid in 1876 when the Banking Act of 1872 was amended to allow profitable banking operations for the first time. All earlier attempts by the government had failed before 1876, but once the profitability of modern banking was assured, banks were established immediately in large numbers.

The long-accepted view, however, has been that:

> The rush of the samurai to found banks stands out in striking contrast to the attitudes of the wealthy merchant houses, which had to be forced to establish the first four national

[81] Tsuchiya quoted Eiichi Shibusawa's remark in which the latter lamented the lack of initiative within the *heimin* (all non-samurai, *i.e.* merchants, peasants, and artisans) class. This particular passage has been quoted *ad nauseam* by the Japanese writers—Tsuchiya, *A Business History Study . . .*, op. cit., p. 189. Contrary to such a view of the samurai class, the following observation by Lockwood seems to put the question of the samurai origin *vis-à-vis* the leadership in a better perspective: "It is incorrect to contrast the Japanese samurai and the Chinese scholar-official class as a whole, and to find here a key to the divergence of the two countries after 1868. Many samurai were as inert and obscurantist as the typical Chinese mandarin in the face of the western challenge. As a class they were more idle, more ignorant, more arrogant. Most of them sank into obscurity once their caste privileges were cancelled."—W. W. Lockwood, "Japan's Response to the West," *World Politics* (October, 1956), pp. 45–46.

[82] Tsuchiya, *A Business History Study . . .*, op. cit., p. 189.

[83] I have examined 38 banks established under the amended Banking Act of 1876 relying mainly on available bank records and histories. For the findings of this examination, see my "The Role of the Samurai in the Development of Modern Banking in Japan," *Journal of Economic History*, XXVII (1967), pp. 198–220; Kōkichi Asakura, *Meiji-zenki Nippon Kinyū Kōzō-shi* (*A History of Early Meiji Financial Structure*) (Tokyo, 1961), and S. Tōhata and T. Takahashi, eds., *Meiji-zenki no Ginkōseido* (*The Banking System in Early Meiji*) (Tokyo, 1965), are the best Japanese sources among the several expressing this view.

banks in 1872. Correspondingly, in this early phase the merchants also fell far behind the samurai as contributors of capital to the whole banking system.[84]

These words by Hirschmeier—and he is being quoted as a representative of many others who wrote in an identical vein—are due, in no small part, to the current view of the Meiji entrepreneurs. When close examinations of available evidence such as the remaining annual reports and bank histories are made, the only possible conclusion is that the main force to establish and operate these banks came from merchants and rich peasants who saw an opportunity for profit, rather than from the samurai class who might have wished to serve the cause of modernization of Japan.

However suited such observations as Hirschmeier's may be to the current view of the Meiji entrepreneurs and to the pattern of economic development suggested by this view, the notion that the success of modern banking in Japan must be attributed to the samurai class cannot be supported. The major "evidence" that the samurai class contributed over three-quarters of the initial capital is inadequate. The fact is that the samurai contributed the commutation bonds they had just received to the establishment of these banks more for lack of alternatives than for any more positive reasons. While the participation of samurai in new banks was thus passive, the *heimin* class participated actively in the majority of new banks by supplying the necessary cash (20 per cent of the intitial capital) and the entrepreneurial energy in the form of directors and initiators in obtaining charters. Even the nominal control of banks by the samurai as majority shareholders shifted in most cases to the hands of the *heimin* a few years after the establishment of these banks.[85] Prof. Patrick, who has studied the Japanese financial institutions and who does not subscribe to the current view of the "community-centred" entrepreneurs, aptly summarized the author's view when he wrote: "it [Japan's financial system] was mainly through the initiative of profit-minded individuals that most Japanese financial institutions were born."[86]

The above is only one example, but it is by no means an isolated case of misinterpretation due to the current view of the Meiji entrepreneurs. The author would go as far as to argue that some aspects of Japanese economic transformation during the early Meiji period have been subjected to an analogous misinterpretation. What is necessary now is to review this period of rapid changes in Japan without the conceptual shackle imposed by the current view.

[84] Hirschmeier, op. cit., p. 58.   [85] See my article cited in note 83.
[86] Hugh T. Patrick, "Banking in the Early Stages of Industrialization: Japan, 1868–1914," in Rondo Cameron, ed., *Banking in the Early Stages of Industrialization* (1967), p. 249.

Though the details of each case could not be elaborated here, the direction this review is to take could be suggested *en gros*. For example, in examining the development of the textile industry, one must now evaluate in a new perspective the desire and efforts of the hard-driving son of a wine merchant, Denhichi Itō, in building a textile mill. What also should not be forgotten is the fact that his interest in textiles predated the entrance of the Meiji government to the industry by several years.[87] What one reads in the biography of Itō, who later established the famed Mie Textile Company, is a story of a struggling entrepreneur in the tradition of Samuel Slater.[88] In the shipbuilding industry, the content of Tomiji Hirano's biography tells a story of a man who in 1861 was an aid to a ship's engineer and who went on to build one of the largest shipbuilding firms in Meiji Japan.[89] He, like Shōzō Kawasaki, the builder of the well-known Kawasaki Shipbuilding Company, who "entered into shipbuilding stimulated by the large profit which could be gained by the government subsidies,"[90] struggled to build the industry by taking opportunities and aids which came as the result of the Restoration. Biographies and company histories related to the paper industry, sugar, flour-milling, mining, and others offer detailed accounts of those men who supplied the entrepreneurial energy of Meiji Japan and who can hardly be categorized under the heading of "the community-centred" entrepreneurs.[91]

Stating it differently, the view of Japanese economic development fostered by the supporters of the current view of the Meiji entrepreneurs overemphasizes the uniqueness rather than the similarities of the incentives and modes of behaviour of these entrepreneurs in the process of industrialization. The stress on uniqueness has resulted in the concept of "community-centred entrepreneurs," which can be repeatedly challenged when close examinations of biographies are made. It has also resulted in statements of so sweeping a character as to imply that the incentive and behaviour patterns of Japanese entrepreneurs are not comparable to their counterparts in any other nation: "The 'spirit of the samurai' not only determined official policies but during the Meiji era also became something of a standard public attitude: a happy mixture of militant patriotism and

---

[87] The Editorial Association of Denhichi Itō's Biography, *Itō Denhichi* (Tokyo, 1936).

[88] Ibid., pp. 11–35.

[89] Mitani, op. cit., pp. 90–101. My thanks are due to Prof. Keiichiro Nakagawa of the University of Tokyo who kindly granted me permission to xerox this rare book.

[90] Mitsuhaya Kajinishi, "Meiji-shonen no Sangyōshihon" ("The Industrial Capital in Early Meiji"), *Shakai Keizai Shigaku (Journal of Social and Economic History)*, XXV (1959), p. 4. See also Mitsuhiko Yamamoto, *Kawasaki Shōzō* (Tokyo, 1918).

[91] This is a summary of the writer's reaction he gained after reading nearly 200 biographies which are available at the Economics Library of the University of Tokyo and the Harvard–Yenching Library. The industries named have more reliable biographies than others.

economically rationalized Confucian ethics."[92] In short, the overemphasis on uniqueness caused many, knowingly or unknowingly, to believe that Japanese economic development came through a route so different as to make it *sui generis*.

But if the view suggested here of the Meiji entrepreneurs is correct, and if the role of the government in the early Meiji years were seen in a proper perspective, as suggested by Prof. Rosovsky,[93] the course of further research is to seek the similarities of the pattern—especially the motivation of entrepreneurs —of Japan's economic development to that of other nations. The emphasis clearly should not be on an often undefined uniqueness but rather on a more globally applicable set of propositions.

PART FOUR: CONCLUSION

Though the author is mindful of the preliminary nature of this article, the following conclusion can perhaps be drawn on the basis of the foregoing. The "community-centred entrepreneur" or "the spirit of the samurai" has long been accepted by many in spite of the fact that the concept is a product of deductive theorizing. The untested concept has been convenient for "explaining" Japan's rapid economic growth. To use a metaphor, the "explanation" offered is no more than a high but spurious correlation coefficient between two variables. The rapid industrialization—uncommon in Asia[94]—and the "community-centred entrepreneurs" with *shikon shōsai* yielded a convenient generalization. One variable seems to be highly "correlated" with the other, giving a comfortable inference of causal relationship. When such variables as Confucian ethics, tradition of loyalty to "higher causes," class structure, and many more were added from the pool of Tokugawa tradition, this process seemed to yield yet a higher correlation of "explanations."

[92] Hirschmeier, op. cit., p. 44.

[93] Prof. Rosovsky would consider the "institutional reform and financial policies" of the government "during the years of transition (1868–1885)" to be of more long-run significance than the fact that the government "operated factories, subsidized certain industries, imported technicians," etc.—Rosovsky, op. cit., p. 113. I agree with this view. As is implicit in this article, I feel that the role of the government during the early Meiji years has been overemphasized to the point of losing sight of the active entrepreneurial activities of the period.

[94] Though Lockwood was frank to note that: "why and how a response of this character [industrialization and modernization] developed so rapidly in Japan, while languishing in China and other neighbouring nations are still elusive issues," the supporters of the current view can find many of their answers to this issue by invoking the community-centered entrepreneurs.—Lockwood, op. cit., p. 37.

The argument of this article is that a fresh re-examination is now in order. However entrenched the current view is, the more globally acceptable profit incentive must now occupy the role of the principal determinant of the entrepreneurial behaviour of the early Meiji years. This is not to say that all the cultural differences between Japan and the West are to be ignored, but it is to say that an entrepreneurial motivation deduced by overemphasizing the cultural uniqueness is clearly in conflict with the evidence seen in biographies, company and bank histories, and other sources. The overemphasis has also contributed, in no minor degree, to what this writer considers as misinterpretations of the process of Japanese industrialization and modernization in its early phase.

14

INDIAN ENTREPRENEURSHIP:
A SURVEY

E. Wayne Nafziger

A number of social scientists have contended that entrepreneurship and other high level human skills are key variables which link the socio-cultural milieu with the rate of economic development. Recently, some economists have shifted the emphasis away from the growth of capital to the growth of high level manpower, such as entrepreneurs, as the major determinant of the rate of economic growth. Despite the evidence of relatively high rates of unemployment and emigration among high level manpower in India, the little information available indicates that the ratio of high level manpower to the population is not high in the country even when compared to other economically less developed countries. Computations based on the data of E. R. Rado and A. R. Jolly point out that the high level manpower ratios in India are below that of Costa Rica, Colombia, Venezuela, Brazil, Turkey, and Greece and above that of Zambia, Kenya, Uganda, and Tanganyika[1] (See Table 14-1). If these ratios are indicative of the relative quantities of entrepreneurship, the productive factor that coordinates the resources used in the production of a good or service, then the ratio of entrepreneurial resources to the

[1] E. R. Rado and A. R. Jolly, "The Demand for Manpower—An East African Case Study," *Journal of Development Studies*, I, No. 3 (April, 1965), pp. 229–230.

287

population is not high in India when compared to other less developed countries.

In this paper, before examining the findings of the studies on Indian entrepreneurship, we shall present introductory sections that deal with the Indian economy, a historical sketch of Indian entrepreneurship, and a synopsis of the leading Indian business communities. After a short exposition on each of the important studies on Indian entrepreneurship, we shall discuss entrepreneurship, caste, and social community; entrepreneurship and the family; entrepreneurship and government; the organization of large scale enterprises; the small entrepreneur; and approaches to future studies.

FIGURE 14-1

TABLE 14-1

High Level Manpower per 100,000 Population—An Inter-country Comparison

Number of Persons Educated to Category I[a] or Category II[b] Level per 100,000 Population

U.S.A. (1950)	17,907.0
Canada (1951)	10,954.0
France (1954)	4,575.2
Italy (1951)	3,550.3
Costa Rica (1950)	3,305.5
Colombia (1950)	2,769.4
Spain (1961)	2,268.3
Brazil (1950)	1,713.7
Venezuela (1950)	1,393.9
Greece (1961)	1,249.5
Turkey (1961)	1,105.5
India (1955)	991.1
Zambia (1961)	572.0
Kenya (1961)	484.5
Uganda (1961)	214.5
Tanganyika (1961)	176.8

[a] Definition: Category I: (a) Professional men and technologists whose work clearly requires a university degree or equivalent training and (b) senior administrators and managers carrying considerable policy and financial responsibility.

[b] Definition: Category II: Technicians, teachers with secondary education, junior administrators and managers, supervisors of clerical staff and of skilled men, fully trained nurses, senior members of the external service with diploma or post school certificate qualifications or the experience and ability to hold equivalent posts.

Source: Rado and Jolly, *Journal of Development Studies*, I, No. 3, pp. 229–230.

SKETCH OF THE INDIAN ECONOMY

According to United Nations data, India, with a gross domestic product (GDP) of $41.9 billion (or 199.6 billion rupees) and a population of 499 million in 1966, ranks substantially below the median in per capita GDP in East and Southeast Asia with $84 (or 400 rupees).[2] The percentage of GDP originating in the manufacturing sector in India, 14 per cent, is the median figure among eleven East and Southeast Asian countries with data in 1965–66.[3] Table 14-2 presents data on the changes in the output and structure of the Indian economy since Independence.

[2] United Nations, Statistical Office, Department of Economic and Social Affairs, *Statistical Yearbook* (New York, 1968), pp. 578–579.

[3] Ibid., pp. 560–567.

TABLE 14-2
Net National Output by Industrial Origin (in 1948–1949 prices and in billions of rupees and percentages)

Sector	1948-49		1950-51		1955-56		1960-61		1964-65	
	Rs. (in billions)	%	Rs. (in billions)	%	Rs. (in billions)	%	Rs. (in billions)	%	Rs. (in billions)	%
Agricultural	42.5	49.1	43.4	49.0	50.2	47.9	59.1	46.4	65.0	43.0
Mining, manufacturing & small enterprises	14.8	17.1	14.8	16.7	17.6	16.8	21.1	16.5	25.5	16.8
Commerce, transport & communication	16.0	18.5	16.6	18.8	19.7	18.8	24.6	19.3	29.7	19.6
Other services	13.4	15.5	13.9	15.7	17.3	16.5	23.1	18.2	31.4	20.7
Net earned income from abroad	-0.2	-0.2	-0.2	-0.2	0.0	0.0	-0.5	-0.4	-1.1	-0.1
Net national output at factor cost (or national income)	86.5	100.0	88.5	100.0	104.8	100.0	127.3	100.0	150.5	100.0

Source: Ruddar Datt and K. P. M. Sundharam, *Indian Economy* (New Delhi: Niraj Prakashan, 1968), p. 33.

A HISTORICAL SKETCH OF
INDIAN ENTREPRENEURSHIP

Indian handicraft industries, such as textiles, enjoyed a world-wide reputation in ancient times, as attested by the use of Indian muslin in wrapping Egyptian mummies.[4] This historical sketch, however, begins in the seventeenth and eighteenth centuries, the period corresponding to the early years of British influence. Despite the lack of systematic data on these centuries, some generalizations are possible. In 1750, India was as urbanized as England, France, and Italy. During the seventeenth century, there were a number of entrepreneurs in major trading areas in the Indus River Valley in northwestern India (much of which is presently a part of West Pakistan), in northeastern India around the Ganges River and its tributaries, and in southern India coastal areas engaged in foreign trade. In addition, in the eighteenth century, Indian merchants and brokers dealt with or were employed by European privileged and chartered companies (such as the English East India Company) or their servants. During the seventeenth and eighteenth centuries, Indians were involved as financiers— in changing money, providing bills of exchange, loaning to government, acting as treasurer and revenue collector for government, and loaning to private parties (including Europeans). In this same period, India lacked sizeable agricultural entrepreneurs in part because of the very high rate of taxation for peasants and the small market resulting from inadequate transportation.[5]

By 1800, the factory system had been developed in England and before 1825, the system had obtained a foothold in a few other Western countries. Although several English businessmen established factories in India in the first half of the nineteenth century, it was not until the middle of the century that such manufacturing enterprises extended beyond initial ventures in a few industries. Around 1850, Indian industrial and financial entrepreneurs became involved, especially in western India, and were instrumental in the substantial progress in modern manufacturing in the last half of the nineteenth century.[6] At the same time, Indian handicrafts, which had had a wide reputation for a long time, declined as a result of the competition of machine-made goods at

---

[4] Ruddar Datt and K. P. M. Sundharam, *Indian Economy* (New Delhi: Niraj Prakashan, 1968), p. 144.

[5] Dhananjaya Ramchandra Gadgil, *Origins of the Modern Indian Business Class—An Interim Report* (New York: Institute of Pacific Relations, 1959).

[6] Phiroze B. Medhora, "Entrepreneurship in India," *Political Science Quarterly*, LXXX, No. 4 (September, 1965), pp. 558–559.

home and abroad, the development of new tastes, and the disappearance of the patronage of princely courts.[7]

In the early part of the twentieth century, some small beginnings were made in the Indian heavy industry—steel, engineering, electric power, and shipping.[8] The rate of growth in industrial output increased in the first half of the twentieth century from that in the last half of the nineteenth century. Between 1912 and 1945, industrial production doubled.[9] Following World War I the colonial government moved slightly in the direction of encouraging local industry. Industrial development was especially rapid and diverse in the 1930s and 1940s, with indigenous enterprise increasingly setting the pace.[10] After independence in 1947 and a period of economic disruption caused by political events, India embarked on a system of economic planning with a high priority on industrial development—especially in the Second and Third Five-Year Plans (1956–1966). The industrial entrepreneurial function has been facilitated by investment in social overhead capital and other programs, such as industrial estates. Government has emerged as a major entrepreneur accounting for almost one-half of industrial investment in recent years.[11] Although in some activities government investment has deterred private investment, in other instances government has stimulated demand for industry by investing so as to alleviate bottlenecks and by creating new linkages with other industries. Finally, since independence, industrialization has widened geographically in the country.

INDIAN BUSINESS COMMUNITIES

The indigenous population of India is divided into several socioreligious communities—Hindus, Sikhs (usually classed with Hindus), Muslims, Jains, Parsis, Christians, and a few others. Within each region and socioreligious community, particularly among the Hindus, the society has been further divided into class, caste and subcaste groups which have been fairly rigidly separated from each other.[12] The Hindu community, which is the largest, is further segmented into classes (or *varna*), which are thought to have been based originally on functional occupational differentiations. In general, four main classes

---

[7] Datt and Sundharam, *Indian Economy*, pp. 144–146.

[8] Helen B. Lamb, "The Rise of Indian Business Communities," *Pacific Affairs*, XXIII, No. 2 (June, 1955), p. 105.

[9] R. Balakrishna, *Review of Economic Growth in India* (Bangalore: Bangalore Press, 1961), p. 102.

[10] Medhora, "Entrepreneurship in India," pp. 571–573.

[11] Ibid., pp. 574–575.   [12] Gadgil, *Modern Indian Business Class*, p. 16.

are recognized—the *Brahmin* or priest, the *Kshtriya* or warrior, the *Vaishya* or trader, and the *Shudra* or artisan—in addition to, in some instances, the "untouchables." The first three classes are twice-born classes (*i.e.* higher classes which have gone through a special ceremony in youth indicating a second or spiritual birth). The four classes are divided into a number of castes (or *jati*) based on geography, kinship, occupation, or ritually determined function. The frequent specialization of economic function by social community means that the business elements of society often coincide with social communities.[13] An analysis of entrepreneurship can, thus, be viewed in terms of the social community and caste of entrepreneurs in various regions.

Let us first consider business communities in the eighteenth century. Despite the fact that the ruling class and the bulk of the population were Muslims, the Khatris and Lohanas, Hindu and Sikh communities, where caste divisions and rules were not rigidly observed, were the leading entrepreneurs in trade and finance in northwestern India. Gujarat and Saurashtra had a highly developed Hindu and Jain [14] trading community, the Banias, in addition to Muslim communities comprising converts from Hindu trading and artisan communities; later in the century, an indigenous Parsi group became active in trade. In Maharashtra, local Brahmins and trading classes from Gujarat, Rajasthan, Saurashtra, and Kutch dominated business. The Banias (later called Marwaris), Hindu, and Jain trading castes from Rajasthan were the leading trading communities in northeastern India around the Ganges River. In Bengal, indigenous Brahmins and Kayasthas, as a result of their positions as assistants and agents for the dominant British businessmen, obtained access to the major entrepreneurial positions instead of the Bengali trading classes. Various Hindu trading communities (such as the Chettis in Madras) dominated business in South India, except for Kerala where Muslims, Christians, and Jews were the chief traders.[15]

Two business communities, the Parsis [16] and the Gujarati (Hindu) trading

[13] Lamb, "Rise of Indian Business Communities," pp. 101–103.

[14] The Jains, an ascetic religious sect originating in the ancient period, became a trading sect for purely ritualistic reasons—only in trading could one practice *ahimsa* (the absolute prohibition of the killing of living things). [Max Weber, *The Religion of India—The Sociology of Hinduism and Buddhism* (New York: The Free Press, 1958), pp. 199–204.] The transition from trading to manufacturing by Jains (especially Marwari Jains) in the second or third decade of the twentieth century was a definite break with scriptural teachings. Medhora suggests that this may have been possible because of the strong influence of the Jain laity. [Medhora, "Entrepreneurship in India," pp. 565–566.]

[15] Gadgil, *Modern Indian Business Class*, pp. 16–21.

[16] The Parsis, followers of Zoroaster which migrated from Iran to western India 1300 years ago, have no basic roots within the country. Medhora, "Entrepreneurship in India," p. 564.

castes, were the dominant Indian entrepreneurs in Bombay's textile manufacturing, finance, and foreign trade and Ahmedabad's textile manufacturing after the middle of the nineteenth century and in the small beginnings in Indian heavy industry early in the twentieth century. Textile mills in the leading southern center, Coimbatore, Madras, were developed by two southern Indian groups, the Chettis, a money-lending community and the Naidus, a local land-owing class.[17]

In the nineteenth century, a large number of Marwaris migrated to Calcutta and vicinity and entered key entrepreneurial positions, especially in trade and finance. However, not until 1920 did the Marwaris begin opening manufacturing plants. Since then, they have risen so rapidly in manufacturing and other sectors that today they are the foremost Indian business community—especially in Calcutta.[18]

Since Independence, refugee Hindu traders from Sindh (now part of Pakistan) are becoming prominent in trade, real estate, and construction in some major cities. If they follow the pattern of a number of business communities in earlier periods, they may eventually become industrialists.[19]

STUDIES IN INDIAN ENTREPRENEURSHIP

In this section, following a brief overview of the major studies on entrepreneurship in India, we shall give a concise synopsis of each of the studies.

The studies by D. R. Gadgil, Helen B. Lamb, Phiroze B. Medhora, and Pritam Singh, which are complementary in scope, survey entrepreneurship in the country as a whole.[20] Gadgil focuses on Indian entrepreneurship in the seventeenth and eighteenth centuries; Lamb (with a historical approach) and Medhora (with a sociological approach) look at the nineteenth and twentieth centuries; and Singh analyzes in some depth the period since Independence in 1947. Except for Singh, who discusses all sizes of firms, the studies stress large scale enterprise. Another study, by Andrew F. Brimmer, examines the impact of the managing agency system on the setting of entrepreneurship in India.[21]

[17] Lamb, "Rise of Indian Business Communities," pp. 104–105.
[18] Ibid., pp. 105–108.   [19] Ibid., p. 109.
[20] Gadgil, *Modern Indian Business Class*; Lamb, "Rise of Indian Business Communities," pp. 98–126; Medhora, "Entrepreneurship in India," pp. 558–559; and Singh, "Essays Concerning Some Types of Entrepreneurship in India" (unpublished Ph.D. dissertation, University of Michigan, 1963).
[21] Andrew F. Brimmer, "The Setting of Entrepreneurship in India," *Quarterly Journal of Economics*, XXIX (November, 1955), pp. 553–576.

Five studies investigate entrepreneurship in specific geographical areas in India. James J. Berna, in an examination of the light engineering industry in Madras state, Leighton W. Hazlehurst, in an anthropological study of entrepreneurs in a Punjabi city, and James T. McCrory, in case studies of small industrial firms in two northern Indian cities, have based their findings largely on empirical data gathered from interviews.[22] Blair B. Kling's study of the lack of entrepreneurship in Bengal and Howard Spodek's research on entrepreneurs in Ahmedabad, Gujarat, rely on the historical method.[23]

Gadgil's study is historical, looking at the origins of the modern Indian business class, with the beginnings of the modern period placed at 1750—close to the beginning of British political and economic influence and in the century preceding the establishment of the factory system in India. Through painstaking effort, Gadgil has brought together the scanty data available on the entrepreneurial history of India in the eighteenth century to paint in broad strokes a picture of the social communities involved in trade, finance, and handicraft industry in various geographical areas. This picture is presented in the context of a background of the political instability accompanying the shift from Mogul dominance to European suzerainty, the pervasive influence of British and European economic power, the high degree of urbanization relative to the rest of the world, the self-sufficiency of the rural economy, the development of the preconditions for a technological and industrial revolution, the rapid increase in internal trade, the specialization of the business function in the *Vaishya* class, and the nature of the organization of caste and trade associations.

Lamb, using a historical approach, analyzes entrepreneurial participation by social community since the advent of the factory system in the middle of the nineteenth century. The stress is on manufacturing and banking entrepreneurs in the major industrial cities, especially in Bombay and Calcutta. Much of the analysis focuses on the three major Indian communities in modern industry and banking, the Marwaris, the Parsis, and the Gujarati trading castes. The rise of social communities (and families) in manufacturing and other large scale industries is explained in terms of factors such as control over several operating firms through the managing agency, community mobilization of resources,

[22] Berna, *Industrial Entrepreneurship in Madras State* (London: Asia Publishing House, 1960); Hazlehurst, *Entrepreneurship and the Merchant Castes in a Punjabi City* (Durham, N.C.: Duke University Commonwealth Studies Center, 1966); and McCrory, *Case Studies in Latent Industrial Potential: Small Industry in a North Indian Town* (Delhi: Government of India, Ministry of Commerce and Industry, 1956).

[23] Blair B. Kling, "Obstacles to Entrepreneurship in India: The Case of Bengal," Paper presented to the *Congress of Orientalists*, University of Michigan, Ann Arbor, Mich., August 1967; and Howard Spodek, "The 'Manchesterisation' of Ahmedabad," *Economic Weekly*, XVII (March 13, 1965), pp. 483–490.

intra-community business linkages, and intra-community marriage networks.[24]

In a sociological examination of the positive and negative influences on the supply of entrepreneurship in India,[25] Medhora borrows heavily from Max Weber's analysis of religion, the caste system, and the family system as factors affecting the emergence of entrepreneurs.[26] The development of indigenous entrepreneurship in manufacturing, finance, and large scale trade is traced with emphasis on three stages: the period of *laissez-faire* capitalism in the nineteenth century, with a sparseness of entrepreneurs; the era of *Swadeshi* and a concern for indigenous industrial development after World War I in which there was a rise in entrepreneurial activity; and the period of economic planning after Independence, when entrepreneurship (both public and private) expanded rapidly. Included is a discussion of the leading families and social communities involved in entrepreneurial activity since the nineteenth century.

Singh's study focuses on empirical findings pertaining to indigenous entrepreneurship after Independence (1947) in the country as a whole. Both the public and private sectors, including both large scale and small scale enterprises, are discussed and evaluated in terms of their contribution to economic development. Although all nonagricultural sectors are mentioned, the primary emphasis is on entrepreneurs in the manufacturing sectors. The major contribution of the study is the assembling of relevant empirical data on entrepreneurship from several different sources, including government studies and documents accessible to Singh as an economist with the Indian National Council of Applied Economic Research.

Among the studies on Indian entrepreneurship, Singh has the most detailed treatment of the concept of the entrepreneur. According to Singh, entrepreneurship involves the actual creation or extension of an organization or institution, which gives rise to various growth-producing phenomena such as increases in productivity, technical change, saving, and investment. The objectives of the organization the entrepreneurs build may be either social service or profit making. The entrepreneur need not be an innovator in the Schumpeterian sense but may be involved in the adaptation of institutions which have been developed in other countries.[27]

Brimmer analyzes the effect of the managing agency system on the setting of entrepreneurship in India. The managing agency system, prevalent among large-scale industrial firms, is a type of industrial organization in which the

[24] Lamb, "Rise of Indian Business Communities," pp. 98–126.
[25] Medhora, "Entrepreneurship in India," pp. 558–580.
[26] Weber, *Religion of India.*
[27] Singh, "Essays Concerning Types of Entrepreneurship," pp. 8–10.

administration, finance and promotion of one or more companies are controlled by a single enterprise.[28]

Berna confines his empirical study, conducted in 1957, to manufacturing enterprises in light-engineering industry in Madras state with fifty to 250 persons employed. His findings are based on interviews with entrepreneurs of fifty-two firms and outside sources familiar with the firms.[29] The sample is based on firms in Madras City and Coimbatore and their vicinities listed in the Madras State Factory List for 1956.[30] Berna focuses on the occupational and socioeconomic background of the entrepreneurs, the origin and growth of their firms, the operational problems of the entrepreneurs, and the mobility of the entrepreneurs.

In the Berna study, the entrepreneur is defined as "the person (or group of persons) responsible for the existence of a new industrial enterprise."[31] However, the discussion implies that Berna includes routine firm management as a part of the entrepreneurial function.[32]

Kling presents a historical explanation, beginning with evidence from the eighteenth century, for the lack of entrepreneurs from the indigenous population of Bengal. His focus is on an analysis of reasons for the antipathy toward business activity by Bengalis.

Spodek's historical study concentrates on the reasons why, unlike most areas in India, Ahmedabad, Gujarat, the textile manufacturing center in India, developed a class of industrial entrepreneurs indigenous to the region. The study, in presenting a brief background sketch and entrepreneurial history of businessmen who pioneered in the textile industry, provides insights into factors related to the success of entrepreneurs in Ahmedabad. The development of a favorable socioeconomic milieu for the rise of industrial entrepreneurship is discussed, with the emphasis on the development of social overhead capital, the improvement in political climate, the high business morality, the establishment of financial and management institutions, and the availability of many complementary factors.[33]

In a study of entrepreneurs in a Punjabi city of 50,000 persons with the pseudonym Ram Nagar,[34] Hazlehurst attempts to analyze the effect of caste,

[28] Brimmer, "Setting of Entrepreneurship," pp. 553–576.

[29] Berna, *Industrial Entrepreneurship in Madras State*, pp. 1–4.

[30] Berna, p. 224.

[31] Berna, p. 2. This is similar to the Schumpeterian concept of the entrepreneur. In *The Theory of Economic Development*, trans. Redvers Opie (New York, Oxford University Press, 1961), p. 66, Joseph Schumpeter indicates that innovations or new combinations are embodied in new firms.   [32] Berna, pp. 101–143.

[33] Spodek, " 'Manchesterisation' of Ahmedabad," pp. 483–490.

[34] In 1966, when the state of Punjab was divided into two states, the city, which is located in Ambala district, became a part of northeastern Haryana.

socio-economic class, kinship structure and social community on the social context in which entrepreneurial activity is undertaken.[35] The study includes entrepreneurship in all the major sectors of the city's economy—trade, manufacturing, and finance. The author's method of acquiring data was through observation and informal interview.

McCrory's findings are based on case studies of fourteen industrial firms that used power and employed no more than twenty workers in two towns in Punjab and Uttar Pradesh in 1955. The monograph accounts for the high mortality rate and lack of growth of firms of this type, and it recommends policies to improve the utilization of resources in the small industry sector.[36]

ENTREPRENEURSHIP, CASTE, AND SOCIAL COMMUNITY

The empirical studies of Hazlehurst, Berna, and Kling investigate the relationship between caste and social community, on the one hand, and entrepreneurship on the other. Some of the issues raised by these studies are discussed in this section.

The displacement of populations as a result of the partition of India into two nation-states in 1947 had a major impact on the structure of entrepreneurship and class, especially in areas close to the India–Pakistan border with relatively large economic opportunities, such as Ram Nagar, the Punjabi city studied by Hazlehurst. The supply of trading entrepreneurs in the city was augmented substantially as a result of the facts that a disproportionate share of refugees from West Pakistan were traders and that administrative arrangements made it more likely for refugees to receive compensation for losses in urban areas.[37] A large majority of the displaced merchants resettled in urban areas in eastern Punjab following the partition were Khatris or Aroras. Many of the subcaste distinctions among these groups have been obscured. One of the reasons for this is the disassociation from orthodox casteism which has resulted from religious reform movement (such as Sikhism and the Arya Samaj), where caste identity has become blurred. A second reason is the high degree of occupational and spatial mobility leading to the erasing of old marriage networks among persons of similar status because of the scattering of possible marriage partners throughout the country. A final reason is the difficulty of assessing the validity

[35] Hazlehurst, *Entrepreneurship and the Merchant Castes*, pp. 1–5.
[36] McCrory, *Case Studies in Latent Industrial Potential*.
[37] Hazlehurst, *Entrepreneurship and the Merchant Caste*, pp. 15–19, 119–120.

of claims to status by refugees. Thus, it may be more accurate to think of the Khatris and Aroras in Ram Nagar as members of occupational groups rather than as members of endogamous caste groups with well defined caste rituals and behavior. Their social status within the city has been influenced primarily by local factors and is more ambiguous and less consistent among local groups than is usually the case.[38]

The arrival of displaced persons from West Pakistan helped weaken the dominant position of the Aggarwal Banias, a *Vaishya* caste, in certain sectors of economy such as trade. In addition, the relative economic position of the Banias declined for other reasons—the loss of Muslim tenants and debtors who fled to West Pakistan during the partition, and legislation passed to restrain entrepreneurs with substantial wealth. Since partition, the Banias have united with a lower caste, the Suds, to control the timber business of the city, in opposition to displaced persons, in order to uphold the social status and economic power of the two major "local" business classes.[39]

Hazlehurst notes that refugee entrepreneurs tend to be more innovative in business than local entrepreneurs, although he offers no explanation.[40] The challenge of a new environment may have beneficial educational and psychological effects. A related factor is that the geographical dispersion of friends, relatives, and neighbors of the refugees may lead to a rejection of local values and sanctions, such as notions of caste propriety, which impede rational business practices.[41]

In his study of manufacturing entrepreneurs in Madras state, Berna discovers that traditional occupation and caste have very little impact in determining entry into entrepreneurial endeavours. The fifty-two entrepreneurs are members of ten different social communities, although forty-one of the fifty-two are from three communities—the Naidu, a land-owning class from the warrior *varna*; the Brahmin; and the Chettiar, a southern Indian trading community. Only four of the sample entrepreneurs are in direct line with the traditional caste-assigned family occupation.[42] This break with the traditional occupation indicates to Berna that in explaining entrepreneurial activity "sociological factors, such as caste, attachment to traditional activities, and approval or disapproval of the social group to which a potential entrepreneur belongs are less important than economic factors such as access to capital and possession of business experience and technical knowledge."[43]

[38] Ibid., pp. 28–33, 40–45.   [39] Ibid., pp. 45–54.
[40] Ibid., pp. 55–59, 118–119.
[41] For a parallel, see Werner Sombart's discussion of Jewish entrepreneurs in the Middle Ages. *Die Juden und das Wirtschaftsleben* (Munich: Verlag von Duncker & Humblot, 1928).   [42] Berna, pp. 42–44, 83–86.   [43] Ibid., pp. 212–213.

This contention has been criticized by Bert F. Hoselitz. If Berna's sample is characteristic of Madras industrial entrepreneurs in general, Hoselitz argues, the social structure of the state must be undergoing a profound change. One important indication of this change, Hoselitz continues, is the decline in occupational choices assigned by caste. Sociological explanations are needed to explain these departures from traditional occupations, he indicates. Brahmins, for example, have been more inclined to become entrepreneurs than previously for a number of reasons: discrimination encountered in universities and government as a reaction against their favored social position in the colonial period, the decline in the number of caste-determined occupations available, an increase in status of business occupations resulting from sociopolitical emphasis on the need for economic growth, and the wealth and influence available for investment in training and new enterprises. In short, with socioeconomic change and the increased emphasis by the government on economic development, entrepreneurship became increasingly attractive for Brahmins as a result of the erosion of their position.[44] A parallel exists in Nigeria, where a large number of Yoruba and Hausa traditional political rulers thwarted possible socioeconomic decline accompanying modernization by using their wealth and influence to establish sizeable trading and manufacturing firms.[45]

Berna, in concluding that sociological factors are less important than economic factors, has raised some important questions. Hoselitz's challenge of Berna's conclusion, together with the prior Papanek–Hagen controversy,[46] has helped clarify some of these issues. The disputations indicate the limitations of the approach of one discipline to a discussion of the determinants of entrepreneurship. Even if a scholar in one discipline has developed a plausible explanation for a relationship between two variables, this does not preclude the possibility that the same relationship can be explained in a different manner by the perspective of another discipline. For example, the Brahmins who were induced by their declining socioeconomic position to turn to entrepreneurial activity had the advantage of access to capital and a good education resulting from wealth and influence. In this instance, social and economic variables interacted.

[44] Bert F. Hoselitz, "Entrepreneurship and Traditional Elites," *Explorations in Entrepreneurial History/Second Series*, I (Fall, 1963), pp. 36–39.

[45] E. Wayne Nafziger, "Nigerian Entrepreneurship: A Study of Indigenous Businessmen in the Footwear Industry," (unpublished Ph.D. dissertation, Department of Economics, University of Illinois), pp. 23–77.

[46] Gustav F. Papanek, "The Development of Entrepreneurship," *American Economic Association Papers and Proceedings*, LII, No. 2 (May 1962), pp. 46–58, and Everett E. Hagen, "Problems of Economic Development—Discussion," Ibid., pp. 59–61.

Berna found that the largest group of entrepreneurs (twelve of fifty-two), when classified according to immediate vocational background, were graduate engineers, although he finds this difficult to explain.[47] It is perhaps not so surprising that graduate engineers have had a high rate of participation in industrial entrepreneurial positions in the post–World War II period, in light of the relatively large output of engineers and their relatively low average salary and high rate of unemployment. One notices, for example, that very few industrial entrepreneurial positions are filled by persons with backgrounds as civil servants, who as a group have relatively high salaries, good working conditions, attractive fringe benefits and secure tenure. To explain entrepreneurial participation among groups such as graduate engineers and civil servants, it is useful to consider the alternative remuneration available.

Two points need to be considered when generalizing on the basis of the Berna study. First, more class fluidity would be expected in Madras than in most states, since the caste system is less rigid in Madras. Second, recruitment to new occupations which are created through industrialization and not in the caste hierarchy is more likely to be open to all castes and classes.

In Bengal, as Kling points out, the Marwaris and other non-Bengali business castes have dominated modern manufacturing and trade. As a result of the lack of economic opportunity in Rajasthan for the Marwaris and the lack of indigenous entrepreneurship in Bengal, the Marwaris began entering key entrepreneurial positions in trade and finance in Bengal, especially Calcutta, in the nineteenth century.[48]

The lack of indigenous entrepreneurship in Bengal at present stems in part from the discrimination and duplicity of the British in the nineteenth century and the low esteem placed on business occupations. In the early nineteenth century, participation of Bengalis in activities competitive with the British, such as international trade, resulted in the subsequent exclusion of Bengalis from modern business. In a number of cases in the 1880s, Bengali firms with established reputations were defrauded by British partners, an action that led many Bengali businessmen to retreat from trade and commerce. In addition, although Bengalis admired the boldness and daring of the ancient romantic merchant-prince and the modern industrialist, they placed a low value on the mundane pursuits of traditional businessmen such as the petty trader. The Bengali business classes, having spurned traditional business and being excluded from modern business, could find no middle ground suitable for their talents. This lack

---

[47] Berna, pp. 60–70.
[48] Kling, "Obstacles to Entrepreneurship," pp. 4–5, and Lamb, "Rise of Indian Business Communities," pp. 105–108.

of participation in traditional business virtually precluded upward mobility to modern business.[49]

On the other hand, the activities of the Marwaris in domestic trade in the nineteenth century complemented British business pursuits. Once the Marwaris had achieved a footing in the Bengali economy, they were able to rise rapidly as a result of their hard work and commercial acumen, their family solidarity conducive to mobilizing capital and entering entrepreneurial positions, and the fact that as aliens, local business values and sanctions did not inhibit them. They moved from a position subordinate to the British before World War I to a dominant position in a diversified modern industrial economy at present.[50]

Many observers contend that the caste system and its series of obligations (which reinforce the practice of following a family occupation) tend to reduce occupational mobility, technical change, and innovation, which are considered to be objectionable and ritually dangerous.[51] As Hoselitz states it, industrial "entrepreneurship can develop only in a society in which cultural norms permit variability in the choice of paths of life, and in which the relevant processes of socialization of the individual are not so completely standardized and demanding conformity to a prescribed pattern that the bases for appropriate personality development leading to productive orientation are absent."[52] In a society which emphasizes that each person has a duty (*dharma*) appropriate to his station in life —a duty which depends upon the caste into which he is born[53]—very little variability would seem to be possible.

However, Baldwin points out that in "Indian industry, the caste system seemed to be considerably looser and more flexible than it often appears to outsiders at first glance. Its novelty, quaintness, and historical importance produce an exaggerated estimate of its present role in the cities, where disintegration may proceed rapidly."[54] Despite the powerful socioreligious sanctions given the caste system, there are several dynamic factors making fluidity and flexibility in occupational and caste structure possible.

Migration, such as that by displaced persons during the India-Pakistan

[49] Kling, "Obstacles to Entrepreneurship," pp. 1–17.

[50] Lamb, "Rise of Indian Business Communities," pp. 105–109; and Kling, "Obstacles to Entrepreneurship," pp. 4–5, 12.

[51] Gadgil, *Modern Indian Business Class*, p. 16; Weber, *Religion of India*, p. 24; and Medhora, "Entrepreneurship in India," pp. 558–580.

[52] Bert F. Hoselitz, *Sociological Aspects of Economic Growth* (New York, The Free Press, 1960), p. 155.

[53] Irawati Karve, *Hindu Society—An Interpretation* (Poona: Sangam Press Private Ltd., 1961), pp. 94–95; and Weber, *Religion of India*, pp. 24–25.

[54] George B. Baldwin, *Industrial Growth in South India—Case Studies in Economic Development* (New York: The Free Press, 1959), p. 338.

partition, tends to obscure old marriage networks necessary to preserve the endogamy of castes and subcastes. In addition, the status claims of immigrant groups may be difficult to appraise. Also, immigrants are less likely to be bound by the restrictive sanctions of the local community and more likely to be stimulated by the tradition-breaking forces of a new environment.[55]

Second, the rise of new religious sects or reform groups frequently may erase some of the old caste distinctions, as in the case of the Sikhs and Arya Samaj.[56] However, in some cases converts find that their caste identification is carried with them to their new sect.[57] In addition, socioreligious groups, such as the Parsis, with no established or defined position in the social structure, may have more flexibility in moving to new and nontraditional forms of occupations.[58]

Third, the caste system is capable of making certain accommodations to changes in the composition of demand for occupations resulting from technical change and economic structural change. Families in castes with shortages may adopt young males from castes with surpluses. In some cases, persons may be released from the occupational duties of the caste, while being expected to fulfill the ritual obligations of the caste occupation. Also, it is possible for the conception of the occupational duties of the caste to evolve over time. In addition, religious injunctions are flexible enough and the inducements of the modern industrial system powerful enough so that caste and religious taboos and sanctions can change.[59] A further point is that certain nontraditional occupations such as modern industry, government service, and day labor can recruit from all classes. And in certain circles in the big cities, there are a number of rich well educated Westernized persons who ignore caste regulations and whose occupations bear no relation to the traditional occupation of the caste into which they were born.[60]

Fourth, the position of each caste in any given area is not defined precisely. The vagueness of caste position results in greater potential mobility for individual castes.[61] Wealthy castes or wealthy families of low castes have tried to adopt the symbols and rituals of high classes as a means of moving up the caste

[55] See Hazlehurst, *Entrepreneurship and the Merchant Castes*, pp. 26–54; and Weber, *The Protestant Ethic and the Spirit of Capitalism*, trans. Talcott Parsons (London: G. Allen and Unwin, Ltd., 1930), p. 191.

[56] Hazlehurst, *Entrepreneurship and the Merchant Castes*, pp. 35–40.

[57] M. N. Srinivas, "Mobility in the Caste System," *Structure and Change in Indian Society*, eds. Milton Singer and Bernard S. Cohn (Chicago: Aldine Publishing Co., 1968), p. 194.

[58] Medhora, "Entrepreneurship in India," p. 564.

[59] Ibid., p. 566.

[60] Srinivas, "Mobility in the Caste System," p. 97.   [61] Ibid., p. 198.

hierarchy. In some cases, dominant castes have used physical violence and economic boycott to prevent the low castes from adopting the symbols of high castes. In other cases, however, the dominant classes have been unsuccessful in preventing the adoption of high caste symbols and subsequent upward mobility of a previously low caste.[62]

At this point, it is useful to discuss Hazlehurst's distinction between the cultural and structural dimensions of caste. Entrepreneurs "participate in numerous cross-cutting social relationships and pursue diverse economic interests while still maintaining the cultural boundaries of caste."[63] In some cases, the ritual ranking of a caste may be relatively rigid, whereas its socioeconomic ranking may be flexible. Indeed, it is possible that individuals and subgroups within the caste may be relatively mobile in socioeconomic status and power. Moreover, structural changes arising from development may lead to realignments of castes. New inter-caste cooperation can result in changes in social status and economic power of groups.[64] Finally, the status of caste and occupational groups is frequently a local matter. Caste ranking—especially socioeconomic ranking—is not completely ascribed but is based in part upon the power and achievement of the group.

Since India is a parliamentary democracy where political strength depends more on numbers than on caste ranking, castes have been able to rise by procuring favorable government legislation and policy. Castes successful in being labelled "backward" have been given financial assistance or relatively high quotas in educational institutions and government positions. In addition, certain occupational groups with a high priority in the economic plan have been assisted, whereas certain occupational groups thought to be retarding socioeconomic development have been restrained.[65]

Studies available indicate that despite the impediments to mobility resulting from the caste system, it does have some elements of flexibility which make it possible for the system to adapt to aggregate and structural economic change. However, more research is needed on the dynamic elements affecting the caste system and occupational structure, and on the socioeconomic explanation for differentials in the rates of entrepreneurial participation among socioreligious communities and castes.

[62] Srinvas, "Mobility in the Caste System," pp. 193–194.

[63] Hazlehurst, "Caste and Merchant Communities," *Structure and Change in Indian Society*, eds. Milton Singer and Bernard S. Cohn (Chicago: Aldine Publishing Co., 1968), p. 295.

[64] See Hazlehurst, *Entrepreneurship and the Merchant Castes*, pp. 26–54.

[65] Srinivas, "Mobility in the Caste System," pp. 194–196; and Hazlehurst, *Entrepreneurship and Merchant Castes*, pp. 49–51.

ENTREPRENEURSHIP AND
THE FAMILY

For a large proportion of firms in India, the basic unit of entrepreneurship is the extended family. India's industrialists, for example, are usually members of old trading families, which frequently exercise control of a number of firms through the managing agency firm. This tendency will be discussed below. Many prominent Indian business families are involved in several companies, which in some cases represent complementary interests. The companies in which the family is involved may or may not be controlled through one managing agency firm. Frequently, there is specialization by family members according to industrial activity, geographical division, or management function.[66] The advantages of a family controlled business are its ability to mobilize large amounts of resources, its quick unified decision making, and its access to trustworthy personnel to oversee operations.[67] The disadvantages are that the business may not obtain the most talented persons for positions within the firm.

Few data are available on the general impact of the Indian extended family on entrepreneurial activity. However, the Indian case might be expected to be similar to the Nigerian case, where one study indicates that the extended family, with its ability to mobilize large resources, facilitates the acquisition of entrepreneurial training and the establishment of firms. On the other hand, like the Nigerian case, the joint family in India would be likely to hinder the expansion of firms by diverting resources for current consumption which might otherwise have been reinvested in the business.[68] However, research is necessary to assess the relative significance of the positive and negative effects of the Indian extended family on entrepreneurial activity.

Auspicious marriages for children in business families are generally considered important for both social and economic reasons. Of course, in most parts of Hindu society, marriage arrangements, though based on clan exogamy, are based on caste endogamy so that the purity of the group or caste is maintained. An individual's status depends upon the maintenance of endogamy within the caste or subgroup.[69] However, for the business family more may be required of the marriage than just caste endogamy.

For one business class in Ram Nagar (the Bania, like many other classes),

[66] Lamb, "Rise of Indian Business Communities," p. 102.

[67] Spodek, " 'Manchesterisation' of Ahmedabad," p. 488.

[68] See E. Wayne Nafziger, "The Effect of the Nigerian Extended Family on Entrepreneurial Activity," *Economic Development and Cultural Change* (forthcoming).

[69] Hazlehurst, *Entrepreneurship and the Merchant Castes*, pp. 42–45, 97.

the marriage ceremony has economic significance in addition to ritual significance. Business saving is often used for marriage expenditures, which are generally well calculated to lead to advantageous interrelationships. Access to credit and avenues for mobility are dependent upon the complex network of relationships arising from marriage. Marriage ceremonies and the payments of dowry serve as public statements to the local community—especially local creditors—of one's financial position and are observed closely. Nonkinsmen who have economic interactions with the family are concerned about the family's total lineage and marriage network. A major offense, such as the marriage of a daughter into a lower caste, can result in the family being outcast from the Banias and leads to the prohibition of economic relationships, business partnerships, and marriage partnerships in the community. On the other hand, the respect and prestige deriving from an auspicious marriage may be important in improving the status of the family and setting the course for future business transactions and endeavors.[70]

In much of village India, a person is granted credit as a member of a particular caste of family, rather than as an individual. Frequently, the creditor-debtor relationship has a social significance beyond the economic relationship. The relationship between creditor and debtor takes on a "*jajmani*-like" character or semipermanent patron–client relationship, in which the creditor provides virtually unconditional access to credit for goods and services for the customer in return for the customer's continuous loyalty and patronage.[71]

To summarize, in many cases the extended family is the unit of entrepreneurship, supplying managerial and financial resources needed for business operations. The fact that the extended family may also be the basic consumption unit means that resources may frequently be diverted from business investment to support family members with little or no earnings. Finally, the interrelationships provided by the marriage networks of the family can help determine the access to credit and opportunities for mobility by family members in entrepreneurial endeavors.

ENTREPRENEURSHIP AND GOVERNMENT

Before World War I, government responsibility in economic affairs was confined primarily to the establishment of peace and justice, and the provision

[70] Hazelhurst, *Entrepreneurship and the Merchant Castes*, pp. 45, 109–118.

[71] Ibid., pp. 47–48. Compare Robert A. LeVine's discussion of the patron-cliental relationship among the Hausa in northern Nigeria in *Dreams and Deeds: Achievement Motivation in Nigeria* (Chicago: The University of Chicago Press, 1966), pp. 25–32.

of basic public services. Although the Indian Industrial Commission, appointed in 1916, recommended that the government play an active role in the industrial development of the country, little initiative was taken by the central government. However, the recommendation of the Fiscal Commission in 1921 did lead to the protection of certain industries such as iron and steel, cotton textiles, sugar, paper, matches, and heavy chemicals. In 1945, the government announced a policy in which the state accepted the responsibility for developing the basic social overhead investment needed for growth and entering the field of basic industries in cases where private firms were lacking.[72]

In 1931, the Indian National Congress promised government ownership or control of industries in an independent India, while in 1938, a Congress committee studied state planning. When India received its independence in 1947, its leaders decided it was necessary for government to have a major role in directing economic development because of the low savings ratio, the lack of values and institutions oriented toward growth, and the lack of growth and diversity in the economy—especially in the industrial sector. Particular emphasis was placed on the establishment of government enterprises to alleviate the lack of production of basic capital goods—a lack that was exacerbating the long run balance-of-payments problem. Over time, the share of net national product contributed by government enterprises grew as the public sector was extended to include more basic industries (see Table 14-3). The growth in importance of state enterprise, however, was viewed as a way to correct existing structural imbalances rather than as a goal in itself for ideological reasons.[73]

In the decade after independence, public investment, through linkage effects, stimulated the growth in private investment. For example, the 72 per cent increase in private investment, from the First Five-Year Plan (1951–1956) to the Second Five-Year Plan (1956–1961) was associated with a 103 per cent increase in public investment from the first plan to the second one.[74]

Even after the Industrial Policy Resolution of 1956, which extended the number of basic and strategic industries in the public sector, the size of the public sector was not large. Government enterprises accounted for 4 per cent of net national product (in 1960–1961), 4 per cent of the total working force (in 1957–1958); and 54 per cent of the net investment in the Second Plan (1956–1961).[75]

Singh's conception of the entrepreneurial function is the building of institutions. In this sense, the government has been heavily involved in entrepreneurial endeavours in such activities as the creation of institutions for rural

[72] Singh, "Essays Concerning Types of Entrepreneurship," pp. 18–22.
[73] Ibid., pp. 22–29.   [74] Ibid., pp. 33–36.   [75] Ibid., pp. 38–40.

TABLE 14-3

Government Share in Net National Output (in current prices and in billions of rupees and percentages)

	1948–49		1950–51		1955–56		1960–61		1962–63	
	Rs. (in billions)	%	Rs. (in billions)	%	Rs. (in billions)	%	Rs. (in billions)	%	Rs. (in billions)	%
Total share of government sector	6.4	7.4	7.2	7.5	9.9	9.9	14.8	10.4	18.4	11.9
1. Net output of government enterprises	2.4	2.8	2.9	3.0	4.2	4.2	5.7	4.0	6.7	4.3
2. Net output of government administration	4.0	4.6	4.3	4.5	5.7	5.7	9.0	6.4	11.7	7.6
Net output of the private sector	80.3	92.6	88.3	92.5	89.9	90.1	127.3	89.6	136.4	88.1

Source: Datt and Sundharam, p. 34.

community development; credit organizations for firms of various sizes and types; export promotional schemes; and new organizations to develop transportation and communication, education, health services, and scientific and technological research.[76] Even though Singh explicitly denies that state planning agencies perform entrepreneurial functions,[77] state planning agencies do perform entrepreneurial functions according to his definition, for they assist in the creation of new institutions.[78]

Government enterprises have been characterized by low profit rates and low savings rates, even where the projects are directly productive activities as opposed to social overhead programs. This would seem to indicate a lack of entrepreneurial skills in the public sector. However, one relieving feature is that, as India's experience with the public sector has increased, profit rates and savings rates have grown.[79]

India has one of the most progressive tax rates in the world. One peculiar feature of the system is that the combination of liabilities on income and wealth taxes imposes a virtual ceiling on individual wealth accumulation. At very high levels of income resulting from wealth, the combined increment in taxes exceeds the increment in income.[80] Many economists believe that the highly progressive nature of the tax discourages business activity and investment.

THE ORGANIZATION OF LARGE-SCALE ENTERPRISES

Because of the importance of the managing agency system, a system unique to India, we shall discuss the system and the way it affects the context of entrepreneurial endeavours. The institution, which originated in the first half of the nineteenth century,[81] is the dominant type of organization for the joint stock company, the prevailing form of enterprise among large scale firms (*e.g.*, firms with over 250 persons employed).[82]

In the managing agency system, a system which especially pervades modern industry, trade, and agriculture, the administration, finance and promotion of one or more legally separate companies are controlled by a single firm.[83] The

[76] Singh, "Essays Concerning Types of Entrepreneurship," pp. 40–43.
[77] Ibid., p. 16.   [78] Ibid., p. 9.   [79] Ibid., pp. 46–56.   [80] Ibid., pp. 140–144.
[81] Cf. Brimmer, "Setting of Entrepreneurship," pp. 559–560; Blair B. Kling, "The Origin of the Managing Agency System in India," *Journal of Asian Studies*, XXVI, No. 1 (November, 1966), pp. 37–38; and Singh, "Essays Concerning Types of Entrepreneurship," pp. 58–59 on the origins of the system.
[82] Singh, "Essays Concerning Types of Entrepreneurship," p. 57.
[83] Brimmer, "Setting of Entrepreneurship," p. 554.

distinguishing feature of the system is the contractual agreement between the managing agents and the board of directors of the operating company, in which the agents receive commissions and fees for providing management over a specified period of time, usually twenty years or longer. In practice, the managing agents usually undertake entrepreneurial responsibility beyond the routine management function.[84] The managing agency firm, which frequently controls more than one operating enterprise, often in the same or related industry, generally can be thought of as the basic entrepreneurial unit.[85]

In most cases, the Indian managing agency firm has been an extension of relationships in an older family firm. Most of the members of the agency are relatives or at least members of the same caste.[86] Generally, the managing agents and their friends comprise the board of directors of the operating company that contracts with the managing agency firm.[87]

The major advantages of the managing agency system are the economies of large scale organization—economies in production, marketing, management, financial services, and vertical linkages.[88] The system especially helps to conserve scarce entrepreneurial talent and to mobilize venture capital. Entrepreneurial skills can be utilized more effectively because of specialization and economies of scale in entrepreneurial endeavor.[89] A small group of businessmen can concentrate their capital in a new operating firm, arrange a contract between the firm and a managing agency, attract capital from other sources as the operating firm becomes established, withdraw capital from the firm while retaining control through the managing agency firm, and begin the process again in a new operating firm.[90]

One of the disadvantages of the system is that it increases the concentration of economic power within and across industries. In recent years, there has been a shift on the part of new companies away from the managing agency system to more direct forms of management as a result of the attempt by government to discourage economic concentration by increasing competition from the public sector and tightening regulation of the agencies.[91]

Despite the argument by Joseph Schumpeter that economic concentration may be associated with internal economies of scale and technological innova-

[84] Singh, "Essays Concerning Types of Entrepreneurship," pp. 59–61.
[85] Brimmer, "Setting of Entrepreneurship," pp. 554–555.
[86] Ibid., p. 558.
[87] Singh, "Essays Concerning Types of Entrepreneurship," pp. 59–61.
[88] Ibid., pp. 61–62.
[89] Brimmer, "Setting of Entrepreneurship," pp. 560–561.
[90] See Singh, "Essays Concerning Types of Entrepreneurship," pp. 59–61.
[91] Ibid., pp. 71–73.

tion,[92] I consider the shift in emphasis away from the managing agency system to be desirable. *Prima facie* evidence would seem to indicate that a large number of managing agency firms have reached a level of output well beyond the realization of internal economies of scale. The fact that the managing agency system was frequently being used to acquire control of well established businesses, to operate several enterprises in one industry, and to increase the concentration of wealth in a few families[93] would seem to indicate that further encouragement of the system was inconsistent with the objectives of the state to decrease economic inequalities and increase efficiency of resource allocation.

Large scale public firms are usually organized in one of the three following forms: a departmental undertaking, a public corporation, or a joint stock company. Departmental undertakings, such as postal, telegraph, telephone, and railway services, frequently lack the autonomy and flexibility desirable for quick decision making and risk taking. In addition, the personnel belong to the civil service. As such, the personnel are subject to rules of recruitment and promotion of the civil service—which are not as conducive to initiative. The public corporation, created under a Parliamentary or state legislative statute, has the advantage of a separate legal entity from government and exemption from most of the complicated regulatory procedures and audit rules of government departments. The majority of public firms, however, have been established as private joint stock companies, which are given maximum autonomy.[94]

THE SMALL ENTREPRENEUR

According to official sources, almost 90 per cent of the enterprises in India in 1955 were small enterprises, if these are defined as enterprises with power which employ less than fifty or enterprises without power which employ less than 100. About two-thirds of all enterprises were included in the category of enterprises "employing less than ten persons with power, or less than 20 persons without power, using mainly household labor" (see Table 4).

A 1962 study of urban households throughout India indicates that 27.3 per cent of all urban household heads are self-employed persons[95] in non-farming

[92] Joseph Schumpeter, *Capitalism, Socialism and Democracy* (New York: Harper and Row, 1942), pp. 87–106.

[93] Singh, "Essays Concerning Types of Entrepreneurship," p. 73.

[94] Ibid., pp. 43–46.

[95] Professional, technical, and related occupations, which comprise about 14 per cent of the self-employed heads, are included in this category.

TABLE 14–4

Distribution of Employment by Type of Enterprise and Urban or Rural Residence, 1955

	Number Employed (in thousands)		
Type of Enterprise	Rural	Urban	Total
1. Employing less than 10 persons with power, or less than 20 persons without power, using mainly household labor	8,068	2,821	10,889
2. Employing less than 10 persons with power, or less than 20 persons without power, using mainly hired labor	833	897	1,730
3. Employing 10–49 persons with power, or 20–99 persons without power	197	298	495
4. Employing 50 or more persons with power, or 100 or more persons without power	1,438	1,650	3,088
Total	10,536	5,666	16,202

Source: P. N. Dhar and H. F. Lydall, *The Role of Small Enterprises in Indian Economic Development*. (New York: Asia Publishing House, 1961), p. 3.

activities—although 80 per cent of these self-employed persons have no employees. If urban household heads are divided into occupational groups—self-employed with no employees, self-employed with employees, government employees, and private employees—the self-employed with employees have the highest average income and an average educational attainment just slightly below the highest group, government employees; the self-employed with no employees have the lowest average income and the lowest average educational attainment. Self-employed persons with some employees have the highest average propensity to save—23.9 per cent—which is substantially higher than that of self-employed persons with no employees—6.1 per cent, and all government and private employees—3.7 per cent.[96]

Over 40 per cent of the self-employed persons are associated with businesses with a net worth less than 200 rupees, which in most cases is only enough to survive. Most of these persons are in business only because they are unable to find other forms of employment. Starting a petty business with 100 rupees or so may be the easiest occupation to enter.[97]

The major sources of capital for expansion of the firm were reinvested earnings in both the Singh and Berna studies.[98] For new businesses, personal or family funds were the most frequent sources of initial capital in the Berna sample.[99]

[96] Singh, "Essays Concerning Types of Entrepreneurship," pp. 89–99.

[97] Ibid., pp. 95–96.

[98] Ibid., pp. 104–105; and Berna, pp. 153–158. The information in the Singh study was based on the urban household survey discussed above. The Berna sample included manufacturing firms with 50 to 250 persons employed.   [99] Berna, pp. 91–93.

The prototypic small urban businessman in the Singh study is a shopkeeper with no employees who does not reveal any entrepreneurial qualities such as saving, innovation, and improvements in productivity. The small rural entrepreneur is also not likely to exhibit any entrepreneurial qualities, although he serves a function because of the employment he provides and the way he satisfies local requirements. However, the small self-employed urban businessman with some employees is more likely to demonstrate these entrepreneurial qualities, such as a high propensity to save. Some of these businessmen are successful in mobilizing small savings from themselves or their friends and relatives which would otherwise not have become available for productive uses.[100]

In recent years, the Indian government, through the administrative control of the Central Small Industries Organization, has increased its assistance to small industry. Included in the program are: managerial and technical assistance through state service institutes; extension centers; common facility services; financial assistance; supply of basic materials; marketing assistance; technical, managerial, and vocational training; and industrial estates. Although Singh expresses confidence that these programs have had a positive impact on the rate of growth of small-scale industry in India,[101] empirical data on the overall cost and benefit of these programs are lacking.

APPROACHES TO FUTURE STUDIES

There are a number of fruitful areas for future research on Indian entrepreneurship. In previous contexts, we have mentioned the need for studies on the socioeconomic explanations for differential rates of entrepreneurial participation among social communities and on the dynamics which influence the caste system. Let us consider a few other areas that might be explored—achievement motivation in India, determinants of entrepreneurial success, and the market for entrepreneurs.

According to David C. McClelland, India ranks very high in measurements of n Achievement or the need or concern for achievement.[102] Very little research has been completed on the relationship between n Achievement and

[100] Singh, "Essays Concerning Types of Entrepreneurship," pp. 106, 124–129, 135, 137.

[101] Ibid., pp. 114–115.

[102] David C. McClelland, *The Achieving Society* (Princeton, N.J.: D. Van Nostrand Company, Inc., 1961), p. 100.

entrepreneurship at a more disaggregated level, although some studies are in progress.[103]

Except for Singh's analysis at a high level of aggregation and Berna's study of factors related to the growth in the hiring of factors in firms, there have been no systematic studies of determinants of entrepreneurial success. In large part, the reason for this lack is that none of the studies on entrepreneurship utilize measures of entrepreneurial and firm success. The lack of these measures is only partly because of the difficulty of obtaining access to firm records. Usually data are at least available on output or value-added, so that it can be related to other variables.[104] For example, Berna had access to data on output which were not utilized.[105] Although Berna does discuss firm growth, it is the growth of inputs, capital, and labor. This growth is no measure of firm performance unless one assumes fixed input–output coefficients, in which case entrepreneurship has no effect upon output.

From the perspective of the economic analyst, the entrepreneur is a factor of production, a factor that combines the resources used in the production of a good or service. Thus, in the study of entrepreneurship, analyses of markets for entrepreneurs and other productive resources are important. The studies of Indian entrepreneurship have placed little emphasis on such concepts as markets for inputs of entrepreneurship, technical and managerial skills, labor, and capital; differences in entrepreneurial remuneration; the alternative cost of entrepreneurial training and endeavor; investment in training; and resource substitutability.

An approach to the market for entrepreneurs is possible. The demand for entrepreneurs is determined by the schedule of the expected returns to entrepreneurship, which is dependent upon the economic environment. The supply of entrepreneurs is a function of entrepreneurial capacity, which depends upon motivation, training, experience, and the sociocultural milieu. Determinants of the supply of entrepreneurs can be found on the basis of differences between data on the characteristics of entrepreneurs and characteristics of the population as a whole, which has an extremely small percentage of entrepreneurs. The large

---

[103] A. D. Pabaney, Elliot Danzig, M. S. Nadkarni, Udai Pareek, and David C. McClelland, "Developing the Entrepreneurial Spirit in an Indian Community," Small Industries Extension Training Institute and Harvard University, Working Report, Hyderabad, India, September 20, 1964.

[104] In my study of Nigerian entrepreneurship, I obtained reliable data on value of output and rate of profit of the firm, which were used as measures of entrepreneurial success. Nafziger, "The Effect of the Nigerian Extended Family on Entrepreneurial Activity, and "Nigerian Entrepreneurship: A Study of Indigenous Businessmen in the Footwear Industry."

[105] Berna, p. 146.

number of Indian entrepreneurs who have migrated to Southeast Asia and South and East Africa in the past[106] might indicate that the lack of indigenous entrepreneurs in India stems more from the low expected returns to entrepreneurship in the country than from the lack of supply. This is in contrast to Nigeria, where the fact that foreign owned and managed enterprises have been substantially more successful than indigenous enterprises suggests that the lack of entrepreneurial capacity and experience, and not an unfavorable economic environment, may be the explanation for a deficiency in entrepreneurship.[107]

Variables which may affect entrepreneurial supply and success are caste, socioeconomic class, social community, family structure, other politico-sociocultural attachments, time perspective, education, training and work experience of the entrepreneurs, the nature of the labor and capital markets, marketing institutions, and government policies. Another key variable which may influence the supply of entrepreneurs is remuneration in competing occupations. Socioeconomic inducements and barriers to the migration, occupational mobility, and vertical mobility of entrepreneurs may affect the distribution of entrepreneurs between subgroups of the population.

Consider how the variables indicated may affect entrepreneurial supply and success. Sociocultural variables such as caste and family structure, by influencing the responsiveness of persons to entrepreneurial incentives and the extent of experiences and resources appropriate for entrepreneurial activity, affect the position and elasticity of the supply of entrepreneurship and the success of the entrepreneurs. Education, training, and experience can increase the supply and success of entrepreneurs by making available more skills which are suitable for entrepreneurial endeavors or can decrease the supply by raising the alternative costs of persons.

Entrepreneurial supply and success are expected to be a direct function of the quality and an inverse function of the costs of inputs, labor, and capital. The supply and success of entrepreneurs from certain subgroups of the population, such as a social community, may be dependent upon the composition of the participants in the marketing and distributive network of goods and the nature of credit relationships within the network. The longer the time perspective (or the lower the discount rate of the future) of the entrepreneur and his reference group, the more likely he would be expected to engage in manufacturing, a venture which requires relatively large amounts of fixed capital, and the less

---

[106] See Medhora, "Entrepreneurship in India," p. 565.

[107] Gerald K. Helleiner, *Peasant Agriculture, Government, and Economic Growth in Nigeria* (Homewood, Ill.: Richard D. Irwin, Inc., 1966), p. 265; and John R. Harris, "Industrial Entrepreneurship in Nigeria" (unpublished Ph.D. dissertation, Department of Economics, Northwestern University, August, 1967), pp. vii–41.

likely he is to be in trade. In the long run, the supply of entrepreneurs may be expected to be a direct function of the remuneration of entrepreneurs relative to that in occupations which require a comparable level of skills.

Differences in social community may impede migration. Occupational and vertical mobility can be expected to be dependent upon the rigidity of the caste system, the nature of the social structure, and the availability of knowledge about economic opportunities.

Social scientists have begun to recognize the importance of the quantity of high level manpower, such as entrepreneurship, as a major determinant of the rate of economic growth and social progress. However, conceptual problems in gathering data and identifying and defining the entrepreneur have limited the number of scholars studying the problem in developing countries such as India. The concepts and tools of many disciplines—economics, sociology, anthropology, psychology, political science, history, management science, and others —are needed so that scholars can have a clearer view of factors related to entrepreneurship in India.

15

THE DEVELOPMENT OF ENTREPRENEURSHIP

Gustav F. Papanek

Discussion of economic development, since the revival of interest in the late forties, almost invariably starts with the acknowledgement that economic growth depends on a complex of interrelated factors. With this out of the way, the tendency is to focus on a single key factor—not the only, but the most important, determinant of growth. The emphasis at various times and by various authors has been on technical knowledge, ideological fervor, natural resources, governmental organization, motives and attitudes, and capital. Emphasis has recently shifted to the key role of decision-making innovators, particularly in industry—in a word, entrepreneurs.

PAST AND CURRENT VIEWS OF ENTREPRENEURSHIP

Stress on the importance of entrepreneurs hardly qualifies one as an innovator in economics. Writings old and new agree not only on this importance but also on five other propositions:

1. The industrial entrepreneur is a distinct personality type. At the least,

Reprinted by permission of the author and the publisher from American Economic Review, *Supplement (May, 1962) pp. 45–58.*

he must believe that change is possible and can be brought about by individuals, and he must be motivated to action bringing it about.

2. Within any society only a limited number of individuals have entrepreneurial attributes in sufficient degree to be actual or potential entrepreneurs.

3. These individuals do not act entirely or even primarily from pecuniary motives. For instance, they may try to achieve recognition in the economic sphere because other avenues are not open to them.

4. A significant number of them will turn from potential to actual entrepreneurship only if the noneconomic obstacles they face are not too severe. Among such obstacles are lack of security for person and property.

5. Entrepreneurs must be able to obtain command over resources by obtaining credit or by other means.

To these propositions, much of the recent discussion of entrepreneurship and development has added others, with wide implications:

1. Potential entrepreneurs are not randomly distributed in societies, as suggested by Schumpeter's analogy with the ability to sing. Instead, entrepreneurial characteristics develop in a significant number of people only from a change in the motives of a society or of a substantial group in it.

2. Such a change in motives results only from fundamental alterations in a society. Changes in economic incentives or disincentives are neither a necessary nor a sufficient condition.

3. The required alterations have not yet taken place in many underdeveloped countries; they are likely to come about slowly and uncertainly; they are difficult to influence or accelerate by conscious government policy.

4. Such industrial entrepreneurs as do exist find it difficult to obtain command over real resources, in the absence of ideological imperatives—such as the Protestant or the Communist ethic. In underdeveloped countries the propensity to consume is high, and such savings as do take place are used for inventory speculation, other short-term commercial ventures, and investment in agricultural land, in urban real estate or abroad. These preferences affect not only landlords and commercial groups but even the few industrial entrepreneurs, since both consumption and nonindustrial investment are prestigious, involve less risk, trouble, technological knowledge and above all less change in habits and customs than does industry.

These propositions, stressing psychological factors and largely ignoring economic ones, are implicit in much of the recent discussion of entrepreneurship and economic development.

Everett Hagen, in his book published in 1962, argues that the emergence of a substantial number of entrepreneurs depends on the suppression of a previously prestigious group and the slow changes in personality this brings about rather than on changes in economic environment.

A. O. Hirschman in the *Strategy of Economic Development* concludes that *the* scarce factor in development is the ability to make decisions. In underdeveloped countries change is considered possible either only at the expense of others, or only if a whole group changes. In either situation, individual ability to make entrepreneurial decisions is severely limited. Development programs and policies must, therefore, maximize induced or routinized decisions.

David McClelland in *The Achieving Society* has accumulated impressive documentation for his thesis that the development of entrepreneurship depends primarily on the strength of a clearly defined psychological variable—the need for achievement. This in turn depends on child-rearing practices, which may be affected by changes in ideology or other factors.

Ragnar Nurkse and J. J. Spengler suggest that enterprise and initiative have come largely from the middle class, which is virtually non-existent in underdeveloped countries.

A number of policy conclusions have been derived from the assumption that the genesis of entrepreneurship is primarily a slow psychological phenomenon. One conclusion, frequently drawn, is that industrialization depends very largely on government funds and government sponsorship. It will, in any case, be difficult to carry out because the entrepreneurs to make the diffuse decisions required will not be available and therefore emphasis needs to be placed on programs where change is more directly in government hands. Furthermore, many government policies can only be implemented by the use of direct physical controls, since the response to indirect price incentives will be inadequate. In any case, direct controls have few undesirable consequences, for even without their inhibiting effects few effective entrepreneurs will emerge. Another policy implication is that the ability to absorb foreign aid is limited by the absence of entrepreneurs to use the capital and technical assistance supplied. One could list other conclusions with respect to research needs, government policies and analysis that follow from the view of entrepreneurship explicit or implicit in much of recent literature, but those listed should suffice to demonstrate the far-reaching consequences. To what extent is this view not only logically plausible but also empirically accurate?

TESTING HYPOTHESES IN PAKISTAN

Pakistan is a good country for testing hypotheses on industrial entrepreneurship, since it had little industry, even for an underdeveloped country, at independence in 1947 and has since experienced an extremely high rate of industrial growth. Except for a few traditional enterprises in the simple processing of agricultural products, practically all industrialists are entrepreneurs in the Schumpeterian sense, innovators who set up industries not previously in existence, with factors not previously in industry, to enter markets not previously supplied from domestic production—all under rapidly changing circumstances. The background, characteristics, and sources of finance of the men who were responsible for the rapid industrial change of the last ten years should throw considerable light on the genesis of entrepreneurship in Pakistan and perhaps elsewhere.

To obtain the necessary data, lengthy interviews were held with a stratified random sample of over 250 industrialists throughout Pakistan and all its industries. The results were checked against other data. Several checks for internal consistency were included in the interview. The sample covered nearly 10 per cent of all firms with about 50 per cent of the capital of Pakistan's industry. It included the industrialists who control some 75 per cent of the capital. The sample and this paper exclude firms not using power or employing less than twenty workers. This is a serious drawback only in some respects. In general, firms below these limits are traditional enterprises, occur only in a few industries, are likely to play a rapidly decreasing role, and do not involve entrepreneurship in the Schumpeterian sense.

The results inevitably have a substantial margin of error due to inadequate records and biased responses. Only gross differences are, therefore, significant. All subsequent figures are derived from the preliminary results of the survey, usually expanded to represent the universe, unless otherwise noted.

The development of Muslim industrial entrepreneurs in Pakistan has proceeded at a phenomenal rate. In prepartition India, Muslims were traditionally peasants, landlords, soldiers, artisans, and, to some extent, government employees. Only a small proportion engaged in trade and an insignificant number were in manufacturing, other than in small or handicraft enterprises. In 1947, industry (firms using power and employing at least twenty workers) contributed about 1 per cent to national income in Pakistan and more than half of this was controlled by Hindus, government or foreigners. Yet by 1959, industry's contribution to a much larger national income was over 6 per cent. Industrial assets had increased ninefold and value-added more than tenfold. Private firms owned by Muslims controlled two-thirds of these assets.

Even these figures do not fully reflect the radical change that took place, since potential industrial investment exceeded actual investment. Investors have applied to the government for permission to set up new industries and to import machinery in amounts that consistently exceeded available foreign exchange.

They have applied pressure, offered bribes, and were willing to pay a legal surcharge of over 100 per cent to import machinery. Investment plans of existing firms would result in more than doubling 1959 industrial assets over the next three to five years. Investment plans of several firms each involve the equivalent of 20 million dollars or more.

Much of the early investment was in cotton and jute products, but by 1958 about 20 per cent of investment was in such long-gestation-period, capital-intensive, or complex-technology industries as chemicals, paper products, cement products, machinery and assembly or manufacture of transport equipment. More signicant, investment plans were heavily concentrated in these lines.

There is thus considerable evidence that in the span of roughly ten years, the Muslims of Pakistan developed a vigorous entrepreneurial group. They did so, at least in part, in response to strong economic incentives and disincentives.

THE DEVELOPMENT OF ENTRE-PRENEURSHIP IN PAKISTAN

At independence, vast opportunities for Muslim traders—especially in importing —opened up because of the separation from Indian industry, the exodus of Hindu traders, and the limited role of foreign ones. With the Korean boom, export profits increased with rising international prices, much larger imports could be financed and some importers/exporters began to deal in substantial sums and to accumulate large profits. Some traders invested their trade earnings in industry, especially if they already had some investment or experience in it. With the end of the Korean boom came a dramatic change in the situation— export earnings declined sharply, imports in some lines practically disappeared, and opportunities for profit in domestic industry greatly increased. Other traders now shifted resources from trade to industry. At the same time, it became increasingly difficult to import the machinery and other items required for investment; and only the more energetic and ruthless were in a position to become industrialists or to expand industrial holdings.

Almost any industrialist was guaranteed a profit, for imports offered little competition, domestic production was inadequate, and those able to import machinery were subsidized by undervalued foreign exchange. In some industries, annual returns of 100 per cent on investment were usual. For a number of reasons, the bulk of industrial profits were reinvested. Government was able to prevent large-scale illegal transfers abroad. Consumption was discouraged by the inadequate supply of imported or domestic luxury goods and building materials, by traditionally limited wants, by some feeling against conspicuous consumption, and, above all, by the desire to reinvest earnings while profits were high. Industrialists had little urge to invest in agricultural land, partly for fear of land reform, partly because the ex-traders earning high profits had not done so for two or three generations. Investment in urban real estate was limited by shortages of building materials and perhaps even more by greater and equally certain profits in industry. Import regulations discriminated in favor of investment goods. As a result of all these factors, most firms invested in industry, not only a large share of great industrial profits, but also generous depreciation allowances, management earnings, and legal and illegal trade profits.

The commitment to industry was not reversible. The rate of return has declined in the last few years, with the increase of domestic competition, some easing of import restrictions, and more effective enforcement of tax and other laws. Nevertheless, investment has continued to be vigorous. The desire for industrial investment has continued to exceed foreign exchange availabilities. Investment plans indicate no flagging of entrepreneurial spirit. Ninety-six per cent of the children of present industrial decision-makers are expected to enter industry.

The lower returns in some industries have stimulated interest in investment in other industries—and in efficiency. The entrepreneurs had always relied heavily on foreign technicians to set up plants and initially run them. At least 60 per cent of the investment in larger firms involved some foreign technical staff. Entrepreneurs thus had overcome the limits on expansion that lack of technical manpower would otherwise have imposed. But, until recently, most of them were little concerned with efficiency. This was sound profit-maximizing behavior, since the returns from increased efficiency were likely to be less than from the promotion of new enterprises and from coping with and trying to evade government regulations. As profits fell, as competition increased, and as laws were better enforced, efficiency received more attention. The trend is from family management to professional management and toward the employment of technical staff regardless of family or "community" connections. The more promising young family members are receiving training in engineering and sometimes business administration. By 1959 at least one-quarter of the investment in larger firms was controlled by families who had provided or planned a technical education for some members. In short, in a period of less than a decade, the robber barons and promoters of early industrial development are beginning to give way to the organization men.

SOME QUANTITATIVE EVIDENCE

Evidence that this description of the process at least approximates reality is given in the following tables.

The rapid growth in industrial assets, accelerated by the Korean boom and even more sharply by its end, would be even clearer in Table 15-1 if industries owned by Hindus, the government, and foreigners were excluded. They accounted for over half of industrial assets in 1947 and only one-quarter in 1958.

TABLE 15-1

Growth in Industrial Assets

	Crores^a	Index
1947	58	17
1949	82	23
1951	128	36
1953	203	57
1955	351	100
1957	436	124
1959	502	143

^a One crore rupees is roughly 2 million dollars.

TABLE 15-2

Reasons for Entering Industry (Numbers of Firms)

	All Firms	Larger Firms^a
Family or individual in industry before	25%	16%
Poor prospects for trade	25	45
Expected profits	27	14
Incidental to trade (e.g., jute baling)	5	6
Industry superior; patriotism	9	5
Government policy; accidental; other	10	14

^a Capital $200,000 equivalent and over.

Entrepreneurs overwhelmingly indicated pecuniary motives for entering industry. *Ex post facto* explanations are not always reliable, but any bias in this case is more likely to lead to stressing of altruistic than profit motives. Table 15-2 also lends support to the thesis that many traders, especially those who are larger industrialists now, were pushed out of trade by declining profit possibilities or attracted to industry by increasing ones. Responses in these two respects are biased downward, since many traders with industrial sidelines in 1947 did not indicate why they shifted resources from trade to industry, but only that they had already been in industry.

Persons whose primary occupation before 1947 (or before entering industry, if this was later) was trade, furnished almost half the entrepreneurs for

TABLE 15-3

Industrialists Occupations Prior to 1947 or to Entering Industry (If Later)

	Previous Primary Occupation		Previous Secondary Occupation		Father's Occupation
	Proportion of In- dustrialists	Present Investment	Proportion of In- dustrialists	Present Investment	Proportion of Industrialists
1. Large and medium industry	17%	16%	4%	30%	8%
2. Small industry, handicrafts	18	6	23	7	17
3. Traders—import, export	17	40	30	25	12
4. Traders—internal	28	29	39	24	34
5. Employees, professional, other	16	6	4	12	16
6. Agriculture	3	3	—	1	12

TABLE 15-4

Sources of Finance for Industry

	Crores	Per Cent
Prepartition industry (Pakistan and India)	27	5
Import trade	31	6
Other trade—export, internal, government suppliers	41	8
Agricultural land (and real estate)	10	2
Government and semigovernment; equity and credit	66	13
Foreign (including India)	21	4
Commercial banks, other creditors	64	13
Other (employment, professions, transport, religious, scattered share- holders)	20	4
Industrial earnings reinvested in the same or new enterprises	221	44
Total	501	

Pakistan's industry. They set up the larger or more rapidly growing firms and now control nearly 70 per cent of capital. On the other hand, individuals in small industry or handicrafts before 1947 have mostly remained small industrialists. Although 18 per cent of present industrialists were from this background, they control only 6 per cent of capital at present. A large proportion of all entrepreneurs had fathers and grandfathers in trade. Trading was their traditional occupation and a change to industry was an entrepreneurial decision.

The very small total of industrial assets in Pakistan in 1947, plus proceeds from industrial assets disposed of by Muslims in India (5 per cent), indicates the insignificant role of Muslims in industry. Government investment includes railway and other workshops, credit institutions whose contributions were of little significance, and about 33 crores of investment by a semigovernmental corporation which played an important pioneering role in the fifties in some industries and geographic areas. Trade profits were crucial for starting private industry, but expansion was supported by reinvested earnings. Excluding government and foreign funds, reinvested earnings provided over half the capital invested by private indigenous enterprise in about ten years. Clearly both profits and reinvestment rates were high.

The evidence in all the tables would be further strengthened if they excluded small firms, traditional processing industries (tea, jute and cotton baling, etc.), and firms set up in the late fifties when several landlords became industrialists. Earlier, larger firms in new industries were generally set up by former traders, who obtained capital from their trade earnings and from reinvested profits. Some of these traders had had industrial holdings as a sideline. (The only significant exceptions are in the metal working industries, where there was some tradition of Muslim participation before 1947.) Traders, unlike landlords, artisans, or employees, were accustomed to buying and selling, to employing others, and to contracts, though mostly on a small scale. In short, they were operating in a market economy and responding to economic incentives. Given an opportunity to expand greatly their trading operation, the more energetic seized it. Later they were suddenly faced with a sharp loss of income and scope if they continued in their accustomed occupation, but could make large profits at little risk in industry. However, to a large extent only those with some foresight, ability, and ruthlessness could make the shift in the face of various obstacles. It is really not surprising that these economic incentives and disincentives called into existence a new, able, ruthless group of industrial entrepreneurs. What is more startling is the speed with which traders became industrial entrepreneurs and with which they became accustomed to this role.

THE SOCIAL BACKGROUND

If firms owned by foreigners, Hindus, and government and semigovernment agencies are excluded (one-third of the total), over half of the industry is controlled by five small "communities" (quasi-castes) of traditional traders, totaling about one-half per cent of the population. Perhaps another quarter of investment is also in the hands of members of traditional trading communities. On the other hand, groups which had little experience with trade or industry, such as the Muslims of Bengal, are underrepresented among industrialists to a startling extent.

Though about three-quarters of industry is in the hands of members of traditional trading communities, these groups have little else in common. (Legend has it, however, that when the great majority of present-day Muslims

TABLE 15-5

Distribution of Muslim Industrial Investment and Population by "Community"

Community	Industrial Investment	Population[a]
Halai Memon	27%	0.3%
Chinioti	9	0.05
Dawoodi Bohra	5	0.04
Khoja Ismaili	5	0.1
Khoja Isnashari	6	0.04
Bengali Muslim	4	50.0
Other Muslim	44	49.0

[a] Estimates of community membership very rough. These figures and most information on trading communities from Hanna Papanek, "The Khoja Ismailis of Karachi" (unpublished).

were converted from Hinduism, these communities were converted from trading castes.)

The more significant of them (Memon, Chinioti) are Sunnis, the majority division among Muslims, and are distinguished primarily by geographic origin. Most of the groups are only economic innovators, not social innovators; they have followed their own tradition in social customs and religious observance, including the attitude toward education and the role of women. None had a large investment in industry before 1947 and all derived their income primarily from trade. What evidence exists does not suggest that these groups had high status in the past; on the contrary, they were traders and stood midway in the social hierarchy. There is no evidence of any sharp change in their attitudes, motives or child-rearing practices in the period before 1947. Conversation with them indicates no strong feelings of nationalism. As a matter of fact, less than 10 per cent of all industrialists suggested any nonpecuniary motives for entering industry (including patriotism, nationalism) and one might assume that there is a strong upward bias in such a figure. While partition of the Indian subcontinent meant a change of domicile for many, it uprooted very few from a traditional environment. Most had left their native town or village earlier to trade in the cities. At least in the case of the two communities most important in industry, there was no selective migration to Pakistan. Chiniotis originate in present Pakistan; entire townships of Memons left India after partition. The only obvious major change that took place in 1947 was in the economic environment: the sudden increase in economic opportunity.

It is not surprising that a few trading communities took advantage of increased opportunities while the bulk of Muslims did not. Among Indian Muslims few except traders were primarily market oriented. They were a small fraction of the Muslim population and most of them belonged to trading "castes" or "communities." Ascriptive community membership facilitated the change from trade to industry, because others from the community were more trustworthy as partners, assistants, managers, technicians, and accountants. Fellow community members might also provide funds, scarce materials, knowledge, and influence. Most Muslim trading communities have participated in industrialization. They were the first to respond to increased industrial opportunities as the result of their market orientation, the support provided by community membership, and the sharp curtailment of their customary trading activities. Other groups were not exposed to the same incentives. The peasants produced primarily for subsistence or barter. Artisans and operators of small workshops often disposed of their products through traditional arrangements with employers or merchant-traders and were not directly in touch with the market. Their opportunities increased little with partition, since few of their competitors were Hindus. They did not obtain either the great capital resources or the experience with large operations of the traders who participated in international trade after 1947. The economic opportunities and social status of landlords, civil servants, and professionals were improved greatly by the Hindu exodus and they had little incentive, therefore, to try new industrial ventures. However, landlords have entered industry in larger numbers recently, when land tenure reform became a real possibility.

CONCLUSIONS

Conclusions should not be drawn from Pakistan's experience without an explicit recognition of some favorable noneconomic conditions that existed in Pakistan and that may be necessary for the development of entrepreneurship: (1) a government and civil service able to maintain law and order, to prevent massive capital flight, to enforce import controls, and to provide reasonably adequate overhead facilities; (2) at least a very small proportion of the population accustomed to responding to market incentives; (3) a value system and institutions that were not so hostile to entrepreneurial activity that only a strongly deviant group would be prepared to undertake it; (4) a political system which did not collapse despite high prices to consumers, high profits for industrialists, and the presence of many foreign technicians. Given these conditions, there is considerable evidence of a rapid development of industrial entrepreneurship in response to powerful economic incentives—whatever may have been the deeper motives satisfied by economic rewards. In a decade, a country with little industry and few industrialists has achieved a vigorous industrial development, limited primarily by inadequate foreign exchange. Many of the new industrialists came from families of traditional traders, but in a few years seemed committed to industry, no longer in need of strong economic stimuli, and ready to pay more attention to efficiency. There was no evidence that they were innovators in noneconomic matters, that they came from suppressed groups, that they differed from other Pakistanis in child-rearing practices or extent of nationalism.

The high rate of industrial growth was sustained from reinvestment of a very large proportion of all earnings. At least part of the explanation for this lies in the high rate of returns expected and the limits placed on consumption by import and other restrictions.

This discussion of Pakistan does not analyze social change which took place before 1947, and particularly the mechanism by which various groups originally became responsive to market influences. However, with respect to the shift from other market activities to industrial entrepreneurship, Pakistan does not lend support to the propositions earlier suggested as reflecting much recent work. It is difficult to interpret what happened in Pakistan in terms of a slow, fundamental change in motivation, or in ideology, or in customs, which then caused alterations in economic behavior. Instead, changed economic incentives were effective in altering economic behavior, given specified favorable noneconomic circumstances.

To generalize from Pakistan's experience for all underdeveloped countries would be tempting, but not justified.

First, other countries may not have in the same degree the four noneconomic conditions suggested as necessary and as existing in Pakistan.

Second, there undoubtedly are other noneconomic factors, which, in other countries and under other circumstances, would be important and might be crucial. A tribal society, with communal ownership, might not develop industrial entrepreneurs even if some of its members are involved in the market on behalf of the group. In the absence of careful study, one must also concede a possibility that even in Pakistan other noneconomic factors, including changes in the Muslim society of India, were more significant for entrepreneurship than here suggested.

Finally, the economic incentives and disincentives making for industrial entrepreneurship will often not be as clear and strong as they were in Pakistan.

Perhaps the recent stress on noneconomic factors in the development of entrepreneurship derived implicitly from societies that did differ from Pakistan in these respects. A primitive society with few market transactions would need to experience fundamental changes before a number of people respond to market incentives. Even in more sophisticated societies, the shift from traditional activities to industry does require strong incentives. Where powerful economic incentives are absent and social obstacles are great, industrial entrepreneurs may not develop in substantial numbers unless either the social obstacles are reduced by changes in the society or a deviant group is willing to surmount them for moderate economic rewards. This may well have been the situation in many countries in the past.

At present, the experience of Pakistan does suggest that, in other countries as well, the development of industrial entrepreneurs may depend largely on economic incentives which are determinable by government policy. In most underdeveloped countries industrialists may not be accorded the highest status—they were not in Pakistan—but the successful native entrepreneur will not be ostracized. Many countries have individuals in touch with the market and accustomed to respond to economic incentives, even at a moderate cost in social status: traditional traders, or money lenders, or growers of plantation crops. Most countries possess a civil service able to affect incentives by controlling foreign exchange and foreign competition and to provide reasonably satisfactory overhead facilities. At least a few countries should find high profits and high prices politically bearable so long as returns from industry are largely reinvested and contribute primarily to development, not conspicuous consumption. If economic incentives are sufficiently clear and strong, other factors can be less favorable than in Pakistan and some individuals or groups are still likely to respond to them.

In short, in Pakistan and probably elsewhere, social change in the past may have been adequate to create the necessary conditions for the emergence of industrial entrepreneurs. A substantial change in economic incentives and disincentives is then a sufficient condition to bring it about.

16

NIGERIAN ENTREPRENEURSHIP
IN INDUSTRY

John R. Harris

THE participation of Nigerian entrepreneurs in the economic development of their country has been striking in comparison with the experience of most other African countries. Internal trade, importing, road transport, non-financial services, building and construction, commercial agriculture, and industry have been areas of active growing entrepreneurial effort by Nigerians in recent years. It is true that the vast majority of large scale enterprises have been in the hands of expatriates or government agencies, yet the many small and medium scale indigenous firms have played an important part in the structural transformation of the economy. This paper will attempt to isolate the principal determinants of Nigerian entrepreneurial activity in industry.

All of the field work on which this paper is based was carried out during 1965; hence, no indication can be given of the possible repercussions of the military coups of January and July 1966 and the ensuing civil war. Detailed interviews were conducted with some 250 wholly Nigerian private firms and

Reprinted with minor alterations by the permission of the author and the publisher from Growth and Development of the Nigerian Economy, *edited by Carl Eicher and Carl Liedholm, Michigan State University Press, East Lansing, 1970.*

19 joint ventures in which Nigerian private interests were dominant.[1] On the basis of (1) a high proportion of Nigerian owned firms, (2) dispersal of the industry in more than one geographical region, and (3) a range of firm sizes, sawmilling, furniture, printing, rubber processing, and garment making were the industries selected for intensive study. Baking and shoe manufacture also met these criteria but were excluded outside of Lagos since they had recently been the subject of comprehensive industry studies.[2] Several other industries comprised of only a very few firms such as beverages, lime making, bone crushing, pipeline welding, gramophone record pressing, brick making, sign making, metal working, electrical equipment, transport equipment, perfume blending, and tanning were also included. We are confident that this sample included more than 80 per cent of the Nigerian owned firms with over 20 employees and about 25 per cent of those with more than 10 but less than 20 employees in each of these industries selected for study.[3] The individual who was primarily responsible for the founding of the firm or, in a few cases, the present principal owner (in the cases of inherited or purchased firms) was interviewed.

Tables 16-1 through 16-3 show the distribution of the 269 firms according to various characteristics. These tables are self-explanatory and will be useful for reference throughout the rest of this paper.

TABLE 16-1
Distribution of Firms by Industry

Industry	Number of Firms
Sawmilling	65
Furniture	34
Rubber Processing	10
Printing	48
Garment Making	30
Baking	38
Other Industries	44
Total	269

Space does not permit a detailed exposition of the theoretical framework underlying the rest of this paper. It will have to suffice to say that I think in terms of a modified supply and demand analysis in which potential oppor-

[1] Mrs. Mary P. Rowe conducted all of the interviews in Lagos; all other interviews were conducted personally by the author.

[2] Peter Kilby, *African Enterprise: The Nigerian Bread Industry* (Stanford University: The Hoover Institution, 1965); and E. Wayne Nafziger, "Nigerian Entrepreneurship: A Study of Indigenous Businessmen in the Footwear Industry" (unpublished Ph.D. dissertation, University of Illinois, 1967).

[3] Detail concerning the sample selection and interview procedure can be found in J. R. Harris, "Industrial Entrepreneurship in Nigeria" (unpublished Ph.D. dissertation, Northwestern University, 1967), Ch. 1.

TABLE 16-2
Distribution of Firms by Number of Employees

Number of Employees	Number of Firms
Less than 20	123
21–30	46
31–50	38
51–100	37
101–500	22
Total	266[a]

[a] This information was not available for 3 of the firms.

TABLE 16-3
Distribution of Firms by Geographical Region

Geographical Region	Number of Firms
Greater Lagos[a]	168
Western Region	35
Mid-West Region	16
Eastern Region	39
Northern Region	11
Total	269

[a] This includes the areas of Mushin and Ikeja which were formally included in the Western Region in 1965. All other regions denote the political organization of Nigeria in 1965.

tunities provide the demand for entrepreneurial services while various social, psychological, and political factors along with education, training, experience, and access to conventional factors of production affect the supply (or responsiveness) of entrepreneurial services. The latter factors listed under supply explicitly affect the demand side as well. This framework allows one to examine the many aspects of entrepreneurship, without resorting to a "single factor" psychological, social, political, or economic approach to the problem. All such factors are important and we can try to identify their interactions.

PART ONE: ENTREPRENEURIAL MOBILITY

First let us examine the geographical, occupational, and social mobility of Nigerian entrepreneurs. If entrepreneurship were found only in some few minority groups within the society, one would expect considerable geographical mobility; potential entrepreneurs would move from their homeland in search of opportunities. Table 16-4 shows a cross-classification between the region in which the business is located and the entrepreneur's region of birth.

TABLE 16-4

Cross-Classification of Entrepreneur's Region of Birth and Region in which Business is Located

Region of Birth	Greater Lagos	Western	Mid-West	Eastern	Northern	TOTAL
Greater Lagos	34	0	0	0	0	34
Western	92	35	0	1	2	130
Mid-West	12	0	16	0	0	28
Eastern	22	0	0	38	2	62
Northern	3	0	0	0	7	10
Total	163[a]	35	16	39	11	264

[a] Region of birth could not be ascertained for 5 of the entrepreneurs in Lagos.

Aside from movement into Lagos, the Federal Capital and largest commercial center, the lack of geographical mobility is indeed quite striking. Interregional mobility is practically nil. Only five of the entrepreneurs in the various regions were operating businesses outside of their region of birth. Further analysis has shown that inter-provincial mobility within the regions is surprisingly limited—only natives of Ijebu province in the Western Region and natives of Onitsha and Owerri provinces in the Eastern Region have migrated in any appreciable proportion. Within the Western Region only Ibadan, the commercial center and capital, draws a significant proportion of migrants as is the case with Port Harcourt, the principal industrial center of the Eastern Region. Some 77 per cent (126) of the Lagos industrialists were born in Lagos or the immediately adjacent provinces of the Western Region, Ijebu and Abeokuta.

There are several possible reasons for this lack of mobility. If entrepreneurial resources are widespread, it is to be expected that opportunities will be exploited by entrepreneurs already living in the area since they are in the best position to become aware of the possibilities. Hostility of residents to "outsiders" may also be a deterrent to the migration of potential entrepreneurs, yet geographical mobility in other entrepreneurial activities such as trade and transport has been much more important than in industry. This is explicable both in terms of greater security for a fixed investment in one's home area, and of the dependence of industrialists on personal contacts in the procuring of materials and marketing of goods in a country in which many markets are still relatively rudimentary. These constraints tend to be less binding in Lagos, with its system of land registration and the important role of the Federal Government as a major purchaser of goods.

Another indication of potential entrepreneurial responsiveness is the willingess of individuals to move from one occupation to another. Table

16-5 reveals considerable intergenerational and individual occupation mobility. Coming from a group of grandfathers who were preponderantly farmers or chiefs, and fathers who were farmers, craftsmen, or traders, these men started

TABLE 16-5

Occupational Background of Entrepreneurs, their Fathers, and Grandfathers

Occupation of Entrepreneur	Grandfather's Occupation	%	Father's Occupation	%	Own First Occupation	%	Own Previous Occupation	%
Subsistence Farmer	92	44.0	66	25.1	7	2.6	0	0
Cash-Crop Farmer	39	18.7	51	19.4	3	1.1	1	0.4
Small Scale Trader	9	4.3	11	4.2	16	6.0	10	3.7
Large Scale Trader	24	11.5	46	17.5	3	1.1	37	13.9
Employed Artisan	1	0.5	10	3.8	74	27.8	31	11.6
Self-employed Artisan, Contractor or Transporter	12	5.7	44	17.0	46	18.5	116	45.5
Clerical	0	0	4	1.5	59	22.2	19	7.1
Teacher	0	0	2	0.8	32	12.0	6	2.2
Gov't. Svc.	2	1.0	14	5.4	17	6.4	30	11.5
Professional	4	1.9	5	1.9	6	2.3	10	3.7
Traditional High Rank	26	12.4	9	3.4	0	0	1	0.4
Total	209[a]	100.	262[a]	100.	263[a]	100.	261[a]	100.

[a] Totals of less than 269 result from non-responses.

their economic lives as craftsmen, clerks, small-scale traders, teachers, and government servants, and were primarily self-employed as craftsmen, contractors, transporters, and large-scale traders immediately prior to founding their industrial enterprises. It is particularly significant to note the movement of these individuals from "modern" occupations such as clerical work and teaching into self-employment. When compared with the general occupational structure of Nigeria it becomes clear that agriculture (with approximately 78 per cent of the labor force in 1952)[4] has been less "productive" of industrial entrepreneurship in Nigeria than have been trade and craft activities.

[4] Federation of Nigeria, *Annual Abstract of Statistics 1964* (Lagos: Federal Office of Statistics, 1965), Sec. 2.

Closely related to occupational mobility, but not the same, is status mobility. A rough index of status was constructed based on occupation, income, and positions of leadership within society.[5] Table 16-6 gives a cross-classification of the entrepreneur's status with that of his father.

TABLE 16-6

Cross-Classification of Entrepreneur's Status and That of his Father

Status of Entrepreneur	Highest	Upper	Status of Father Middle	Lower	Lowest	Total
Highest	13	9	8	6	0	36
Upper	8	12	6	21	2	49
Middle	3	7	36	35	11	92
Lower	1	5	17	26	24	73
Lowest	0	0	0	1	3	4
Total	25	33	67	89	40	254[a]

[a] It was impossible to obtain rankings for father's status in 15 cases.

There is a significant positive relationship between the father's and the entrepreneur's status (Goodman-Krushkal's Gamma has a value of .493 which is significant at the $p < .001$ level), indicating that entrepreneurs with high status ranking tended to come from fathers with relatively high status.[6] Nevertheless, entrepreneurial activity has been an avenue of upward status mobility for many entrepreneurs. An examination of Table 16-6 shows that 122 observations lie above the principal diagonal, indicating that the entrepreneur is now of

[5] Harris, op. cit., Ch. 9.

[6] As shown by H. L. Costner in "Criteria for Measures of Association," *American Sociological Review*, XXX, 3 (June, 1965), pp. 341–353, Gamma can be interpreted as the proportional reduction in error of estimation made possible by the ordinal relationship. Linton Freeman, *Elementary Applied Statistics: For Students in the Behavioral Sciences* (New York: John Wiley and Sons, 1965) contains a discussion of Gamma in Chapter 8 and a table of significance for Gamma is reproduced in Appendix B.

On breaking Table 16-6 down by Lagos and non-Lagos, it becomes apparent that the status ranking of both entrepreneurs and their fathers is much lower for Lagos. This may reflect the different structure of Lagos society, dominated as it is by the national elite of politics, the civil service, and professions, or it could also reflect interviewer bias in the construction of the scale (crude and subjective as it is). Nevertheless, the conclusions hold: for non-Lagos respondents, Gamma has a value of .506 with 53 cases above the diagonal and 8 below; for Lagos respondents Gamma has a value of .425 with 70 cases above the diagonal and 34 below. A further explanation of the difference between the two scales is the smaller average size of the Lagos firms (median employment in Lagos firms was 15; in non-Lagos firms it was 25).

a higher status than his father, while only 42 observations lie below the diagonal. It is quite clear that entrepreneurial activity is a means of moving one or two "notches up the ladder" which is consistent with mobility patterns in observed western countries. Furthermore, this scale tends to underestimate the degree of upward mobility because many of the individuals now of lower status than their father are young men whose businesses are still expanding—hence it is to be expected that their wealth and leadership position will increase as they get older.

In summary, Nigerian entrepreneurs in industry have been geographically immobile but highly mobile in terms of occupation and status. Given the explanations preferred for the lack of geographical mobility, the evidence is not consistent with the existence of a "traditional society" of the sort described by Hagen for Nigeria as a whole.

PART TWO: CULTURAL AND ETHNIC VARIATIONS

A great deal of interest has been aroused in recent years by theories which relate entrepreneurial response and performance to psychological or social variables. Space precludes detailed examination of these theories here, but the important point to be drawn from them is that entrepreneurial response should vary systematically among ethnic or cultural groups according to their social structure and child-rearing patterns.

On the basis of recent work by LeVine[7] and examination of ethnological studies of groups not covered by this study, we would predict the following order of responsiveness (ranged from high to low) of the major ethnic groups of Nigeria: Ibo, Ibibio, Yoruba, Edo, and Hausa.[8] Let us examine these theories in terms of our sample.

In Table 16-7 the relative proportions of entrepreneurs from each ethnic group are compared with the distribution of ethnic groups within the entire Nigerian population. The table indicates that the Edo, Yoruba, and Ibo groups are over-represented in our sample, while Ibibio, Efik, and Ijaw, Hausa-Fulani and other groups are under-represented. The order of representation is: Edo, Yoruba, Ibo, Ibibio, Efik, Ijaw, Hausa-Fulani, and other groups. Although this ranking is inconsistent with the prediction based on psychological and sociological theories, one must be very cautious in giving any weight to this "test."

[7] Robert A. LeVine, *Dreams and Deeds* (Chicago: University of Chicago Press, 1966).
[8] Harris, op. cit.

TABLE 16-7

Distribution of Entrepreneurs by Ethnic Grouping Compared with that of the Nigerian Population

Ethnic Group	(1) % of Entrepreneurs	(2) % of Nigerian Population (1952–53 Census)	(3) Index of Representation (1)/(2)
Ibo	21.6	17.9	1.2
Ibibio, Efik, and Ijaw	1.9	2.5	.8
Yoruba	63.5	16.6	3.8
Edo	9.3	1.5	6.2
Hausa-Fulani	2.6	18.2	.2
Other ethnic groups	1.1	43.3	.03
Total	100.0	100.0	

First of all, the census is out of date and of questionable reliability, though it is unlikely that errors in the census would change these findings. The sampling procedure, however, does not allow much confidence in these estimates.

The investigation was restricted to a limited number of industries in major urban areas, therefore this is not a representative sample of *all* Nigerian industry. Even if it were, it would not provide a significant test of the hypothesis. Industry represents a very small portion of the economy, and geographical differences are confounded with ethnic groupings (note that the Edo are concentrated entirely in rubber processing and sawmilling—the Mid-West being the principal area of high forest and rubber cultivation). Therefore, one cannot claim that participation in industry is an appropriate test for entrepreneurial responsiveness. Trade, transport, and services are all quantitatively more important outlets for entrepreneurial energy.

Rather than mere participation, qualitative differences between entrepreneurial performance of different ethnic groups might shed more light on the hypothesis under question. Table 16-8 presents a cross-classification between ethnic grouping and size of firm (measured by number of employees). Although there is clearly some tendency for the Ibibio, Edo, and Ibo entrepreneurs to have larger firms than the Yoruba or Hausa, the relationship is not statistically significant (after further grouping, a chi-square test was not significant at the .10 level).

One of the obvious difficulties that arises in evaluating Table 16-8 is whether or not size of firm is an appropriate measure of entrepreneurial

TABLE 16-8
Ethnic Group of Entrepreneur and Number of Employees in Firm

Ethnic Group	Less than 20		21–30		31–50		51–100		More than 100		TOTAL	
	%	No.	%	No.	%	No.	%	No.	%	No.	%	No.
Ibo	39.7	23	13.8	8	13.8	8	20.7	12	12.1	7	100	58
Ibibio, Efik, and Ijaw	20.0	1	20.0	1	20.0	1	20.0	1	20.0	1	100	5
Yoruba	52.4	88	18.5	31	13.1	22	10.1	17	6.0	10	100	168
Edo	29.1	7	8.3	2	25.0	6	25.0	6	12.5	3	100	24
Hausa	14.3	1	57.1	4	14.3	1	0.0	0	14.3	1	100	7
Other	66.6	2	0.0	0	0.0	0	33.3	1	0.0	0	100	3
Column Total as % of Grand Total / Total	46.1	122	17.4	46	14.3	38	14.0	37	8.3	22	100	265

TABLE 16-9
Ethnic Group of Entrepreneur and Success of the Firm Index of Success

Ethnic Group	Very Successful		Successful		Average		Marginal		Unsuccessful		TOTAL	
	%	No.	%	No.	%	No.	%	No.	%	No.	%	No.
Ibo	22.6	12	41.5	22	24.5	13	5.7	3	5.7	3	100	53
Ibibio, Efik, and Ijaw	20.0	1	60.0	3	0.0	0	20.0	1	0.0	0	100	5
Yoruba	14.1	23	35.0	57	25.8	42	20.2	33	4.9	8	100	163
Edo	14.3	3	33.3	7	9.5	2	38.1	8	4.8	1	100	21
Hausa	20.0	1	60.0	3	0.0	0	20.0	1	0.0	0	100	5
Other		0		0		2		1		0	100	3
Total	16.0	40	36.8	92	23.6	59	18.8	47	4.8	12	100	250

performance. A measure of firm growth and/or profitability might be better.[9] A rough index of success based on the rate of growth of assets and profitability was constructed which gives a reasonably accurate and useful ordering of the firms with regard to these variables. (Sixteen of the firms could not be evaluated because they were too new or major reorganizations had recently been made.) Table 16-9 shows the distribution of entrepreneurs by success and ethnic group.

Table 16-9 reveals that Ibo and Ibibio entrepreneurs tend to be relatively more successful than Yorubas and Edos. Hausas perform about the same as the average of all groups, but the small number makes this difficult to interpret. Application of a chi-square test for association reveals that the relationship in Table 16-9 is even weaker than that in Table 16-8. Other measures of differential entrepreneurial performance include innovation, changes made within the firm since founding, and plans for future expansion. On each of these measures Ibibios, Ibos, and Hausas ranked higher than the other groups. The most highly significant relationship is that for innovation as shown in Table 16-10. While only 18 per cent of all entrepreneurs had innovated, 71 per cent of Hausas, 60 per cent of Ibibios, and 29 per cent of Ibos had done so.

However, both size of firm and the index of success may well be correlated with the particular industry and access to credit, both of which may be

---

[9] Most of the larger firms kept formal books although their accuracy was frequently called into question; few of the smaller firms maintained proper accounts. One could usually get fairly good information about fixed assets and manage a reasonable estimate of their replacement value. Most entrepreneurs had keen recollections of the time of purchase and cost of major assets. Current assets are much more problematical to estimate. Through questioning one could usually determine the value of fixed assets at the time of establishment of the firm as well. With this information it is possible to calculate an average rate of growth of assets. Similarly, it is fairly easy to get an accurate indication of the number of employees, both at the time of establishment and at the time of interview. Problems are raised by seasonality in some industries and sometimes casual (daily-paid) and family workers were not included in the totals given, but careful questioning can overcome these difficulties. One then has estimates of growth both of assets and employment.

It is much more difficult to obtain data on profitability. Frequently the least obtainable piece of information is that of gross sales during the previous period. One can try to establish average rates of output and average selling price to construct an estimate. Then by a similar process purchased inputs can be estimated. Labor costs can be computed fairly directly. Most entrepreneurs were willing to indicate how much money they withdrew from the business during an average month (special attention has to be paid to months in which school fees fall due) and what new assets were purchased. One can then perform some rough calculations for consistency of the data and question further when inconsistencies appear. With this information one can estimate rough rates of return to investment after imputing the entrepreneur's labor at an appropriate opportunity wage. Even when formal records are kept, this same line of questioning was followed. It should be abundantly clear that such data on profit are extremely crude. Nevertheless they seem to give a reasonably consistent ranking of different levels of success between firms.

TABLE 16-10
Ethnic Group of Entrepreneur and Degree of Innovation

	Innovated		Did Not Innovate		TOTAL	
Ethnic Group	%	No.	%	No.	%	No.
Ibo	29.3	17	70.7	41	100	58
Ibibio, Efik, and Ijaw	60.0	3	40.0	2	100	5
Yoruba	12.1	20	87.9	145	100	165
Edo	8.3	2	91.7	22	100	24
Hausa	71.4	5	28.6	2	100	7
Other	33.3	1	66.7	2	100	3
Total	18.3	48	81.7	214	100	262

Chi-square $= 29.968$, 5 d.f., $p. < .001$.

importantly influenced by the economic structure of the particular region. Given the relative geographical immobility of these entrepreneurs, a better test of the hypothesis that entrepreneurial performance differs among ethnic groups would be an examination of the ethnic distribution of entrepreneurs by size of firm and success in Lagos only. Tables 16-11 and 16-12 show these data.

Both tables show a tendency for a greater proportion of Ibos to have large and successful businesses than is the case for Yorubas, but the relationship is even less strong than it was for the entire sample. Further tests were performed in which the particular industry was controlled and in which both region and particular industry were controlled. In each case, the relationship was in the same direction: Ibos and Ibibios higher than Yorubas and Edos, with Hausas occupying an intermediate position. However, the effect of controlling for additional variables was always to further weaken the relationship.

In summary, on the basis of social structure and psychological testing we were led to predict the following ordering of entrepreneurial performance by ethnic grouping: Ibo, Ibibio, Yoruba, Edo, and Hausa. Our data do not contradict this prediction but neither do they lend strong support to it. An alternative hypothesis that the differences in economic structure of the regions, exposure to western education, and "modern" occupational experience are responsible for the observed ethnic differences cannot be rejected.

PART THREE: EDUCATION, OCCUPATIONAL EXPERIENCE, AND TECHNICAL INFORMATION

Perception of opportunities, gaining command over resources, and managing the ongoing enterprise are primary functions of entrepreneurship. Regardless of the individual's willingness to undertake entrepreneurial activities, these

TABLE 16-11
Ethnic Group of Entrepreneur and Number of Employees in Firm (Lagos Only)

Ethnic Group	Less than 20		21–30		31–50		51–100		More than 100		TOTAL	
	%	No.	%	No.	%	No.	%	No.	%	No.	%	No.
Ibo	60.8	14	8.7	2	8.7	2	17.4	4	4.3	1	100	23
Yoruba	58.8	74	15.6	20	11.7	15	9.4	12	5.5	7	100	128
Bini	37.5	3	25.0	2	25.0	2	12.5	1	0.0	0	100	8
All others[a]	60.0	3	20.0	1	0.0	0	20.0	1	0.0	0	100	5
Total	57.3	94	15.2	25	11.6	19	11.0	18	4.9	8	100	164

[a] "All others" consists of 2 Ibibio-Efik and 3 "others."

TABLE 16-12
Ethnic Group of Entrepreneur and Success of the Firm (Lagos Only)

Ethnic Group	Index of Success										TOTAL	
	Very Successful		Successful		Average		Marginal		Unsuccessful			
	%	No.	%	No.	%	No.	%	No.	%	No.	%	No.
Ibo	23.8	5	28.6	6	33.3	7	14.3	3	0.0	0	100	21
Yoruba	16.0	20	36.0	45	23.2	29	20.0	25	4.8	6	100	125
Bini	12.5	1	25.0	2	25.0	2	37.5	3	0.0	0	100	8
All others[a]	20.0	1	40.0	2	20.0	1	20.0	1	0.0	0	100	5
Total	17.0	27	34.6	55	24.5	39	20.1	32	3.8	6	100	159

[a] Five Lagos entrepreneurs could not be rated on the success scale because of recent changes in the firm.

desires will not be realized if the necessary capacity to carry them out is lacking. Education, occupational experience, and access to technical information should each play a crucial role.

It must first be remarked that the level of schooling of entrepreneurs in our sample is high by Nigerian standards. According to the 1952–53 Census, only 5.8 per cent of the population over 7 years of age had completed more than four years of schooling. This percentage ranged from 0.9 per cent in the Northern Region to 10.6 per cent in the Eastern Region and 33.7 per cent in Lagos, the Federal capital. Although there has been great expansion of education since 1952[10] the census figures give a reasonable picture of educational levels of these

TABLE 16-13
Education of Entrepreneurs

Highest level of formal education	No. of responses	%
None	34	12.7
Less than 6 years	36	13.5
6 years	93	34.7
Some secondary schooling	64	23.9
Secondary school certificate	22	8.2
Some post-secondary schooling	7	2.6
University degree	5	1.9
Post-graduate training	7	2.6
Total	268	100.1

entrepreneurs' cohorts since all were over 7 years of age in 1952. By contrast, 73.8 per cent of this sample had 6 or more years of formal schooling.

Education is seen to be positively but weakly correlated with size of firm (Gamma = .161), strongly correlated with innovation (Gamma = .454), and with plans for expansion (Gamma = .342). However, the relationship between formal education and size of firm is insignificant for the Lagos sample (Gamma = .07)— there is no ready explanation.

With respect to the index of success, there is a nearly significant positive correlation (Gamma = .154). Controlling for industry, education and success are positively correlated in sawmilling, furniture, printing, and garment making, essentially uncorrelated in baking and other industries, and *negatively* correlated in rubber processing.

The relationship between formal education and entrepreneurial performance is much weaker than had been expected. There are at least three possible explanations. First, those entrepreneurs with less formal education are more

[10] F. Harbison, "From Ashby to Reconstruction: Manpower and Education in Nigeria," in *Growth and Development of the Nigerian Economy*, edited by Eicher and Liedholm (East Lansing, Michigan State University Press, 1970).

likely to have had longer periods of apprenticeship and on-job training than those with more education. Secondly, there may well be a compensatory mechanism at work. Two of the most successful entrepreneurs had left government service because their limited educations precluded promotion to higher posts and they felt determined to show that they could succeed in spite of this handicap. One of the entrepreneurs with no formal education taught himself to read after he had started his own tailoring business and later travelled to England to take a course in cutting—he is perhaps the best record keeper of the whole group! Finally, size of the firm may not be the appropriate test of the effect of education. Kilby found a similar lack of relationship between formal education and success in the Nigerian baking industry.[11] He attributed this to the fact that more educated entrepreneurs are likely to undertake several businesses. If this is the case total employees in all enterprises controlled by the entrepreneur is the relevant variable. The correlation between this variable and education is considerably higher (Gamma = .402).

Other recent studies of entrepreneurship have identified two types of industrial entrepreneurs—the trader-entrepreneur and the craftsman-entrepreneur.[12] Generally speaking, the craftsman-entrepreneur has emerged earlier in the process of industrialization, but has remained primarily a traditional artisan. The larger and more rapidly expanding enterprises have been founded by former traders. This is usually explained in terms of the traders' greater familiarity with the market and his general commercial and managerial experience. Table 16-14 classifies the entrepreneurs by number of employees and previous occupation prior to founding the industrial enterprise.

It can be seen that these entrepreneurs came from a wide variety of backgrounds. The self-employed category demands some explanation—it includes both craftsmen who were working on their own (these dominate in the smaller firms) as well as contractors and transporters. Although a greater proportion of former traders are found in the largest size firms, individuals coming from governmental and professional backgrounds also tend to have larger than average firms.

According to performance on the index of success, traders have done better than average, but there is no strong relationship between previous occupation and success. In a country such as Nigeria, highly skilled workers

[11] Kilby, op. cit., *African Enterprise: The Nigerian Bread Industry*. It is interesting to compare these findings with Harbison's discussion of the need for a reorientation of education in Nigeria to meet the needs of small-scale industry and agriculture. See Harbison, op. cit.

[12] J. J. Carroll, *The Filipino Manufacturing Entrepreneur: Agent and Product of Change* (Ithaca: Cornell University Press, 1965); A. Alexander, *Greek Industrialists* (Athens: Center of Planning and Economic Growth, 1964); and G. Papanek, "The Development of Entrepreneurship," *American Economic Review*, LII (May, 1962), pp. 46–58.

TABLE 16-14

Classification of Entrepreneurs by Number of Employees and Previous Occupation

Previous Occupation	Number of Employees												
	Less than 20		21–30		31–50		51–100		More than 100		TOTAL	
	%	No.	%	No.	%	No.	%	No.	%	No.	%	No.
Farmer			100.0	1							100	1
Trader	36.2	17	25.5	12	12.8	6	8.5	4	17.0	8	100	47
Employed Craftsman	48.6	17	17.1	6	22.9	8	8.6	3	2.9	1	100	35
Clerical, Teaching and Professional	40.0	16	17.5	7	17.5	7	15.0	6	10.0	4	100	40
Self-Employed	56.0	56	15.0	15	9.0	9	18.0	18	2.0	2	100	100
Government	42.0	13	16.1	5	16.1	5	12.9	4	12.9	4	100	31
Total	46.8	119	18.1	46	13.8	35	13.8	35	7.5	19	100	254

and supervisors are difficult to find; the man with experience in the shop tends to have an advantage. By and large, the former traders had considerable difficulties in the management of production, quality control, and equipment maintenance. The technical experience of the former craftsmen, and their tendency to concentrate on a single business, has compensated for their relative lack of commercial acumen. The importance of specific occupational experience differs between industries. Timber contractors have founded the largest sawmills; traders in rubber have gone into rubber processing; former craftsmen have predominated in furniture and printing; the miscellaneous industries (which have tended to be more innovative) have drawn entrepreneurs from government, professions, clerical work, and trade.

Access to technical information has been rather haphazard. The most important source is one's own training and experience, followed by suppliers and repairmen, observing other firms, hiring experienced Nigerians, hiring expatriates, and making trips abroad. New ideas, when shown to be profitable, spread quickly through informal channels of communication.

Levels of technical competence in Nigeria are very low. Technical training has lagged far behind literary training in the schools and most apprenticeships are served under traditional craftsmen operating with hand methods and producing a low quality product. Only recently has engineering training been offered in the Nigerian universities and the need for sub-professional technicians is still largely unmet.[13] Industries into which Nigerian entrepreneurs have entered are relatively simple technologically. Indeed, the lack of technical training and experience effectively bars the entry of Nigerians into lines which require more advanced technical skills. Although some Nigerian entrepreneurs have overcome this problem to some extent by the hiring of expatriate personnel, this has not been uniformly successful.

Education, occupational experience, and access to technical information are each important in enabling an individual to perceive that a potentially profitable opportunity exists. Whether or not the perceived opportunity is actually exploited depends on the motivation of the individual and his ability to marshall the necessary resources.

PART FOUR: PROFITABILITY, ACCESS TO CAPITAL, AND MANAGEMENT

Standard economic reasoning assumes that the principal motivation to entrepreneurial behavior is the quest for profit. Other writing has stressed drives

[13] Harbison, op. cit.

for power, recognition, and immortality through founding a dynasty as motivating factors. In either case pecuniary gain becomes important since it is instrumental for achieving any of the latter goals.

The vast majority of these Nigerian entrepreneurs stated pecuniary reasons for undertaking entrepreneurial activity. In some cases industry exerted a pull by offering higher potential earnings than they had previously achieved. In other cases there were "push" effects, particularly in periods of depressed trading profits.

Indeed, these entrepreneurs have been quite successful by Nigerian standards of earnings. Half were earning more than £50 per month from the industrial enterprise and two-thirds of them earned more than this from all of their combined businesses. Keeping in mind that average wages paid by these entrepreneurs is under £7 per month and only 31 of them paid *any* employee over £40 per month, it is clear that they have done well by themselves.

Total personal assets of these entrepreneurs ranged from £1000 to over £1,000,000 with the median being near £15,000. One cannot help but be impressed with the general drive for wealth in Nigeria, wealth and status being virtually synonymous at least in the Southern regions.[14]

Much has been made in the literature of "trader's mentality" deterring investment in industry because of an irrational desire for high liquidity. Although there may be some truth in the statement, it appears that the two principal deterrents to industrial undertakings are the greater technical and managerial requirements and slightly lower average profits than in trade or transport. After making allowances for implicit payments to owned factors, the return to investment in industry ranges from substantial losses up to 50 per cent per annum. The median return in the sample is between 8 and 12 per cent.[15] This is slightly higher than the average net return to investment in urban rental dwelling units which is between 5 and 10 per cent. It was impossible to obtain reliable data for returns in trade and transport although industrialists who were also engaged in these activities suggested that returns from industry are slightly lower on average but fluctuate less. It is significant to note that real estate was usually explained to be a secure investment which would provide an "annuity" if the individual were to become sick and unable to manage his other undertakings. Thus it would appear that Nigerians do respond to prospective profits subject to discounting for risk. One does not have to resort to irrationality to explain the observed behavior.

Furthermore, it was evident that profits were substantially higher in newly

[14] LeVine, op. cit.; and H. Smyth and M. Smyth, *The New Nigerian Elite* (Stanford: Stanford University Press, 1960).

[15] This is consistent with the findings for shoe manufacturing by Nafziger. Nafziger, op. cit.

introduced industries. Profitable ventures rapidly attract emulation, forcing returns down by competitive pressures. This pattern has been particularly noticeable in tire retreading, rubber processing, sawmilling, and offset printing. The most successful entrepreneurs attributed much of their success to an ability to keep "one jump ahead" of their competitors in finding new products or processes.

Out of the 269 entrepreneurs in this sample, only 48 could be considered as having innovated even under a very loose definition of innovation. Four opened up a new market for a good, two introduced the use of a new material, twelve introduced new production processes, twenty-five introduced new products, and five pioneered new business methods. All of the innovations represented adaptation of products or processes to Nigeria which were already in use in industrialized countries. Examples are: introduction of tire retreading; starting the manufacture of rubber and plastic foam; being the first to start processing a raw material which was being exported; or being the first to manufacture gramophone records in the country.

The relative lack of innovation does not mean that these businesses have been stagnant. Only 43 firms reported having made no changes since establishment and the majority of those were less than two years old. One hundred and six of the firms had made major changes such as installing new and improved machinery or introducing new product lines, while another one hundred and fifteen had expanded the scale of operations. This kind of rapid response to changing opportunities is also an important characteristic of Nigerian traders. Katzin has remarked, "Whatever the final judgment may be of Africans as innovating entrepreneurs, there can be no doubt of their proficiency as imitating entrepreneurs. . . . The search for new ways of earning a profit is unremitting."[16] The returns to innovation are sometimes high but usually short-lived; the demonstration that a line of activity can be profitable considerably reduces the subjective risk to potential imitators.

Gaining access to capital is a major hurdle in starting any business. Table 16-15 shows that initial assets in these firms ranged from below £1000 (several started with less than £50) to upwards of £100,000. The median value is less than £1000. While not inconsiderable by Nigerian standards, the initial capital requirements in these industries are still quite modest. The median value of present assets of these firms is close to £10,000. It is obvious that the majority of the firms have experienced substantial growth of assets since founding.

[16] Margaret Katzin, "The Role of the Small Entrepreneur," in *Economic Transition in Africa*, edited by M. J. Herskovits and M. Harwitz (Evanston: Northwestern University Press, 1964).

TABLE 16-15

Assets of Nigerian Industrial Firms

Value of Assets £	Initial Assets (No. of Firms)	%	Present Assets (No. of Firms)	%
Less than 1,000	154	58.3	19	7.2
1,000–5,000	53	20.0	86	32.4
5,001–10,000	23	8.7	50	18.9
10,001–20,000	16	6.1	41	15.5
20,001–50,000	17	6.4	45	17.0
50,001–100,000	0	0.0	12	4.5
More than 100,000	1	0.4	12	4.5
Total	264[a]	100.0	265[a]	100.0

[a] Totals less than 269 are caused by non-responses.

TABLE 16-16

Type of Loans Received by Entrepreneurs

Term of Loan	Number of Loans	%
No loan	62	23.9
Overdraft	28	10.8
1–5 years	120	46.4
Over 5 years	49	18.9
Total	259	100.0

Self-finance is of overwhelming importance in Nigerian industry. Strengthening this argument is the observation that 76 per cent of the respondents indicated that their own savings was the single most important source of initial capital; 61 per cent of those respondents who had expanded their businesses relied on reinvested profits as the single most important source of funds for the expansion.

Credit, however, has been more available than is usually believed to be the case. Loans from banks, government, and suppliers (in the form of hire-purchase agreements) have played a part in the financing of 76 per cent of these Nigerian industries. Table 16-16 shows the length of term for which loans have been made.

Although a shortage of capital is frequently asserted to be a major impediment to the development of indigenous industry, and the respondents claimed inability to raise capital as their most serious problem, I am loath to accept this proposition. If capital is the principal bottleneck it will have two main effects. First, if economies of scale are important, firms without access to sufficient capital will be of less than optimal size. These firms would be less profitable than those which are able to start out on a larger scale. With profits providing the major source of capital for further expansion, the smaller firms would then tend

TABLE 16-17
Success of Firms by Amount of Initial Assets

Evaluation	Less than 1,000 No.	%	1,000–5,000 No.	%	Initial Assets (£) 5,001–10,000 No.	%	10,001–20,000 No.	%	More than 20,000 No.	%	TOTAL No.	%
Very successful	24	15.7	8	16.3	3	15.0	1	7.7	4	26.7	40	16.0
Successful	55	35.9	18	36.7	6	30.0	7	53.8	5	33.3	91	36.4
Average	38	24.8	11	22.4	6	30.0	3	23.1	2	13.3	60	24.0
Marginal	32	20.9	6	12.2	4	20.0	2	15.4	3	20.0	47	18.8
Unsuccessful	4	2.6	6	12.2	1	5.0	0	0.0	1	6.7	12	4.8
Total	153	100.0	49	100.0	20	100.0	13	100.0	15	100.0	250	100.0

to also have lower rates of growth. Table 16-17 shows that firms starting out on a small scale did just about as well in terms of profitability and growth as those firms starting out with greater assets. This implies that economies of scale are unimportant in the industries *contained in this sample.*

Secondly, if there are no economies of scale, or if all firms are of optimal size, capital shortage would be reflected by a high rate of return to existing capital and we would expect to observe intensive utilization of this stock. Table 16-18 indicates that the existing capital stock is worked at relatively low intensity. Our measure of utilization is per cent of effective 3 shift operation and while it is an inadequate and unsatisfactory measure, the conclusion is inescapable that considerably more output could be produced without increasing investment in additional fixed equipment. This reflects both a lack of cooperating factors and the rapid response of potential entrepreneurs to profitable opportunities.

TABLE 16-18

Per cent of Capacity (based on 3 shift operation) Utilized

% Capacity Utilized	No. of Firms	%
Less than 5	8	3.1
6–10	7	2.7
11–25	103	39.6
26–50	98	37.7
51–75	21	8.1
More than 75	23	8.8
Total	260	100.0

These two findings (lack of relation between initial assets and success, and the existence of considerable excess capacity) give some substance, although certainly not conclusive proof, to the assertion that capital shortage is not a principal barrier to development of industry *of the type represented in this sample.* It has been possible to start with relatively limited capital and expand through reinvestment; this has been the pattern of growth of most of the successful firms in this study.[17]

Perceiving an opportunity and gaining command over the resources to establish a firm are not the sole functions of entrepreneurship. Management of the ongoing concern is an equally important entrepreneurial function and it is this skill which appears to be most lacking in Nigeria.

Generally, the level of efficiency within the firms was very low. Substantial

[17] S. Schatz, *Development Bank Lending in Nigeria: The Federal Loans Board* (Ibadan: Oxford University Press, 1964), Ch. 6; and S. Schatz, "The Capital Shortage Illusion," *Oxford Economic Papers*, XVII, 2 (July, 1965), pp. 309–316. Schatz concluded that capital shortage is more apparent than real under existing institutional arrangements.

increases in output could be achieved without additional investment. This has previously been shown by the author in a paper on the Nigerian sawmilling industry, and by Kilby in two studies of Nigerian industry.[18] Closer supervision, better organization, improved layout, and quality control are desperately needed on the production side. The low levels of capacity utilization shown in Table 16-18 are largely a result of management deficiencies.

Most of the firms were one-man operations. When the business expands beyond the point that the owner can personally control everything, serious problems are encountered. Admittedly, it is difficult to find capable subordinates and managers in Nigeria, but little has been done by these entrepreneurs to train and develop such personnel. Many have now sent sons overseas for training in engineering, accounting, or business management which suggests that the problem will ease over time. In the meantime some have hired expatriate managers but the experience has been largely unhappy. Recruitment of capable and trustworthy expatriates is difficult and the ability to delegate authority to such personnel while still keeping adequate control is generally lacking. This inability to delegate authority successfully is attributable primarily to a lack of experience in large-scale organizations.

A factor that has been frequently claimed to be a serious impediment to the development of successful Nigerian management is the widespread dispersal of effort over several businesses.[19] It has not been uncommon to find entrepreneurs trying to juggle three or four firms with inadequate management control over any one of them. This may represent an attempt to pool risk through diversification, or it may be that limited markets prevent the further expansion of any one of the businesses. One hundred-thirty-three of our entrepreneurs had interests in additional businesses, but most of them were in related fields. For instance, sawmillers engaged in timber contracting; rubber processors were involved in the rubber trade; furniture makers were also building contractors; and garment manufacturers were large wholesalers of garments. Only 52 of these entrepreneurs indicated that less than 50 per cent of their working time was devoted to the industrial enterprise. Dispersal of effort may be common, but it does not seem to be a major problem for the entrepreneurs in this sample. Industry is a full-time operation for the majority, and it is a part of a rationally integrated business for most of the others.

[18] J. R. Harris and M. P. Rowe, "Entrepreneurial Patterns in the Nigerian Sawmilling Industry," *Nigerian Journal of Economic and Social Studies*, VIII, 1 (March, 1966), pp. 67–96; and Peter Kilby, "Organization and Productivity in Backward Economies," *Quarterly Journal of Economics*, LXXVI (May, 1962), pp. 273–291.

[19] Schatz, op. cit., *Development Bank Lending in Nigeria: The Federal Loans Board*; and Kilby, op. cit., *African Enterprise: The Nigerian Bread Industry*.

The principal obstacle now facing these firms is finding sufficient markets at present levels of capacity and costs. Each of the major industries in this study has expanded considerably since 1955, and productive capacity has been increasing more rapidly than demand for the products at existing prices. Profits have been made even at relatively low operating levels, although they seem to have been declining. It remains puzzling that in these industries, each having several firms, prices are relatively inflexible while entry is free. The result is that profits are driven down to "normal" through new entrants and expansion of existing firms giving rise to excess capacity at constant product prices. Kilby has documented similar behavior in the baking industry with overcapacity giving rise to occasional price wars and withdrawal of capacity.[20]

It may well be that the competitiveness of these industries gives rise to such rapid response to price changes by competitors that each entrepreneur believes the demand curve facing him to be downward sloping. The situation is rather like the standard kinked demand curve analysis of oligopoly. It is unlikely that the action of one sawmiller in Lagos to reduce price would not be known by his 29 competitors by the next day and they would be forced to match his price or lose a large part of their business. Therefore, it may be quite rational for each sawmiller to view his demand as one thirtieth of market demand and the the failure to cut price arises from profit maximization. When asked about price cuts entrepreneurs reply in terms of not wanting to "spoil the market" for everyone.

The point is that response is extremely rapid to industrial opportunities characterized by low levels of technology and insignificant economies of scale. For the most part these firms produce low price–low quality goods, There is potential for rapid expansion of low price–high quality goods although much of the expansion would be at the expense of existing producers. In fact the vast majority of these entrepreneurs are potentially vulnerable to competition from efficient competitors since their present operations are quite inefficient.

Technical and managerial personnel appear to be the primary bottlenecks to increasing the efficiency of existing firms although considerable improvement may be expected in the near future. Problems of machinery procurement and maintenance have declined in importance as sales and servicing facilities have improved greatly in recent years.[21] Nevertheless, 103 out of the 269 firms in this

---

[20] Kilby, op cit., *African Enterprise: The Nigerian Bread Industry*, Ch. 6.

[21] S. Schatz, "Economic Environment and Private Enterprise in West Africa," *The Economic Bulletin of Ghana*, VII (December, 1963), pp. 42–56. Schatz argues that entrepreneurs in developing areas face greater problems than businessmen in industrialized countries. He particularly stresses problems of ordering, maintaining, and replacing machinery. He also argues that skilled labor such as machinists present a critical bottleneck.

sample have well developed plans for further expansion within the next eighteen months. It remains to be seen if markets will support such expansion.

In summary, it appears that Nigerian entrepreneurs have been somewhat more successful in identifying opportunities and gaining command over resources than they have been in the management of the enterprises they have founded. Nigerians are not unresponsive to economic opportunity and are capable and willing to change and adapt their businesses as circumstances require. Kilby stated this same conclusion nicely in his study of the Nigerian baking industry:

> We have identified the dominant favorable characteristics exhibited by the majority of Nigerian bakers as a keen perception of and response to economic opportunity, willingness to adapt to changing market conditions, and marked competitive abilities. To their debit, most of these Nigerian entrepreneurs showed less skill in carrying out the organization functions of business enterprise, a lack of persistence in everyday supervision and little effective interest in improving product quality. . . . Indeed, it is the veritable surfeit of such perception of economic opportunity which threatens the established entrepreneur: in the employment of his skilled journeymen he is but training his soon-to-be competitors. Where he is not protected by a high investment threshold for entry into the industry, the entrepreneur's prime defense must lie in the extent of his own technical mastery and the quality of his product.[22]

PART FIVE:
POLICY IMPLICATIONS

The principal findings and policy implications are as follows:

1. Observed ethnic differences in entrepreneurial response and performance were generally consistent with the predictions of both psychological and sociological theories of entrepreneurship but had little explanatory power. The alternative hypothesis that observed differences arise from variations in the structure of economic opportunities, occupational experience, and educational levels in each of the regions cannot be rejected.

2. Education and previous occupational experience in trade, craft, or clerical work make some contribution to entrepreneurial success. The importance of these variables would appear to lie with their conditioning the individual's ability to perceive opportunities and to manage the ongoing firm.

3. Nigerians have responded quite promptly to profitable opportunities in industry which they have the capability to exploit. At the present time sufficient

[22] Kilby, *African Enterprise: The Nigerian Bread Industry*, pp. 111–112.

markets and the shortage of personnel with technical and managerial skills appear to be the principal obstacles to further expansion of this sector.

4. Availability of capital has not been a serious obstacle to the expansion of industries which are technologically simple and have a fairly low investment threshold.

5. Standards of management in Nigerian owned industries are very low. This stems primarily from a lack of experience in large scale organizations. Improvement can be expected as individuals gain technical and managerial training and experience.

It appears that in Nigeria *ability* to respond, rather than *willingness*, is the primary deterrent to the expansion of effective entrepreneurship. If this is the case, the development strategy called for is one of increasing opportunities for potential entrepreneurs, while at the same time upgrading their capacity to exploit more demanding opportunities.

Government can play a strategic role in making the perception of opportunities easier. Pilot plants, market studies, foreign aid assistance, and dissemination of technical information can each play a part. Even more important, as public and expatriate corporations undertake strategic investment programs which lead to fundamental structural changes in the economy, additional ancillary projects will be opened up for private entrepreneurs. This is in fact Hirschman's unbalanced growth proposal.[23] His point is that as imbalances develop, the investment priorities become more obvious, hence more easily perceived, and decision making becomes easier. A clear example of this process is seen around the oil industry in Port Harcourt. Nigerian owned firms making furniture, printing, clearing drilling sites, welding pipelines, and supplying specialized heavy transport equipment have all sprung up since 1960 to meet the demands of the expanding oil industry. The response has been prompt.

It has been demonstrated that Nigerians can be expected to exploit additional opportunities in industries characterized by simple technology and low investment thresholds. In the longer run, technical training, improved capital markets, and the gaining of managerial experience should considerably increase the ability of Nigerians to respond to opportunities that are now beyond their competence to exploit. These measures are likely to be far more effective than the unsuccessful credit arrangements to date.

[23] A. O. Hirschman, *The Strategy of Economic Development* (New Haven, Yale University Press, 1958).

17

DEVELOPING ENTREPRENEURSHIP: ELEMENTS FOR A PROGRAM

Eugene Staley and Richard Morse

THE fostering of vigorous industrial entrepreneurship in under-developed countries requires action in two areas. First, the overall environmental setting must be one which provides stability, an adequate level of reward for private business initiative, and a well functioning system of price signals which accurately reflects society's economic needs. Second, positive programs are needed to aid the emerging small industrial entrepreneur (a) to upgrade critical skills, (b) to increase his access to important technological and market knowledge, and (c) to benefit from better quality, less expensive factor inputs by means of improved institutional arrangements.

THE ENVIRONMENTAL SETTING

Although this chapter is concerned with the second area, setting out the elements for a positive program, we will briefly review those environmental factors which powerfully condition the ease and scope of entrepreneurial activity.

Reprinted by permission of the authors and the publisher from Modern Small Industries for Developing Countries (*New York: McGraw-Hill, 1965*), Ch. 13, with abridgements.

Good Government

Can citizens feel reasonably confident about security of persons and property, fairness of law enforcement, and justice in the courts? Is the government providing leadership in the spread of education, improvement of agriculture, development of natural resources, provision of transport and communication, and other community services? Modern industry, whether large scale or small scale, requires long-term investment and continuity of operation. The speculator with his quick in-and-out operations may perhaps prosper in an atmosphere of uncertainty, civil disorder, and arbitrary decisions, but not the constructive builder of permanent industry. Government must provide a framework of stability and progress which encourages foresighted private planning. It must also take the lead in developing the human and material foundations for economic modernization and growth.

An Expanding Economy

Is the market for manufactured goods growing? Can a potential entrepreneur who thinks of taking up manufacture of bicycle parts, tools, clocks, sewing machines, or something else reasonably expect to find larger sales opportunities for this product year by year?

Human Resources Development

Are there a fair number of local people who have attained the level of energy, education, motivation, and skill required for modern-type economic achievement as entrepreneurs and managers, technicians, and skilled workers? Are measures being taken to increase the number of such people? The answers to these questions depend on health, family upbringing, opportunities for schooling and trade training, opportunities for adult education in the broadest sense (adult courses, news media, educational work by political leaders, etc.), and the stimuli which outstanding opinion leaders, in government and out, can impart.

Natural Resources Development

Are natural resources available which lend themselves to industrial use, and are they being developed? Farm products, forest products, clay, limestone, and many other industrial materials, if properly developed, provide a resource base for specific lines of industry. Resource surveys, followed by developmental action, help to create a favorable environment for industrial undertakings.

Basic Utilities and Services

Are there reasonably good facilities for transportation, communication, water supply, and power supply? Are there plans for developing these further as industry expands? Can small industrial firms find reasonably adequate services in such fields as banking, insurance, wholesale trade, construction, and the installation and repair of equipment? Obviously, utilities and services for industry have to develop parallel with industrial growth; it is wasteful to push them too far ahead, and equally wasteful to inhibit growth by letting them fall too far behind. These facilities constitute one more environmental factor that must be carefully assessed and, if necessary, improved at the time of launching a small industry development program.

Laws, Regulations, Procedures

Do the laws, governmental regulations, and administrative procedures which apply to small manufacturing firms permit and encourage the legitimate business activities which are necessary for modernization and growth? Not infrequently it happens that there is an unintentional bias which works against the further development of a growing small firm. In most cases this bias takes the form of a handicap; however in some instances it appears as an incentive to remain in the unregulated small scale sector, *e.g.*, avoidance of minimum wage law, Provident Fund taxation, safety standards. We will consider the cases of factory licensing, allocation of quotas and profit taxation.

Industrial laws of newly developing countries oftentimes require that factories above a certain minimum size be registered. Where this is a mere routine procedure for statistical and regulatory purposes, the only barrier to growth which it imposes is that small industrialists may hesitate to graduate into the registered group for the reasons just noted. However, in some countries approval is necessary, in the form of a license which is more than a routine procedure, for establishing an industrial unit larger than a certain small size, or for expanding production beyond the previously licensed limit. Such approvals involve delay and require entrepreneurs to spend time and effort convincing government officials of the soundness of their proposals. The effect is to place yet another barrier in the way of growth.

Newly industrializing countries are generally short of foreign exchange, which causes scarcities of imported components and of imported equipment needed by manufacturers. Key materials and services produced within the country may also be in short supply (for example, steel, cement, transportation). In an effort to distribute the scarce items equitably and in accordance with the development plan, governments sometimes impose a system of allocations. They may also fix prices of these items below their true scarcity price, which results in a black market where prices are substantially higher than official prices. Such control systems almost inevitably favor large-scale over small-scale firms, stagnant firms over growing firms, inefficient firms over efficient firms, and entrepreneurs that cultivate political influence or engage in bribery over those that concentrate on doing a straightforward job of production and business management.

Tax laws and regulations sometimes discourage growth of firms or even promote artifical fragmentation. In India we learned of cases where small manufacturers of storage batteries, finding their business expanding, had split their operations into two or more separate units held in the names of members of their families; this was because an excise tax was levied only on the output of producers with more than four employees. In Turkey, under the Income Tax Law of 1961, small artisans and certain categories of small businessmen whose gross receipts were less than a stipulated figure were permitted to pay their income tax according to a simplified fixed assessment or lump sum method, and not required to keep books. The ineffectiveness of controls resulted in gross underassessment. It was alleged that many small businessmen paid one-twelfth the tax paid by salaried employees with the same income. From the viewpoint of the Turkish small industrialists, whose knowledge of modern industrial possibilities and motivation for industrial achievement may have been limited in any case, this tax system provided strong incentives not to expand.

With this very brief survey of environmental and general policy factors, we now turn to our principal concern: how to design an effective program to encourage indigenous industrial entrepreneurship.

A POSITIVE PROGRAM

Before embarking on a discussion of concrete measures which public, quasi-public, and private agencies can pursue, we want to stress three principles we have come to employ when analyzing how to upgrade the performance of the entrepreneurial unit. We believe these to be, in fact, general principles of development, applicable in many fields besides industry.

The Principle of Combinations and Interactions

A leading soil scientist has written: "The response of a soil to management is always a response to a combination of practices, interacting with one another and with the soil characteristics. . . . This principle of *interactions* is the most important principle of soil management."[1]

For example, in the Punjab of northwest India, introducing the seed of a higher-yielding corn (maize) variety without changing other practices increased the yield about 12 per cent. Proper water and fertilizer, while still using the un-improved seed, also increased the yield about 12 per cent. But the *combination* of better seed with better water control and fertilizer gave an explosive increase in yield of some 300 per cent. *Single* measures to increase yield cost more than the results were worth, but a suitable combination of measures more than repaid the effort and expense.

Another illustration, less spectacular, and perhaps for that reason sounder as an analogy, comes from experiments with sugarcane in the Cauca Valley of Colombia. Apparently water, not soil nutrients, was the chief limiting factor, but when water was supplied the cane also responded markedly to fertilizer.

It is our thesis that the productiveness of small and medium size manu-facturing plants—like the productiveness of a field of corn or sugarcane—depends on a combination of interacting factors. If a development program improves only one of these factors, the results may be quite meager, perhaps not worth the effort and expense. To improve a properly selected *combination* of factors may, on the other hand, prove highly effective. The yield, in terms of the development of the country, may then be much more than the cost. Some-times, however, there is one limiting factor of key importance, like the water in the sugarcane experiment. Improvement in such a limiting factor will permit other factors already present to work more effectively and hence will bring large results.

What are the interacting factors on which the development of modern small factories depends in newly industrializing countries? Some of them surely are capital and credit, managerial training, technical advice, market information, product design, raw materials supply, an entrepreneurial spirit of innovation and drive for achievement, a social and political climate encouraging to business

[1] Charles E. Kellogg, "Basic Theory of Soil Conservation Plans," *Soil Conservation*, Vol. 26 (February, 1961), p. 151.

growth, and so on. It is not possible to set up experimental situations like the trial plots of the agricultural scientists, to test the effects of altering these factors singly and in combination. But there is a good deal of evidence, from comparing the results of various kinds of development measures in many countries and from logical analysis, that the principle of combinations and interactions does apply. Hence, *any single-factor approach to indigenous industry development in a newly industrializing country is likely to be ineffective and wasteful. An integrated program that works on a carefully selected combination of factors simultaneously—the exact combination depending on local conditions—is much more likely to prove worthwhile.*

For example, training in modern labor skills is obviously important. But such training takes effect only in the presence of other factors. In Honduras, an industrial school was established with United States aid, to teach the manufacture of metal and wood products such as hand tools, bicycle frames, household and office furniture, and various kinds of craft and repair work. But a large proportion of the graduates were unable to apply their training because there were no firms manufacturing the items in question, and the graduates lacked funds to establish their own small firms.

Better access to capital and credit is certainly one of the requisites for industrial development. There are situations in which it really is true that improvement in access to capital and credit will enable a substantial number of industrialists to forge ahead. This is most likely to be the case in countries where there is already a fair amount of industrial experience and a substantial number of active, well-informed businessmen. In Colombia, for example, a team which evaluated the growth potential and growth needs of 106 small manufacturing firms found that 70 of these (two-thirds) seemed capable of significant expansion. It was judged that over 60 per cent of these more promising firms could probably expand with financial assistance only. However, for two-thirds even of these outstanding firms, financial assistance should include counsel in financial planning. Other kinds of assistance, especially production management counsel, were deemed essential or important to nearly 60 per cent of the entire group of firms with growth potential.[2]

Ghana, on the other hand, represents quite a different situation. There, the Industrial Development Corporation undertook to advance small industry mainly by supplying capital. This program, at least in its early phase, was a failure. The making of loans for political rather than economic reasons was a

[2] *Small and Medium Industry in Colombia's Development: A Survey and a Recommended Program*, Report of an inquiry organized by Banco Popular, aided by a team of consultants from Stanford Research Institute, Banco Popular (Bogotá, 1962), Ch. I.

major factor in this result. But also, nearly all Ghanaian manufacturing enterprises lacked other elements requisite for growth, not merely capital. Subsequent recommendations for a new policy emphasized manager and worker training programs, advisory services, industrial research services, and other small industry aids as well as financing.

The principle of combinations and interactions suggests serious doubts about the validity for development purposes of one fairly common practice. That is the tendency to "give" one area a technical school, another a power plant, and another a branch of an industrial financing agency. Such scattering of developmental measures arises out of political pressures from the various localities and from a desire to be fair. But the result can be wasteful, like a farmer putting improved seed in one field, fertilizer in another, and water in a third. Measures for small and medium industry development in any locality should rarely be taken singly. Instead, if any effort is to be made at all, it should be thoughtfully planned to constitute an integrated attack on those factors which prior investigation suggests be capable of yielding the greatest combined response.

The Principle of Adaptation

In the rest of this chapter we intend to analyze the many elements that deserve to be considered by designers of practical small industry development programs. We do not mean to recommend, however, that any particular device, much less any total program, be copied exactly by the development planners of another country. No two countries have exactly the same economic opportunities, business traditions, labor and managerial skills, political presuppositions, administrative capabilities, educational foundations, and cultural backgrounds. Hence, almost any social invention that is borrowed from another country will have to be adapted in various ways, sometimes very important ways in order to work well in the new environment. A good motto for development planners who are borrowing ideas on social technology from abroad is: *Adapt, do not simply adopt.*

The Principle of Selectivity

The elements in a well-designed program will be different, or combined in different proportions, in each country. Just as local investigation is needed to identify promising products, so the key limiting factors facing small firms need to be correctly assessed in each country. To ensure that developmental benefits are commensurate with their costs, programs should initially be tailored to the critical local factors, expanding or changing to meet new obstacles or opportunities as small firms begin to emerge and to grow. A practical implication of the above principles is that program planning should be sufficiently comprehensive to identify the main forces affecting small manufacturers and the interactions among these forces in the local environment.

A GUIDE TO PROGRAM PLANNING

Ten major types of developmental measures for small and medium size industry are grouped below under under the headings that emphasize first the key managerial elements, and second the provision of finance and other developmental facilities.

The management improvement triad

1. Industrial advisory services (extension of counseling services)

2. Training of entrepreneur-managers and supervisory personnel

3. Industrial research services

Developmental facilities

4. Developmental finance

5. Factory sites and buildings (industrial estates)

6. Common facility services

7. Facilitating the procurement of materials and equipment

8. Marketing aids

9. Labor relations services

10. Interfirm contracts and assistance

Our purpose now is to assess each of these types of developmental measures, considering critically the circumstances in which it may be helpful and the methods that can make it most effective.

The rise of an energetic and skillful group of creative, innovating, achievement-motivated entrepreneur-managers is a key to widespread industrial growth, whether in a private enterprise economy or one that depends heavily on publicly managed enterprises. Ways of increasing the number of such persons in a society were explored in the previous chapter. Now we consider the increasingly effective methods that have been developed in several countries for enhancing the competence and initiative of existing entrepreneur-managers.

Experience is clearly the principal and the best school for management. Experience alone is rarely enough, however, to ensure the most effective management of a small business facing the complexities of a modern economy. In newly industrializing countries, lacking the institutions and communications media which spread modern practices in industrialized economies, management experience is typically fragmentary and "catch-as-catch-can." Strengthening managerial abilities in such circumstances is a central requirement for modernization and expansion.

Poor management causes not only low labor productivity but also, even more critical in capital-scarce countries, "underemployment of capital,"[3] and wastage of materials. Substantial potential for increased output without large new investment has been dramatically demonstrated by productivity improvements in many small as well as large plants. "Skill-intensive" measures for management improvement, as contrasted to "capital-intensive" physical facilities, therefore assume highest importance in most developing regions.

The modernizing triad of extension, training, and research, which has proved to be a valuable instrument of agricultural improvement in many countries, has important applications for industrial management improvement as well.

Management training relevant to the local scene can hardly be accomplished without preliminary management diagnosis and extension work in existing firms. The "feedback" of practical problems raised by factory managers and industrial extension agents gives a realistic focus to training and research activities, directing them to timely and useful topics. Research findings, in turn, whether technical, economic, or managerial, are useless unless effectively communicated to industrialists through sound extension practices.

[3] Richard S. Roberts, Jr., *Economic Development, Human Skills, and Technical Assistance: A Study of I.L.O. Technical Assistance in the Field of Productivity and Management Development*, Librairie Droz (Geneva, 1962).

Industrial Advisory Services (Extension or Counseling Services)[4]

The need for advisory services stems basically from the small firm's lack of management specialization, in an era when specialized knowledge and techniques underlie most industrial progress. The entrepreneur-manager may have a number of assistants with some special knowledge, but generally he himself has to make most of the firm's decisions, covering such diverse fields as product planning, production techniques, purchasing, sales, personnel, labor relations, and finance. Gaps in the manager's own experience which would be filled by specialists in a large firm must be overcome by measures which help him to gain new understanding, to train assistants in new functions, or to institute new procedures.

An industrial extension service will be called on for (1) economic guidance on promising new lines of manufacture, for expansion of existing firms or entry of new ones; (2) technical advice on such problems as selection of machinery, improved processes, and better use of machines and materials; (3) production and business management counsel on plant layout, costing, marketing, financing, and personnel management, to give just a few examples; and (4) assistance in product design and improvement.

The focus of advisory services deepens as industrialization proceeds and experience is gained. At an early stage, managers are usually most aware of specific technical problems: installing a new machine, case hardening of bicycle bell covers to ensure resonance, suitable clay mix and firing processes to achieve brilliant glaze on ceramic articles, or correct use of jigs and fixtures. Production management methods are less often a felt need but are crucial for cost reduction, especially once substantial fixed assets are in place: preventive maintenance of equipment, plant layout and work flow improvement, work simplification, production scheduling and control, inventory controls. Moreover, such industrial engineering procedures often find effective response from the many owner-managers who started as craftsmen or technicians and can therefore readily appreciate and assimilate practical improvements in work methods.

Financial management problems, including accounting, costing, and cash-flow budgeting, are typically cloaked by the felt need for greater working capital. Loan applicants must often be denied until they can be assisted in establishing basic records. When the enterprise seeks to expand, its credit needs

[4] See Joseph E. Stepanek, *Small Industry Advisory Services: An International Study*, a publication of the International Development Center of Stanford Research Institute, Free Press of Glencoe (New York, 1960). Also see Jean Marie Ackermann, *Communicating Industrial Ideas: An International Handbook for Industrial Extension*, Stanford Research Institute, Menlo Park, Calif., 1962.

may lead to financial consultation that uncovers problems of inventory control, accounts receivable, and balance between fixed and working capital expansion.

As industries diversify, the individual firm is pressed to introduce new products, improve product design and quality, meet market trends more closely, and develop new sales initiative. Such marketing problems require new forms of analysis and counsel.

Finally, growth to medium size raises new problems. There is the psychological hurdle of a possible change from a proprietary or private limited organization to one that is incorporated. Problems of enlarged administrative span can be eased by sound guidance. Help can be given in preparing specialists —in accounts, stockkeeping, sales, etc.—to assume delegated departmental responsibilities. As workers and owner lose their personal touch, when the work force grows beyond 35 or 40 to 75 or 100 persons and more, deterioration in labor relations can be averted through proper development of supervisory personnel and labor-management consultation.[5] Longer-term and more detailed planning procedures can be instituted. In all these moves, the capacity and drive of the entrepreneur is the real key to growth, but he needs to be in touch with sources of self-help as well as advice in order to advance successfully.

This enumeration of the interlocking management needs of a small firm makes it clear that the first requirements of an industrial advisory service is high-quality personnel. Both generalists and specialists are needed. A generalist in this sense is one who can take a view of the firm that is as broad and thorough as necessary to diagnose its key problems, calling on a specialist for advice beyond the generalist's own competence. Advisory service specialists vary with local needs and resources but generally include persons skilled in industrial engineering, finance, marketing, economic research, and those branches of technology that are most important to small industry in the region.

How can such high caliber extension staff be developed, especially in countries where scarcity of skilled personnel is a major bottleneck? Some lessons on staff development are offered by the recent experience of developing economies:

(a) Initial quality of staff is far more important than their numbers. In East Pakistan it is now recommended that the director of an advisory service centre should have a minimum of ten years business experience, preferably in manufacturing, and that junior staff should have at least three years. Adequate salary and professional status are necessary to attract such men.

---

[5] For evidence on the gross waste of time, output, and industrial morale due to poor labor relations in medium-sized firms (50 to 250 workers), see James J. Berna, *Industrial Entrepreneurship in Madras State, India* (Asia Publishing House, Bombay, 1960), pp. 106–124.

(b) The high status to be accorded senior extension staff does not mean that theirs is a desk job. Nor are quick, certain answers a mark of their professional growth as counselors. Their first work is in the plants and business offices of small firms, learning management strengths and weaknesses through give-and-take discussion. The senior counselor should not be a person who feels loss of face when he does not know as much as the industrialist about all operating details. He will serve his professional purpose, and gain respect, by listening carefully to the industrialist's problem, interpret it against his own wider knowledge of management principles and industrial techniques, and helping the manager devise a specific solution for the firm's situation.

(c) Consulting work is the best school for counselors. Given a small initial staff with the aptitudes and attitudes stressed above, intensive advisory work with promising local managers will establish the level and content of services needed. Extension workers are intended to be adaptive or innovating agents in the industrialization process, and must therefore build from where local entrepreneurs are, toward objectives they can reasonably hope to attain.

(d) Direct demonstration of tangible in-plant improvements is the best way to spread progress.

(e) The tests of success in counseling are productivity gains and sound growth in the firm assisted. Even though these can be gauged only crudely, such objectives must be held in view and not displaced by more measurable but less significant criteria, such as the number of plants visited.

Once initial success has been achieved through individual work with representative growing firms, the ground is laid for reaching larger numbers of entrepreneur-managers through well-designed group training programs. These we now examine.

Training of Entrepreneur-Managers and Supervisory Personnel

Formal and informal training measures for small manufacturers include short courses, self-education aids, and preparatory training.[6] The substance of training should be more than a reduced version of management training for large firms, since the tasks of one-man management are in many respects quite different. Many modern management techniques have been evolved mainly to cope with the complexity of big organizations. Flexibility and face-to-face control in the small firm make some of these techniques unnecessary or self-

---

[6] See Joseph E. Stepanek, *Managers for Small Industry: An International Study*, a publication of the International Development Center of Stanford Research Institute, The Free Press of Glencoe, New York, 1960.

defeating.[7] Simplified and adapted, however, such techniques as work study, costing, budget control, or inventory management are invaluable to the small manufacturer. He must have a reasonable grasp of the principles involved in the types of problem handled by specialists in large firms, in order to know how to locate his own problems and get outside help where needed.

It follows that training topics should be chosen and course materials designed, with small firm needs in mind. In particular, we suggest:

(a) For existing managers, effective course content, can be developed on the basis of the key problems that repeatedly arise during in-plant diagnosis and counseling.

(b) Courses should not be offered until training leaders are available who can translate management principles into practical applications for local small firms. Course scheduling may well be intermittent. Between courses, instructors should strengthen their practical knowledge through in-plant counseling and research.

(c) Training aids and case materials pertinent to local industry are required. Extension workers, staffs of productivity centers, and university or research personnel can help develop such aids. Case studies prepared by the Industrial Development Center in the Philippines[8] illustrate issues on which data from an industrially developed country would be largely inapplicable:

Freight differentials in imported raw materials, parts, and subassemblies

Inventory control in a rapidly growing bottled gas company when new bottles are not obtainable

Need for careful planning when notes receivable are discounted at 16 per cent per year

Critical problem of locating and training salesmen

The daily work of an advisory service will suggest many local problems that can be adapted as realistic training aids for managers, taking care to protect confidences.

[7] For a discussion of differences between small and large firm management problems, see "The Adaptation of Management Techniques to Small Undertakings," an agenda paper for the ILO Technical Meeting on Small-scale and Handicraft Industries, at New Delhi, 1961. Geneva, International Labour Office, Document SSHI/1961/2 (II).

[8] Stepanek, op. cit., pp. 204–205.

(d) A training director who has a clear overall appreciation of small firm management problems will find ways of mobilizing and orienting local talent for seminar leadership and lectures. If successful local industrialists, private consultants, or university personnel are enlisted as part-time trainers, adequate time and budget should be assured for them to adapt their experience to small firm needs.

(e) Advantage should be taken of productivity center courses now available through ILO or AID assistance in many countries. Although typically aimed at larger firms, their short courses in work study, production planning and control, quality control, and supervisory techniques have attracted small firm managers and have led to numerous in-plant improvements. A country with an effective on-going productivity program will need to supplement it by training in financial management, marketing, and general or overall management of small enterprises.

(f) Preparatory training for future small enterprise managers needs to be significantly improved. Business management programs now being developed by universities in several industrializing countries should give due weight to small enterprise needs. One or more courses in industrial management should be included in engineering and economics curricula.

In a community or country with little previous business responsibility, post-secondary school training below the university level can also be an important step toward commercial and industrial activities.

(g) Finally, self-education manuals and other aids are needed, both to stimulate initial interest in modern techniques and for managers' continuing self-improvement. One guide, replete with practical aphorisms, was written out of five years' experience as management counselor and trainer in Bombay.[9] Others, including a translation of a Japanese "self-diagnosis" questionnaire, are cited by Stepanek.[10] Ratio analyses and management manuals prepared in industrialized countries constitute a pattern for such self-education aids, but only a pattern. To strike home to the entrepreneur-manager, such aids to self-analysis must embody local practices and data.

Industrial Research Services

Research by qualified specialists is one of the management aids which large enterprises can afford but small ones cannot. However, many types of applied

[9] F. A. Ryan, *Efficiency for Small Manufacturers* (Bombay, etc., Asia Publishing House, 1962).
[10] Stepanek, op. cit., Ch. 7 and pp. 238–242.

industrial research lend themselves to collective performance for the benefit of several firms simultaneously. Development agencies in quite a number of newly industrializing countries have perceived this and have established industrial research institutes. Too often this has been done without an industrial extension service to disseminate the results and to bring industry problems to the research organization. This gravely limits the usefulness of the research, particularly so far as small industry is concerned. The converse mistake is almost equally grave —that is, to establish an industrial extension service without supporting research activities.

The valuable, indeed indispensable, role of research in modern industry is well known. In newly industrializing countries, the payoff from properly directed industrial research can be particularly rapid because much of the research can consist of selecting from the world reservoir of already existing scientific and technical knowledge those ideas most immediately applicable in the country concerned and then adapting them somewhat to make them truly workable under local conditions. Without this local adaptation, products and techniques that work perfectly in their place of origin may fail when transferred to a different environment.

Applied industrial research undertakes to integrate the economic, engineering, and often certain management aspects of specific industrial opportunities and problems. Economic research for small industry has two distinct clients: the manufacturer himself, who needs information about market, cost and other factors that affect his own situation, and the government policymaker, who needs data for program planning and review. Separate research techniques are required for each purpose, though data and results overlap.[11] For entrepreneurs, economic research focuses on competitive conditions and anticipated market growth in important small plant products, cost factors and cost-reducing methods, minimum size of economic plant, breakeven projections, and opportunities in particular regions and locations. The economic research service will often be called upon to assess the industrial potential of particular regions or districts. Thorough grasp of the technoeconomic characteristics of the country's important small plant industries must normally precede effective area development research of this kind. Engineering collaboration in economic studies for small firms is particularly important in assessing cost factors, economies of scale, possible substitution of labor for capital, and other production factors.

[11] For a comprehensive discussion, see S. Nanjundan, H. E. Robison, and Eugene Staley, *Economic Research for Small Industry Development: Illustrated by India's Experience*, a Publication of the International Development Center of Stanford Research Institute (Asia Publishing House, Bombay, 1962).

Conversely, economists and management specialists should cooperate closely with engineers in the preparation of technical schemes or plant requirement reports, ensuring adequate treatment of costs, market feasibility, financial requirements, etc. This area of collaboration should be particularly active when research and counseling are developed in direct cooperation with financing programs, which are dealt with below.

Within the applied research program, establishment of a technical information service is of key importance. Problems raised by small and large industrialists, extension staff, and research specialists are the origin of most technical inquiries. Ingenuity combined with systematic knowledge of technical literature and information retrieval methods is needed to obtain, screen, and adapt information that will be relevant to such local situations.

In existing industrial research institutes, which have quite naturally been planned with the needs of medium and large firms at the forefront, the applied research problems of small manufacturers are usually under-represented. Without an industrial extension service, the recurrent research needs of small firms are not likely to be known. Small firm managers, moreover, like other managers in an environment where research is a new phenomenon, must be educated in the use of outside research facilities.

For countries which have yet to develop applied industrial research facilities the above combination of economic, engineering, and managerial research, linked to an industrial extension service, appears to offer a sound foundation for planning more specialized and elaborate research facilities. The work of the advisory service, supported by research personnel, will reveal the most pressing problems of the country's native manufacturers, which should be incorporated with those of larger firms in designing the program of an applied industrial research institute.

DEVELOPMENTAL FACILITIES

The educative nature of the services just described makes strict calculation of benefits against costs impossible. Fees for services will be discussed elsewhere here, but often fees are not expected to cover full costs in view of the long-run returns to society from such educational measures. The next four measures, in contrast, are susceptible to cost-benefit tests. Since they involve higher capital expenditure than the above *skill-intensive* measures, a cost-benefit consciousness is essential in their planning, execution, and evaluation.

Developmental Finance

Adequate access to capital and credit is a key requirement of any industrial program oriented to development—that is, toward helping existing small enterprises to modernize and grow, and new ones to start. The usual sources of funds for small, privately owned industrial ventures in newly industrializing countries are personal savings of the proprietor and his family and borrowings from relatives and friends. Institutional financing for this class of borrower is generally most inadequate. Such institutional financing is beset with difficulties because the cost of making many small loans is greater than the cost of making one large loan and because the risk on loans to small enterprises is substantial. The risk is heightened by deficiencies of managerial skill and technical knowledge on the part of small industrialists.

There is considerable ferment in the field of institutions and techniques for industrial financing, though nowhere have fully satisfactory solutions been found for the inherently difficult problems. Without entering in detail into the complexities of this field, which are treated in a companion study,[12] some salient points may be noted:

(a) Central bank rules or legislation governing bank practices may either inhibit or encourage bank lending to industry, and to smaller firms in particular. Experience in Germany, Japan, Sweden, the United States, and certain other countries shows that the commercial banking system can be a key source not only of short-term but also of intermediate-term finance (one to five years), if regulations or incentives are conducive to such lending operations.

(b) Specific gaps in finance for small firms—for example, seasonal working capital, working capital for expansion, equipment credit, etc.—may be ascertained by field inquiries.[13] It is important to recall that "quite different types and combinations of finance are essential to the development of different types of enterprises,"[14] and that these needs change dynamically in periods of either growth or contraction, whether of the economy or the enterprise. Hence the importance of "fostering multiple sources of finance,"[15] to give better assurance of meeting all types of need, to meet new contingencies, and to provide a degree of competition among institutions.

(c) Commercial banks are a substantially underutilized potential source

[12] Robert W. Davenport, *Financing the Small Manufacturer in Developing Countries* (McGraw-Hill, 1966).

[13] An example of such field appraisal is Banco Popular, *Small and Medium Industry in Colombia's Development*, Report of an inquiry assisted by Stanford Research Institute, English and Spanish (Bogotá, 1962).

[14] Ibid., p. 74.   [15] Davenport, op. cit.

of industrial short-term and medium-term finance in most industrializing economies. They make a greater contribution in countries such as those named under point (a). Normal incentives typically pull commercial bank resources toward forms of lending that have higher turnover or deposit generation. To stimulate bank lending to industry, particularly to small firms, other incentives and aids are necessary, such as favorable rediscount policies and collateral requirements, development of credit information and exchange, credit insurance, and training of industrial loan appraisal officers.

(e) For medium- and long-term credit, and even for short-term loans in many instances, supplementary institutions specially geared to small industry financing are needed in most countries to pioneer new lending techniques, to assure that financial counsel is provided in conjunction with credit, or to meet the special needs of new or rapidly growing firms. The Industrial Development Bank in Canada is a successful prototype in this field.[16] Development banks established in newly industrializing countries have generally found it necessary to focus on larger firms, in an effort to stabilize themselves in the face of innumerable initial difficulties. Where successful, such banks may constitute a base for building a medium- or long-term credit program adapted to the specific objectives and techniques required for lending to small enterprises.

(f) Effective substitutes for direct lending have evolved in the form of hire-purchase or installment purchase schemes, especially for machinery and equipment. Such schemes have been used to provide medium-term credit in India, Burma, and Indonesia. The Banco Cafetero finances equipment imports in Colombia, where proposals have also been made to permit local equipment manufacturers to extend three-year equipment credit to small firms by rediscounting bills with the central bank.[17]

(g) The advantages of industrial estates as a means of long-term capital assistance to small firms are noted in the next section.

(h) Finally, and of key importance, it is by now widely recognized that the financial problems of small manufacturers are hardly ever just financial. While a certain percentage of well-managed, outstandingly promising small firms may be able to benefit decisively merely from better finance (see the findings of the Colombian survey mentioned earlier), shortage of finance is in most cases a symptom of other problems—poor planning, outmoded technology, ineffective marketing, bad product design, lack of cost accounting, and so on. In such cases, *no purely financial solution will really help.* Serious experimentation is

[16] Davenport, op. cit.
[17] Banco Popular, op. cit., p. 99.

needed in newly industrializing countries to evolve a more intimate combination of financing with technical and managerial counsel and other developmental aids.

Factory Sites and Buildings (*Industrial Estates*)

Small factories are often housed in cramped, dark, and dirty quarters which are not conducive to good work by human beings or by machines. Often they have very inadequate access to industrial utilities—transport, water and electricity supply, sewage disposal, and other services. Better factory sites and buildings can stimulate managers and workers to make other improvements, and the effect on productivity and general initiative may be considerable.

A comparatively recent device which has already become an important tool of industrial and community development in many countries is the industrial estate.[18] The industrial estate can aid small industry development in several important ways. The provision of suitable factory premises on rental or hire-purchase is as good as a loan, if the enterprise would otherwise have to finance its own building. The risk of loss to the sponsoring agency can be kept to a minimum because premises can be rented to some other firm if one fails. The clustering of several firms fosters complementary transactions among them and also facilititates bulk purchases and shipments. Moreover, an industrial estate reduces the costs—and relieves the small industrialist of the time-consuming tasks—of getting title to land, having buildings designed and constructed, arranging for road, power, and water connections, and the like.

Vigorous promotional use of industrial estates in several newly industrializing countries, including India, Pakistan, Nigeria, and Puerto Rico, has resulted in valuable lessons which should be taken into account in other countries:

(a) Proper location is of paramount importance. Choice of a region having good industrial potential, and of a site that offers real advantages for the industries concerned, is necessary in order to have the estate plots taken up and to set in motion a self-reinforcing attraction of new industry and capital. Alone, industrial estates cannot overcome locational disadvantages, particularly in small towns or remote places which lack entrepreneurs, good transport, and

[18] See William Bredo, *Industrial Estates: Tool for Industrialization*, a publication of the International Development Center of Stanford Research Institute (Free Press of Glencoe, New York, 1960); United Nations, *Establishment of Industrial Estates in Under-Developed Countries*, New York, 1961; P. C. Alexander, *Industrial Estates in India* (Asia Publishing House, Bombay, 1963).

other industrial requisites. Estates have in some cases been too large for the center chosen or were developed too far ahead of demand, resulting in high vacancy rates and sizable losses.

(b) Industrial estates appeal to certain types of industry but not to others. They seem especially suited to light assembly operations, end products of food, wood, and apparel, light metalworking and electrical industries, and some kinds of service establishments. Industrial estates can be an effective tool of small and medium industry development in conjunction with existing or planned large plants, if the latter present opportunities for subcontracting or further manufacturing relationships.

(c) Because of such locational requisites, the planning of an industrial estate should be dovetailed with overall industrial planning for the region. Such planning entails prior research in considerable detail. Allocation for industrial estates should not outpace the capacity of sponsoring agencies to make realistic plans for their location, design, and management.

(d) Variety and flexibility in factory sizes should be achieved, permitting growing firms to shift to larger worksheds when needed. Undeveloped land adjacent to the initial site should be reserved for estate expansion. In some instances, a combination of small and medium factory types will be appropriate, and plans should not overlook possible linkages with large-scale plants.

(e) The need to improve factory standards over existing slum-congested conditions, while keeping costs and rents as close as possible to current rentals for equal space, presents difficult challenges to architects and estate planners. Better productivity in the new space will ultimately justify rent differentials over the old, but this productivity may take time to be achieved and to be realized by the small firm. Strict economy in estate construction is therefore essential if vacancy rates and rent defaults are to be minimized. This implies that:

(i) Factory design must be skillful, achieving austerity yet with better layout, lighting, space per worker, foundations, and access than in existing premises used by small industry.

(ii) Local and inexpensive building materials should be used as far as possible, with effective subsitutes for imported materials.

(iii) Advance cost estimates must be reliable in order to set realistic rent quotations as a basis for canvassing demands for space, so that rent levels will not later have to be changed.

(iv) Roads, unbuilt space, and administrative buildings (if any) should be kept to the minimum commensurate with factory requirements. Costs of official structures beyond those directly allocable to estate operation should be kept out of the rent base. If extra facilities such as a rail siding, post office branch, or fire station are to be provided, their planning should be integrated with that of the surrounding community so that they will be used to full capacity. Their costs should be partially covered by local taxes or by the agency concerned, rather than being borne only by estate occupants.

(f) It is usually desirable to permit instalment purchase of factories, as an alternative to rent. This draws in private capital, releasing public funds for estate expansion or other developmental use.

(g) Where private initiative is ready, or the success of industrial estates has been demonstrated by one or more examples, it is frequently possible to attract an association or cooperative of small firms or private investors into estate development.

(h) Occupants of industrial estates should not be subsidized by setting rents at less than the true cost of the space, except where explicit objectives are to be met. Any such departure should be temporary and planned ahead, so that dates for termination or reduction of the subsidy are understood by all concerned. Justification for subsidy may exist if the estate is designed to serve a catalytic function in an industrially undeveloped area that has real potential for industrial growth, or if it is viewed as a training ground for promising local entrepreneurs who are handicapped mainly by lack of experience and resources. Techniques exist to tailor the subsidy to the objective, administering it on a business basis that enhances its catalytic or training purpose. One way is to lengthen the amortization period. Another is to postpone payments on the principal for the critical first three to five years of the enterprise, covering only interest and maintenance charges in the rent initially levied. Whatever the level or method, it is imperative that proposed timing of changes be spelled out clearly in the original rental agreements with estate occupants.

Common Facility Services

We saw earlier the important role of small firms which specialize in support-type or jobbing activities for other firms. Heat treatment, forging, electroplating, precision die casting, tool and diemaking, and welding are examples of such service facilities. Apart from individual firms operating such specialty services, groups of firms may join to sponsor them. In Japan, thousands of common facility cooperatives have been organized by the voluntary action of small businessmen in such industries as textiles, lumbering and woodworking, ceramics, handmade paper, and food processing, often with governmental assistance.

In the initial phases of development, private initiative to set up service or jobbing units is often slow to crystallize. This is true in the less industrialized parts of a modern economy as well as in the less industrialized countries. In a major Canadian city, for example, large industry was until recently handicapped by the absence of a specialized facility for sharpening hardened steel cutting tools. An immigrant having excellent craftsmanship but lacking funds or business background was assisted by the provincial Department of Industry and Commerce in founding such a plant. His special tool center now runs profitably, doing job work for many firms of all sizes, which thereby achieve substantial savings in their tool cutting.[19]

When an essential common facility does not arise as a result of normal market forces, the community or government faces a choice: to establish it directly, or to encourage private or cooperative sponsorship. Widespread experience over the past decade or more suggests that a valid criterion for judging this issue is the following: Does the operation involve a variety of jobbing and business transactions with many firms? If so, stimulus to private sponsorship is likely to be more effective than government operation for the following reasons: (1) government procedures are inherently unsuited for rapid and flexible pricing decisions, the hallmark of competitive jobbing units; (2) if an advisory service is drawn into such operations, more and more time of senior officers must typically be devoted to operating or business-type problems, to the detriment of the main extension function; (3) service-type operations, as we have seen, are a principal field for small firms. Since the overall objective is normally to stimulate the efficient growth of a complement of well-run, flexibly managed firms, needed in any developing industrial complex, government operation of such a facility in effect counters the aims of its own program. Although the common facility is often viewed as a catalytic unit, to be transferred to private or cooperative enterprise when ready, experience shows that it is exceedingly difficult to withdraw from such commercial-type activities once they are built into a governmental structure.

In contrast, application of the above criterion suggests that testing facilities, charging standard fees on a given material or product, may appropriately be operated under government auspices where a private laboratory is unavailable. Since test equipment may often be provided in conjunction with a government standards or quality control institute, test fee procedures can often be routine and relatively unresponsive to market influences.

[19] Confidential report.

Facilitating the Procurement of Materials and Equipment

Handicaps of small manufacturers as compared to large in purchasing industrial raw materials and equipment are aggravated by two basic conditions in newly industrializing countries, First, the business network of suppliers and sales agencies is much less developed than in highly industrialized countries, where it usually provides comprehensive and effective services to industry. Second, except for those few fortunate countries with favorable long-term foreign exchange prospects, most developing economies face chronic and heavy shortages of materials and equipment as they strain to catch up with decades of unfulfilled but increasing wants. These circumstances tend to reinforce the inherent advantage of large firms in acquiring supplies, namely, their economies in bulk purchases, the planning and purchasing abilities of their specialized procurement staffs, and the greater political, social, and financial influence which they can bring to bear on the governmental or trading network.

There are no quick or simple solutions to these inherent developmental problems. Attempts to control the effects of scarcity by an elaborate system of governmental licensing, allocations, and import permits have in important instances increased rather than decreased the disadvantages of small firms. Small firms have been able to obtain a smaller share of their needs than large firms through authorized channels, and have been forced to resort much more heavily to the black market at premium prices. Is there a more promising line of attack?

It would appear that any basic improvement can be achieved only by a combined approach to the two underlying conditions: (1) by positive measures to increase the efficiency of the distributive network and (2) by fundamental policies (relating to inflation, foreign exchange, capital formation, etc.) to mitigate or at least confine the pressure of scarcities.

The efficiency of the regular business supply system in serving small industrialists may be increased by wider dissemination of information on demand and supply conditions, by training both industrialists and distributors in techniques of inventory planning and control, and by encouraging the entry of enough independent private distributors to avoid monopolistic control of supply channels—without at the same time encouraging fragmentation of distributive functions that require at least a minimum scale for efficient operation. A more widespread awareness of inventory management should help to counteract the speculative and hoarding practices that multiply the effects of scarcities. It must be assumed that major distributors and import houses, particularly in the early phases of industrial development, will possess a sharper knowledge of short-

and long-run market trends, seasonal and other fluctuations, than most governments or smaller firms, and will thereby be able to take maximum advantage of any monopoly or speculative position which they may hold. Governments, industrial associations, banks, dealers, and consumer groups concerned with orderly industrial expansion can improve the terms and conditions of internal trade by steps to strengthen the reliability and timeliness of relevant market information and to widen understanding of its use for business planning.

Scarcity is endemic in a poor country but takes specific form in the marketplace through the inflationary process that typically accompanies development. Expansionary policies release submerged demands for consumer goods, including a heavy bill of consumer durables in countries where income distribution is highly unequal. Foresight is necessary if equipment imports for new factories to produce goods locally are not to run far ahead of the economy's continuing capacity to import materials to feed these factories. A price-tax policy which curtails the demand for nonessential goods may have advantages over the licensing and allocation procedures which have attracted postwar development planners in many new nations.[20] Instead of attempting to channel investment by requiring licenses, investment decisions might be guided by applying high excise taxes to end products—particularly consumer durables or luxury goods—for which indigenous raw materials are limited and little export promise exists. (Corresponding duties would be required to curtail imports of such goods.) Positive encouragements, on the other hand, would be given to manufacturing investment in product lines having substantial promise in terms of the country's basic endowment.

Within a framework of moderate inflation, selective guidance to manufacturing investment through taxes and incentives could reduce if not eliminate the need now felt in many developing countries for close materials allocations and import permits.

Marketing Aids

The small industrialist, especially if he enters manufacturing from the craftsman or engineering side, oftentimes fails to do an adequate job of marketing. He can be helped in a number of ways.

Among these, better market information will usually offer the greatest

[20] For an extended discussion, see *Development of Small-scale Industries in India: Prospects, Problems and Policies*, Report of the International Perspective Planning Team, sponsored by the Ford Foundation, Government of India, Ministry of Industry, New Delhi, 1963, pp. 2–3 and Ch. III.

opportunity for benefit at least cost. A relatively simple but basic first step is the compilation and publication of trade directories in which information about small manufacturers is provided under a standard product classification, with manufacturers listed alphabetically and cross-indexed by geographical area to guide the inquirer to potential suppliers. Joint catalogs, in which each manufacturer takes a page or a few pages in a looseleaf volume to describe his products, are also fairly simple but useful promotional devices. Use can be made of announcements or advertisements in technical journals as these gain in circulation.

The needs of small firms for market research in order to reveal trends in consumer demands and test the market for new products or for expanded sales of old products have already been noted. Often a government development agency must take the lead in initiating market analyses and disseminating market information specifically useful to small firms. Such an agency can also foster the development of market research activity by industrial associations, by individual firms, or through encouragement of competent private consulting firms—for example, by providing free training in market research techniques.

Joint market promotion efforts on behalf of small manufacturers should focus primarily on strengthening their marketing position in normal commercial channels, whether domestic or export. Although the traditional high-markup, low-volume wholesaler has often exploited his strong bargaining position *vis-à-vis* the small firm, forward-looking distributors oriented to high sales volume and to competitive price-quality relationships are beginning to emerge in several newly industrializing countries. These distributors offer important outlets for expanded small firm sales, leading in turn to a stronger and more independent position for the manufacturer. Association efforts can aid small firms in establishing sound trade and credit terms with vigorous wholesale houses. In marketing the technical products of small firms, manufacturers' representatives or agents have acquired an important role in industrialized countries in the past few years, a role that should be paralleled in developing countries as their manufacture of producer goods expands.

It is important to improve the access of small manufacturers to two special types of market. One is purchases of larger manufacturers. On p. 383 we consider methods for promoting mutually beneficial contracts for supplies and component parts between large and small manufacturers. The other is government purchases. In some countries, an organized effort is made by the government to channel a part of its own buying to smaller manufacturers. The United States has an outstanding program of this sort, and officials concerned with it claim that it not only provides smaller manufacturers with new opportunities but, once these manufacturers have learned to make the required items, actually saves the government money. India has introduced a similar program, using procedures based partly on United States experience.[21]

Labor Relations Services

Any program should give attention to improvement of human relations in factories. This aspect of industrial progress is too often neglected in development planning. Working conditions, labor-management relations, and government regulations in these fields are sometimes viewed solely from the angle of social welfare. This is, of course, an important aspect. But the treatment of people in industry—the problems of recruitment, employment terms, training on the job, incentives, collective bargaining, handling of grievances, and the whole broad range of industrial relations—is one of the most fundamental elements in the attainment of high industrial productivity. Modern human relations techniques are as important in successful industrial development as modern mechanical techniques. Failure to perceive this truth can be a source of serious weakness in development programs.

It is our impression that the entrepreneur managers in many newly industrializing countries need as much help in improving their handling of human organization and human relations in the factory as in improving their technical production processes. Three factors intensify the need.

First, there is the transition underway in these countries from traditional to modern types of personality and work relationships. Authoritarian, status-conscious, paternalistic relations between master and worker are in process of being displaced by more democratic, merit-conscious, individualistic relations. All this demands unaccustomed new ways on the part of employers and employees.

Second, if a small industrialist is successful and his factory grows, he finds himself facing a situation where the problems of organization and communication between management and workers can no longer be cared for quite so informally. More sophisticated and consciously planned devices have to be introduced, or the organization may founder.

Third, the sweep of social and political ideas introduces trade unions into newly industrializing countries at an early stage, before either workers or

[21] See for details, Kennard Weddell, *Aiding Small Industry through Government Purchases*, a publication of the International Development Center, Stanford Research Institute, Menlo Park, Calif., 1960.

managers are prepared to operate responsible collective bargaining. While small factories are generally less unionized than large and often are relatively immune to the labor and social laws—by exemption or nonenforcement—this is not a situation that will last, especially for the successful firms that grow.

The development agency should not normally assume the direct function of mediating labor disputes, nor will it have the staff experienced for this purpose. Industrial harmony within a firm entails deep-seated, on-going attitudes and relationships, which can generally not be adequately comprehended by a short-term consultant not specialized in this field. Faced with such issues in firms that otherwise have growth potential, a small industry advisory service should assume the role of a generalist itself, enlisting assistance from a labor department or conciliation service for direct exploration and counseling on the problem.

Interfirm Contracts and Assistance

The mutual benefits from direct and indirect complementarities between large and small manufacturers have been emphasized throughout this book. Such possibilities often go unrecognized. Conscious fostering by government agencies and by associations of manufacturers may be necessary if they are to develop on a sound basis.

Practical steps in this direction include the following:

(a) Liaison between individual small and large firms may be informally effected by a small industry advisory service. Personal contacts through a competent and disinterested technical counselor can establish a basis for confidence and satisfactory negotiations, overcoming doubts about reliable performance or delivery schedules, often the main barrier to subcontracting by large firms.

(b) More formally, exchange of information on large firm subcontracting needs and small firm capabilities should be instituted on a systematic basis. Initially, the government could meet part of the costs of advertising small firm machine time in newspapers and technical journals, or in a periodic bulletin. Information should be published on the type of work small firms can do, tolerances attainable on their machines, and volume or scheduling that they can accept. In turn, large firms should register components or items needed, specifications, and required deliveries.

(c) As experience increases, large firms should be encouraged to provide technical assistance to existing and prospective subcontractors as a means of strengthening sources of supply.

(d) A further step is suggested by Japan's experience in modernization of selected machinery industries. Small firms with the general competence to meet large firm specifications, but lacking a necessary specialized or high-volume machine, are assisted by government loans or tax write-downs to equip themselves for production standards that meet large firm requirements. Close cooperation in planning such modernization is called for on the part of all the parties concerned—the small firm, the large firm, the government loan or credit insurance agency, and in some cases the small firm's bank.

We would underscore the voluntary element in such arrangements. Satisfactory interfirm relationships are based on performance and mutual confidence. They cannot be forced. Once standard quality and reliable deliveries are attained, the advantages will promote the spread of specialized subcontracting and interfirm services throughout an increasing range of industries.